£ 3.38

OUR TIMES

VOLUME V

OUR TIMES

VOLUME V

OUR TIMES

THE UNITED STATES
1900-1925

V

OVER HERE
1914-1918

BY

MARK SULLIVAN

CHARLES SCRIBNER'S SONS
NEW YORK · LONDON
1946

CONTENTS

4 / 0 0 2

CONTENTS

CONTENTS

ILLUSTRATIONS

ARMAGEDDON
1914-1918

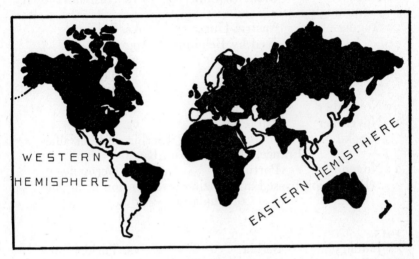

The World War.

The parts of the earth's land surface shown in black are those of countries which in one degree or another were involved, most of them taking a part in the fighting. The small number of countries which stood off from hostilities are shown in white. Of these, a few, such as China, declared war but did not contribute fighting troops; others severed diplomatic relations.

DECLARATIONS OF WAR

CHRONOLOGICAL LIST

1914		
28 July	Austria-Hungary	vs. Serbia
1 August	Germany	vs. Russia
3 August	France	vs. Germany
3 August	Germany	vs. France
4 August	Germany	vs. Belgium
4 August	Great Britain	vs. Germany
6 August	Austria-Hungary	vs. Russia
6 August	Serbia	vs. Germany

1914

7 August	Montenegro	vs. Austria-Hungary
8 August	Austria-Hungary	vs. Montenegro
9 August	Montenegro	vs. Germany
12 August (midnight)	France	vs. Austria-Hungary
12 August (midnight)	Great Britain	vs. Austria-Hungary
22 August	Austria-Hungary	vs. Belgium

(Received by Belgium 28 August)

23 August	Japan	vs. Germany
29 October	France	vs. Turkey
3 November	Russia	vs. Turkey
5 November	Great Britain	vs. Turkey
11 November	Turkey	vs. Allies

(Spoke of it as a holy war against Serbia and her allies)
France, Great Britain, Russia)

23 November	Portugal	vs. Germany

(Resolution passed authorizing intervention as an ally
of England)

1915

8 January	Serbia	vs. Turkey

(Treaties declared terminated from 1 December, 1914)

19 May	Portugal	vs. Germany

(Military aid granted)

24 May	Italy	vs. Austria-Hungary
21 August	Italy	vs. Turkey
14 October	Bulgaria	vs. Serbia
14 October	Serbia	vs. Bulgaria
15 October	Great Britain	vs. Bulgaria
16 October	France	vs. Bulgaria
19 October	Russia	vs. Bulgaria
19 October	Italy	vs. Bulgaria

1916

9 March	Germany	vs. Portugal
27 August	Roumania	vs. Austria-Hungary

(Allies of Austria also considered it a declaration of war)

28 August	Germany	vs. Roumania
28 August	Italy	vs. Germany

1916
29 August   Turkey   vs. Roumania
 1 September   Bulgaria   vs. Roumania
24 November   Greece (Provision-   vs. Germany
                   al Government)

1917
 6 April   United States   vs. Germany
 7 April   Cuba   vs. Germany
 7 April   Panama   vs. Germany
 2 July   Greece (Govern-   vs. Bulgaria
                   ment of Alexander)

 2 July   Greece (Govern-   vs. Germany
                   ment of Alexander)

22 July   Siam   vs. Austria-Hungary
22 July   Siam   vs. Germany
 4 August   Liberia   vs. Germany
14 August   China   vs. Austria-Hungary
14 August   China   vs. Germany
26 October   Brazil   vs. Germany
 7 December   United States   vs. Austria-Hungary
10 December   Panama   vs. Austria-Hungary
16 December   Cuba   vs. Austria-Hungary

1918
20 April   Guatemala   vs. Germany
 7 May   Nicaragua   vs. Germany
 8 May   Nicaragua   vs. Austria-Hungary
23 May   Costa Rica   vs. Germany
12 July   Haiti   vs. Germany
19 July   Honduras   vs. Germany

OVER HERE

"Now tell us what 'twas all about,"
  Young Peterkin he cries;
And little Wilhelmine looks up
  With wonder-waiting eyes.
"Now tell us all about the war,
And what they fought each other for."
    .   .   .   .

"But what good came of it at last?"
  Quoth little Peterkin.
"Why, that I cannot tell," said he;
"But 'twas a famous victory."
        —"The Battle of Blenheim," Robert Southey.

PROLOGUE

America Learns of the War. A Reproduction of the Ways in Which News of the War, and Awareness of It, Came to America; That Is to Say, through Short Newspaper Dispatches, Headlines, and the Vivid Brevities Which Newspapers and Motion Pictures Have Come to Call "Flashes"; Followed by Some Longer Accounts, Which Were Read Eagerly by the America of That Day, for We Were Avid to Know about the War, Thinking of It as a Spectacle Which, While Distant, Was Fascinating. Including Some Vivid Descriptions by American Writers, Among Them a Classic by Richard Harding Davis and an Evocative Picture by the American Author Who, When the War Broke, Was Minister to Belgium, Brand Whitlock. Beginning with an Inconsequent Small Episode Which Illustrates How Casually, with What Surprise, America Learned of the Outbreak of the War.

IN the pleasant midsummer of 1914, a local banker in Monterey, Calif., Charles D. Henry, went with some friends on a fishing trip into the remote heights of the California Sierras. A few weeks later, on his way down the slopes in early August, he was hailed from across a ravine by an in-going party who called out, "Any news of the war?" Mr. Henry, puzzled, asked the stranger to repeat. Again came the question, "Have you any news of the war?" Mr. Henry, mystified, turned queryingly to his companions. They all concluded they were being subjected to a not particularly funny attempt at "kidding." Thereupon Mr. Henry, entering as fully into the spirit of the occasion as his appreciation of its wit would permit, groped among his materials for repartee, recalled a phrase of his boyhood in Civil War times, and shouted back, "All's quiet along the Potomac." With that he dismissed the incident. Not until he and his friends had reached a town several days later did he learn of the outbreak of the Great War.

The coming of the War to Mr. Henry — he was an average American, not distinguished[1] from millions of others and he does not figure again in this history — was, in its unexpectedness and its casualness, typical of its coming to America as a whole.

II

The War did not come to America as it came to Europe. No Oregon rancher working in his field of a peaceful afternoon was disturbed by an odd whirring in the sunny air, and looked toward Mount Hood to see an airplane spitting fire upon his neighboring village. In no New England town did children huddle in the windows and peer at exultant Uhlans prancing down the maple-shaded street. No Maryland farmer from his hill-top field saw a thing that sent him hurrying to the house to gather his children into his cart and take to the road in fear. No city of ours walked for days in anxiety, listening to the rise and fall of a fateful cannonade. War did not thunder at our doors as at the forts of Liége.

It was not in the shape of violence of any sort that the war, in its early phase before America became a belligerent, came to us. Its coming took a form hardly physical at all; it came as newspaper despatches from far away, far away in distance and even farther away in spirit. The despatches were as if black flocks of birds, frightened from their familiar rookeries, came darting across the ocean, their excited cries a tiding of stirring events. The despatches, printed under heavy black headlines smudged across the first page of the country's newspapers, gave an impression as if Europe by some dark enchantment had

---

[1] Except that some years later it happened that his son-in-law, Herbert Hoover, became the thirtieth President of the United States.

Tribune

NEW YORK, WEDNESDAY, JULY 29, 1914 • • PRICE ONE CENT In City of New York, Newark, Jersey City and Hoboken. ELSEWHERE TWO CENTS

AUSTRIA DECLARES WAR, RUSHES
VAST ARMY INTO SERVIA; RUSSIA
MASSES 80,000 MEN ON BORDER

New York Tribune

Vol. LXXIV No. 24,781. NEW YORK, SUNDAY, AUGUST 2, 1914. SIX PARTS 42 PAGES PRICE FIVE CENTS

GERMANY DECLARES WAR ON RUSSIA;
FRANCE PREPARES TO JOIN HER ALLY;
ITALY QUITS THE TRIPLE ALLIANCE

| U. S. TRANSPORTS FOR RELIEF OF MAROONED AMERICAN TOURISTS | LATEST NEWS OF THE WAR
Berlin, Aug. 1.—The German Emperor declared war on Russia at 7:30 p. m., two hours after signing an order mobilizing the army. The last line of reserves has been called up, bringing the strength of the Kaiser's forces to close upon four million men. | KAISER MOBILIZES TO HIS LAST MAN; 4,000,000 IN ARMS |

New York Tribune

Vol. LXXIV....No. 24,783. NEW YORK, TUESDAY, AUGUST 4, 1914. • • • PRICE ONE CENT In City of New York, Newark, Jersey City and Hoboken. ELSEWHERE TWO CENTS

BRITISH ULTIMATUM TO GERMANY;
JOHN BURNS QUITS THE CABINET;
GERMANS ADVANCE THROUGH BELGIUM

| RUSSIAN FLEET DRIVEN BACK; 1 SHIP ASHORE; THREE TOWNS SEIZED | LATEST NEWS OF THE WAR.
London, Aug. 3.—John Burns, the ex-Labor leader, resigned from the British Cabinet, indicating that the war party is in the ascendant. Berlin, Aug. 3.—The invasion of Russian Poland by German | INVASION OF THE LUXEMBURG BY KAISER'S TROOPS SWIFTLY COUNTERED BY SIR E. GREY |

How America learned of the War through headlines.

become a witch's cauldron brewing mephitic shapes which flying westward in an unending black slash across the clean skies of the Atlantic came to roost in the newspapers of America:

Vienna,[2] July 25. — Diplomatic relations between Austria-Hungary and Servia were formally broken off to-night. . . . The portentous news of Servia's decision [with respect to Austria's ultimatum of the day before] was made known to the public by extra editions of the evening papers and at 8 o'clock to-night half the population of the city seemed to be on the

[2] New York *World*, Sunday, July 26, 1914.

streets. They fought eagerly for the papers, and processions were formed which marched through all the thoroughfares, *singing national hymns and cheering*[2a] for Emperor Francis Joseph, Emperor William, and the army.

St. Petersburg,[3] July 29. — A great patriotic demonstration took place on the Nevsky Prospekt this afternoon. A procession was formed and with banners flying marched to the Servian Legation, where there were speeches, *singing, and cheering.* Thence the procession moved on to the French and British Embassies where similar scenes of enthusiasm were indulged in, the crowds still growing. . . .

St. Petersburg,[4] August 1. — Enrollment of the reservists of the army started at a hundred corners in St. Petersburg at 6 o'clock this morning and was accompanied by stirring scenes. Crowds of women and children accompanied their husbands and fathers to the assembling stations, while priests everywhere blessed the reservists as they marched through the streets *singing* hymns.

St. Petersburg,[5] August 3. — . . . When it became known that a special service of prayer was to be celebrated at the Winter Palace, where the Emperor was to show himself to the people, an extraordinary wave of exultation passed over the city. . . . When the imperial yacht, with the Emperor and his family, arrived from Peterhof at 4 o'clock in the afternoon, they received a tremendous ovation, the people all kneeling and *hurrahing* as the imperial party passed to the palace. The Emperor addressed the representatives of the Army and Navy: "I here declare solemnly that I will not make peace while a single soldier of the enemy remains on Russian soil — [there was not a German soldier in Russia at the time]." While the Emperor was speaking all in attendance fell to their knees. . . .

Berlin.[6] — The memory of that turbulent night [August 3] in Berlin will never fade from my mind. The Kaiser's beautiful Capital was converted in the twinkling of an eye from a phlegmatic, pleasure-seeking summer metropolis into a community raging mad for war. Unter den Linden filled, as if by magic,

[2a] The italicizing of passages in all these despatches describing singing and cheering is the author's.
[3] New York *World*, July 30.
[4] New York *World*, August 2.   [5] New York *World*, August 4.
[6] From an account by Frederick William Wile, Berlin correspondent of the New York *Times*, in the New York *Times* "Current History of the War."

lsace. The red trousers are again seen on our plains and
ountains. The gay bugles of France sounded the charge at
ltkirch and Muhlhausen."
There were few who were not in tears as the speaker con-
uded. The *singing* of the "Marseillaise," followed by *cheers*
r Belgium, Russia, and England, ended the ceremony.

London,[9] August 5. — The crowds last evening and this
orning began to betray growing excitement. A procession of
ung men marched along by Whitehall and up the Strand,
eering. It was headed by a squad carrying the Union Jack
England and the tri-color of France. As it passed Trafalgar
quare there was some booing, but the *cheering* outweighed it.
eet Street last evening was jammed by crowds watching the
illetins. Occasionally they *sang* "The Marseillaise" and "God
ve the King."

The practically universal refrain in all the despatches
om all the European capitals, "singing . . . cheer-
g," was varied — but very rarely — by a chord of real-
y, sober apprehension of what was ahead. From Lon-
on came a despatch quoting the warning of a distin-
ished English man of letters[10] to his countrymen:

Let us not put on paper caps and march through the streets
ving penny flags, breathing beer and singing "Britons never
all be slaves." Let us not sing boastful songs! Honor may
ll us to fight, self-preservation may force us into the slaugh-
-house; but let us wear on our sleeves the crape of mourning
a civilization that had the promise of joy, and strike our
emy without a hiccup or a curse.

III

Besides "singing . . . cheering," there was through-
t the despatches another theme:

HELP US, GOD

t. Petersburg,[11] August 3. — Emperor Nicholas to-day is-
d this manifesto:
'By the grace of God we Nicholas II, Emperor and Autocrat

New York *Times*, August 5.
) Harold Begbie, in the London *Daily Chronicle*, August 5. Printed in Amer-
in *The Literary Digest*, August 29, 1914.
New York *World*, August 4, 1914.

with shrieking, *singing* processionists. "War! \
shouted. "Down with Russia!" "War with Ru
yelled, between verses of "God save Franz, the I
Austrian national anthem) and "Deutschland, I
über Alles," Germany's boastful battle *song*. . . .

Munich,[7] July 31. — This city is feverish with
over the prospect of war. We arrived from Berli
den, where the mobs in the streets and procession;
singing "Die Wacht am Rhein," and other war I
of such magnitude that old residents said nothir
had been seen since the beginning of the Franco-I
flict of 1870. We had just been driven out of the
ture-gallery by the four-o'clock closing bell, wh
excited throngs eagerly calling for immediate a
mobilization of all reserves and indicating that t
ropean war . . . had come.

Paris,[8] August. — Never has Paris been more
the summer tourist than we found it upon our a
afternoon of Sunday, July 29. We were driven
crowded gay streets to the Hotel Regina, just ac
Louvre and overlooking the Tuileries Gardens. .
About midnight, Friday, August 3, I heard a ¡
tion on the streets and, having a room on the cc
out in the hall to see what had happened. . . . A
presumably of students, had marched down tl
(Rue des Pyramids) next to our hotel, had dra
of Arc statue in the centre of the Place de Riv
and were *singing* the "Marseillaise." This was r
4 o'clock in the morning.

Paris, August. — The crepe festoons which f
have hung from the monument of the city of St
ital of Alsace-Lorraine, which stands in the Pla
corde, were torn down to-day and replaced wi
palm branches, while a tri-colored sash was dra
figure. The ceremony was conducted by 2,000 r
Federation of Alsatian Societies in Paris. Jose
Mayor of the Eighth Arrondissement, embrac
and then, addressing the gathering, said:
"The hour of revenge for which we have pray
for forty-four years has at last struck. The Fre

[7] New York *Evening Post*.
[8] Miss Ona Brown, in the Philadelphia *Public Ledger*.

In this picture the French are removing the mourning festoons, which for years had draped the Strasbourg Monument in Paris.

Recruiting in London during the early days of the War.

America was eager for War photographs.

of all the Russians, King of Poland, and Grand Duke of Finland, &c, &c, to all our faithful subjects make known that Russia, related by faith and blood to the Slav peoples and faithful to her historical traditions. . . .

"With a profound faith in the justice of our work, and with a humble hope in omnipotent Providence in prayer, we call God's blessing on holy Russia and her valiant troops.

"NICHOLAS."

It was the German Kaiser, however, even more than the Czar or any of the others, who excelled in linking God to his army and himself, dragged God from His throne and made Him a personal ally, invoked God's aid

Alle deutschen Herzen schlagen heute höher.

Reden, die gestern Kaiser und Kanzler hielten, haben in ganz Deutschland lebhaften Widerhall gefunden.

When the Kaiser made his parting speech to German troops, leaving Berlin for the front, a German-American newspaper, *The New Yorker Herold*, August 1, 1914, had a headline reading, "All German hearts beat higher today."

for one army, His vengeance for the other. Almost the Kaiser had a manner as if, should God prove a reluctant or unenthusiastic ally, the Kaiser would deal with Him as with any one else who dared stand between Germany and the place in the sun to which she aspired — the Kaiser would show God the mailed fist. To America, on August 1, newspaper despatches brought the words of the Kaiser's address delivered from the balcony of his palace in Berlin to a hundred thousand of his subjects:

A fateful hour has fallen for Germany. Envious peoples everywhere are compelling us to our just defense. The sword

Photograph by Underwood & Underwood.

Recruits drilling in Hyde Park, London, during the early days of the War.

is being forced into our hand. I hope that if my efforts at the last hour do not succeed in bringing our opponents to see eye to eye with us and in maintaining peace we shall with God's help so wield the sword that we shall restore it to its sheath again with honor. War would demand enormous sacrifices of blood and property from the German people, but we should show our enemies what it means to provoke Germany.

And now I commend you to God. Go to church. Kneel down before God and pray for His help for our gallant army.[12]

A few days later came the Kaiser's blessing to his soldiers as they took their way to the fighting:

Remember that the German people are the chosen of God. On me, the German Emperor, the spirit of God has descended. I am His sword, His weapon, and His viceregent. Woe to the disobedient, and death to cowards and unbelievers.[13]

And by mid-August cables brought to American newspapers His Imperial Majesty's congratulations on a successful battle of German troops, in Upper Alsace:

Grateful to God, Who was with us. I thank you and your troops for the first victory. Please convey to all the troops which took part in the fight my Imperial thanks in the name of the Fatherland.[14]

YOUR CHIEF WAR CAPTAIN.

IV

Presently came despatches giving accounts of the leaving for the front, the march toward the battle-line, early clashes, refugees. In the yellowed newspaper files of nearly twenty years later these despatches and headlines

[12] The translation here given is as printed in the New York *Times* "Current History of the War," Vol. I, p. 209.

[13] This is the most extreme of the Kaiser's invocations of God. As printed here, it is taken from the New York *Times* "Current History of the War," Vol. I, page 341, where it appears as part of a speech by Lloyd-George, who took it from the *British Weekly*.

[14] New York *Times* "Current History of the War," Vol. I, p. 212.

Photograph by Underwood & Underwood.

All the early despatches about German troops leaving for the War mentioned their singing.

appeared as vivid facets of the picture that the America of 1914 saw:

GERMANY GOES
SINGING TO WAR

In Trains Labelled "Special to Moscow," "Excursion to Paris"

Scheveningen, Holland, August 7. — The Germans are going to war in the liveliest good spirits, smiling, singing, and cheering. "Die Wacht am Rhein" and "Deutschland, Deutschland über Alles" echoed unceasingly from them.[15]

KITCHENER'S CALL
BRINGS LEGIONS

Rush of Volunteers to Army Surpasses Anything in England's Military History

SWAMP RECRUITING OFFICES

Men in Silk Hats Stand Shoulder to Shoulder with Laborers in Waiting Throngs[15a]

FRENCH SINK CRUISER
PANTHER OFF
ALGERIAN COAST[16]

London,[17] August 7. — There is a queer and touching mixture of enthusiasm and pathos in the scenes at the departing Continental trains taking French and Belgian reservists. The termini are packed with cheering crowds, while wives and daughters of the men leaving break down utterly and have to be led away by their friends.

TWO GERMAN ARMIES
INVADE FRANCE WHILE
RUSSIAN ARMY EN-
TERS GERMANY; BRIT-
ISH TROOPS HURRY-
ING TO COAST

[15] Frederick W. Wile, New York *Times*. August 8.
[15a] New York *Times*, August 8.
[16] New York *World*, August 5.   [17] New York *World*, August 7.

Before Declaration of War Is Made 100,000 of Kaiser's Forces Enter Luxembourg, Breaking Neutrality Treaty, and Advance on Longwy Fortress. . . .

TWO BRITISH MERCHANTMEN SEIZED BY GERMAN WAR VESSELS.

In their Eagerness to Get Away from the Perils of War, Americans Even Abandon All Their Belongings, Fought for Places on the Last Train from Paris and Arrived in London Starved and Moneyless. President Wilson Devising Means to Provide Gold and Ships to Bring Them Home. Steamship "President Grant" Returned to Port on Hearing of a Mysterious Craft Hovering Off the Coast.[18]

London,[19] August 7. — The whole Franco-German frontier is being patrolled by rival airplanes, which are flying parallel and within easy sight of each other.

ITALY WILL NOT HELP ALLIES; AMERICANS IN PANIC TRY TO QUIT EUROPE; BANK OF ENGLAND RUN CONTINUES[20]

RUSSIANS BEGIN INVASION OF GERMAN TERRITORY[21]

Paris, August. — The first battle of the air[22] occurred at

[18] New York *World*, August 3. [19] New York *World*, August 8.
[20] New York *World*, August 2. [21] New York *World*, August 3.
[22] New York *Sun*. Was this "the first battle of the air"? The author, after trying to find out, does not know. Indeed, he is doubtful whether the event recorded ever happened at all; it sounds "fishy." From the very beginning of the war, propagandists of the various belligerents, inventive souls, sent out stories

Cirey-les-Forges, on the French border. The French aviator
deliberately sacrificed himself. The big Zeppelin was seen first
at Cirey-les-Forges late in the afternoon. It had been recon-
noitering the frontier for some time when a whirr of an aeroplane engine was heard and the French machine was seen
rising.

The aviator went up until he was close to the big gas-bag of
the Zeppelin. Then he pointed his machine straight at the
German airship. The powerful engine drove the aeroplane
into the bag. There was an explosion and the two machines
crumpled up. The force with which the aeroplane had struck
the airship carried it clear through the gas-bag, but as it came
out on the other side it was seen that it, as well as the airship,
was mortally hurt. The Zeppelin crumpled up, staggered for a
moment, and then dashed straight to the earth. Almost every
one of the twenty-five men of the crew were thrown out at the
first shock and dashed to death far below.

The French aeroplane, shattered from her encounter, went
crashing to earth, too, taking along the body of France's first
hero of the war.

GREAT FLEETS IN BAT-
TLE, LONDON HEARS
MINE SINKS BRITISH
CRUISER, 131 LIVES
LOST[23]

Brussels, August 5. — Thousands of dead and wounded German soldiers and a repulsed German army are the results to-
night of an all-day battle near Liège, a Belgian city close to the
German and Dutch frontiers. . . . The Belgians lost few men
by death or wounds. In the foreguard of the invaders came
1500 German soldiers in 150 automobiles, making what was
perhaps the first "motor cavalry" sortie of history. But the
Belgian artillery and infantry met this spectacular rush in

designed to aid each their own cause. These in many cases were apocryphal. The
Germans, like the French, made a claim to the first air victory (at Wesel),
which, like the French one, must be regarded with suspicion.

The reader will understand that all the newspaper despatches reproduced in
this chapter are given as they appeared in American newspapers, without attempt
to verify the facts they purport to recite. Most, I do not doubt, were accurate.
Some may have been colored by propaganda, or even invented by it. But as details of the picture of the war that America received, they are authentic.

23 New York *World,* August 7.

Russian troops in the early days of the War.

"stonewall" fashion and slowed up and stopped the motor forces.[24]

Brussels,[25] August 6. — With the beginning of the German artillery attack on the forts at Liége, women and children, weeping, were hurried away in every possible kind of vehicle and many on foot, staggering along, trying to run and hardly able to walk because they were carrying so many things.

Huiry, France, September 8.[25a] — The road which leads east to Montry was full of the flying crowd. It was a sad sight. The procession led in both directions as far as we could see. There were huge wagons of grain; there were herds of cattle, flocks of sheep; there were wagons full of household effects, with often as many as twenty people sitting aloft; there were carriages; there were automobiles with the occupants crowded in among bundles done up in sheets; there were women pushing over-loaded handcarts; there were women pushing baby-carriages; there were dogs and cats, and goats; there was every sort of vehicle you ever saw, drawn by every sort of beast that can draw, from dogs to oxen, from boys to donkeys. Here and there there was a man on horseback, riding along the line, trying to keep it moving in order and to encourage the weary. Every one was calm and silent. There was no talking, no complaining. . . . The next morning — that was September 2 — I woke just before daylight. There was a continual rumble in the air. At first I thought it was the passing of more *réfugiés* on the road. I threw open my blinds, and then realized that the noise was in the other direction. I listened. I said to myself, "If that is not artillery, then I never heard any." Sure enough, the English soldiers were at the Demi-Lune.

Fear of spies, hatred of aliens resident in enemy countries, soon a mania in all the warring nations, was reflected in many despatches to America:

Brussels,[26] August 7. — Half a dozen Germans pretending to be English made their way to the office of the Governor after

[24] On the heels of this came a despatch from Berlin:
"August 6—It is announced that a report that German troops operating on Belgian territory had been compelled to retire is unfounded."
This sequence of assertion by one combatant, denial by the other, was familiar throughout the war.
[25] *Literary Digest*, August 22, 1914.
[25a] Mildred Aldrich, in *The Atlantic Monthly*.
[26] New York *World*, August 8.

From the beginning of the War, almost to the end, photographs of refugees, similar to these, aroused sympathy in America.

the battle [at Liége]. They were found to be armed and were shot. A German officer disguised as a nun was arrested on the battlefield. Five men dressed as preachers were arrested to-day at the Liége railroad station suspected of being spies.

ANTWERP MOBS DRIVE GERMANS FROM CITY; LOOT THEIR HOMES

GERMANS CLOSE ENGLISH SHOPS; HURL CORRESPON-DENTS IN JAIL[27]

Paris, August 6. — The most extraordinary discovery [in connection with German spies] was that a company designating itself the "Bouillon Kub" (Bouillon cube), a German firm doing an immense business in France with compressed meat essences, was using its billboard advertisements for illicit purposes. Various arrangements of its cubes on the lithographs, so that they appeared in groups of different numbers, or bore certain geometrical relations to each other, all carried hidden messages intended for the German invaders, such as: "This village has so many inhabitants, so many armed men, so many cattle [which may be seized], so many bakeries."[28] . . . All over France to-day city and village authorities are tearing down billboards.

Paris, August 6. — To-night half a dozen searchlights are sweeping the sky from the top of the Eiffel Tower, nearly 1000 feet above the ground, and more are lighting the heavens from the roof of the automobile club. . . .

Paris, August 6. — Great indignation followed the news that M. Jules Cambon, who was French Ambassador to Germany, was not even given the means of transportation when he received his passports at Berlin. He had to pay from his own pocket transportation to Denmark where he still is. The French government gave a special train to the German Ambassador as far as the German border.

[27] New York *World*, August 9.

[28] The author feels called on to repeat that while these despatches are authentic as details of the picture of the war which America received in despatches from Europe, the authenticity of the facts recited may be doubtful.

V

Presently the war in Europe, spreading in widening waves of repercussion, gave rise to incidents in the ocean off the American coast, which, recited in the newspapers, became vivid details of the picture of the war as it emerged before American eyes. While it yet seemed that war would be avoided, a great new ship of the North German Lloyd, the *Kronprinzessin Cecilie*, embarked from New York for Germany with a full passenger list and a large sum in gold aboard. For days nothing was heard from her. Interest in her fate grew in proportion as the time lengthened since her departure. After a week, the suspense was broken by a news flash:

Bar Harbor, Maine, August 4.[29] — Rushing through a dense fog, at the utmost speed of her powerful engines, with every light on board covered, the *Kronprinzessin Cecilie* finished a desperate four-day run and dashed into this port and safety at dawn this morning. Her $13,000,000 treasure and her crowd of passengers were safe from the clutches of French and British warships. . . .[30]

New York *Press:* From Ellis Island to Tottenville, in the Upper Bay [of New York Harbor], there is to be seen to-day a sight not equalled anywhere in the world. In this greatest port of this greatest neutral nation lie strings of ships flying the flags of all the countries now grappling to the death in Europe. They are so close together that the proverbial biscuit could be tossed almost from one to the other, so close that scowls and hard words are communicated easily enough by the crews. Yet they lie in amity; the mantle of this nation covers all alike.

29 New York *World,* August 5, 1914.

30 The war gave rise in America to many moods, including a levity of a kind which a decade later came to be called "wise-cracking." There had been widespread apprehension over the safety of the passengers on the *Kronprinzessin Cecilie* and a sporting hope that the vessel, one of the fastest afloat, might succeed in her dash to Germany. Nevertheless, jokesmiths wrote, and editors published, and the public enjoyed such facetieties as:

"The prediction of a prosperous season for American summer resorts as a result of the European war has already been vindicated. Bar Harbor has ten million dollars in gold."—New York *Evening Post.*

Here are British tramps and German liners, Russian emigrant ships and French freighters, Austrian hookers and many others, their ensigns all fluttering. Some may grow weary of inaction, perhaps, and slip out past Sandy Hook, to brave the dangers of destruction or capture. How many will be afloat a year from now?

VI

By mid-August and toward September first, longer despatches began to come, detailed descriptions, narratives of battle. The best American war correspondents, hurrying to Europe by what means they could find, had arrived at the front or near it. Their accounts, in weekly periodicals as well as daily newspapers, were eagerly received by the mounting American appetite for pictures of the incredible scene. The New York *Tribune* printed an eye-witness account of the Germans crossing the river Meuse to storm Liége:

General von Emmich had barely ridden back across the bridge over the River Meuse, and was still in sight, cantering across the beautiful valley, when there was a long roar, a cracking crash and splash. The bridge had been blown up. General von Emmich was seen to turn on his horse and watch the cloud of dust which went up into the air far above the cloud of smoke from the explosives. . . .

The German troops could be seen approaching. Just as the first line came into view, the guns of the German artillery, posted somewhere far behind them, started booming. The shells could be heard coming as they hummed through the air. They were not aimed at the city, but at the forts which lie in a crooked line quite some distance out. Some of the shells went wide, buried in the earth, and then kicked up a vicious, spiteful kick. Some hit the forts, but buried themselves in the sand outworks and sputtered out. The forts did not reply.

Ahead of the German column galloped some wagons. They pulled up alongside the river, near the wreckage of the blown-up bridge. The soldiers, looking in the distance like busy ants at work, seemed to be pulling their wagons apart and throwing the parts into the river. Other men picked them up, and in what seemed an amazingly little while a pontoon bridge began growing in jerks across the river.

The first rank of the German soldiers, crossing the bridge, were about twenty feet from the Belgian side, swinging with the bridge, and had just broken from a quaint, slow, waddling march into a run, when the Liége guns let go. When the frightful roar stopped, the only part of the pontoon bridge left was about fifty feet of it on the side where the Germans were, and the surface of the river was wiggling with German soldiers, struggling horribly to free themselves from the dead and the shattered and swim to the side. . . .

The other German soldiers [on the bank] appeared to take no more notice of what had happened than if it had been part of the arranged programme. Another set of wagons galloped up and another pontoon bridge was thrown across the Meuse. Before it was completed at least a hundred of the men building it were shot. As they fell into the river others took their places and went on building the bridge.

Then the battle began. The Liégeois waited for the troops. The slaughter was terrible. Every time the advancing line jumped up to run a few yards nearer to us we could see men fall, dead or wounded. I doubt if I could have watched it much longer, even if I could have stayed. And yet it was absolutely fascinating. No more war for me. No, sir, never.

Of the American correspondents who "covered" the war, Richard Harding Davis had an extraordinary gift of vividness. His picture — it was almost literally pictorial — of the entry of the German army into Brussels was eagerly read by the America of that day, and deserves to be regarded as classic among accounts of the war:

The entrance of the German army into Brussels has lost the human quality. It was lost as soon as the three soldiers who led the army bicycled into the Boulevard du Regent, and asked the way to the Gare du Nord. When they passed the human note passed with them.

What came after them, and twenty-four hours later is still coming, is not men marching, but a force of nature like a tidal wave, an avalanche, or a river flooding its banks. At this minute it is rolling through Brussels as the swollen waters of the Conemaugh Valley swept through Johnstown.

At the sight of the first few regiments of the enemy we were thrilled. After, for three hours, they had passed in one unbroken steel-gray column, we were bored. But when hour after hour passed and there was no halt, no breathing time, no open spaces in the ranks, the thing became uncanny, unhuman. You returned to watch it, fascinated. It held the mystery and menace of fog rolling toward you across the sea.

The gray of the uniforms worn by both officers and men helped this air of mystery. Only the sharpest eye could detect among the thousands that passed, the slightest difference. All

Richard Harding Davis (*left*), American war correspondent, whose account of the Germans entering Brussels was a classic.

moved under a cloak of invisibility. Only after the most numerous and severe tests at all distances, with all materials and combinations of colors that give forth no color, could this gray have been discovered. That it was selected to clothe and disguise the German when he fights is typical of the German staff in striving for efficiency to leave nothing to chance, to neglect no detail.

After you have seen this service uniform under conditions entirely opposite, you are convinced that for the German soldier it is his strongest weapon. Even the most expert marksman cannot hit a target he cannot see. It is a gray-green, not the blue-gray of our Confederates. It is the gray of the hour just before daybreak, the gray of unpolished steel, of mist among green trees.

I saw it first in the Grand Place in front of the Hotel de Ville. It was impossible to tell if in that noble square there was a regiment or a brigade. You saw only a fog that melted into the stones, blended with the ancient house fronts, that shifted and drifted, but left you nothing at which you could point.

Later, as the army passed below my window, under the trees of the Botanical Park, it merged and was lost against the green leaves. It is no exaggeration to say that at a hundred yards you can see the horses on which the Uhlans ride, but cannot see the men who ride them.

If I appear to overemphasize this disguising uniform it is because, of all the details of the German outfit, it appealed to me as one of the most remarkable. These men passing in the street, when they have reached the next crossing, become merged into the gray of the paving-stones and the earth swallows them.

Yesterday Major-General von Jarotsky, the German Military Governor of Brussels, assured Burgomaster Max that the German army would not occupy the city, but would pass through it. It is still passing. I have followed, in campaigns, six armies, but, excepting not even our own, the Japanese, or the British, I have not seen one so throughly equipped. I am not speaking of the fighting qualities of any army, only of the equipment and organization. The German army moved into this city as smoothly and as compactly as an Empire State Express. There were no halts, no open places, no stragglers.

This army has been on active service three weeks, and so far there is not apparently a chin-strap or a horseshoe missing. It came in with the smoke pouring from cook-stoves on wheels, and in an hour had set up post-office wagons, from which mounted messengers galloped along the line of column, distributing letters, and at which soldiers posted picture postcards.

The infantry came in in files of five, two hundred men to each company; the Lancers in columns of four, with not a pennant missing. The divisions of quick-firing guns and field pieces were one hour at a time in passing, each gun with its caisson and ammunition-wagon taking twenty seconds in which to pass.

The men of the infantry sang "Fatherland, My Fatherland."

Between each line of song they took three steps. At times two thousand men were singing together in absolute rhythm and beat. When the melody gave way, the silence was broken only by the stamp of iron-shod boots, and then again the song rose. When the singing ceased the bands played marches. They were followed by the rumble of siege-guns, the creaking of wheels, and of chains clanking against the cobble-stones, and the sharp, bell-like voices of the bugles.

For seven hours the army passed in such solid column that

Photograph © Underwood & Underwood.

Belgian civilians made prisoners by the Germans, entering Brussels under German guard.

not once might a taxicab or trolley-car pass through the city. Like a river of steel it flowed, gray and ghostlike. Then, as dusk came and as thousands of horses' hoofs and thousands of iron boots continued to tramp forward, they struck tiny sparks from the stones, but the horses and the men who beat out the sparks were invisible.

At midnight pack-wagons and siege-guns were still passing. At 7 this morning I was awakened by the tramp of men and bands playing jauntily. Whether they marched all night or not I do not know; but now for twenty-six hours the gray army

The German entry into Brussels.

For twenty-six hours the gray army rumbled by with the pertinacity of a steam roller.

has rumbled by with the mystery of fog and the pertinacity of a steam-roller.[31]

The grayness — and also another aspect of war, the smell — was emphasized by Will Irwin:

We had seen three days of the German army by now; and it seemed to me . . . that the whole world had turned into a gray machine of death — earth and air and sky. The gray transport wagons rattled past, carrying gray machines of men. The gray motor-cycles and automobiles streaked past, the mufflers cut out, chugging the message of death. Overhead, the gray biplanes buzzed with a kind of supernatural power. The very singing of the regiments, as they swung in behind the baggage-wagons, seemed no more a human touch. It was mechanical, like the men who sang — the music of a music box.

And over it all lay a smell of which I have never heard mention in any book on war — the smell of a half-million unbathed men, the stench of a menagerie raised to the nth power. That smell lay for days over every town through which the Germans passed.[32]

At Brussels was the American Minister, Brand Whitlock. He too wrote a description:

Lovely Brussels was lovelier than ever, but somehow with a wistful waning loveliness infinitely pathetic. All over the Quartier Leopold the white façades of the houses bloomed with flags, their black and red and yellow colors transparent in the sunlight; in the Foret the sunlight filtered through the leaves, irradiating the green boles of the trees, and through the hazy sunlight that lay on the fields the mound of Waterloo was outlined against the sky. In the Bois, in the midst of woodland peace, the children were playing and lovers whispered still their marvellous discoveries. Who . . . can think of those days without the memory of that wonderful sunlight which filled them to the brim? Day after day went by, with each new morning the miracle was renewed. . . .

The crash of the music of a military band, high, shrill with the fierce, screaming notes, the horrid clang of mammoth brass cymbals, not music, but noise of a calculated savagery, to strike terror. The Prussian officers with cruel faces scarred by duelling. Some of the heavier type with rolls of fat, the mark of the

[31] New York *Tribune*.   [32] *Collier's Weekly*.

The German goose-step, soldiers entering Brussels.

German Uhlans leading the advance into Belgium.

Wounded English marines coming from the trenches in Belgium.

French Poilus, before trench hats and the later style of uniform were issued.

beast, as Emerson calls it, at the back of the neck, and red, heavy, brutal faces looking about over the heads of the silent, awed, saddened crowd, with arrogant, insolent, contemptuous faces! The heavy guns that lurched by, their mouths of steel lowered toward the ground. It became terrible, oppressive, unendurable, monstrous, those black guns on gray carriages; those field-gray uniforms, the insolent faces of those supercilious young officers; those dull plodding soldiers, those thews and sinews, the heels of those clumsy boots drumming on the pavements.

Richard Harding Davis wrote, from the window of a car in which he was held prisoner by the Germans, a description of the destruction of Louvain.

For two hours on Thursday night I was in what for six hundred years had been the city of Louvain. The Germans were burning it, and to hide their work kept us locked in the railroad carriages. But the story was written against the sky, was told to us by German soldiers incoherent with excesses; and we could read it in the faces of women and children being led to concentration camps and of the citizens on their way to be shot.

The Germans sentenced Louvain on Wednesday to become a wilderness, and with the German system and love of thoroughness they left Louvain an empty, blackened shell. The reason for this appeal to the torch and the execution of non-combatants, as given to me on Thursday morning by General von Lutwitz, military governor of Brussels, was this: On Wednesday, while the German military commander of the troops in Louvain was at the Hotel de Ville talking to the burgomaster, a son of the burgomaster with an automatic pistol shot the chief of staff and German staff surgeons. Lutwitz claims this was the signal for the Civil Guard, in civilian clothes on roofs, to fire upon the German soldiers in the open square below. Fifty Germans were killed and wounded. For that, said Lutwitz, Louvain must be wiped out. . . .

Money can never restore Louvain. Great architects and artists, dead these six hundred years, made it beautiful, and their handiwork belonged to the world. With torch and dynamite the Germans have turned these masterpieces into ashes, and all the Kaiser's horses and all his men cannot bring them back again.

When by troop train we reached Louvain, the entire heart of the city was destroyed and fire had reached the Boulevard

Tirlemont, which faces the railroad station. The night was windless, and the sparks rose in steady, leisurely pillars, falling back into the furnace from which they sprang. In their work the soldiers were moving from the heart of the city to the outskirts, street by street, from house to house. . . .

On the high ground rose the broken spires of the Church of St. Pierre and the Hotel de Ville, and descending like steps were row beneath row of houses, roofless, with windows like blind eyes. The fire had reached the last row of houses, those on the Boulevard de Jodigne. Some of these were already cold, but others sent up steady, straight columns of flame. In others at the third and fourth stories the window curtains still hung, flowers still filled the window-boxes, while on the first floor the torch had just passed and the flames were leaping.

An account of life — and death — in the trenches was sent from an English source:[33]

Figure to yourself (as Wells says, isn't it?) a country of flat plowed field, pollard willows and deep muddy ditches. Then we come along, and in military parlance "dig ourselves in." That is, with the sweat of the brows of hundreds of Tommies working by night narrow trenches five feet deep at least and with the earth thrown up another two and a half feet as a bank on top. These trenches are one and a half to two feet wide, and curl and twist about in a maddening manner to make them safer from shell-fire. Little caves are scooped in the walls of the trenches, where the men live about four to a hole, and slightly bigger dug-outs where two officers live. All the soil is clay, stickier and greasier than one could believe possible. It's like almost solid paint, and the least rain makes the sides of the trenches slimy, and the bottom a perfect sea of mud — pulls the heels off your boots almost. One feels like Gulliver walking along a Liliputian town all the time. The front line of trenches — the firing-line — have scientific loopholes and lookout places in them for seeing and firing from, and a dropping fire goes on from both sides all day long, but is very harmless. . . .

I don't believe there is a man living who, when first interviewing an 11-inch howitzer shell, is not pink with funk. After the first ten, one gets quite used to them, but really, they are terrible! They hit a house. You can see the great shell — a black streak — just before it strikes; then, before you hear the

[33] Originally printed in the London *Times*, December 18, 1914. Reprinted in the New York *Times* "Current History of the War."

explosion, the whole house simply lifts up into the air, apparently quite silently; then you hear the roar, and the whole earth shakes. In the place where the house was there is a huge fountain-spout of what looks like pink fluff. It is the pulverized bricks. Then a monstrous shoot of black smoke towering up a hundred feet or more, and, finally, there is a curious willow-like formation, and then — you duck, as huge pieces of shell, and house, and earth, and haystack tumble over your head. And yet, do you know, it is really remarkable how little damage they do against earth trenches.

VII

Thus—first by brief despatches, flashes of startling news, later by vivid narratives and descriptions in periodicals and newspapers, accompanied by photographs of soldiers marching, cities ruined, men in trenches, tragedy at sea — thus did America learn of the war. It gave rise among us to many moods, expressed in Isaiah-like sermons with Europe's "insanity" as text, pontifical editorials which combed the dictionary for synonyms of "senseless," "barbaric"; man-in-the-street debate, cigarstore oraculation. Present among the echoes, sure to appear in any American reaction to any event or condition, was a characteristic national humor, compounded of wit and pungent sageness, the newspaper quip. "This European war," said the *Buffalo Courier*, "suggests that maybe the white man's burden is the white man himself." . . . "The French and German waiters returning to Europe as reservists in the armies should be able to charge well."[34] . . . "It may yet become necessary to land marines to protect Mr. Carnegie's Peace Palace at the Hague."[35]

Those were off-hand whimsies. Quips that went deeper, reflected a fundamental American feeling, proving that jest may contain many a true word, were in the

[34] Columbia (S. C.) *State.*   [35] Indianapolis *Star.*

The early photographs of trench-life, which were widely printed in American newspapers, interested everybody because of this novel aspect of this War.

After the first call to the colors.

French soldiers marching to the front along vineyards in which the civilian population continued busy.

vein of the Chicago *Herald's*, "Peace-loving citizens of this country will now rise up and tender a hearty vote of thanks to Columbus for having discovered America." That was the humorous way of putting what was the uni-

Photograph from Underwood & Underwood.

An early photograph of a scene destined to be duplicated throughout much of France and Belgium.

versal serious feeling and expression of America's attitude toward the war — "Thank God we are not mixed up in it!" Perhaps the most accurate and comprehending reflection of the American attitude — the more characteristic because voiced by a mid-West, small-town newspaper, was that of the Wabash (Ind.) *Plain Dealer:* "We never appreciated so keenly as now the foresight exercised by our forefathers in emigrating from Europe."

1

WAR KNOCKS AT WILSON'S DOOR

And Finds Him Not Disposed to Welcome So Rude a Visitor. Perfunctorily Wilson "Tenders His Good Offices" to the Belligerents, but Finds Them Preoccupied. He Makes the Usual Declaration of Neutrality, Proclaims a "Peace Sunday," Urges His Fellow Citizens to Be "Impartial in Thought as Well as in Action," and Assures Congress that the War Is a Thing "with Which We Have Nothing to Do."

To President Wilson the contentions and responsibilities, domestic and foreign, which came with the war, were a rude intrusion. Wilson's way of treating an unwelcome intruder, if an individual, was to assume a manner of gazing at the stars over the offender's head. But the war could not be snubbed.

To deal with the problems the war raised was, in the early phases, uncongenial to Wilson's temperament. It was a kind of duty distant from what he had in mind when he sought the Presidency. He resented the war; tried to put it away from him, not in a spirit of timorousness but rather of irritation.

Yet it came to be that the war was Wilson's greatest responsibility; and, later, that Wilson was, in the whole world, the figure about whom the war raged and the peace swirled. For some five years, 1914–1919, the history of the United States, as respects the Great War, was mainly the history of Woodrow Wilson's mind. For the last two years, 1917–1919, the history of the whole world was the history of Wilson's mind. And the results of Wilson's acts lay upon the world for more than a decade after the end of the war. For at least nine years[1] after his death[2] the world was racked by ideas that Wilson had introduced; steps that he had taken or

Something New for the Barbarians to Look At

The early inclination of President Wilson was to snub the war, turn his back upon it. He had disdain for the war, regarded it as barbarous, a thing with which America should have nothing to do. As this cartoon suggests, Wilson's attitude was approved, during the early days, by much of America.

—*Darling in the Des Moines (Iowa) Register and Leader.*

attempted continued to be the concern of statesmen, the preoccupation of nations and of peoples.

Wilson's mind, the evolution through which it passed,

[1] Up to the time these words are written, July 10, 1933 — with prospect that the condition would continue.
[2] February 3, 1924.

was the largest single factor in the war. And the first phase of Wilson's attitude toward the war was distaste for it, wish to keep it at arm's length, as something shameful to the world, odious to him personally.[3]

II

Wilson's Pre-War Domestic Program

Wilson had been elected[4] with a mandate almost limited to, certainly with heavy emphasis on, internal reform — a series of policies, chiefly economic and all domestic, called by Wilson the "New Freedom," meaning freedom for the average man against big business and high finance.

In fulfilment of his domestic program, Wilson, taking high satisfaction in the process, sponsored and aided in getting through Congress a bill reorganizing the banking structure of the United States into the Federal Reserve System, designed to frustrate what he and the Democrats called the "Money Trust." He brought about creation by Congress of the Federal Trade Com-

[3] "Wilson, the lifelong student of domestic problems . . . It was his dread of being diverted from his main business, his dread of becoming entangled in the meshes of European powers, that lent so much earnestness to his repeated announcements of American neutrality."—"Woodrow Wilson and His Work," William E. Dodd.

"I find the President singularly lacking in appreciation of the importance of this European crisis . . . more interested in domestic affairs. I find it difficult to get his attention centred upon the one big question." — Diary of Colonel E. M. House, September 28, 1914.

"Had Wilson been called upon to deal only with American affairs, as he hoped he would, during his terms of office, his idealism would have been wholesomely kept in touch with practicality by his knowledge of the psychology and history of his own countrymen. But when he had to do with foreign nations, his lack of sound knowledge let his idealism fly loose, like a balloon whose string has been cut and which floats away from the solid earth." — "The March of Democracy," James Truslow Adams.

[4] November 4, 1912, with 6,286,214 votes to 3,483,922 for William H. Taft as candidate of the Republicans, and 4,126,020 for Theodore Roosevelt, as candidate of the Progressive party.

During the early part of Wilson's administration, before the war broke, Wilson
was engaged with a legislative program of business and financial
reform, which he called "The New Freedom."

—*Ketten in the New York Evening World.*

mission,[5] to prevent unfair methods of competition in
business and to aid in executing the anti-trust laws. He
initiated and pressed through Congress a farm loan act
setting up government and quasi-government banks to
loan money to farmers at rates lower than 6 per cent (in
practice 4 to $5\frac{1}{2}$ per cent) as against pre-existing rates
of private local bankers sometimes twice as high. He
broadened the scope of the Sherman anti-trust law of

[5] See "Our Times," Vol. IV.

1889 by the Clayton Act, which prohibited the selling
of commodities at different prices to different purchasers
when such discrimination tends to lessen competition, and
in other ways curbed unethical business practices. He
initiated, and successfully pushed through Congress, a
downward revision of the tariff.[6] He brought about the
enactment, as an amendment to the Tariff Bill, of a
measure imposing a graduated tax on incomes.[7] He advocated and had enacted into law a measure limiting the
workday of interstate railroad employees to eight hours.
He encouraged the passage of the Seaman's Act, written
by Senator Robert M. LaFollette, which in the judgment of its advocates "freed the men in the forecastle
from the tyranny of the bridge." (But in the judgment
of its critics, "prescribed such rules for wages, food,
and accommodations of sailors as made it impossible for
the United States to compete with foreign shipping.")
He secured the consent of Congress for the building of
a government-owned railroad in Alaska, and had an act
passed authorizing the Government to engage in the
shipping trade.[8]

This program of domestic legislation was practically
finished before the war began. Wilson, confident and
serene, was able to say to Congress, in his Message of
December 8, 1914: "Our program of legislation with

[6] The Underwood Tariff Act of 1913, so named for its principal author, Representative Oscar Underwood of Alabama. This lowest tariff bill in more than
a generation was never given an opportunity to demonstrate whether in the long
run a low tariff is advantageous or otherwise to the country's business. Within
a year of its enactment the war in Europe broke out, which had an effect more
prohibitive than any tariff in diminishing the shipment of goods to the United
States.

[7] The Constitutional amendment empowering Congress to levy a graduated income tax was proposed to the States on July 12, 1909, and declared ratified
February 25, 1913, seven days before Wilson took office. All the states ratified
except Utah, Connecticut, Florida, Pennsylvania, Rhode Island, and Virginia.

[8] The summary of Wilson's administration here given is confined to measures
embraced in his "New Freedom," his policies of domestic reform in the fields
of business and finance. Other events in Wilson's administration are mentioned
in the chronological chapters at the end of this volume.

respect to business is now virtually complete. . . . The road at last lies clear and firm before business."

III

The War Comes to Wilson

Into this preoccupation of Wilson with domestic affairs, agreeable to his temperament, congenial to his talent and experience; into this complacency with its completion and assurance about the future, intruded the war.[9]

It found him by the bedside of his sick wife. She died August 6, 1914, without knowing war had broken out. Her death, and the coming of the war, combined to a peculiar degree to make a break in Wilson's life, tragic in the personal sense, having far-reaching consequences in the public sense. One who knew Wilson well, James Kerney, thinks the death of his wife had an effect on the spirit with which he met his and the world's crises: "There was never a time when Wilson so needed the steadying influence of Ellen Axson as the months that immediately followed her death. And the world needed it even more. . . . Who can say how the death

---

[9] Before the Great War, Mars intruded upon Wilson in the less aggressive form of a revolution in Mexico. About 2:30 o'clock on the morning of April 21, 1914, Wilson was awakened by the ringing of a telephone bell in his bedroom. He found Secretary of State, Bryan; Secretary of the Navy, Daniels; and private secretary, Tumulty, all on the phone at once. They recited to him a despatch received from Admiral Mayo of the American fleet off Vera Cruz, Mexico, reporting a condition disturbing to the United States. Wilson, after a brief conversation with his advisers, said: "Daniels, send this message to Admiral Mayo: 'Take Vera Cruz at once.'" Then Wilson went back to bed. Awaking the next morning he sent for the White House chief usher, Irwin Hoover. Still in his night-shirt, a shaving-brush in one hand, Wilson shook a minatory finger at the usher: "I wish you to give orders that under no circumstances am I ever to be called on the telephone at night." Softening his imperativeness, he added in explanation: "No man aroused from sleep in the middle of the night can have his best judgment about him."

He was destined to experience many occasions when the imperative urgencies of war came upon him suddenly, demanded his best judgment instantaneously.

of this modest, self-effacing, self-denying woman affected the future of the world?"[10]

The intrusion of war upon Wilson came on the evening of July 28 in the form of a despatch, serious and

President Wilson and his first wife, Ellen Axson Wilson. She died August 6,
1914, just after the war began, and her death had a material effect on the
spirit in which Wilson met the impact of the war in Europe.

imperative, from Ambassador Myron T. Herrick in
Paris:

Situation in Europe is regarded here as the gravest in history. It is apprehended that civilization is threatened by de-
moralization which would follow a general conflagration. . . .
It is felt that if Germany once mobilizes no backward step will
be taken. There is faith and reliance on our high ideals and
purposes, so that I believe expression from our nation would

10 "The Political Education of Woodrow Wilson," James Kerney.

have great weight in this crisis. I believe that a strong plea
for delay and moderation from the President of the United
States would meet with the respect and approval of Europe,
and urge the prompt consideration of this suggestion. I would
not appear officious but deem it my duty to make this expression
to you.

The spirit of high urgency in Herrick's note failed
to infect Wilson. Perfunctorily, after several days during which he consulted Ambassador Page in London,
Wilson on August 4 sent notes to the heads of state of
the five powers then involved in the war, chiefly crowned
ones. It was no more than the customary "tender of
good offices." The wording was Wilsonian: "I feel it
to be my privilege and my duty to say to Your Majesty
that I should welcome an opportunity to act in the interest of European peace . . . to serve Your Majesty and
all concerned in a way that would afford me lasting cause
for gratitude and happiness." Majesty King George
of England "expressed most earnestly his thanks"; Majesty Emperor Wilhelm of Germany was "most grateful for the President's message." Both had a manner of
being busy with other matters than peace.

August 6, Wilson attended to his other routine function, issued the formal proclamation of neutrality, the
customary American formula, devised in the administration of George Washington: Americans must not enlist in the army of either belligerent nor aid in fitting
out any armed vessel to be used in the service of either
belligerent. Belligerents in their turn must conform to
our status as a neutral, must not permit their vessels of
war to engage in hostile operations within the waters
of the United States, nor make use of our ports to facilitate attack upon their enemy.

These formalities attended to, Wilson, following his
wish rather than his reason, "looked upon the war as a

distant event, terrible and tragic, but one which did not concern us closely in the political sense.[11]

Both combatants, like fighting boys appealing to an

All the combatants in the European war sought, through propaganda and directly, to persuade Uncle Sam that their respective sides were in the right.

—*May in the Cleveland Leader.*

older bystander, cried out to Wilson to see the justice of their respective sides. The Kaiser: "I solemnly protest to you about the way this war is being waged by our opponents." President Poincare of France: "Germany is trying to deceive and make use of pretexts and lies."

11 "Intimate Papers of Colonel House," Charles Seymour.

Belgium[12] sent a delegation with documentary evidence of Germany's crimes.

To both sides Wilson made the same reply. To the

One of the wisest Americans of the time was Doctor Charles W. Eliot, president emeritus of Harvard University. Within a week after the war began Doctor Eliot suggested to President Wilson that we should unite with the British and other Allies in a blockade "to rebuke and punish Germany."

Kaiser: he was honored that the Emperor should turn to him "as the representative of a people truly disinterested" — the Kaiser, he was sure, would not expect him "to say more." To the Belgians: "I am honored that your King should have turned to me. . . . You will, I am sure, not expect me to say more."

In the United States Wilson was beset with contradictory advice. The man who perhaps was the wisest American of his time, Doctor Charles W. Eliot, President Emeritus of Harvard University, wrote him:[13]

[12] The delegation arrived September 16, 1914.   [13] August 8, 1914.

Has not the United States an opportunity at this moment to propose a combination of the British Empire, the United States, France, Japan, Italy, and Russia in offensive and defensive alliance to rebuke and punish Austria-Hungary and Germany for the outrages they are now committing by enforcing against those two countries non-intercourse with the rest of the world by land and sea? . . . The proposal would involve the taking part by our navy in the blockading process.

On the other side, the principal man in public life other than the President himself, ex-President Theo-

PRESIDENT URGES PEOPLE TO BE IMPARTIAL IN THOUGHT AND ACTS.

Declaring that the Spirit of the Nation in European Crisis Will Be Determined Largely by What Individuals Do and Say, He Warns Them as Americans Against that "Deepest, Most Subtle, Most Essential Breach of Neutrality Which May Spring Out of Partisanship, Out of Passionately Taking Sides"—Resents Efforts to Embroil the United States in the War and Denies that the Kaiser Has Complained of Unfairness to Germany in This Country.

Newspaper headline announcing President Wilson's proclamation that America should be "neutral in thought as well as in act." New York *World,* August 19, 1914.

dore Roosevelt, wrote:[14] "We should remain entirely neutral and nothing but urgent need would warrant breaking our neutrality and taking sides one way or the other."

To both kinds of advice and all kinds, and to everybody, Wilson replied August 19, with a proclamation:

My Fellow Countrymen: I take the liberty of addressing a

14 *Outlook.* September 23, 1917. Later, Roosevelt changed his attitude.

few words to you[15]. . . to urge very earnestly upon you [that] we must be impartial in thought as well as in action. The United States must be neutral in fact as well as in name.

Finally, he decreed a Peace Sunday:

I, Woodrow Wilson, President of the United States of America, do designate Sunday, the 4th day of October next, a day of

WILSON READY TO RENEW PEACE OFFER WHILE NATION PRAYS

Thousands Join in Plea of Universal Creed at President's Request—Bryan Makes Two Diplomatic Addresses.

SOME PREACHERS SEE NEED OF WAR

U. S. Looked To for Solution of Conflict—Cardinal Farley, Bishop Greer and Others Review Horrors of Strife.

HONOR FOR FIRST AVIATOR TO DROP BOMB ON LONDON

(By Cable to The Tribune.)

Amsterdam, Oct. 4.—Information has been received here from Berlin that the Kaiser has promised to confer a special decoration of the second class of the Order of the Red Eagle on the first German aviator who succeeds in dropping explosives on London. Other lesser, but still unusual honors, are promised to the German aviators who succeed in dropping explosives either on a British warship or on some other town in England.

ITALIANS REPORTED LANDED IN AVLONA

London, Oct. 4.—A Reuter dispatch from Rome says a rumor is in circulation there that Italian sailors were landed Friday at Avlona, a seaport of Albania on the Adriatic.

A Stefani Agency dispatch from Rome says a telegram received fr.

Wilson's proclamation of a "Peace Sunday." The N. Y. *Tribune,* October 5, 1914.

prayer and supplication, and do request all God-fearing persons to repair on that day to their places of worship, there to unite their petitions to Almighty God that . . . He vouchsafe his children healing peace and restore once more concord among men and nations.

The proclamation was very generally carried out. "WHOLE NATION PRAYS FOR PEACE," said a New York *Times* headline, October 5. "The response to the Presi-

---

[15] Throughout this book the appearance of three dots (. . .) in a quotation indicates that something has been omitted. Where there is more than one omission, the dots are in some cases not repeated, in order to avoid awkwardness to the eye. Occasionally the order of sentences or clauses in a quotation is changed. In all cases, of course, there is care not to change the meaning.

dent's call for a day of prayer could not have been more general or more fervent. . . . Enormous numbers of persons went to the doors of the churches at an early hour: thousands tried in vain to obtain admission." Secretary of State Bryan went to New York to speak in the morning at Carnegie Hall, in the evening at Broadway Tabernacle.   In Chicago, Governor Dunne of Illinois, speaking at a meeting with Bishops Fallows and

Mr. Bryan to Urge Peace To-Day in Carnegie Hall

Secretary of State Will Address Free Synagogue and Mr. Oscar S. Straus Will Make an Address from the Same Platform.

ALL CHURCHES TO HOLD SPECIAL SERVICES

Headline from the N. Y. *Herald,* October 4, 1915, announcing that Bryan would speak on "Peace Sunday."

Anderson, observed, with a slight touch of self-righteousness, that "if this Republic can live in peace, others ought to be able to do the same." About the reaction of the battlefields to Mr. Wilson's "Peace Sunday," there is no record, except that the lists of dead and wounded did not diminish.

To Congress, when it came into its first session[15] following the beginning of the war, Wilson spoke with a manner of petulance against those who felt we should take notice of the war by preparing for the eventuality that we might be drawn into it: "This is the time above all others when we should wish and resolve to keep our

[15] December 8, 1914.

strength by self-possession. . . . [To engage in pre-
paredness], permit me to say, would mean merely that
we had lost our self-possession, that we had been thrown
off our balance by a war with which we have nothing
to do, whose causes cannot touch us."

Wilson felt strong, superior, felt that the right is so
mighty it can look after itself without exercise of physical might. Wilson at this time, in this attitude about
the war, was even more the intellectual aristocrat than
usual.

That was the first stage in the evolution of Wilson's
mind with respect to the war. It was an attitude of
proud detachment — the war was a barbarous thing, in-
decent, with which America and Wilson should have
nothing to do. The attitude of America was parallel
with that of Wilson. The country, without quite sharing Wilson's high disdain, felt that the war was, in the
colloquial phrase, "none of our business."

2

AMERICA LOOKS ON AT THE WAR

Being a Picture of the United States during, Mainly, the
Early Months, from August 1, 1914, to About January 1,
1915, More Than Two Years Before We Entered. Our Pre-
occupation with Our Own Affairs, of Which We Were Sure
the War Was Not one. Efforts of Both Groups of Com-
batants to Capture American Sympathy. The Invasion of
Belgium Causes American Sentiment to Crystallize Against
Germany. Complacent Prophecies That "the War Cannot
Touch Us," Which Were Pleasing to Our Prevailing Wish
to "Keep Out of It." Other Prophecies, Saying the War
Could Not Possibly Last More Than Three Months. Some
New Words, Very Strange, That We Were Obliged to
Learn. The Early "Atrocity" Stories. The Singing of "Tip-
perary." Together with Other Episodes of the Period
When We Were Quite Sure the War Was None of Our
Business.

AMERICA was self-contained and self-contented. Our
sense of remoteness from Europe, habitual at all times,
our preoccupation with our own conditions and concerns,
had been accentuated during several years by an enthrall-
ing adventure we were making toward social altruism,
expressing itself in movements toward forbidding labor
by children, limiting employment of women in factories,
prohibiting absolutely the manufacture and sale of alcoholic drinks, giving women the suffrage, enlarging the
direct participation of all citizens in the mechanisms of
government through Direct Primaries, Direct Election
of United States Senators, Initiative and Referendum,
Recall of Judicial Decisions.

All that, and more like it, and controversies arising
out of it, engaged American interest to a degree and in a
manner which we thought of as having a martial quality

47

of its own. *The Literary Digest*, epitome of current events, in its issue of August 8, 1914, seven weeks after the assassination at Sarajevo and eleven days after the opening declaration of war, devoted two pages to "NEW ALIGNMENTS AT ARMAGEDDON." But the historian of 1933, looking in those *Digest* pages for comment about alliances between Russia and France, Kaiser Wilhelm and Emperor Franz Josef, finds, instead of those worthies, a photograph of an obscure New York politician, Harvey D. Hinman, whose title to eminence at Armageddon rested on his candidacy for Governor of New York, which was expected to bring about fusion of the Republican and Progressive parties. The fight between Republican and Progressive, now three years old, was what America in August, 1914, understood to be Armageddon.

II

We had heard, with only listless attention to its ominousness, the shot at Sarajevo;[1] we had read the despatches, sketchily brief in most American newspapers, especially in the interior, about exchanges of angry notes, ultimatums, threatened mobilizations of troops; and we had been aware, rather dimly, that several European nations—we were not quite clear just which ones—were "giving each other the dog-eye."[2] Even when the first of the declarations of war came, July 28, we thought of conflict between Austria and Servia as little more than "another mess in the Balkans," of a sort that had been intermittently chronic as long as any of us could remember. When Germany declared war on Russia, August 1, and the New York Stock Exchange appraised its signifi-

---

[1] June 28. See "Our Times," Vol. IV, Ch. I.

[2] American slang of the day, vivid in the picture it conveyed of dogs as they circle about each other with hair bristling, teeth bared, and eyes that express the emotion of belligerency rather more than they really intend the overt act.

cance by closing for the first time since 1873 (for a period that lasted more than four months — it was reopened on December 12), a few of the more sophisticated among us were impressed; but even yet many Americans paid only casual attention to it, as something far away, and not necessarily conclusive — at all times we thought of most of the European nations, especially those east of the Rhine, as constantly shaking

BELGIAN GOVERNMENT RETIRES TO ANTWERP AS BEGINNING OF NEAR-BY BATTLE IS REPORTED; KAISER AND CROWN PRINCE JOIN THE ARMY

FRANCE MOVES CAPITAL BACK TO BORDEAUX TO LET ALLIES PIVOT THE LEFT WING ON PARIS; PARISIANS SEE THE FIRST BATTLE IN THE AIR

Top: From the N. Y. *Times,* August 18, 1914. *Bottom:* Farthest point reached by the first German drive. From the N. Y. *Times,* September 3, 1914.

mailed fists at each other.[3] American newspapers had a phrase, "saber-rattling," with which they were accustomed to explain that sort of thing, and dismiss it.

It was not until newspaper headlines the morning of August 4 described German troops actually marching

[3] Some who have read proofs of this book think I have overstated American lack of grasp of the meaning of events during July and early August, 1914. But I am sure I am right. One who was far above the average, David Franklin Houston, member of President Wilson's cabinet, wrote, in a memorandum made at the time:

"I had noted with passing interest the news of the assassination of the Austrian Archduke and his wife at Sarajevo, on June 28th, Austria's ultimatum to Serbia on July 23d, Russia's mobilization on the 29th, and Germany's declaration of war against Russia the day before I left Washington. But as . . . there was no clear indication that the developments would be brought very near home to us, I decided to take a short vacation. There had been so much fighting and turmoil in the Balkans that I had become accustomed to them."

"The weather was warm in July, and it was time for the annual holiday. What? Another little war in the Balkans? Serbia is in the Balkans, isn't it? A lot of fuss over an archduke. Called himself Francis Ferdinand. He probably didn't amount to much; he couldn't have with a name like that."—"Wilson the Unknown," by Wells Wells (a pseudonym).

into Belgium on their way to France, that we realized
something formidable and portentous was really under
way.

III

The average American saw Germany's invasion of
Belgium in the simplest possible terms, as big dog pounc-

Photograph by Underwood & Underwood.

Belgians, retreating in front of the German invaders, left their addresses pen-
cilled on bulletin boards for the information of their families.

ing on little one. In such a contest it was an American
trait to take, rather aggressively, the side of the smaller
and under dog — that was a quality of our temperament
and a tenet of our national traditions. Recalling our own
earliest experience as a nation, a small people fighting for
independence against a powerful one, we had usually
sympathized with the little contendent against the in-
vader or oppressor: with Ireland against England, with
the Boers against the British, with Cuba against Spain,

with all the Latin American peoples against Spain and Portugal, with Greece against the Turk. Practically every American school-boy had recited "Marco Bozzaris," had thrilled with sympathy for "Greece, her knees in suppliance bent," and now thought of Belgium in the same appealing rôle. When we read, later, that Germany's invasion of Belgium was something even more flagrant than wanton attack upon a small nation, that Germany was a guarantor of Belgian neutrality, had been bound by specific treaty (with France and Britain) to respect Belgium as neutral, that deepening of the offense, and the indignation that arose against the German Chancellor's scornful reference to the treaty as a "scrap of paper,"[4] added little to the American feeling which had already flamed up against Germany. America's attitude had been fixed the hour that Germany's army projected the first stiff goose-step of its vanguard's toe across the boundary-line of Belgium. With average Americans all the legalisms about right and wrong, all the arguments about original responsibility, weighed little. Only a few scholars in colleges read the official "Books"[5] — White Book, Yellow Book, Red Book — in which the various belligerents tried to fasten blame upon each other. The average American did not look farther into the evidence

[4] The phrase was von Bethmann-Hollweg's, in a conversation with the British Ambassador to Germany, Sir Edward Goschen, late in the evening of the day Britain declared war on Germany. Bethmann-Hollweg, overwrought, forgot restraint in his indignation at England's course. Afterwards he said to a friend: "I did not know I could speak English so fluently; I spoke right out." For his indulgence in the luxury of angry candor he and his country paid a considerable price — his phrase, as propaganda, was as useful to the Allies as an army corps. The context of this phrase was: "Just for a scrap of paper Great Britain is going to make war on a kindred nation." This incident was typical of the blundering statesmanship of Germany throughout the war. Those who wish to read more deeply about the "scrap of paper" will find an account in "The Coming of the War 1914," by Professor Bernadotte E. Schmitt.

[5] The complete spectrum of official accusation and denial, counter-accusation and rebuttal, included: the German White Book, the French Yellow Book, the Russian Orange Book, the Austro-Hungarian Red Book, the Servian Blue Book, the Belgian Gray Book, the British White Paper.

than the simple newspaper picture of the opening blow, a powerful, militarist nation sending a great army into a country we knew was small and believed to be peaceful. That, and Belgium's gallant defense, followed by her succumbing to overwhelming force, fixed American opinion or emotion, crystallized it for the duration of the War, adverse to Germany.

IV

It need not have been so. Had Germany realized, as in her confidence she did not, that the war would be so prolonged as to make American opinion as important as armies and navies; had Prussian insight into American psychology been as accurate as Prussian military science was expert in estimating the quickest path to Paris — in that event Germany might profitably have given up the military advantage of a short-cut[6] through Belgium, for the moral advantage of avoiding alienation of American opinion.

The natural disposition of America was to think well of Germany. Had any one on August 3, 1914, or a week or a month or a year before, said to a group in a cigar store that in any European war, with Germany on one side and France and Russia on the other (as the line-up stood August 3), America would participate, he would have been jeered at. Had the prophet convinced his audience of what then seemed fantastically improbable,

---

[6] Not a short-cut in the sense of materially shorter distance. Germany had hoped and expected that Belgium would interpose no obstacle to the passage of German troops across Belgian territory on their way to France. The fulcrum of the entire German war plan was a swift attack on France, before France had completed her mobilization (and then the concentration of overwhelming forces against the Russians on the Eastern front). Against the French along the narrow, strongly fortified Franco-German frontier, the Germans expected to make but slow progress. To succeed in their campaign they had to go through Belgium.

and had he asked for a cigar-store plebiscite about which side America would take, the response in most cases would have said that in such a line-up America would stand with Germany,[7] against France and Russia.

Every American had neighbors of German birth or ancestry. Germans had been with us in large numbers since the immigration of 1849, and we liked them. Each of us knew a Gus or a Hans, a Heinie or a Rudolf, and had affection and respect for him. Every American, farmer in Iowa or clerk in New York, knew the Germans in America as good citizens and friendly neighbors.

With the French, on the other hand, most Americans had little acquaintance. Vaguely we knew from our school days that Lafayette had fought for us in our war for independence, but that had been a long time ago, and considerations having to do with our early history had begun to become less potent as determining influences on American thought. There were few French among us; and so far as the un-travelled and little-read American knew the French by reputation, he thought of them vaguely as having ways he did not approve — in the lower strata of American folklore, for some reason not easily traceable to its origin, the adjective "French" carried implications of gilded sin, rather than of any particular culture or philosophy. To the average American, a French picture meant one you were more likely to see in a bar-room than in a home. "Slightly Frenchy" meant slightly risqué, or as the common man would have expressed it, "slightly off-color." Certainly "French" did not connote anything you would fight for. As for

[7] This judgment, also, has been queried by some who have read the proofs of this book. But I am writing of August 3, 1914, before Belgium had been invaded and therefore before Britain had entered the war, and before any of the events which alienated American opinion from Germany. I am writing of what American feeling was, other things being equal, as between Germany on one side and France and Russia on the other. It is true that as between Germany on one side and Britain on the other, American opinion was likely to be with Britain.

Russia, we thought of that as pretty far away and a little barbaric.

The Germans on the other hand we thought of as kin to us. Words and phrases of theirs, such as "gemütlichkeit," had passed almost into our own speech, certainly

Many Americans arrived at their view of the French as somewhat "risqué" from magazines such as this.

into our consciousness far enough to carry implications of likable German traits. "Prosit!" and "Gesundheit!" were as common as "To your good health!"; "Auf wiederseh'n!" as frequent as good-bye. Some of the music that was at once the best and most familiar in

America was German, such as "Stille Nacht, Heilige Nacht." Among popular songs, German ones were especially well loved, such as "Ach du Lieber Augustine." Much of our tradition about Christmas had come to us from Germany. German standards of education were

Globe Photograph.

Immediately after the opening of the war, German reservists in New York (as well as French reservists) made their way to the war. This photograph pictures a parade of German reservists. Under the law it was necessary to carry the American flag when the flag of another nation was displayed.

models for many American teachers and colleges. The cleanliness and order and discipline which the Germans called "ordnung" they had brought with them to America, not to so rigid a degree as to repel us, but, rather, sufficient to cause us to think of their ways as somewhat preferable to our own comparative easy-goingness. So far as their Kaiser and their military system carried discipline to an extreme that was repugnant to our conception of government, and to our ideal of individualism, we thought of those German institutions as absurd, to be

laughed at — not by the most fantastic stretch of imagination did we think of German autocracy or German
militarism as things we should ever go to war to destroy.

V

This favorable predisposition on the part of America,
precious possession of the Germans as a people, they lost
the moment their military leaders gave the orders whose
results appeared in American newspaper headlines and
bulletins — the sequence of them was a month-long
drama, a many-act tragedy which America watched
throughout August, 1914, cumulatively stirring our
emotions to indignation against Germany:

August 6:
GERMAN ARMY ATTACKS LIEGE
BELGIANS MAKE HEROIC DEFENSE[8]

August 8:
LIEGE STILL HOLDING INVADERS IN CHECK
BELGIANS FIGHT FIFTY HOURS WITHOUT REST[9]

August 10:
GERMANS CAPTURE LIEGE[10]

August 16:
GERMANS PREPARE TO HURL FULL FORCE ON
CONFIDENT BELGIANS[11]

August 18:
GERMANS CUT THROUGH AT NAMUR;
BELGIANS SHIFT CAPITAL TO ANTWERP[12]

August 21:
GERMAN CAVALRY SEIZES BRUSSELS
BELGIAN ARMY WITHDRAWS TO ANTWERP[13]

[8] New York *Tribune*. Partly paraphrased.
[9] New York *Tribune*. Partly paraphrased.
[10] New York *Tribune*.
[11] New York *Tribune*.
[12] New York *Tribune*. Paraphrased.
[13] New York *Tribune*.

August 22:

GERMANS EXACT FIFTY MILLION DOLLARS
FROM BRUSSELS AND LIEGE[14]

And finally, August 29:

GERMANS SACK LOUVAIN
WOMEN AND CLERGY SHOT[15]

Photograph by Brown Brothers.

Louvain after the German army had passed through. Photographs of ruined
Louvain, printed in the American press, had much to do with the crystallization of American sentiment in favor of Belgium and the Allies.

That conclusion of the subjugation of Belgium, the
sack of Louvain, was the clinching event in the fixation
of American opinion. It was capped, with a convincing-
ness which a tragedy of the imagination would omit as
over-dramatic, by a statement from the Germans,

---

[14] New York *Tribune.*   [15] New York *Tribune.*

Photograph © Underwood & Underwood.

A consultation on the German front in 1914. The figure on the right observing
troop movements through a telescope is one of the Kaiser's sons,
Prince Oscar. America was avid for war pictures.

deemed by them to be justification, but considered by
Americans to be confession by the villain:

BERLIN CONFIRMS LOUVAIN HORROR

Washington, August 28. The German Embassy to-day
gave out the following wireless from Berlin: "Civilians of
the Belgium [sic] town of Louvain made a perfidious attack on German troops while fighting. Louvain was punished by the destruction of the city. . . ."[16]

Civilians attacking troops could never, to the American way of thinking, appear so shocking as it did to the

[16] New York *Tribune.*

Kaiser's militaristic psychology; what seemed outrageous to America was troops attacking civilians.

Louvain was the climax of Belgium, and Belgium the precipitant of American opinion. "For us," said one of the most understanding of American commentators,[17] "the great, clear issue of this war is Belgium. If we see anything right at all in all this matter, Belgium is a martyr to civilization, sister to all who love liberty or law; assailed, polluted, trampled in the mire, heel-marked in her breast, tattered, homeless. . . . The great — unconquerable fact of the great war is Belgium."

VI

Though Germany's invasion of Belgium made us partisan, we were still very distant from thinking of the struggle as a thing we should have any part in. As Germany pressed on into France, and into Russia on the East, we took the rôle of fans in the bleachers, regarding the Allies like the home team, to be sure, and cheering them on, but with no more thought of becoming participants than of descending on the diamond to take part in the game. In this spirit during the early weeks, the war was discussed in corner-grocery forums, on the street and in the home, displacing argument about the relative merits and capacities of Red Sox versus Chicago Cubs, Jack Johnson versus Jess Willard, Democratic versus Republican, Roosevelt versus Wilson.

Favor for the Allies did not blind us to the formidableness of the Germans, nor did heat of feeling deprive us of humor. A quip of the day, one of scores of jokes, legends, and sayings that became a current American

17 Edward S. Martin, editor of *Life*, January 7, 1915.

folklore, took the form of dialogue between two negroes:

"Dem Englishmens has got a gun dat'll kill you at five miles."
"Huh! Dey ain't got nothin' on dem Jummans. W'y, man, wid deir guns, all dey ask to kill you is yo' address!"[18]

Presently, as a kind of newspaper record of the progress of the game, came daily maps with a heavy black line to show the long battle-front from Switzerland to the sea, first-page equivalent of the baseball score on the tenth page. The crude small newspaper maps were supplemented soon by large colored ones hung from the walls of business offices, accompanied by a little tray of pins with which could be marked the wavering of the line from day to day, pins with blue heads for the Allies, red ones for the Germans. Many an American carried for years, as a vivid recollection of the Great War, the emotion, in most cases sad, with which he set blue pins back, red ones forward, until September 3, when soberly he set the blue pins of the Allies almost on the borders of Paris, and read that the French government had removed the capital to Bordeaux. Thereafter, beginning September 6–10, he enjoyed for several days in succession the exultation of setting red pins farther and farther back toward Germany. Toward Germany, but not into Germany. Not until after the armistice did the Allies on the West set foot on German soil.

VII

Adequate expression of our interest in the struggle was handicapped by difficulty of pronouncing places of battles and names of generals — it dawned upon many Americans that another reason for self-congratulation lay in the democratic simplicity which had led us to fight

18 *Life,* June 10, 1915.

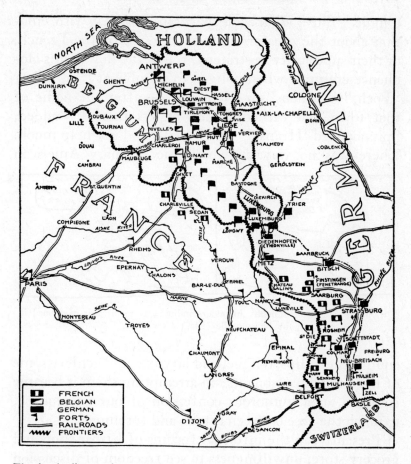

The battle line as it stood August 19, 1914. Maps like this were in every American newspaper and enlarged ones were on the walls of many offices. This map appeared in the N. Y. *Times*.

our American battles at places and under generals having names easily pronounceable by any lips. Bunker Hill and Gettysburg, George Washington and Robert E. Lee, did not require one to twist his tongue into unaccustomed contortions.

German names gave us little trouble. Von Kluck and von Hindenberg, von Moltke and von Falkenhayn, von Bulow and von Mackensen, were easy to the American tongue. But a cigar-store partisan, charged with emotion about the greater right on the side of the French, or their superiority in strategy, found the flow of his eloquence cramped when obliged to stumble at "Joffre" or "Foch," "Amiens" or "Rheims" — after the name of that town and cathedral newspapers tactfully added, "pronounced 'Hrans'," which really did not help much. There was no way by which the ordinary American

Provincial American difficulty in understanding war terms was cartooned in
the Jacksonville (Fla.) *Metropolis.*

equipment of lips, tongue, and larynx could achieve some of the French consonants; in attempting them it became common, as a humorous confession of our inadequacy, to pinch the nose between thumb and forefinger.

Presently, in the informal forums of barber shop and grocery store, unwillingness to see freedom of discussion hampered by an immaterial detail of phonetics, arrived tolerantly at standardized approximations of French, Belgian, and Polish names, which, however they might have surprised the respective nationalities, became valid verbal tender in the cigar-store exchanges. Among the atrocities of the war not undeserving of mention were the varied violences of mutilation practised upon the word "Ypres,"[19] which some impish god decreed should

[19] Not one American in ten thousand ever achieved complete comfort in pronouncing "Ypres," not even those who as members of the American Expeditionary Force came to have personal contact with the place. British "Tommies"

be the place where the battle line crystallized roughly for most of the war, hence the one town most necessary to mention. Only slightly less incommoding were Mons and Aisne, Oise and Ourcq.

As for the scenes of battles between Germans and Russians, a material factor contributing to the lesser American interest in the Eastern front was the difficulty of expressing convictions or emotion in sentences compelled to include "Przemsl," which became, during the early part of the war, almost as much a landmark on the East as Ypres on the West. It was not reasonable to expect Americans, even those with the most wide-ranging interests, to include in their concerns a battle-front which, as reported in the New York *Times*, September 1, 1914, "extends through Przmyslany to Brzozdovitza."

VIII

Many new words, essential vocabulary of the struggle, we could not ignore. They came across the ocean to us in every despatch. To read about the war we had to learn them; to talk about it we had, difficult job for most of us, to pronounce them: "bosche" for German soldiers, later varied by "Fritzy"; "junker" for German caste arrogance; "All-highest," a jeering designation of the Kaiser; "Hun," generic word for all Germans, conveying an implication of barbarism; "poilu" for French soldiers, "Tommies" for British — the last derived from Kipling's "Here's to you, Tommy Atkins." "Allies" for one group of contendents, "Entente" for the other group, became familiar in the printed form, but timorousness about pronouncing them led us to use the term

---

suffered no such embarrassment; confident of the superiority of British ways, they called it "Wipers," and were tolerantly courteous in concealing their surprise at the ignorance of Belgians who failed to understand.

"Germans" for all the Central powers. "Carry on," British term for "close ranks," coming later to signify cheerful endurance under hard circumstances; "cheerio," British word of greeting, meant in part to

A world-wide view about "Kultur" as reflected in an Italian periodical, which pictured "Kultur" as a plant which must be watered often with blood.

convey the effect of an encouraging slap on the back. "Shrecklichkeit," German word for frightfulness, used by their enemies and critics, and to some extent by themselves, to describe their means of reducing to meekness the civilian populations of the Belgian and French towns they occupied. "Der Tag," to which Germans drank toasts, as the day when they should attain their "place in the sun." "Kultur," spelled, according to German usage, always with a capital K; a sinister quality attributed to the word was suggested by a magazine article to which Professor Frank Jewett Mather, Jr., of Princeton University, gave the caption, "Kultur versus Culture." "Gott strafe" — presumed to be an habitual German state of mind, the object of the malediction being England, or the United States, or whatever other country or individual was at the moment an impediment to German purposes. "Deutschland über Alles," denoting German ambition or German exultation. "C'est la guerre," shoulder-shrugging explanation of anything that went wrong, any interruption of the accustomed routine of peace. "Somewhere in France," dictated by military authorities as the only permitted date-line on news despatches or letters, since greater exactness might enlighten the enemy about the location of troops. "Zeppelins," "blimps," "communiqué," "sector," "propaganda."[20]

IX

Almost instantly with the outbreak of the war came recognition by both sides that American public opinion constituted a sector of the battle-front rather more important to capture than Mons or Verdun. To win American opinion, propaganda arose; it came from all the combatants; we were drenched with it. We did not at first call it by that name. Hitherto "propaganda" had been a rather technical word, residing mainly in the world of religion, describing the process and institutions by which churches, especially the Catholic, sought to propagate the Christian faith in non-Christian nations.

[20] This partial list of war words is meant to be confined to ones that arose and became familiar to America during the early months, the summer and fall of 1914. Many others arose later.

Such attempts by interested parties to shape public opinion as we had been familiar with in America had come mainly from the world of business and had been called "publicity." It was by that name, or in that way, that

The first press agent's war, pictured in the Baltimore (Md.) *Star,* Oct. 8, 1914.

we thought, at the early stage, of the attempts of the European combatants to influence us: "This," said a New York *Times* editorial, September 9, 1914, "is the first press agents' war."

"Press agent," however, was recognized instinctively as too lowly a term to describe the personages who presently made us the beneficiary of efforts to influence our opinions. They were very exalted indeed, as exalted as possible, for capture of American public opinion was recognized by every head of state involved to be a major objective of the war. Kaiser Wilhelm, King Albert of Belgium, King George and Foreign Minister Grey of Britain, President Poincare of France, all bestowed upon us repeatedly gestures or messages designed to attract us to their respective sides.

From the heads of state down, varied groups were called to the literary colors, or volunteered. Fifty-three

Berlin Accuses France of Atrocities

Protests Against Mutilation and Killing of Wounded German Soldiers, Charges French Troops Fired on Ambulances and Physicians in the Field, Invaded Hospitals, Arrested Clergymen and Otherwise Disregarded the Rules of War.

New York *Herald,* Oct. 22, 1914.

British authors, including Kipling, Galsworthy, Hardy, Masefield, Barrie (Barrie came to visit us), united in a statement assuring us of the "righteousness" of the Allied cause, "its vital import to the future of the world." Germany countered with twenty-two heads of German universities who sent out a "German appeal to civilized nations against the campaign of systematic lies and slander." One hundred and fifty British professors exchanged literary volleys with "34 German dignitaries . . . thinkers, moralists, philanthropists," who proclaimed "the Truth about Germany, Facts about the War." Forty-five British artists and art-lovers were pitted against ninety-six German professors, "representatives of German art and science" who protested "to the civilized world [especially America] against the lies and calumnies" of the Allies.

"*It is not true,*" the Herr Professors said, with italicized asseveration, "that Germany caused this war. . . . *It is not true* that we trespassed in neutral Belgium. *It is not true* that our troops treated Louvain brutally. . . ."

X

In the competition to capture American favor, Britain had many advantages. British and other Allied propaganda was much "more general than that of the Teutons, and more adroit."[21] Also, Britain, with France, controlled all the cables. Britain cut the only German cable as one of her first acts in the war. By the British control of cables, German communication with the United States (excepting by mail, which hardly counted) was confined to wireless, then still new and imperfect. The two receiving stations in America, at Sayville, Long Island, and Tuckerton, N. J., were taken over and censored by the American government; Germany was permitted to communicate in cipher with its ambassador in Washington, only provided a copy of the code was deposited with the State Department. Anyhow, German messages flying through the air were subject to not difficult picking up and deciphering by the extremely expert British secret service. The only real means left Germany to communicate with the United States was by mail, much too slow for the speed with which events moved. Besides, Britain, by reason of her incomparable advantage, control of the sea, was able to assert the right and exercise the power to seize and hold long enough for examination and censorship, mail between the United States and Germany, even mail directed via neutral countries, and mail originating in neutral countries, including

[21] "Brief History of the Great War," Carlton J. H. Hayes.

© *Underwood & Underwood.*

RHEIMS CATHEDRAL CANNOT BE RESTORED SAYS THOMAS HARDY

Stained Glass Irreplaceable, as Is the Sculpture—Vandalism a Product of Nietzschian Philosophy.

Top: The ruins of Rheims Cathedral. *Lower Right:* A cartoon by Rogers in the New York *Herald* of August, 1914, on German Religious Art.

America.   Britain was ruthless about it.   She seized and
opened official letters addressed to our consuls.[22]

As one result of control of cables by the Allies, the

American opinion was unanimous in regarding as outrageous and intolerable
Britain's interference with our commerce with European countries other
than the Allies. The author of this cartoon, McCutcheon, of the Chicago
Tribune, aptly labeled it: "The Atrocities Still Go On." The sitting figure
is, of course, John Bull.

bulk of the news America got, whether of battle or of
other developments, came from or via London or Paris,
and took on the color of the route it travelled.   American
correspondents at the front were almost always with the

[22] Consul General Skinner at London, in a letter to the Secretary of State,
September 15, 1916: "I have the honor to report that within the last ten days
practically all letters addressed to me or to the Consulate General, of American
origin, have been opened by the censors."

Allied troops, since only from there would they get their accounts to America promptly. Correspondents not at the front were usually at one of the Allied capitals; inevitably they took much of their news from the British and French press — what they did not get from that source, they necessarily could only get from British and French officials. Moreover, practically everything they sent was censored. What the Allies did not want sent to America was not sent.

The limitations on German communication with the United States really mattered little. What the Germans were able to send was ill-designed to be effective — the time came when German Ambassador von Bernstorff at Washington cabled to von Bethman-Hollweg that German propaganda might as well be given up. Germany, through long domination of its schools and all its culture by a militaristic ideal, had developed points of view which to America were not only strange but repugnant. Much of Germany's propaganda, in its impact on American thought, took on a reverse quality, became a boomerang. Hardly any British denunciation of the destruction of Louvain aroused as much indignation as the way the Germans tried to justify it — the Kaiser's explanation that:

> The old town of Louvain . . . had to be destroyed for the protection of my troops. My heart bleeds when I see such measures unavoidable and when I think of the many innocent people who have lost their houses and property as a result of the misdeeds of the guilty [Belgians !]. The cruelties practised in this cruel warfare, even by [Belgian] women and priests, toward wounded [German] soldiers and doctors and hospital nurses, were such that eventually my generals were compelled to adopt the strongest measures to punish the guilty and frighten the blood-thirsty population from continuing their shameful deeds.[23]

[23] Kaiser Wilhelm to President Wilson, September 7, 1914.

XI

Most of all, Germany was eclipsed in American favor
by England through the possession by America and England of a common tongue and common ways of looking
at things, a common background of literature and institutions. When Kipling at the outset of the war wrote,

> For all we have and are,
> For all our children's fate,
> Stand up and meet the war;
> The Hun is at the gate. . . .
>
> There's but one task for all,
> For each one life to give.
> Who stands if freedom fall?
> Who dies if England live?[24]

— that sentiment did not come to America as from an
alien people, most of America felt it as much as the British themselves. Similarly, when Rupert Brooke, as he
went to the war, wrote:

THE SOLDIER

> If I should die, think only this of me:
>   That there's some corner of a foreign field
> That is for ever England. There shall be
>   In that rich earth a richer dust concealed;
> A dust whom England bore, shaped, made aware,
>   Gave, once, her flowers to love, her ways to roam. . . .

— that spirit of gentleness and dedication appealed as
much to America as to England. And when John Masefield wrote:

AUGUST, 1914

> How still this quiet cornfield is to-night. . . .
>
> So beautiful it is I never saw
>   So great a beauty on these English fields
> Touched, by the twilight's coming, into awe
>   Ripe to the soul and rich with summer's yields.

[24] Printed in America as a despatch to the N. Y. *Times,* Sept. 2, 1914.

These homes, this valley spread below me here,
  The rooks, the tilted stacks, the beasts in pen,
Have been the heartfelt things, past-speaking dear
  To unknown generations of dead men.

Who, century after century, held these farms,
  And, looking out to watch the changing sky,
Heard, as we hear, the rumors and alarms
  Of war at hand and danger pressing nigh.

Then sadly rose and left the well-loved Downs
  And so, by ship to sea, and knew no more
The fields of home, the byres, the market towns,
  Nor the dear outline of the English shore.

— that affection-stirring evocation of quiet English scenes and ways of life excited in America, to almost the same degree as in England, common sentiments, common memories of long vistas of English literature back to Chaucer, common visions of English landscapes described in Thackeray and George Eliot.

Milton and Wordsworth, Shakespeare and Shelley were as much a part of the fibre of American emotion as of English. As the war got under way one could realize that without any planning, without any intention of propaganda, with a force that made propaganda a fantastic superfluity, every little red school house in America where on Friday afternoon children recited Gray's "Elegy Written in a Country Churchyard," had been through generations a recruiting post which now produced sympathy for Britain; and every prairie courthouse where judges and lawyers dealt daily with Blackstone and Coke and Magna Charta, had been an unconscious breeding-ground for the conviction that British institutions must not be destroyed.

All this crystallized when Britain entered the war, when the line-up became, in American eyes, mainly Britain versus mainly Germany. We followed the fortunes of the first British Expeditionary Force almost as closely, as poignantly, as if it had been our own; took almost as much pride as the British themselves in turning into a designation of honor the term in which the Kaiser was said to have expressed his jeering scorn of them, "the Contemptibles."[25] When cables told us the British in France, as they marched, sang a ditty that had been current in London music halls when they entrained, America took up the tune almost as universally as the British themselves — "Tipperary" during the fall and winter of 1914–15 was sung in America, and whistled, hummed, danced to and applauded, in public places where "Die Wacht am Rhein" would have led to a riot, and even the gentle "Du Bist Wie Eine Blume" would have drawn scowls.

XII

The appeal to America of such war-verse as Kipling's, Brooke's and Masefield's, partly because of its prevailing gentleness or its superior art, partly because of our own predisposition, was more effective than some efforts in verse that the Germans made. Doubtless Ernest Lissauer's Hymn of Hate Against England[26] ("Hassgesang Gegen England") may have given emotional satisfaction to Germans, may have stirred their people to greater militancy — Lissauer was for the time the mouthpiece

[25] Kaiser Wilhelm said he had never used the phrase attributed to him "the contemptible little army." George Sylvester Viereck thinks it may have been an adaptation of an answer made by Bismarck many years before to the question: "What would you do if England landed an army on the coast of Germany" — "I would call out the police to arrest them."
There is impressive evidence that the phrase was deliberately invented and attributed to the Kaiser by an artful British propagandist; if so that literary combatant should rank with the best of the British military leaders; the three words "contemptible little army," by its stimulation of British morale, its evocation of American sympathy, was very valuable.
[26] This version is as it appeared in the New York Times, October 15, 1914, translated by Barbara Henderson.

of Germany, he was decorated with the Order of the
Red Eagle; his hymn had universal circulation, became

© 1912, B. Feldman & Co.

The first war song coming from Europe to America was "Tipperary," during
the fall and winter of 1914–15. "Tipperary" had been composed and published two years before but did not become popular in America until despatches from the front in France said it was the favorite marching song of
the first British Expeditionary Force.

a folk-song, was distributed among the troops as an army
order by Crown Prince Rupprecht of Bavaria:

> French and Russian, they matter not
> A blow for a blow and a shot for a shot . . .
> We have but one and only hate,
> We love as one, we hate as one,

We have one foe and one alone.
Come, let us stand at the Judgment Place,
An oath to swear to, face to face,
An oath of bronze no wind can shake,
An oath for our sons and their sons to take.
Come, hear the word, repeat the word,
Throughout the Fatherland make it heard.
We will never forego our hate,
We have all but a single hate,
We love as one, we hate as one,
We have one foe and one alone —
        ENGLAND!

You we will hate with a lasting hate,
We will never forego our hate,
Hate by water and hate by land,
Hate of the head and hate of the hand,
Hate of the hammer and hate of the crown,
Hate of seventy millions choking down.
We love as one, we hate as one,
We have one foe and one alone —
        ENGLAND!

As argument the "Hymn of Hate" belonged in the category that gives pleasure to the arguer as a catharsis of his anger, rather than that which converts the hearer, or enlists his sympathy. To America, the violence of the "Hymn of Hate" tended to confirm our impression of German bitterness, German arrogance. The "passionateness of its rhythm, its flashing energy and Old Testament hatred" impressed us — but moved us in a direction opposite to the prayer. From the point-of-view of enlisting sympathy from America, poet Lissauer would have done better had he had, in 1914, the afterthought he expressed in 1928, when he found it "painful to find my name still always associated with killing and destroying . . . I realize to-day that I would have done better to give vent to my feelings not in a Hymn of Hate against England but in a Hymn of Love for Germany."

An American periodical, influential at that time, *Life*, was strongly pro-Ally; in its cartoons it habitually pictured Germans and even German-Americans as repellent persons inimical to the American flag and American institutions. From *Life*, July 15, 1915.

Similarly, when the German-American poet, George Sylvester Viereck, addressed the Kaiser, astonishingly, as "the Prince of Peace":

> May thy victorious armies rout
> The savage tribes against thee hurled,
> The Czar, whose sceptre is the knout,
> And France, the wanton of the world.
>
> But thy great task will not be done
> Until thou vanquish utterly
> The Norman brother of the Hun,
> England, the Serpent of the Sea.

— the common American instinct was to wonder whether to be shocked at the impiety of the Kaiser as Christ, laugh at the absurdity, or get angry at the fierce incitement to hate. A distinguished American editor, Henry Watterson, solved what doubt there might be by calling Viereck a "venom-bloated toad."

German violence repelled us, German humor — let us put it this way — did not appeal to us. Designation of their opponents as the "All-Lies" may have pleased the Germans, but did not convert many Americans.

XIII

Propaganda, at first chiefly that from the Allies, projected "atrocities," in a special meaning, into our rapidly increasing vocabulary of war. Allied propagandists charged that German soldiers had cut off the breasts of Belgian women, the hands of Belgian babies, that London hospital cots contained scores of the maimed Belgian children; that German soldiers had crucified Canadian soldiers, with bayonets stuck through hands and feet; that the Germans, as a detail of efficiency, salvaged all the corpses on battlefields, tied them into bales, and shipped them back to Germany to be made into soap, grease, and fertilizer.[27]

Germans, with equal inventiveness, charged that the

[27] This story did not become current until 1917. The one about Belgian babies, with scores of others, arose during the early occupation of Belgium. The story about crucified Canadians was printed in the London *Times,* May 15, 1915, and asserted in the House of Commons, August 12.

The corpse-factory story arose from the fact that the Germans actually did make use of dead horses. A German newspaper allusion to this use of "Kadavers" was picked up by an official British propagandist who either did not know, or adroitly forgot, that in Germany the word "kadaver" is used about animals only, whereas in English "cadaver" is used about humans only. The propagandist sent the story to Asia for effect on Hindus to whom this use of the bodies of animals was as odious as the same use of human bodies; and on Chinese, who revere their ancestors. From this start the story went around the world.

TOURIST SAW SOLDIER WITH BAGFUL OF EARS

American Salesman Bluffs His Way to Front and Sees Real Fighting.

Super-Dum Dums Inflict Awful Injuries on Victims

Wounds of Soldiers in Hospitals in Belgium Cited as Proof of Use of Prohibited Bullets by Prussians—German Denials and Accusations Ready When War Begun.

N. Y. Herald, Oct. 5, 1914.

Life.

Life, July 25, 1915.

There was much propaganda to the effect that prisoners were mutilated and that the Germans took delight in torturing the weak and helpless.

Allies gouged out the eyes of German prisoners; that the French put cholera germs in wells in territory occupied by the Germans; that a Belgian priest wore a chain of

This picture (from *Life,* March 21, 1918) reflected one of the most widespread "atrocity" stories. It was to the effect that the dead bodies of German soldiers were gathered up on the battle-field, were shipped back to Germany, and were treated chemically to procure lubricant oils, fats, and fertilizers. The story was untrue; explanation of it will be found in the text of this chapter.

German finger rings around his neck; that French priests offered to German soldiers coffee poisoned with strychnine; that a Belgian priest put a machine gun behind the altar to spray German Catholic soldiers who came to Mass.

America, prevailingly, being pro-Ally, believed the stories of German atrocities, rejected the Allies' ones. Many, one felt, seemed to get a perverse pleasure in be-

By courtesy of the Century Company.

To Your Health!·Civilization!

Louis Raemaeker's cartoons furnished the most graphic evidence of the barbarity and waste of war.

lieving the story about the Belgian children without hands. It persisted for the duration of the war. In 1918, an Iowa orator making speeches to stimulate purchase of Liberty bonds, told the story as a personal experience: A childless couple, he said, friends of his, who had sent to Belgium for two children for adoption, found the tots, when they arrived, handless. A Des Moines newspaper man,[28] skeptical, directed a photographer to find and photograph those children regardless of expense. They were never found. They did not exist. The orator finally admitted he had averred his personal knowledge of the story as an invented contribution to stimulate emotion which should express itself in buying more Liberty bonds.

By five years after the war ended, practically every atrocity story from either side had failed, upon investigation, to yield proof. "A lie," said Sophocles, "never lives to be old." But for these atrocity stories, to live for the duration of the war was, as regards effect, to live forever.

XIV

The disposition to believe atrocity stories was part of a disposition to believe anything, and this was in part due to censorship. There was censorship by each of the combatants over everything sent from the front to the home press, an additional censorship over everything sent from Europe to America, and a special censorship by Britain over material sent or attempted to be sent from Germany to the United States. The public was aware of it, and knowledge that censorship was in effect modified the public's attitude. When newspapers are functioning normally, a sensational story received by word of mouth is accepted until the appearance of the next day's newspaper; if the newspaper does not contain the story, it is dismissed as a canard. During the war, however, men heard sensational stories, failed to find confirmation in the next day's newspaper, started in their minds to dismiss the yarn but suddenly thought, "Ah, but the censorship may

[28] Gardner Cowles, publisher of the Des Moines *Register*.

have ruled it out." Thereupon he believed the story, and, passing it on, enlarged and adorned it.

In the absence of newspapers functioning normally as fumigants of sensational rumor, preposterous yarns passed by word of mouth. A familiar one, during the

Photograph by Underwood & Underwood.

Children war refugees from Flanders arriving at the Gare du Nord, Paris, 1915.

first two months of the war, was that an immense Russian army, coming circuitously via Archangel, had managed to unite with the French on the Western front. The size of the Muscovite host was in proportion to the spectacular quality of their being in France at all; a particularly restrained version of the story, in the New York *Times*, September 4, 1914 (on the authority of a passenger just arrived from England on the *Mauretania*), put the number at a modest 72,000. Nearly every person in England, France, and the United States had a friend who had an acquaintance who had seen trainloads of the bearded Russians passing from a port in Scotland, to which they had come from Archangel, across England to France. In variations, the source of the information was a bystander at a railroad depot who had seen the Russians dash into the station restaurant to ask for vodka, or whatever British substitute had the highest alcoholic content; or a wakeful farmer, hearing a special train go by, had looked out to see bearded faces peer out between the slats of drawn car-window blinds.

Explanations of the canard, when explanations came, were as various as the story itself. One said that a British soldier who happened to wear a beard — if there was such a British soldier — when asked where he came from, replied "Ross-shire," easily translated, in those excited days, into "Russia." A plausible explanation said that a British merchant who had imported a car-load of Russian eggs, had unintentionally stirred the imagination of the world by an economy in telegraph tolls which led him to wire "100,000 Russians arrived." Russian eggs may or may not have arrived in England; during the four years of war, no Russian soldier fought in France.

One form of the world-wide credulity attributed to the Germans a talent, in war and for all purposes, which was more than superefficient, almost supernatural. A story from France recited discovery that the Germans, in anticipation of the war, had laid concrete foundations here and there through France and Belgium, which they could use for their great guns so soon as "Der Tag" arrived. With this as a start, the story took the whole world for its field. In every country the Germans had laid similar foundations in anticipation of a later "Tag." About this story, credulity extended to high places. President Wilson, talking with Colonel House during the early months[29] of the war, said there was reason to sus-

[29] November 4, 1914. Intimate Papers of Colonel House.

pect the Germans had laid throughout America concrete foundations for great guns, similar to those they
had laid in France and Belgium, in anticipation of war."

Uncle Sam Has the Chance of His Life

TO SIT TIGHT, KEEP HIS HANDS IN HIS POCKETS AND HIS MOUTH SHUT.

Our impulse in 1914 was "to keep out of it."

—*The Riverside (California) Press.*

Wilson asked General Leonard Wood to investigate, but
warned him to be discreet, for "if the rumor got abroad
it would inflame our people." The rumor did get abroad;
German-born citizens who had concrete floors in their
cellars or garages came under vigilant scrutiny from
their neighbors.

XV

The common American impulse was "to keep out of it." Prediction said this would be easy. Much of the prophecy — there were floods of it — had to do with duration; the common estimate of the length so devastating a war could last was three to five months. Equally frequent among the prophecies was the word "certain" or "permanent" accompanying self-congratulation over America's immunity, our "permanent good-fortune" in not being mixed up in it.

"Our isolated position and freedom from entangling alliances," said *The Literary Digest*, putting the common attitude into words, "inspire our press with the cheering assurance that we are in no peril of being drawn into the European quarrel." The New York *Sun*, confidently and somewhat complacently, asserted that the United States would "suffer inevitably to some extent from the waste and destruction abroad, but it had permanent cause for gratitude in its insulation from the worst." Any timid souls dubious of the soundness of this conviction had reassurance from the professors, the historians. Very generally they agreed with Doctor Roland G. Usher, author of numerous books on history and head of the Department of History at Washington University:[36]

Needless to say, the European war will not involve the United States in actual hostilities. It is highly improbable that either our army or our navy will see service. We are too distant from the seat of war; too entirely devoid of interests the combatants might seriously injure, too completely incapable of aiding or abetting one or the other in arms to cause them to assail us. Even were we not a nation of a peaceful disposition, even had we not a President blessed with a singularly

[36] New York *Times* "Current History of the War."

clear head and able to keep his temper, we should still stand little chance of going to war.[37]

[37] If Doctor Usher's major prophecy, about the war and America, turned out to be matter for smiling, a minor prediction of his, in the field of economics, turned out to be grimly accurate:

"After the close of the European war, when manufacturing and production are resumed, America will find herself over-producing and face to face with another economic readjustment necessary to meet the new situation. Then will ensue a commercial crisis with all its attendant suffering and trouble such as the United States has probably never seen and which will be violent and serious in proportion to the length of the war."

3

WILSON MAINTAINS NEUTRALITY, WITH DIFFICULTY

He Finds, Reluctantly, That Despite His High-minded Intentions the War Can "Touch Us." Britain Violates Our Rights as a Neutral. Germany Does the Same, in Different Ways, Ways Rather More Serious. As to Both, Wilson Is Firm. But His Firmness toward Britain Is Qualified by One of Those Personal Equations That Frequently Play a Large Part in History, the Personality of the American Ambassador to Britain, Walter H. Page.

WHEN Wilson spoke of it as "a war with which we have nothing to do"[1] he was expressing the original attitude with which the evolution of his mind began. "Cannot touch us"[1] expressed his ideal, his wish to keep the war at arm's length, to look on it with disdain; "cannot touch us" was not a clear judgment of facts and probabilities. Within a few months, events forced Wilson to learn that when a human being wishes to have nothing to do with an abstract force, the wish may fail to be mutual; that however firm Wilson's determination (on behalf of himself and America) to have nothing to do with the war, the war failed to entertain the corresponding determination toward America. Thus arrived a material modification of Wilson's mind; he still loathed the war, regarded it as an unqualified barbarism, felt that the best rôle for America was to preserve in the world an island of sanity; but he found that maintenance of neutrality required an affirmative state of mind, could not be achieved by negative aloofness, that it involved constant care, continuous readiness to meet emergencies.

[1] In his address to Congress December 8, 1914.

Left: Warning, by the cartoonist Darling, following the outbreak of war in Europe, of the tragic aftermath that would follow America's becoming a belligerent.—*Des Moines (Iowa) Register and Leader. Right:* Cartoon from *Life* (which was pro-Ally from the start) suggesting that neutrality on the part of the United States could only lead to disaster.

Daily, actions by British and actions by Germans called for action by us.

II

The Allies bought great quantities of munitions in America. This, Germany (and the German-Americans)

"Strictly Neutral"

This cartoon in *Life* hinted sardonically that one of America's reasons for not taking part in the war was our immense profits through remaining neutral and manufacturing supplies for the Allies.

resented. They forgot that, so far as the United States was concerned, the Germans were as free to buy from us as the British.

What moved sympathizers with Germany was a sense

The German submarine *Deutschland*, the only German vessel carrying cargo that reached the United States during the war.

GERMAN U-BOAT REACHES BALTIMORE, HAVING CROSSED ATLANTIC IN 16 DAYS; HAS LETTER FROM KAISER TO WILSON

BOAT AND ERRAND A PUZZLE

Officials in Washington Prepare to Determine Deutschland's Status.

LEGAL QUESTIONS RAISED

If the Craft Is a Merchantman New Problems Will Be Set in International Law.

ENVOY MAY BE ABOARD

Germans Insist U-Boat Carries No Arms and Was Built Solely for the Merchant Service

Special to The New York Times.

BALTIMORE, Md., July 9.—This much can be authoritatively told about the Deutschland: She belongs to the Ocean Rhoderei of Bremen, a corporation formed to attempt the sub-surface crossing of the Atlantic, the possibility of which Germany has been boasting for some time. She was built to carry cargo, mails, and official dispatches, and her agents here assert that she carries no arms whatever.

Special to The New York Times.

WASHINGTON, July 9.—The statement was made tonight in a well-informed German quarter that the submarine Deutschland was sent to this country not as a naval vessel, but as a merchant submarine by the North German Lloyd Company, and that its commanding officer was not an officer on the active list of the German Navy, but a merchant Captain who was formerly in command of the German steamship Neckar.

DODGES ALLIES' CRUISERS

Runs Past Warship Patrols at Cape Henry and Gets Into Port.

VALUABLE CARGO ABOARD

With Dyes and Chemicals, She Gains Port at Night and Will Dock Today.

GERMAN AGENTS ELATED

Remarkable feat of the German U-Boat *Deutschland*. From the N. Y. *Times*, July 10, 1916.

of frustration arising from an inherent handicap under which Germany suffered. Her enemy, Great Britain, controlled the sea. Hence British (and other Allied) ships could come and go to the United States without impediment (until German submarines were able to set up a partial one). But no German ship could venture on the ocean; during the whole four years only one German vessel set out for and arrived at a United States port, a submarine, the *Deutschland*, which, furtively crossing the Atlantic, sailed audaciously into the harbor of Norfolk, Va., with a cargo of dyes and chemicals — the sporting tribute which American feeling gave to the feat was testimony at once to the gallantry of it and its uniqueness, and also a sign of Germany's helplessness on the sea.[1a]

Germans and British alike were free to buy munitions in the United States; the difference was that Britain could take them home, Germany could not. (Except furtively and infrequently, by use of neutral aid.) The Germans were unable to distinguish between their emotion arising from their helplessness and the hard fact of Britain's superior power on the sea.

Because Germany could not get munitions from America, the Germans said, in effect, the Allies should be prevented from buying, by our government. This view, and other complaints, the German-Americans presently embodied in an appeal to Congress, an appeal which, as summed up by the National German-American Alliance, was that Congress should "lay an embargo

[1a] The *Deutschland's* voyage was one of the most spectacular events of the war. After reaching Norfolk she proceeded to Baltimore, whence she sailed August 1, 1916, arriving back in Germany on the 23d. On November 1, she completed another trip, carrying a cargo worth $10,000,000, which she discharged at New London, Conn. November 21, leaving New London at midday, she had little trouble evading the Allied ships lying in wait for her outside the three-mile limit and returned successfully to Germany.

upon all contraband of war (saving and excepting food-
stuffs alone), and thereby withdraw from the contending powers all aid and assistance of this Republic."

With this demand, and their other complaints, the
German-Americans sought out a Senator who had a
large constituency of their race, Stone of Missouri.
Stone, January 8, 1915, laid the complaints, numbered 1
to 20, before Secretary of State Bryan. Bryan — in an
adventure into cold reason so unusual with him as to
suggest that this, like some of his other state papers, may
have been vicarious, the voice of Bryan but the hand
of a State Department lawyer — replied:

Those in this country who sympathize with Germany and
Austria-Hungary appear to assume that some obligation rests
upon this government, in the performance of its neutral duty,
to prevent all trade in contraband, and thus to equalize the
difference due to the relative naval strength of the belligerents.
No such obligation exists; it would be an unneutral act, an
act of partiality on the part of the [United States] government
to adopt such a policy if the Executive had the power to do so.
If Germany and Austria-Hungary cannot import contraband
from this country it is not, because of that fact, the duty of
the United States to close its markets to the Allies.

The markets of this country are open upon equal terms to
all the world, to every nation, belligerent or neutral.

That answer was, in the world of reason, conclusive;
in the world of emotion, of course, it settled nothing.
Germany and the German-Americans continued to feel
the American government was not neutral, that it facilitated success in the war for the Allies, put a harsh
handicap on Germany.

III

In a different class, having a less clear delineation of
legal right and wrong, was a series of episodes that arose
on the sea.

Strictly, there was no such thing as "international law." "Law of the sea" was little more than a set of rules laid down by whatever nation had dominance on the sea, a self-denying concession made by naval power to expediency or humanity. This, plus a few inconsequential treaties between individual nations, and conventions entered into by groups of nations, was all there was of international law. Law of the sea was mainly a self-

The British Navy was a material factor not only in deciding the war but in preventing Germany from buying supplies in the United States, while the Allies were able to buy supplies here and ship them home freely. This illustration pictures a review of the British fleet in the North Sea prior to the war.

imposed code defining the limits of whatever the dominant sea-power chose to do. At all times international law, law of the sea, freedom of the seas, all flow mainly from whatever nation has a navy that dominates the sea. If, in any war, the strongest naval power happens to be a neutral, then neutral rights are held and increased as against rights of belligerents. If the strongest naval power is one of the belligerents, neutral rights shrink. In this war, the strongest naval power was a belligerent, Britain; and Britain proceeded to impinge upon the rights of neutrals, of whom the chief was the United States.

IV

The disputes that arose between Britain and America fell, mainly, into eight categories:

A. To the commodities long accepted as contraband, materials used exclusively or mainly for war, Britain now made many additions. Contending that modern war used many new materials, Britain added to the category of contraband: copper, rubber, gasoline, cotton — some 32 in all.

B. Food, traditionally, was not contraband. But Germany, in the interest of conserving its domestic food supply, seized all stocks of flour, wheat, and corn in the empire, took them over for the imperial government. This act, Britain declared, gave food a military quality, and therefore made it contraband.

C. Direct shipments of contraband from neutral United States to belligerent Germany were subject to seizure — that was accepted. Britain, however, declared that shipments from the United States to other neutrals, particularly Sweden, Norway, Denmark, and Holland, were subject to seizure — if there was reason to suppose the shipments would ultimately reach Germany. "Reason to suppose" on a universal scale was inferred from the enormous increase in exports from the United States to countries bordering on Germany. Exports from New York to Denmark, for example, had risen some 600 per per cent, from $558,000 in November of 1913 to $7,010,000 in the November after the war began, 1914.[2] Britain seized ship after ship carrying copper,

---

[2] Some of the increase was due to Denmark's present inability to get supplies from former sources now involved in the war.

cotton, oil, or other material from the United States to neutral countries.

D. By usage, search of ships for contraband took place on the high seas; the belligerent warship stopped the neutral merchantman and searched it on the spot. Now, Britain took seized ships to British ports to await search there, claiming that German submarines made it dangerous for ships to remain motionless on the ocean.

E. Britain proclaimed the entire North Sea to be "a military zone," in which Britain laid mines, and into which neutral ships, if they entered, must do so at their peril.

F. At the beginning of the war, some German merchant ships in United States ports were interned. Thereafter, some of these ships were purchased from their German owners by Americans, were registered as American, were loaded with cargoes and sent to Germany with non-contraband. Britain challenged the good faith of these transfers.

G. British ships, when in danger of pursuit — and this excuse was broadly interpreted by scared captains — sometimes raised the American flag to deceive German submarines. Britain claimed that when there was actual danger, this was a legitimate ruse of war. In specific cases, dispute arose whether there had been actual danger.

H. Britain made a blacklist of some eighty American firms, suspected by Britain of having traded with Germany, which the firms had a right to do if they could. Britain's blacklisting them prevented them, in effect, from trading with neutral countries.

About these and similar questions, about the law in general and the facts in specific cases, intricate controversy arose between Britain and the United States, carried on in diplomatic notes. That Britain was in the

wrong[3] again and again and again, there was no doubt.
Many of Britain's acts, Secretary of State Lansing said,[4]

Courtesy of the Navy Department.

Two famous German merchant vessels, the *Kronprinz Wilhelm* and *Prinz Eitel
Friedrich,* named for two of the Kaiser's sons. These, with many other German vessels, were interned in the United States during the war, these two
in the Navy Yard at Philadelphia.

were "illegal and indefensive." [*sic*] President Wilson,
vigorously asserting American rights, spoke[5] of "well

[3] "England is playing a . . . high game, violating international law every day."
—Letter written by Wilson's Secretary of the Interior, May 29, 1915.
Some of Britain's violations of American rights were ruthless: "Britain con-
voyed neutral vessels into British ports to search them at leisure; mails were
rifled and American trade secrets filched. . . . It became impossible for an
American firm, not approved by the British government, to do any European
business. American exporters desiring to fill orders for neutral European
countries were obliged to go hat in hand to the British Embassy and beg permission to ship their goods. Before permission was given they were required to
submit a list of their foreign customers, which was referred to London. These
lists were thereafter placed at the disposal of British competitors."—"Wilson the
Unknown," Wells Wells (a pseudonym).
[4] In a note to Britain, October 21, 1915.   [5] July 30, 1916.

defined international practices which the government of the United States deems the government of Great Britain to have too lightly and too frequently disregarded." But though Britain took pains to be placatory, her answer, or the answer implicit in the circumstances, and in the tenuous thing that went by the name of international law, was, "What are you going to do about it?" Britain never put it that way — always in her diplomatic replies to our complaints, she was courteous and considerate. Nevertheless, that is what the circumstances amounted to.

We could do two things: protest or declare war. We limited ourselves to protest — and our protests were not as strong as Britain's acts called for.

Our protests to Britain against her violations of our neutrality were, from the beginning of the war, less insistent than the facts called for. However vigorously our State Department in Washington might write a note, its "punch was pulled" in delivery. Our Ambassador to Great Britain, Walter H. Page, was not an American Ambassador standing firmly for the letter of American rights, but rather a man who believed powerfully in the Allied cause, believed Britain was fighting for us and for civilization; believed, long before others did, that ultimately America would join the Allies, and therefore believed his higher duty was to soften and compromise our complaints against British violation of our neutrality. Page was completely candid about it, allowed the British Government and his own Government at home to know that he was acting in the interest not of our neutrality but of Allied success. So far as our Ambassador to London could deliver us, America was in the war from the day Britain entered it. When it was announced that the steamer *Dacia* would sail from the United States for Germany, the British Government notified Washington that the *Dacia* would be seized, on the ground that she had formerly been a German vessel interned in America, and that her transfer to American ownership could not be recognized by Britain. The situation blazed

Walter Hines Page, American Ambassador to Great Britain. Strongly pro-Ally, his actions had material influence in softening protests made by our government against Britain's violations of American rights.

in the newspapers, the incident was supposed to present a test-case of America's rights as a neutral, a "dare" by America to Britain — all the world was watching what would happen.

In London, Page went to see Foreign Minister Grey. Approaching the subject with genial facetiousness, Page asked Grey:

"Have you ever heard of the British fleet, Sir Edward?"
Grey admitted he had, though the question obviously puzzled him.

"Yes," Page went on musingly. "We've all heard of the British fleet. Perhaps we have heard too much about it. Don't you think it's had too much advertising?"

The Foreign Secretary looked at Page with an expression that implied a lack of confidence in his sanity.

"But have you ever heard of the French fleet?" the American went on. "France has a fleet too, I believe."

Sir Edward granted that.

"Don't you think that the French fleet ought to have a little advertising?"

"What on earth are you talking about?"

"Well," said Page, "there's the *Dacia*. Why not let the French fleet seize it and get some advertising?"

A gleam of understanding shot across Grey's face. The old familiar twinkle came into his eye.[6]

Page knew that if the British seized the *Dacia*, there would be popular anger in America, but that, if France committed the same act, there would be less excitement — there had been no agitation about French violations of our neutrality. So it turned out. Page's suggestion was acted on; a French cruiser seized the *Dacia* and took it into port, where a French prize court promptly condemned it. The proceeding did not cause even a ripple of hostility.

Page, in his frank giving of aid[7] to Britain in her controversies with the United States, had the justification that most of America, wishing for Allied success in the war, would not clamor for strict insistence upon our

[6] This incident is told in the words of Page's biographer, Burton K. Hendrick, "Life and Letters of Walter H. Page."

[7] "Page was so whole-heartedly pro-English that he did not refrain from tampering (and on one important occasion suppressing) some of Wilson's more acid notes to the British government."—Quoted from the London *New Statesman and Nation*, March, 1933.

"Page came to see me at the Foreign Office one day and produced a long despatch from Washington contesting our claim to act as we were doing in stopping contraband going to neutral ports. 'I am instructed [by the American Government],' Page said, 'to read this despatch to you.' He read it, I listened. He then said: 'I have now read the despatch but I do not agree with it; let us consider how it should be answered.' . . . Page's advice and suggestions were of the greatest value in warning us when to be careful, or encouraging us when we could safely be firm."—"Twenty-five Years," Sir Edward Grey.

rights; and the further justification that his judgment about the future turned out to be correct.   After we entered the war, Page had the happier of the two possi-

© *"Jugend," Munich.*

A German cartoon (from *Jugend,* Munich) expressing the German charge that British ships loaded with munitions secured protection for themselves by carrying American passengers. American passengers on such British boats were called by the Germans, "Guardian Angels" of the cargoes of contraband.

ble fates of a rebel, who is crucified if his cause fails but becomes a hero if it prevails.

Historically, Page's course is of high importance, it prevented the possibility — if any could have arisen — of war, or of termination of diplomatic relations or other strain, between the United States and Britain.

And considering the importance of whatever Wilson did, it was fateful that Page was in London to soften the notes which Wilson, living up to the obligation of strict neutrality, must send.   Wilson seemed instinctively to "sense" this. He was fully aware of Page's attitude, spoke of it with disapproval,[8] but he never listened to suggestions that he recall Page.

All this, however, is history after the event.   At the time, the plain fact was we did not insist upon our neutral rights as against Britain so vigorously as against Germany.   The Attorney-General of the United States, Thomas Watt Gregory, said, years later: "Up to the time that Germany began its atrocious submarine warfare culminating in the sinking of the *Lusitania*" — that qualification is important — "we had far less cause for complaint against her than against Britain."[9]

This condition was known, and resented, by Germany and by pro-Germans in America — and by some Americans who were not pro-German but thought we should live up in fact to the neutrality we proclaimed.

IV

The Germans, because of their naval inferiority, had (with immaterial exceptions) no war vessels on the sea except submarines. This distinction caused our disputes with Germany to fall into categories different from our disputes with the British.

A. Germany claimed that the nature of her principal active naval weapon, the submarine, made it impossible to live up to the traditional requirements, that pas-

[8] "Mr. Page actually went so far as to resent our demand that England respect American rights on the high seas."—Wilson, in a conversation with George Creel.

[9] New York *Times,* January 9, 1925.

sengers and crews be taken off before sinking an enemy merchant vessel, and that neutral vessels carrying contraband, when seized, be taken to a port. Submarines usually could only sink such vessels forthwith. Sink them Germany did, and with them, often, their crews and passengers, including, sometimes, American citizens. Germany was, she said,[10] "in a position where her life depends upon her putting into effect the only means she has of saving herself; she must and will use this means."

B. Germany declared[11] the whole of the waters surrounding the British Isles to be a war zone in which she would sink all enemy ships "even if it may not be possible always to save their crews and passengers." As to neutral vessels, Germany proclaimed, because of the "hazards of naval warfare," they "cannot always be prevented from suffering from attacks meant for enemy ships." In fulfilment of this threat many merchant vessels, enemy and neutral, including some American, were sunk by German submarines.

V

To the average American the rights and wrongs of all this were a confusing clamor, a three-cornered, multiple-angled maze of several different controversies intricately intermingled:

America complaining against Britain and Britain replying to America.

America complaining against Germany and Germany replying to America.

Germany complaining to America that our complaints against Britain were not severe enough.

[10] February 16, 1915.   [11] February 4, 1915.

Britain complaining to America that our complaints against Germany were not severe enough.

To the average man the jumble was impenetrable. The technicalities of it, the legal and diplomatic terminology were outside his vocabulary — legalisms about contraband, non-contraband, and conditional contraband; "continuous voyage," "ultimate destination," blockade, cordon blockade, effective blockade, embargo, sea lane, war area, visit and search, search and seizure, radius of activity. To the average man, it was mainly a long parade of names of ships in the newspapers, giving rise to reflections less about international law than about the esoteric variety of marine nomenclature — the ships involved, each figuring excitedly in the newspapers for days and weeks, included the *Orduna*, *Wilhelmina*, *Brindilla*, *Platuria*, *Kronland*, *William P. Frye*, *Falaba*, *Gulflight*, *Dacia*, and scores of others.

The average man understood, however, a fundamental distinction between Germany's violations of our neutrality, and Britain's: British violations injured property almost alone, never human life. (Occasionally Britain deprived an American seaman or passenger temporarily of his liberty, through detaining him on his ship.) When a British warship seized a neutral vessel, with or without right, she took it to a British port. The injuries Britain did us could be compensated in damages later, and Britain contemplated they should. Germany's injuries to us, on the other hand, often included bloodshed, loss of life. The British seized ships; Germany habitually sank them, and with them, in many cases American citizens.[12]

[12] "Property can be paid for; the lives of peaceful and innocent people cannot be. The present German submarine warfare against commerce is a warfare against mankind."—President Wilson (subsequently, in the speech in which he called for declaration of war, April 2, 1917).

The difference was understood by the average man, who therefore applauded occasional phrases in President Wilson's notes to Germany, " . . . hold the Imperial German Government to strict accountability."[13]

Cartoonist John T. McCutcheon, in the Chicago *Tribune,* satirically pictures Uncle Sam's difficulty in remaining neutral.

" . . . secure American citizens full enjoyment of their rights on the high seas."[14] This the average American understood, and he probably thought America's rights were being adequately defended, so far as words could do so — though a member of Wilson's cabinet[15] felt in his heart that Wilson in his notes to Germany

13 February 10, 1915.   14 February 10, 1915.
15 Franklin K. Lane, in a letter to George W. Wickersham, July 18, 1915.

had habitually "been too polite — talking Princetonian English to a water-front bully."

In time there came, May 7, 1915, an event which lifted it all out of the world of legalisms, made it stark for every one to understand.

4

THE LUSITANIA

Of the Sinking of Which an Authority on This Matter Said: "Germany Paid for It with the Loss of the War." A Newspaper Advertisement Which, in Its Effects, Turned Out to Be the Most Important in History. The Occasion of a Phrase Similarly Famous, "Too Proud to Fight."

OF all the motives, the dark emotions and clear-thought purposes that incited Germany to war, of all the envies that tormented her into fighting for her place in the sun, the most concrete was England's dominance, naval and commercial, on the sea. Of all the conditions that now tortured the German soul, the most biting was the consciousness that every ship of hers that had sailed the seas was now in frightened hiding in German ports or interned in neutral ones, while British ships imperturbably carried on: On any day, from the beginning of the war to the end, any American traveller could go down to the Bowling Green section of New York, walk into a British steampship office, talk with a placid English clerk, and get passage to Europe — while, next-door and across the street, the Hamburg-American and other German offices were idle. (Except as the Hamburg-American served as a centre for propaganda and other furtive activities.)

Of all the lines and routes that composed England's world-wide fabric of commercial dominance, proudest and oldest was the Cunard, special pride of the British nation, special concern of the British Admiralty — "the British Navy," said a Cunard agent, on an occasion destined to be recalled, "is responsible for all British ships, especially Cunarders." And of all the ships that flew the Cunarder flag, queen of the fleet was the *Lusitania*.[1]

The *Lusitania* was a splendid ship. A four-stacker, 30,395 gross tons, 755 feet in length and 88 in breadth, largest ship afloat when launched, first four-propellered turbine steamship, with accommodations so ample and

---

SPECIAL ANNOUNCEMENT

In view of the uncertainty of the present European situation, we have decided to postpone sailings of the S. S. Vaterland from New York; Amerika from Boston, August 1st, and Imperator from Hamburg, July 31st. For the same reason we have also ordered the S. S. President Grant, which sailed from New York yesterday, to return.

HAMBURG-AMERICAN LINE

A material factor in the war was the practically complete paralysis of German shipping while British shipping imperturbably "carried on."

—Philadelphia Ledger, August 1, 1914.

---

luxurious for her capacity of three thousand souls (passengers and crew), that ship designers said one-third of her space was prodigal gratuity to comfort. She was the first vessel in the world to be called a "floating hotel." The Cunard were proud of that phrase, and prouder still of her speed record. She was the first ship to steam for twenty-four hours at a higher average speed than twenty-five knots — she did twenty-six and a third. And

---

[1] The *Lusitania's* transatlantic record was 4 days, 11 hours, 4 minutes. A sister ship, the *Mauretania*, had once bettered this, by the tactful margin of one hour and one minute. But the *Mauretania* was now withdrawn for war service.

their cup overflowed when they recalled that the *Lusitania* had fulfilled her British builders' intentions by wresting the ocean speed record from the North German Lloyd's *Kaiser Wilhelm II* on Friday, September 13, 1907, a time when Germany had been content to make her attempt at dominance by honest competition in skill. The *Lusitania* had been built to be empress of the seas, and she was.

Superbly conscious of this prestige, then, on April 30, 1915, the Cunard's accustomed advertisement — simple and dignified as befitted their traditions, announced the sailing of the *Lusitania* for the following morning:

CUNARD
Established 1840
Europe via Liverpool
LUSITANIA
Fastest and Largest Steamer
Now in Atlantic Service
Sails . . .

Directly beneath the Cunard announcement of sailing appeared on Saturday morning, May 1, 1915, the "Notice" reproduced on this page. It excited attention; the Associated Press sent the text of it as a news despatch to papers in the interior.

15
OCEAN STEAMSHIPS.

CUNARD

EUROPE VIA LIVERPOOL

LUSITANIA

Fastest and Largest Steamer
now in Atlantic Service Sails
SATURDAY, MAY 1, 10 A.M.
Transylvania, Fri., May 7, 5 P.M.
Orduña, - - Tues., May 18, 10 A.M.
Tuscania, - - Fri., May 21, 5 P.M.
LUSITANIA, Sat., May 29, 10 A.M.
Transylvania, Fri., June 4, 5 P.M.

Gibraltar—Genoa—Naples—Piraeus
S.S. Carpathia, Thur., May 13, Noon

NOTICE!

TRAVELLERS intending to embark on the Atlantic voyage are reminded that a state of war exists between Germany and her allies and Great Britain and her allies; that the zone of war includes the waters adjacent to the British Isles; that, in accordance with formal notice given by the Imperial German Government, vessels flying the flag of Great Britain, or of any of her allies, are liable to destruction in those waters and that travellers sailing in the war zone on ships of Great Britain or her allies do so at their own risk.

IMPERIAL GERMAN EMBASSY

WASHINGTON. D. C., APRIL 22. 1915.

An advertisement, extraordinary in character, which made much history.

It excited attention — but no one heeded it. The word "unthinkable" is commonly used after an event, as an epithet, an expression of strong disapproval, a synonym for horrible. In this case "unthinkable" had an exact meaning in advance of the event. No one believed the German Government could seriously intend to do the thing this warning implied. No one of the 1257 passengers booked to sail on the *Lusitania*, so far as there is any record — and subsequently this and every other aspect of the event was subjected to minute scrutiny — considered cancelling his sailing. No member of the *Lusitania's* crew of 667 gave it a thought. If any had, he would have ignored it.[2]

The warning[2a] diminished not at all the gaiety and eclat that accompany embarkment on one of the crack liners of the world. The scene was at once festive and distinguished; the passengers included several leading figures in the national life of the time: Charles Frohman, principal American theatrical producer, patron and friend of nearly all the important actors and playwrights of the English- and French-speaking worlds, now off to look after some of his London productions; Alfred Gwynne Vanderbilt, best-known member, because of his interest in horses and sports, of a famous American family, sailing to look over his London rac-

[2] The imperturbability of British seamen, including stewardesses, was a force which throughout the war, at once reflecting British morale and preserving it, contributed powerfully to ultimate victory.

[2a] This narrative seems to imply that the warning by the German Government was directed specifically to passengers on the *Lusitania,* that the warning and the sinking were synchronized, that the sinking of this particular ship was carefully planned. This was widely assumed at the time—the assumption was implicit in the facts. But I think this is not so. I think, after considerable investigation, that the warning was a general one, directed to all Americans sailing on all enemy vessels. George Sylvester Viereck—one of the German "propaganda cabinet" in New York which conceived the warning, wrote a draft of it, and sent it to the German Ambassador von Bernstorff who inserted it—says the warning was a general one.

"Lusitania's" First Cabin List

May 22, 1915

LIST OF
SALOON PASSENGERS
BY THE QUADRUPLE-SCREW TURBINE

R.M.S. "Lusitania"

CAPTAIN
★ W. T. TURNER, R. N. R.

STAFF-CAPTAIN
● J. C. ANDERSON

CHIEF ENGINEER—A. BRYCE   ● CHIEF OFFICER—J. T. PIPER
SURGEON—J. McDERMOTT   PURSER—J. A. McCUBBIN
ASST SURGEON—J. GARRY   ★ 2ND PURSER—P. DRAPER
● CHIEF STEWARD—R. V. JONES

From New York to Liverpool, May 1st 1915.

Mr. Henry Adams	England.
Mrs. Adams	England.
Mr. A. H. Adams	London, Eng.
★ Mr. William McM. Adams	London, Eng.
Lady Allan	Montreal, Can.
and maid (Emily Davies)	
Miss Anna Allan	Montreal, Can.
Miss Gwen Allan	Montreal, Can.
and maid (Annie Walker)	
★ Mr. N. N. Alles	New York, N. Y.
★ Mr. Julian de Ayala ,	Liverpool, Eng.
(Cuban Consul for Cuba at Liverpool)	
Mr. James Baker	England.
Miss Margaret A. Baker	New York, N. Y.
Mr. Allan Barnes	Toronto, Ont.
Mr. G. W. B. Bartlett	London, Eng.
Mrs. Bartlett	London, Eng.
★ Mr. Lindon Bates Jr.	New York, N.Y.
Mr. J. J. Battersby	New York, N.Y.
Mr. Oliver Bernard	Scarport, Eng.
Mr. Charles P. Bernard	Boston, Mass.
Mr. Albert C. Bilicke	New York, N.Y.
Mrs. Bilicke	
Mr. Henry ?	

★ Mr. Fred. J. Gauntlett	New York, N. Y.
Mr. Mathew Gibson	Glasgow, Scot.
Mr. George A. Gilpin	England.
Mr. Edgar Gorer	London, Eng.
★ Mr. Oscar F. Grab	New York, N. Y.
Mrs. Grant	Chicago, Il.
Mr. Frederick S. Hammond	Toronto, Canada.
★ Mrs. F. S. Hammond	Toronto, Canada.
★ Mr. O. H. Hammond	New York, N.Y.
Mrs. O. H. Hammond	New York, N.Y.
★ Mr. C. C. Hardwick	New York, N. Y.
★ Mr. John H. Harper	New York, N. Y.
★ Mr. Dwight C. Harris	New York, N.Y.
★ Mr. F. W. Hawkins	Winnipeg, Man.
● Miss Katberyn Bickson	New York, N.Y.
Mr. Charles T. Hill	London, Eng.
● Mr. William S. Hodges	Philadelphia, Pa.
Mrs. Hodges	Philadelphia, Pa.
● Master W. S. Hodges Jr.	Philadelphia, Pa.
★ Master Dean W. Hodges	Philadelphia, Pa.
● Master F. W. G. Holt	Montreal, Can.
● Mr. Thomas Home	Toronto, Canada.
● Mr. Albert L. Hopkins	New York, N.Y.
★ Dr. J. T. Houghton	Saratoga Springs N Y
Mr. Elbert Hubbard	E. Aurora, N V
Mrs. Hubbard	E. Aurora, N V
Miss P. Hutchinson	England.
★ Mr. C. T. Jeffery	Chicago, Ill.
★ Mr. Francis B. Jenkins	New York, N. Y.
★ Miss Rita Jolivet	Paris, France.
● Miss Margaret D. Jones	Honolulu, Hawaii
★ Mr. W. Keeble	Toronto, Cana.
Mrs. Keeble	T.
★ Mr. Francis C. Kellett	
★ Mr. Maitland Kempson—	
★ Dr. Owen ?	

Miss Amy W. W. Pearl	New York, N.Y.
Miss Susan W. Pearl	New York, N.Y.
Master Stuart Duncan D. Pearl	New York. N.Y.
(and maid (Alice Lines)	
Mr. Edwin Perkins	England.
Mr. Frederick J. Perry	Buffalo, N. Y.
● Mr. Albert Norris Perry	Buffalo, N. Y.
Mr. Wallace B. Phillips	New York, N. Y.
Mr. Robinson Pirie	Hamilton Ont.
Mr. William J. Pierpoint	Liverpool, Eng.
● Mr. Charles A. Plamondon	Chicago, Ill
● Mrs. Plamondon	Chicago, Ill.
Mr. Henry Pollard	Washington, D. C.
Miss Theodate Pope	Farmington Ct.
and maid (Emily Robinson)	
★ Mr. Eugene H. Peon	London, Eng.
★ Mr. George A. Powell	Toronto, Ont.
★ Mr. Norman A. Ratcliff	England.
★ Mr. Robert Rankin	New York. N.Y.
★ Mr. A. L. Rhys-Evans	Cardiff Wales.
★ Mr. Chas. E. Robinson	Philadelphia, Pa.
Mrs. Robinson	Philadelphia, Pa.
★ Mr. Frank A. Rogers	Toronto, Canada.
★ Mrs. Rogers	Toronto, Canada.
★ Mr. Percy W. Rogers	Toronto, Canada.
★ Mr. Thos. W. Rumble	Toronto, Can.
Mrs. C. Sterling Ryerson	Toronto Canada
★ Miss Laura Ryerson	Toronto Canada
★ Mr. Leo M Schwabacher	
★ Mr. August W G?	

Part of the passenger list of the *Lusitania* on her fatal sailing when 1198 were lost out of 1924 aboard. Among the lost were 63 infants and children. Americans aboard numbered 188, of whom 114 were drowned. Survivors are indicated by a star; identified dead by a circle.

ing-stable; Elbert Hubbard and his wife — Hubbard was known to all America as head of the "Roycrofters," a school of genial iconoclasm expressed by Hubbard in incessant popular lecturing and in a pungent, humorous little periodical, *The Philistine;* Justus Miles Forman,

The *Lusitania,* premier ship of the British passenger service at this time, called, fairly, "Empress of the Seas."

an author just coming toward the top rank — a recent play of his, "The Hyphen," had irritated German-Americans; Charles Klein, leading playwright, producer of the "Music Master" and now contemplating production of "Potash and Perlmutter in Society"; Herbert Stone, son of Melville Stone, head of the Associated Press; other persons eminent in business, the arts, and professions. The *Lusitania's* passenger list was a microcosm of Americans well-known, well-liked.

Passengers and friends of passengers crowded dock

and decks. Messenger boys carrying flowers, baskets of fruit, and books rushed up the gangplank. The ship's musicians played the latest fox-trots and one-steps. As the hawsers of the great liner were cast off and a dozen puffing tugs manœuvred her into midstream, crowds lining the pier waved and shouted good-byes, not at all in the spirit of parting, but, as usual, in the spirit of cheering the fortunate travellers on to a happy voyage.

The trip across was exceptionally agreeable. Except for a few hours of fog the second morning out, the weather was perfect, the sea smooth. For six soft sunny days the passengers enjoyed an exceptional experience of the pleasure of a transatlantic voyage on the most luxurious liner afloat. Nights, the port-holes were closed and lights on deck forbidden — any passenger who struck a match for his cigar found his arm seized by a steward, deferential and polite but firm, who reminded him he was breaking a ship's rule. That, however, had become the universal and commonplace precaution of war-time travel on the sea and, if commented on at all, was used only as a peg upon which to hang a witticism. Within, in the parlors and smoking-rooms, passengers danced, played cards, drank cocktails and champagne, made bets on the day's run; with no thought of insecurity, they enjoyed an ocean trip under the most agreeable conditions afforded by the modern world.

Friday, May 7, passengers finishing lunch came on deck to see, some eight or ten miles away, the green fields, sloping hills, and white-washed cottages of the southern point of Ireland, the Old Head of Kinsdale. They called to each other to look. Between expressions of pleasure at the sight of one of the most alluring bits of land in the world, there were occasional allusions, nearly all humorous, to the possibility of submarines now that the *Lusitania* had reached British waters. There had been momentary expectation that fast British destroyers would appear to escort the *Lusitania* into port, as was the custom. Indeed, failure of a convoy to appear suggested assurance that danger from submarines was past. Elbert Hubbard, feeling relief over the *Lusitania's* safe passage through the submarine-infested waters farther out, spoke with humor to a fellow passenger of a personal reason the Kaiser had for "getting" him — Hubbard had written and published in *The Philistine* an article about the Kaiser and the War bearing the suggestive title "Who Lifted the Lid Off Hell?"

Suddenly, there was a sound, heavy, muffled; and a shock, a tremor through the ship, the smash of glass from port-holes. The bow began to dip, forward and to the side.

Of what followed there is a description by the only person, except perhaps God, who looked on from outside the *Lusitania*. His name was Schwieger, his title *Leutnant-Kapitän*. He was in command of *U-boat 20* of the German submarine fleet. In his log[3] (made public years later) he set down, with Teutonic thoroughness, notes of his periscope observations:

Right ahead appeared four funnels and two masts of a steamer. Clean bow-shot from 700-meter range. Shot hits starboard side right behind bridge. An unusually heavy detonation follows with a very strong explosion cloud. . . . The superstructure over point struck and the high bridge are rent asunder. The ship stops immediately and quickly heels to starboard, at the same time diving deeper at the bow. She has the appearance of being about to capsize. Great confusion on board. Life-boats being cleared and lowered to water. Many boats crowded, come down bow first or stern first in

[3] Here condensed from a translated copy in an article by Robert L. Duffus in the New York *Times*, May 3, 1925.

the water and immediately fill and sink. The ship blows off. In the front appears the name *Lusitania* in gold letters. It appears as if the vessel will be afloat only a short time. I submerge to 24 meters and go to sea. I could not have fired a second torpedo into this throng of humanity attempting to save themselves.

Of the total of 1924 aboard, only 726 were saved. Among the 1198 lost were 63 infants and children. Out

International News Photograph.

Leutnant-Kapitän Schwieger, Commander of German *Unterseeboot 20,* which sank the *Lusitania.*

of 35 babies only 4 were saved. One family of eight was completely wiped out. Americans aboard numbered 188; 114 were drowned.

Humanity is in *Leutnant-Kapitän* Schwieger's debt. Had it not been for that surge of humane forbearance inspired in his breast by the sight of the "throng of humanity attempting to save themselves," he might have sent torpedo after torpedo into the torn hull of his victim, sinking her in ten, or five, or three minutes, instead of twenty. It was in his power, if he had wished, to bring *Unterseeboot 20* to the surface, and, with entire safety to himself and crew, to have dropped shells from his deck-rifle into every lifeboat that stayed afloat after the *Lusitania's* final plunge. Then there would have been no survivors at all.

It was not, one judges from his diary entry, a matter of remorse on Schwieger's part for the heartrending scenes his "clean bow shot" had caused, that stayed his hand. It was not his conscience that had been revolted at thought of the thirty-one babies whose tiny bodies had been crushed by the "unusually heavy detonation" of the boilers that had followed his torpedo's impact, or who, clutched in the arms of frantic mothers, had been hurled into the sea by the *Lusitania's* final convulsion. It was not because consciousness suddenly came to him that what he had done was unspeakably wicked. No hint is to be found in Schwieger's unctuously precise diary notes that a sudden overwhelming sense of personal guilt held him back from further slaughter. Considering the *Leutnant-Kapitän* an average product of Prussian frightfulness, why should he have been conscience-stricken, remorseful? What difference is there, except in degree, between killing only 1198 defenseless people, and killing all the 1924 who were aboard? For him there was nothing immoral, nothing reprehensible, in sinking the *Lusitania;* he had acted entirely within the rules of war laid down by his superiors, the German war lords. To withhold firing "a second torpedo into this throng of humanity attempting to save themselves" may be regarded as what in strict truth it was: kind-hearted Teutonic forbearance, the kind of chivalry to be expected in a gangster who, having fatally wounded his victim, turns away without bothering to make death complete. One can hardly conceive, nevertheless, that Schwieger's self-restraint will mitigate greatly the judgment of mankind upon his deed.

The other eye-witness accounts of the *Lusitania's* sinking had one advantage over Schwieger's. They were written or related to ship reporters by persons who had been aboard the vessel when Schwieger's torpedo exploded against its side and who consequently had opportunities to view the tragedy at close hand, whereas Schwieger's observations were made from the safe, deep sanctuary of the periscope tower of *U-boat 20*, 700 meters away.

Robert Rankin, of Washington, D. C.:[4]

We saw what looked like a whale or a porpoise rising about three-quarters of a mile to starboard. We all knew what it was, but no one named it. Immediately a white line, a train of bubbles, started away from the black object. It came straight for the ship. It was obvious it couldn't miss. It was aimed ahead of her and struck under the bridge. I saw it disappear. We all hoped for the fraction of a second it would not explode. But the explosion came clear up through the upper deck, and pieces of the wreckage fell clean aft of where we were standing. We ducked into the smoking-room for shelter from the flying debris. The boilers exploded immediately. The passengers all rushed at once to the high side of the deck — the port side. There was such a list to starboard that all boats on the port side swung right back inboard and could not be launched.

Oliver P. Barnard, an Englishman, who at the moment the *Lusitania* was struck mounted to the flying-deck and from there watched the launching of lifeboats:

I could see them making an awful mess of getting the boats

4 The stories of passengers on board here quoted are taken from issues of the New York *Tribune* following the *Lusitania's* sinking.

out. They were cutting and hacking at them. The first boat floated away empty. The next three were smashed. I slid off the flying-deck onto the boat-deck, and from there fell into a boat lying alongside. As I got into the boat she was swept away by one of the funnels falling across her, and we only managed to push clear. I saw a woman sucked right down one of the funnels and shot out again, looking like a piece of burned coal. We managed to save her. I rowed for some time with a woman between my knees before discovering that she was dead. Most of the women tried to keep cool, and, except for occasional screams of "Where is my husband?" "Where is my child?" they acted bravely.

Ogden H. Hammond, of New York:

The man at the bow of the lifeboat let the rope slip through his hands, while the man at the stern paid it out too slowly. The situation was terrible. We were dropping perpendicularly when I caught the rope and tried to stop the boat from falling. My hands were torn to shreds, but the boat fell and all in it were thrown into the water — a dense struggling mass. I went down and down and down, with thirty people on top of me. I thought we never would come back to the surface. I must have been partly unconscious then, for I can only remember getting almost to the surface and then sinking back, and doing this three or four times. Finally, I was hauled into some boat, but no one else from the boat that fell was ever seen again.

Finally there is the account of a St. Louis man, a drummer probably — his name was not given in the cable that transmitted his story — whose Missouri sense of humor was so sinewy that it stayed by him throughout all the horror of the *Lusitania's* sinking:

We had been playing poker ever since the trip began, and some one had just ordered a round of beer. As we started to drink, one of the fellows said: "What would you do if a torpedo hit us?" I said: "I am unmarried, and I'd finish my beer." Just then the torpedo struck and the others bolted, but I finished the beer and went over to the bar and called for another bottle and said to the bartender: "Let's die game, anyway." But he said: "You go to hell," and bolted, leaving me all alone. I had another drink, and just as I was finishing it the boat

Death of a man-of-war.

Two photographs which in their mute depiction of stark tragedy were among the most poignant that came out of the war.

turned over. When I woke up I was being hauled into a small boat.

Watches recovered later from floating bodies were stopped at a few minutes after half past two. Allowing twenty minutes for the sinking of the ship and the drowning of the passengers, the time when the torpedo struck was eight minutes past two. 2:08 P.M. of May 7, 1915. That was the precise moment — more nearly than the inception of most wars can be fixed — when war between America and Germany became inevitable.

II

The average American, after reading his newspaper[5] at breakfast Saturday morning, May 8, looked about hoping to see a German whom he could fight, or at the least express his opinion to. The immediate feeling was reflected in the Des Moines (Iowa) *Register and Leader*[5a] in an editorial which began:

The sinking of the *Lusitania* was deliberate murder

and ended impressively with the same affirmation:

The sinking of the *Lusitania* was deliberate murder.

That was the emotion of America as a whole. No event since the sinking of the *Maine* had so stirred the country. The phrase used by a distinguished historian[6] to describe the country's emotion, "mingled horror and rage," was not too strong.

Popular anger was increased by the attitude of the German-American press, which had a manner of shrug-

---

[5] Reading the newspaper account of the *Lusitania's* sinking was to many Americans the most vivid experience of the war, remained in their memories most clearly. They were able to remember the surroundings in which they read it, the emotion they had, their actions the rest of the day.

[5a] May 9, 1915.

[6] John Bach McMaster, "The United States in the World War."

"VELL, VE VARNED 'EM!"

THE ANNOUNCER.

GERMAN EMBASSY'S ADVERTISEMENT GAVE WARNING ONE WEEK AGO

The American press printed hundreds of such angry cartoons as these. The one on the left was printed in the Brooklyn *Eagle* on the anniversary of the *Lusitania's* sinking, May 8, 1916. The one in the middle was printed in *Life*, May 27, 1915. The one on the right in the New York *Herald* the day after the *Lusitania's* sinking, May 8, 1915.

ging its shoulders and saying, "War is war"; by stories
that groups in German-American restaurants had broken
into cheers at the news and drunk toasts to the U-boat

Medal struck off in Germany in celebration of the *Lusitania* sinking.

commander and sung "Deutschland über Alles"; by
other stories that in Germany school children had been
given a holiday and that a medal had been struck off to
commemorate the sinking; and by the indisputedly
authentic remark of an official German representative in
America, Doctor Bernhard Dernburg — ironically his
official function was one of mercy, he was the head of
the German Red Cross work in America:

The death of the Americans might have been avoided if our
warning had been heeded; we put in advertisements and were
careful to put them next the announcements of the Cunard
Line's sailing dates; anybody can commit suicide if he wants to.

7 "United States in the World War," John Bach McMaster.

As resentment rose and surged, all thoughts, all eyes, turned to President Wilson. Here, every one thought, was the thing — worse than the thing — he had warned Germany against when he had said he would hold Germany to "strict accountability."[8] It was now "inconceivable we should refrain from action," said Theodore Roosevelt; "we owe it not only to humanity but to our own national self-respect."

III

It happened that Wilson some time before had made an engagement to speak in Philadelphia, Monday, May 10. The fact that the audience was to consist of some 4000 foreign-born persons recently nat-

[8] February 10, 1915.

The Destruction of the Lusitania

A Marching Song. (Tune: Upidee, Upida.)

By RUDOLF KUHN.

I.
Carrying shameful contraband,
From New York to the English land,
Bearing thousands, on she came:
But the U-boat sniffed its game.

II.
Sailed the Lusitania gay
Further on her felon way;
Off Ireland's coast the U-boat peers,
See the course her quarry steers!

III.
Passengers from every shore—
English, Greek, and Dutch galore,
Americans and sons of France
Sail along to death's fell dance.

IV.
Ah! The U-boat's aim was good;
Who doesn't choke, drowns in the flood.
Vanderbilt was there that day,
The only one we missed was Grey.

V.
Each one gives his nose a wrench
At the gases' awful stench.
"They're our shells, our very own,"
Cries the Yankee Mr. Kohn.

VI.
The old water-nymphs below
Straight begin to curse and blow;
"What chuck ye then so carelessly
On the bottom of the sea?"

VII.
There lay the dead in Neptune's jaws,
Most of them with scalded paws—
Sons of England with their wives;
Ne'er so still in all their lives!

VIII.
Chant we now the funeral chant,
More U-boats is what we want.
To a chill grave with the enemy!
Till he stop bothering Germany.

Exultation by German sympathizers over the sinking of the *Lusitania* contributed to inflaming American emotions. This doggerel asserts that the *Lusitania* carried "shameful contraband." That the *Lusitania* carried "contraband" in the broad sense, is true, for "contraband" had come to describe a wide variety of goods. As to whether the *Lusitania* carried munitions there has been prolonged dispute. There is some evidence that her cargo included a small quantity of materials for munitions, such as unfilled cartridge cases.

uralized aroused expectation that Wilson would speak
in the vein of patriotism. Now, with the speech coming
three days after the *Lusitania* sinking, anticipation was
confident and excited.

    Wilson made the speech. He did not use the word

Queenstown, 7. Mai 1915.
Der Cunarddampfer „Lusitania" ist torpediert worden und gesunken.

International Film Photograph.

    Reproduction of a picture post card sold by the millions in Germany following
the sinking of the *Lusitania*. In the inset is Admiral Von Tirpitz, author of
Germany's submarine campaign. The inscription, translated, reads: "Queenstown, May 7, 1915. The Cunarder *Lusitania* has been torpedoed and sunk."

"Germany." Conspicuously he did not use the word
"Lusitania," nor make any remotest allusion to what was
in every American mind. The nearest he came to
alluding to anything controversial was an appeal to the
newly naturalized citizens that they should not think
of themselves as "groups," meaning, by implication —
he did not use any word so provocative as "hyphenated"

— that they should not think of themselves as British-Americans, nor Swedish-Americans, nor Irish-Americans, nor German-Americans. Wilson did not use these terms, only the generalization "groups." His speech was not about the war, his topic was Americanism in an

"SO SAY WE ALL OF US"

A cartoon from the Cleveland *Leader* which reflected a view widely held in America, especially the rural portions, that Wilson was right in treating the *Lusitania* sinking not as an immediate cause for war but as a matter for diplomatic protest.

idealistic sense. Without having the war in mind, he expressed an ideal of his own. To be mixed up in fighting is a thing that a proud man disdains. Expressing that ideal, Wilson used a phrase that startled every ear:

The example of America must be a special example. The example of America must be the example not merely of peace because it will not fight, but of peace because peace is the healing and elevating influence of the world and strife is not. There is such a thing as a nation being so right that it does not need to convince others by force that it is right. . . . There is such a thing as a man being *too proud to fight*.

Press and public, having anticipated drama in Wilson's speech in the form of allusion to the *Lusitania*, and having failed to find that, now made drama of "too proud to fight." To those who wanted to go to war with Germany, it was poltroonery on Wilson's part, national humiliation on the part of America — in huge type the New York *Herald* exclaimed: "WHAT A PITY THEODORE ROOSEVELT IS NOT PRESIDENT!" But to those who did not want war, "too proud to fight" was magnificent self-restraint. Persons and parts of the country who were normally for peace but had been moved to willingness for war by the *Lusitania* sinking, now, through Wilson's silence and through his "too proud to fight," were swung back to peace. The Des Moines (Iowa) *Register and Leader's* editorial "Deliberate Murder" of May 9, became on May 13, "TRUST THE PRESIDENT." "It is because the President has the courage to hold himself in restraint and not because he is wanting in courage, that everybody turns to him. . . . Trust the President."

By Wilson's silence and his "too proud to fight," the momentary impulse of the nation to go to war was turned back to cautious waiting. "Trust the President," "Sit Tight," became the majority state of mind.

IV

The "sitting tight" was long and tedious. The series of notes by the United States, answers by Germany, counter-notes by the United States, rebuttal notes by Germany, which figure in our State Department files as the "Lusitania Correspondence" covered almost exactly a year. Alternating roughly with the notes were further sinkings of vessels by German submarines under much the same circumstances as that of the *Lusitania*, the fresh sinkings rather more numerous than the notes: The American steamship *Nebraskan*, struck without warning by a torpedo — the Germans explained that their

This cartoon, by Jay N. Darling a week after the *Lusitania* sinking, bore upon the theory that American travellers should not go upon vessels of belligerents, that either they should remain at home or go only on American vessels. This view led to an unsuccessful attempt to have Congress withdraw protection from Americans traveling on ships of belligerents.

—*In the Des Moines Register and Leader.*

submarine had mistaken the *Nebraskan* for a British merchantman, it was "to be considered an unfortunate accident"; the German Government expressed its regret and was ready to make compensation for damages. The American ship *Leelanaw*, torpedoed and sunk — although the crew were taken aboard the submarine with the lifeboats in tow, its American ownership made its destruction a violation of treaty. The British steamer

Germany's promise to modify her submarine warfare was violated and during the year of diplomatic correspondence over the sinking of the *Lusitania,* German submarines continued to sink ship after ship.

—*Rollin Kirby in the New York World.*

Arabic, torpedoed and sunk without warning off the south coast of Ireland (not far from where the *Lusitania* went down); of the 423 passengers and crew, 44, including two American citizens, lost their lives — since the *Arabic* was on her way to New York and therefore carried no contraband, this case fulfilled President Wilson's definition of an act "deliberately unfriendly to the United States." The British steamer *Hesperian,* 350 passengers and a crew of 300, torpedoed while bound from Liver-

pool to Montreal; the vessel remained afloat and all were
saved by rescue steamers called by wireless; in the crew
were 2 Americans. The Italian liner *Ancona*, with
400 passengers and a crew of 170, torpedoed and sunk
by an Austrian submarine, carrying down 200 persons,
including 9 of the 12 Americans on board. The French
passenger steamer *Sussex*, with a crew of 53 and 325
passengers, of whom 25 were Americans; though the
Sussex did not sink, some 80 persons were killed or injured by the torpedo; the German Government, in a
note, "frankly admits that the assurances given to the
American Government that passenger vessels were not
to be attacked without warning, has not been adhered
to in the present instance." The German Government
expressed "its sincere regret regarding the deplorable
incident, and declared its readiness to pay an indemnity,"
and the German Government expressed the "hope that
the American Government will consider the case of the
Sussex as settled by these statements."

With each of these new sinkings, the new offense was
included as an addendum to whatever note happened to
be the current instalment of the *Lusitania* serial.

Finally, April 18, 1916, after the *Lusitania* had
rusted for more than eleven months at the bottom of the
Atlantic, the notes from our State Department reached
the climax of an ultimatum — of a sort. Wilson
thought his note strong; he quoted long passages from
it in an address he made to Congress the same day. In
a kind of heavy-footed solemnity it had, the final American note really was strong:

[The] roll of Americans who have lost their lives upon ships
thus attacked . . . has grown month by month until the omi-
nous toll has mounted into the hundreds. [The government of
the United States had] been willing to wait until the facts became unmistakable and were susceptible of only one interpretation. . . . It now owes it to a just regard for its own rights

to say to the Imperial German government that that time has
come. . . . Unless the Imperial German government should
now immediately declare and effect an abandonment of its

—From *Punch, London.*

Wilson's treatment of the *Lusitania* sinking through diplomatic notes was
   fiercely satirized by some American newspapers and even more by British
   periodicals. This cartoon from *Punch,* London, pictures Wilson at a time
   when Austria had sunk yet another vessel, calling to his secretary to "Bring
   me a copy of our No. 1 note to Germany—humanity series."

present methods of submarine warfare the government of the
United States can have no other choice but to sever diplomatic
relations with the German Empire altogether.

To this American ultimatum — of a sort — Germany
replied May 4, 1916, with a pledge — of a sort. The
Imperial German Government "notifies the Government

of the United States that German naval forces have received the following orders":

Merchant vessels . . . shall not be sunk without warning

Wilson's course in dealing with the *Lusitania* sinking by diplomatic notes to Germany was lampooned by *The Bystander*, London.

and without saving human lives unless those ships attempt to escape or offer resistance.

To this, a rider was attached — "a string was tied to it," said American popular comment. Since Germany was promising to live up to American demands in regard to the submarine, she, Germany, would expect America to insist that Britain live up to America's demands in regard to other violations of international law.[9] If America should not so demand, or if Britain should refuse to agree, then "the German Government would be facing a new situation, in which it must reserve to itself complete liberty of decision." That was the familiar game in all the controversies about violations of international law, Germany hitting at Britain through the United States (and Britain hitting at Germany through the United States).

Quickly the American State Department told Germany that our controversy with her must be considered alone, on its own merit, Germany's condition respecting Britain was a thing the "United States cannot for a moment entertain."

The Germans said nothing. But for nine months Germany sank no ships under the kind of circumstances that America had outlawed. From May 4, 1916, until January 31, 1917, Germany restricted her submarine warfare within the limits that Wilson insisted on. It was, for the nine months, a diplomatic victory for Wilson. He had not gone to war over the *Lusitania*, but, after a year of correspondence, he had secured a pledge that Germany would cease unrestricted submarine warfare.

Wilson had won the victory by his skill in dialectics (plus, of course, the right of his cause), an art which was to serve him well later on.

As respects the evolution of his mind, Wilson had now passed from an original passive neutrality to an active, affirmative, determined neutrality. He would not allow the war to touch us, he would fight it off.

9 See p. 95.

5

EVOLUTION OF AMERICAN THOUGHT

Which Consisted to Some Extent at First of a Falling into Groups. America Divided between Pro-Ally and Pro-German, with the Largest Group of All Being neither Pro-Ally nor Pro-German, but Just American, and Determined to Be Neutral, though the Feeling of a Majority of Them Was That Germany Was in the Wrong, the Allies in the Right. And a Very Conglomerate Division of Races, Italian-American, Irish-American, Polish-American, Hungarian-American, and What-Not, Each Having Its Own Allegiance as between the Belligerents. And a Sectional Cleavage, East versus West. And a Quite Acute Division between Preparedness Advocates and Pacifists, the Latter Having General Subdivisions.

It was commonly said later, and frequently at the time, that Wilson, the day after the *Lusitania* sinking, could have carried America into the war. Von Bernstorff thought so, and he should have been a good judge: Wilson needed only to "nod to induce his country to fight after the *Lusitania*."[1]

But this should be added: It was on the Atlantic seaboard mainly, and perhaps only, that willingness for war prevailed to a degree sufficient to make a declaration by Wilson practicable. The East was the section, principally, that expressed itself in execration of "too proud to fight." For whatever reason, whether because of the greater quantity of war news in the Eastern big-city newspapers, whether because of greater nearness to the scene, or the larger number of persons who had direct associations with England and France, it was a definite

[1] "My Three Years in America," Johann Bernstorff.

and important fact in the evolution of American thought about the war that the East arrived at readiness to enter long before the rest of the country. On the Pacific coast, Secretary of Agriculture David F. Houston, being in Los Angeles on the day news came of the sinking of the *Lusitania*, found that the members of a local delegation who came to see him "talked for a few minutes about the *Lusitania* tragedy without excitement," and then

PROF. MUENSTERBERG ASKS FAIR PLAY FOR KAISER AND GERMANY

—New York Globe, Aug. 6, 1914.

turned to "irrigation, citrus fruit, roads, water power, and forest-fire protection. . . . Nor did any reporter of any Pacific coast newspaper seek to interview me on the *Lusitania*, and no citizen brought it up during the remainder of my stay in the West, which lasted several weeks."

This cleavage between East and the remainder of the country was but one of several divisions into which the country had fallen. The cleavages criss-crossed each other, intricately.

II

One strong line of division arose almost with the very outbreak of the war. Propagandist energy directed upon America by German professors in Germany incited some

German professors resident in America, serving as teachers in our own universities — conspicuously Edmund von Mach, formerly of Harvard and Wellesley; Doctor Kuno Francke, Professor of the History of German Culture at Harvard University; Doctor Hugo Munsterberg, Professor of Psychology at Harvard University

"GERMANY FIGHTING FOR CIVILIZATION"

Charles Vezin Outlines for The Eagle German Viewpoint of War.

KAISER STOOD FOR PEACE.

Either Glorious Victory or Glorious Death of Great People to Be Result.

—Brooklyn Eagle, Aug. 6, 1914.

— to give us light about the greater virtue of the German cause. That most of us resented. We ought not to have resented it. Nothing any German-born Professor in our colleges said upon the German side was more provocative than what British and French-born persons among us said on the Allied side. And many of us who resented pleas for Germany by German-born professors or leaders of thought among us, did not at all resent, but on the contrary applauded, pleas for the Allies by college teachers of native birth. A statistically-minded authority, after due investigation, reported[1a] that in 25 educational insti-

1a J. J. McCook in the New York Evening *Post*, August 15, 1915.

tutions, only 1 professor in 15 was pro-German; in 9 theological schools 1 professor in 17; in 7 law schools, 1 in 40.

The truth is, America was not neutral; American thought, opinion, emotion was strongly pro-Ally. President Wilson in his heart sympathized with the Allies (though he was conscientiously careful to keep his personal feelings separate from his public duty and his official attitude, which was one of strict neutrality). Vice-President Thomas R. Marshall was pro-Ally — when Wilson said that Americans "must put a curb upon our sentiments" Marshall obeyed the injunction of his superior, but said "I am the only American possessed of a voice who followed that request."[2] Chief Justice of the Supreme Court Edward D. White, officially neutral and mute, was in heart strongly pro-Ally; once he said to a member of Wilson's cabinet:[3] "I wish I were thirty years younger, I would go to Canada and enlist." The leading Republican, ex-President Theodore Roosevelt, was pro-Ally (though at the beginning he did not feel we should take part). One of the most distinguished leaders of thought in America, President Emeritus Charles W. Eliot of Harvard University, was pro-Ally; he spoke of "ultimate defeat of Germany and Austria-Hungary" as "the only tolerable result of this outrageous war."[4] Most of our men of letters were pro-Ally; a representative one, William Roscoe Thayer, biographer of Roosevelt, Hay, and Cavour, proclaimed: "I make no spurious claim to neutrality; only a moral eunuch could be neutral in the sense implied by the malefic dictum of the President."

So general was pro-Ally sentiment in America, that

[2] "A Hoosier Salad."   [3] David F. Houston, Secretary of Agriculture.
[4] In a letter to President Wilson, August 6, 1914.

many of us came to feel that to be not pro-Ally was to be not patriotically American. In our overwhelmingly pro-Ally emotion, our conviction that Germany was in the wrong and should be defeated, our latent impulse to help, if only vicariously, in the pro-Ally cause — in that condition the pleas of the German-born professors gave

The Fatherland
FAIR PLAY FOR
Germany and Austria-Hungary

Edited by
GEORGE SYLVESTER VIERECK
FREDERICK F. SCHRADER
European Representative:
LOUIS VIERECK, Berlin, Suedwest Korso 8.

A weekly published and owned by The International Monthly, 1123 Broadway, New York City. Telephone, Farragut 9938. Cable Address, Viereck, New York. President, George Sylvester Viereck; Vice-President, Joseph Bernard Rethy; Treasurer, M. Binion; Secretary, Curt H. Reisinger. Terms of Subscription, incl. postage in the United States and Mexico $2.00 per year; $1.00 for six months. In Canada, $2.25 per year; $1.25 for six months. Subscription to all foreign countries within the postal union, $2.25 per year. Single copies, 5 cents. Newsdealers and Agents throughout the country supplied by The International News Company. Manuscripts, addressed to the Editor, if accompanied by return postage, and found unavailable, will be returned. The Editor, however, accepts no responsibility for unsolicited contributions.
Copyright, 1914, by The International Monthly, Inc.   Entered at the Post Office, New York, N. Y., as Second Class Matter.

When you have finished reading this number, don't lay it aside, but pass it on to your American friends who may be anxious to know the other side of the great European conflict.

LIES, LIES, LIES.

IF we are to believe the mendacity mills of St. Petersburg and London, the German Army is bent on carrying out on a large scale the theory of a pessimist philo-

again and again in official reports from Paris and London. It was not until the 19th of September that the German dispatch was verified by London. The Sayville station is the only source of reliable information.

GREAT BRITAIN REPRIMANDS PRESIDENT WILSON.

SIR LIONEL GARDEN, formerly Great Britain's representative in Mexico, now on his way to his new post in Brazil, severely reprimands President Wilson for his order withdrawing our troops from Vera Cruz. The British diplomat does not hesitate to characterize President Wilson's action as "a shame." The interview is printed in the New York Sun and is vouched for by one of that newspaper's ablest reporters and two of his colleagues. The subsequent perfunctory denial by Sir Lionel isn't taken seriously by any one acquainted with the editorial integrity of the New York Sun, and this minister's past record for impertinence toward the President of the United States.

English warships have seized and destroyed the mail of American citizens addressed to Germany without regard to neutrality, in flagrant violation of the conventions of international law. This act of piracy is almost a casus belli.

Evidently British statesmen look upon the United States as a province of the British Empire. Else they would not dare to strain to the breaking point the neutrality proclaimed by President Wilson.

The German side of the argument as presented by *The Fatherland*.

us something concrete to complain against, something occurring on our own soil.

Complain many of us did, and presently we extended our complaint to include our German-American citizens generally. They, in natural resentment against being treated so, and partly on account of the spokesmanship given them by the German professors, partly on account of the sum of all the conditions, became self-consciously pro-German, vocal, and organized. Some of them acted through the "National German-American Alliance," which urged German-Americans to "organize press bureaus and combat the attitude of the English language press." A conspicuous American of German parentage, George Sylvester Viereck, conducted a weekly paper, *"The Fatherland,* devoted to Fair Play to Germany." The quite considerable German language press in America, hitherto a rather innocuous medium of news from the homeland and of neighborhood items for German immigrants and their descendants, became aggressively pro-German. Many, though not all, ministers of Lutheran churches called meetings, adopted resolutions: "We German-Americans" protest "against the common calumnies against the head of a nation friendly to us . . . [brand as false the charge] that Germany and its Emperor have sought and forced this war."

Between German-Americans and pro-Germans and, on the other hand, anti-Germans, academic war, kept within oral and polemic limits, went on constantly. Friends of Germany, thinking mainly in terms of the German people, pointed to their kindliness, quoted their poets, cited German achievement in science. Anti-Germans, thinking mainly in terms of the German ruling caste, the Hohenzollerns, the militarists, and the Kultur they had fastened on the people, pointed to the Kaiser's bombast, cited some of the German philosophers and about all the German authors of treatises on military science, the schrecklichkeit they preached or condoned. Philosopher Nietzsche, through quotations from his "Will to Power" and other works, became almost as familiar a name as that of the contemporary holder of the highest batting average in professional baseball. Source for the most bloodthirsty quotations was von Bernhardi — that name, too, became as familiar to readers of editorials as the name of any of the generals at the front. Some of Bernhardi's sentiments were, to the American point-of-view, pretty shocking. An often quoted one — "Weak nations do not deserve to exist and should be absorbed by powerful ones" — ran counter to a deep American sentiment, and seemed to explain Germany's invasion of Belgium, which, to America, was the outstanding wrong of the war.

As the tension grew, activities of some pro-Germans went to a point inconsistent with our neutrality, inconsistent indeed with loyalty to the United States. They established connections with the German government,

In the 1916 campaign the political parties at one and the same time desired and looked askance at the German vote (personified in this *Life* cartoon as a dachshund).

received money which they spent on propaganda, in some cases on criminal conspiracy, even criminal violence.[4] This, as it became known, excited strong feeling. The cleavage between pro-Germans and the rest of the people became tense.

The Germans were joined by some Irish, comparatively few but very much moved, and with a racial capacity for making their emotion vocal; the beginning of the Great War had happened to coincide with an acute outbreak of the seven-centuries-long struggle of the Irish against England. An organization of Irish-Na-

[4] For an account of German spying, sabotage, and violence in America, see Chapter 8.

tionalists, meeting in Philadelphia, "pledge ourselves to do all in our power . . . to bring Irishmen and Germans together to fight for a common cause, the national welfare of Germany. . . ." One Irish organization that became active and resourceful in pro-German propaganda was called "The American Truth Society." At many an exalted meeting "The Wearing of the Green" mingled, rather incongruously, with "Die Wacht am Rhein."

As feeling grew, race-consciousness became infectious. In the bedevilling cleavages by which America was thus beset, an intricate line of division separated various foreign groups each from each: Italian-Americans, Irish-Americans, Polish-Americans, Russian-Americans, Hungarian-Americans, and other groups from the peculiarly polyglot Austro-Hungarian Empire. All began to organize, take sides, and express their emotions in foreign-language newspapers, including demands that their adopted country should take one side or the other. Thus arose another war-created term, "hyphenated American." The phenomenon disturbed us, caused many to wonder if our policy of unrestricted immigration had been wise, whether America was really a nation, or just an international boarding-house. It was not a happy time for average Americans — occasions arose when they were obliged to wonder whether they existed, whether there was such a thing as "the average American." Some, conspicuously Theodore Roosevelt, then ex-President, took the situation very seriously, started movements for "Americanization" — Roosevelt popularized a phrase, "hundred per cent American." One more tolerant, or more timorous, expressed himself in poetry, at least in words that rhymed, in the New York *Sun:*

The barber to the right of me was hoching for the Kaiser.
The barber to the left of me was hacking for the Czar.

A gentleman from Greece was shearing off my fleece,
While very near a swart Italian stropped his scimitar.
And when presently discussion, polyglot and fervid,
On political conditions burst about my chair,
I left the place unshaven — I hope I'm not a craven,
But I sort of like to wear a head beneath my hair!

III

Along another line, there was cleavage between preparedness advocates and pacifists. Both these groups, however, must be subdivided.

Some preparedness partisans aimed at universal military training, others merely at having a larger army and a quite strong navy.

Pacifists were divided between two factions. One opposed preparedness for this war — these were to some extent identical with or parallel in their aims with the pro-Germans. The other group, pacifists in the more exact sense, opposed preparedness on principle, opposed it for any war at any time with anybody, the peace-at-all-times-and-at-any-price people. Argument and quarrel between pacifists and preparedness advocates was rather less violent than that which had its origin in racial affiliations. Preparedness advocates could as a rule satisfy their emotions adequately by speaking of their meek opponents as "milk-faced grubs." Pacifists retorted, "jingo" and "bloody-minded militarists." Millions of individual arguments posed the question, "Would you fight if a foreign soldier struck your mother?" Much of the emotion of the pacifist-preparedness jibing centred about a song, its sentiment taken perfectly seriously by those who liked it, fiercely jeered at by those who did not: "I did not raise my boy to be a soldier!"

IV

The cleavages that beset the country were far more intricate than could be described as three pairs of antitheses: Preparedness advocates versus pacifists, pro-Germans versus pro-Allies, and East versus West. One lists the groups only with much qualification; each line of division was cross-cut by other lines.

At all times there was a large group, the largest of all, into which the lines of cleavage did not penetrate. This group were comparatively detached about the war; they either mildly favored the Allies or took neither side; so far as they reflected at all upon what we should do, their instinct said we should stay out of it, the war was none of our business. To mind one's own business, or as expressed in an imperative, "mind your own business," was a traditional American attitude of mind, a corollary to our strong individualism; it had almost the force of folk-lore. Now it was expanded from a personal rule of life to a national one. Only upon some extremely strong incentive, such as assurance from Wilson that we should fight, would the majority of Americans consider entering the war.

V

To Wilson, the cleavages among the people presented a delicate job of leadership. To remain neutral, yet not to achieve neutrality by supine yielding of American rights, was a task which required him not only to keep a firm face toward the belligerents abroad, but to be watchful at home. On occasion, pro-Germans and pacifists united in a common purpose. In pursuit of this purpose they insisted that American travellers should avoid belligerent vessels, so as to avert such causes for

complaint against Germany as arose out of the sinking of
the *Lusitania*. Pro-Germans and pacifists actively
pushing this proposal received tacit support from many
citizens, chiefly un-travelled rural residents of South and
West, who, without being excited over the war, felt that

Cartoon chiding anti-war sentiment.—*From the News Press, St. Joseph, Mo.*

Americans ought to keep out of danger, and by keeping
out of danger save America from being involved in the
war.

The demand was pushed forward in Congress, in the
form of a resolution[5] warning citizens they must not take
passage on vessels belonging to belligerents, meaning of

[5] Presented in the Senate by Gore of Oklahoma, in the House by McLemore
of Texas, February 22, 1916.

course Allied vessels, mainly British, since there were no German vessels on the sea. The resolution as introduced in the House was inspired by a fiery young Irish-American associated with German propaganda.[6] It was supported, however, by large masses of the people who were neither pro-German nor pro-Ally. Both sponsors of the resolution in Congress and most of its supporters, were members of Wilson's party. Speaker Champ Clark, also a Democrat, led a delegation to Wilson to tell him the resolution would pass Congress by 2 to 1. Wilson, in a public letter to Senator Stone of Missouri, declared that "I shall do everything in my power to keep the United States out of war" — but

I cannot consent to any abridgment of the rights of American citizens. . . . To forbid our people to exercise their rights for fear we might be called upon to vindicate them would be a deep humiliation indeed. If in this instance we allowed expediency to take the place of principle, the door would inevitably be opened to still further concessions. Once accept a single abatement of right, and many other humiliations would follow. . . .

As the result of this letter, the House, after a debate which consumed four and a half million words (it would fill 300 volumes as large as this history) "tabled" the resolution 275 to 135. The incident increased Wilson's prestige, strengthened his leadership, showed that very probably America would at any time take whatever course about the war Wilson might lead toward.

[6] This statement is made on the authority of George Sylvester Viereck, who should know, since he was the leading German propagandist in America.

6

BRYAN, RESIGNING, LEADS THE PACIFISTS

Having at Last Got into Office He Continues to Lecture on the Chautauqua Platform, Serves Grape Juice at Dinners He Gives to Diplomats, Coins an Unfortunate Phrase "Deserving Democrats," Writes Some Thirty Useful Treaties. Finding the Duties of the State Department Boring and Unpalatable, He Resigns, Explosively, thereby Giving Comfort to Pacifists and Pro-Germans and Making Things More Difficult for Wilson.

THE first of the *Lusitania* notes and all the preceding notes to all the belligerents had been signed — as a rule signed but not written — by William Jennings Bryan as Secretary of State.

Bryan had been taken into the Cabinet by Wilson partly in the spirit of getting him on the inside to keep him from being on the outside; partly in gratitude for past services, partly in anticipation of future usefulness — but a usefulness which was not expected to include skill in the post of Secretary of State, nor adaptation to it.[1]

The first of many and important services by Bryan

---

[1] "Mr. Wilson did not want Bryan in his Cabinet and did not believe him fitted for the Secretaryship of State . . . but Bryan's influence in the party was such that he could effectively block the Wilson legislative programme and perhaps wreck the administration."—"The Intimate Papers of Colonel House," Charles Seymour.

"There was no doubt, from the beginning, that William Jennings Bryan was to be the Secretary of State. His distinguished position in the party and his great service to Mr. Wilson at Baltimore and during the campaign entitled him to recognition. But over and beyond all that, there was a manifest political advantage in having him in the Cabinet. A very large element of the Democratic party stood squarely behind Bryan. His co-operation with the Administration meant the smoothing-out of many diverse views about the currency and the tariff." — William G. McAdoo, Secretary of the Treasury and son-in-law of President Wilson, in "Crowded Years."

to Wilson had been a forgiveness. Wilson, years[2] before, while still President of Princeton with little thought of ever being anything else, had written, in a casual letter. to a friend[2] about the fortunes of the Democratic party, "Would that we could do something, at once dignified

Cartoon by Kemble in *Harper's Weekly* at the time of the 1912 Democratic convention, showing Bryan deciding which of the candidates for the Presidential nomination he should favor. In the end he favored Wilson and by doing so had a dominating hand in elevating Wilson to the Presidency.

and effective, to knock Mr. Bryan, once for all, into a cocked hat." As Wilson emerged into national politics, the letter was made public. Had Bryan chosen to hold the sneer to his heart, Wilson's upward career would have stopped. Bryan, however, not only overlooked the slight; he became the decisive agent in nominating Wilson for the Presidenecy. At the Democratic National Convention in which Wilson was a candidate, Bryan, as

[2] April 29, 1907. The letter was to Adrian Joline.

a delegate instructed in binding manner to support
Champ Clark, and further bound to Clark by old friendship, broke his instructions, flouted his friendship, sensationally charged Clark with having support from "the

Photograph © Underwood & Underwood.

A photograph of Wilson's Cabinet as it stood in the beginning. On the left at
    the top of the table is Wilson. On Wilson's right in the foreground is Sec-
    retary of State Bryan. The other members beginning at Wilson's left are
    William G. McAdoo, Secretary of the Treasury; James Clark McReynolds,
    Attorney-General (subsequently an Associate Justice of the Supreme
    Court); Josephus Daniels, Secretary of the Navy; David F. Houston, Sec-
    retary of Agriculture; William Wilson, Secretary of Labor; William C.
    Redfield, Secretary of Commerce; Franklin K. Lane, Secretary of the In-
    terior; Albert S. Burleson, Postmaster General, and Lindley M. Garrison,
    Secretary of War.

interests" — and threw his own strength behind Wilson.
    Such services commend men strongly for Cabinet posts.
Besides, Bryan had political capital, a personal following larger than that of any other Democrat except Wilson himself. Wilson knew that in getting his legislative
programme through Congress, the difference between

support and opposition by Southern and Western adherents of Bryan in Congress might be determined by Bryan's presence in, or absence from, the Cabinet. Particularly, Wilson meant to establish a banking and currency system, the Federal Reserve, which Bryan outside the Cabinet might oppose as contrary to his well-known radical views on finance, but which Bryan within the Cabinet could not decently resist.

Bryan was tendered the post of Secretary of State, accepted, and made good on the implied obligation[2a]: When the Federal Reserve bill was before the House, and Democrats from West and South, Bryanite in their views about banking, were about to make enactment difficult or impossible, Bryan was cajoled, argued with, and persuaded by Wilson and members of the Cabinet until, without ever fully understanding the measure, and without wholly believing in the parts he did understand, Bryan gave to Carter Glass in charge of the bill in the House a complete franchise to use his name and influence in behalf of the measure:

You are authorized to speak for me and say that I appreciate so profoundly the service rendered by the President to the people in the stand he has taken on the fundamental principles involved in currency reform that I am with him in all the details. If my opinion has influence with anybody . . . I advise him to stand by the President.

II

As Secretary of State, Bryan constantly generated hot water round himself, constantly embarrassed the President. He had told Wilson, when Wilson offered him the post, that his personal investments were unproductive, and that, therefore, he would like the privilege of

[2a] "No lash of the Administration whip could have compelled Congress to pass the Federal Reserve Act without Bryan."—Colonel E. M. House.

lecturing. With a curious indirectness which defeated its own purpose he said he could see there might be indelicacy in requiring the public to pay a specific admission fee to hear the Secretary of State talk, but that it seemed to him it would be all right if he were one of

Photograph by Brown Brothers.

While Bryan was Secretary of State he continued to be a professional lecturer at Chautauquas, giving rise to much deprecatory comment.

half a dozen grouped attractions on an inclusive programme for which Chautauqua patrons should pay a season fee. In consequence, Bryan periodically left Washington, followed by a retinue of reporters — not wholly free from malice — to appear on programmes alongside other performers who sometimes included acrobats, jugglers, female impersonators, and Swiss yodellers, until newspapers laughing at him and Senators seriously reproving him and threatening official admonition, led him to admit, even if he could not see, that there was dubious taste in it.

As a second condition of accepting the post, Bryan had told Wilson that as a conscientious Prohibitionist he could not serve wine at the formal meals which, as Secretary of State, he would be expected to give to foreign ambassadors. At his first diplomatic lunch (in honor of Ambassador James Bryce), Bryan rose and "with full consciousness of how this would ultimately be reported to the outside world,"[3] explained at length that he shared the conviction of millions of Americans against alcoholic drinks and that "to be true to his principles and traditions," he was obliged to limit the liquid refreshment of his guests to water and grape juice. The innovation, or deprivation, became the occasion of a thousand quips;[4] it was said that European diplomats learned a technique of acquiring saturation to last the evening before they left their homes for Bryan's dinners; occasional inaccuracy in estimating the quantity led to regrettable consequences. But if Bryan's rule led to rather more drinking by some of his guests, the publicity attending it as a pious example led the public to drink less, became, indeed, one of the forces that, stimulating dry sentiment in the West and South, brought national prohibition.

Bryan, in office for the first time since he had been in Congress more than twenty years before, was avid for patronage. He was, he told a fellow Cabinet member,

[3] Bryan's admiring biographer, J. C. Long, thus expresses it in "Bryan the Great Commoner."

[4] Apocryphal legend at the time said that the Russian Ambassador, startled by Bryan's announcement, tried to remember the last time he had drunk water; meditative research into his memory brought back an occasion when he was a young attaché in Rome in the year 1879.

David F. Houston,[5] in an unusual position: "Six million people had voted for him for President three times, and many of them would like to serve the nation." He asked Houston if he could find a place for "Coin" Harvey, a venerable fanatic who had been prominent as a free silver advocate in Bryan's first campaign.[6] To one of his subordinates, an American official acting as receiver of customs in the Republic of Santo Domingo,

THE FATHERLAND
Fair Play for Germany and Austria-Hungary
Edited by GEORGE SYLVESTER VIERECK and FREDERICK F. SCHRADER

VOL. II, No. 13   MAY 5, 1915   PRICE, 5 CENTS

THE WORK OF THE GRAPE JUICE

BECAUSE the British Ambassador was busy issuing instructions to the American Ambassador in London, Secretary Bryan had to reply to Count Bernstorff's note himself. It is true that Mr. Wilson assisted him and that it took both these distinguished gentlemen more than three weeks to concoct some excuse for their surrender of the United States Government to, Great Britain. Nevertheless, Mr. Bryan's answer is absolutely untainted by reason. The laboring mountains have brought forth a preposterous mouse. A sillier or more dishonest statement was never issued by an American official. In fact, the reply of the Administration to Count Bernstorff is the most dishonest document that was ever submitted by one great Government to another. It is not merely a slap in the face of the German people, but a slap in the face of truth.

the good faith of the United States in its performance of its duties as a neutral." Count Bernstorff cannot have impugned the good faith of the United States for the simple reason that good faith on the part of the United States in its relations with Germany is a thing that does not exist. The Administration has shown bad faith, and nothing but bad faith, from beginning to end, from the suppression of the wireless to the attack on the Odenwald, from its early subservience to Great Britain to its present insolence toward the representative of the Kaiser.

Does Mr. Wilson think that Germany is Mexico? Does he dream the German people and the Kaiser will accept insults from him that even Huerta resented? Does Mr. Wilson seriously imagine that he can censure the German Ambassador like a school boy? Mr. Bryan

Bryan as a loyal prohibitionist, while Secretary of State, served only grape juice at dinners to foreign diplomats. This became the basis of much ridicule. In the article here reproduced from the German-American propagandist organ *The Fatherland*, Bryan is accused of being unfair to Germany. The accusation, as it subsequently turned out, was very incorrect.

Bryan wrote a letter which, when impishly exploited by the Republican press, gave satiric currency to the phrase "deserving Democrats" — a deserving Democrat being, in Bryan's eyes, one who had voted for Bryan all three times:

Now that you have arrived and are acquainting yourself

5 "Eight Years With Wilson's Cabinet," David F. Houston.
6 See "Our Times," Vol. I.

with the situation, you can let me know what positions you
have at your disposal, with which to reward deserving Democrats. . . . You have had enough experience in politics to know
how valuable workers are when the campaign is on: and how
difficult it is to find rewards for all the deserving.

If Bryan as Secretary of State had ineptnesses inherent in his personality and experience, they were partially balanced by services, likewise of a sort that only
his expansive good-will would be likely to achieve. At
a time of dangerous tension with Japan, beginning with
passage by California of laws forbidding Japanese to
own land and otherwise humiliating them, Ambassador
Chinda concluded a tense conversation with Bryan by
rising and saying: "I suppose, Mr. Secretary, your decision is final." Bryan, with characteristic genuineness,
impulsively extended his hand, cried out emotionally,
"Between friends, there is nothing final," and brought
the conference to a happier end, the relations with Japan
to a better status.

In international arbitration Bryan brought about a
unique and important advance, which, twenty years
later, stood as a pioneer landmark of the movement toward prevention of war. His plan, when proposed to
Wilson and others, was given perfunctory encouragement, as a project unlikely to succeed. But Bryan, after
evolving his plan fully, called a meeting of foreign ambassadors and ministers and persuaded some 34 nations
to adopt treaties of which the essence was that none
would go to war without permitting a year's time for
discussion between the arising of a dispute and the going
to war.

III

With the opening of the war, Wilson found that a
Secretary of State chosen for considerations other than

fitness for conducting foreign relations may be a handicap when foreign relations become important. From
the moment serious responsibility descended on Wilson,
Bryan became to him not merely a weak crutch but an
impediment.

On the very first day of the war, August 1, 1914,

Photograph by Underwood and Underwood.

Characteristic photograph of Bryan on the platform.

when Wilson contemplated at least a perfunctory gesture
toward peace-making, Colonel House warned him: "Do
not let Mr. Bryan make any overtures to any of the
powers involved; they look upon him as absolutely
visionary, and it would lessen the weight of your influence if you desire to use it yourself later. Make it clear
that what we have done was at your own instance; if the
public, either here or in Europe, think that Mr. Bryan
instigated it, they would conclude it was done in an impracticable way and was doomed to failure."

IV

Compulsion upon Wilson to be his own Secretary of State[7] did not trouble him greatly. The nearly two years of notes to Britain about her violations of international law, and the early notes to Germany as well, passed without material embarrassment from Bryan. When, however, Wilson read to the Cabinet his first note to Germany about the *Lusitania*, Bryan querulously asked why we were more stern with Germany than we had been with Britain — why did we not check Britain's violations of our neutrality? When other Cabinet members supported the note, Bryan showed heat, charged there were "some members of the Cabinet who were not neutral. The President turned to him and said, with a steely glitter in his eyes: 'Mr. Bryan, you are not warranted in making such an assertion; we all doubtless have our opinions in this matter, but there are none of us who can justly be accused of being unfair.' Mr. Bryan apologized and the incident passed."[8] But Bryan, clinging to his view and purpose, prepared a draft of a supplementary letter or postscript to be sent to the Germans and to inform them of our willingness to submit the issue to a commission. The postscript, as described by another Cabinet member,[9] had the spirit of telling Germany that she "should not consider the note seriously, that it was meant in a Pickwickian sense." Wilson thoughtlessly was about to sign the supplementary letter when other members of the Cabinet heard of it and showed the

[7] "It was Wilson's habit to write out important state papers himself and have Bryan sign them."—"The Political Education of President Wilson," James Kerney.

[8] This Cabinet episode was told by Attorney-General Thomas W. Gregory to Colonel House, and is here quoted from "The Intimate Letters of Colonel House."

[9] Attorney-General Thomas W. Gregory, whose account of the incident, as told by him to Colonel House, is here quoted.

President that such a letter "would have been saying to the American public, 'We are standing firm in demanding our rights,' and behind their backs it would be saying to the German government, 'We merely send this note to pacify the American people and do not mean what we say.' "[9]

—*From The World, New York.*

After Bryan resigned as Secretary of State and became leading spokesman of pacifist sentiment in the United States, he was represented by cartoonist Rollin Kirby of the New York *World* as receiving applause from the Kaiser —but no attention from America generally.

Wilson, once his attention was focussed on it, suppressed the letter. Bryan, still clinging to his purpose, told the Austro-Hungarian ambassador that America

9 Attorney-General Thomas W. Gregory, whose account of the incident, as told by him to Colonel House, is here quoted.

did not really mean as much as the *Lusitania* note said. The Austro-Hungarian was quick to transmit such authoritative and important information to Berlin, with the effect of causing the Germans to feel they ran little risk in continuing their submarine warfare.

V

When Wilson, in his second *Lusitania* note, went still farther in the direction of sternness toward Germany, Bryan, listening to the reading of it in the Cabinet meeting, sat back, silent, his eyes half closed. Afterward he said he could not sign it, he must resign. Wilson asked McAdoo to labor with him. McAdoo gave two days to it, asked Bryan to go out of the room while he talked with Mrs. Bryan, persuaded Bryan to go with Mrs. Bryan to the country over the week-end before finally deciding. Rest merely buttressed Bryan's determination: he "had to abide by his own feeling, his own conscience." McAdoo warned him that resignation at so critical a time would be bitterly resented by the country as an embarrassment to Wilson — "You will destroy yourself." Prospect of martyrdom increased Bryan's determination: "I believe you are right. I think this will destroy me, but I must do my duty according to my conscience."[10]

At a final lunch with several members of the Cabinet, Bryan sat silent, "seemed to be communing with himself." At the end, "Gentlemen," he said — addressing half a dozen friends he had to be oratorical — "I have valued our association and friendship. I have had to take the course I have chosen. . . . The President has one view, I have a different one. I cannot go along with him in this note. I think it makes for war. I can do

[10] "Crowded Years," William G. McAdoo.

more on the outside to prevent war than I can on the inside." Dramatically he continued: "I go out into the dark; the President has the power and prestige on his

Bryan's leadership of the pacifist movement (after he had resigned as Secretary of State) gave rise to this picture in *Life* (July 29, 1915), and the following doggerel:

I want to be a neutral and with the neutrals stand,
A smile upon my ego, the German vote at hand.

side." Breaking down completely he concluded, irrelevantly, "I have many friends who would die for me."

VI

Bryan on the outside, working for peace, now provided spokesmanship and leadership for the pacifists, a group not identical with the pro-Germans but in part having a common objective. Bryan, accepting the fol-

[11] "Eight Years with Wilson's Cabinet," David F. Houston.

lowing of both, was careful to keep himself in the classification of pacifist.

The preparedness advocates and pro-Allies, and in

The cartoonist's anger at Bryan for his theatric withdrawing from President
Wilson's Cabinet at a time of acute crisis—an emotion shared by probably
the great majority of Americans—is reflected in the white feather the artist
has stuck in Bryan's hat and by the altogether unattractive appearance he
has given to the likeness of the retiring Secretary of State.

—*Carter in the New York Evening Sun.*

general all who believed in supporting Wilson in whatever course Wilson's sense of responsibility led to — all
these denounced Bryan with a vehemence to satisfy the
most hardy appetite for a hair shirt. They had good

reason. Bryan's resignation weakened Wilson's hand seriously, enabled the pro-Germans to claim, as their organ *The Fatherland* put it, "The President in his present course has not behind him the majority of the Amer-

A German cartoon ridiculing the attempt of pacifists to bury the war hatchet in an ink pot.

ican people, since even his own advisers desert him." Bryan's defection was denounced by the New York *World*, leading Democratic organ, as "unspeakable treachery not only to the President but to the nation."

VII

Bryan, stepping into leadership of the pacifists, made an appeal "To the American people," timing it to appear the same day as the *Lusitania* note he had refused to sign. "Although," he said, "the jingoes have got the rabies from the dogs of war, shall the opponents of organized slaughter be silent while the disease spreads?" Another appeal he addressed "To the German-Americans." He addressed, in New York, a meeting held under the auspices of the "Friends of Peace" — inclusive title for groups specifically designated as the German-American Alliance, United Irish Societies, American Truth Society, American Independence Union,

---

The Commoner

WILLIAM J. BRYAN, EDITOR AND PROPRIETOR

VOL. 15, NO. 12   Lincoln, Nebraska, December, 1915   Whole Number 680

WRITE, WRITE NOW, WRITE OFTEN

The tide in favor of a big army and a big navy has passed its flood; the ebb has begun.

As senators and congressmen assemble in Washington they bring reports from the several states and congressional districts to the effect that the masses are opposed to frenzied preparedness. The scare that has been worked up by the representatives of munition factories has exhausted itself, and even the metropolitan papers are beginning to select the things that they will INSIST upon in view of the impossibility of getting all that they demanded. The newspaper estimates as to the strength of the opposition are increasing, but the danger is not past. The retreat has commenced, but the opposition must not be over confident.

Every American citizen who is opposed to the proposed increase in the appropriations for the army and navy ought to write to his congressman, both of his senators and to the President. Individual letters are better than petitions because they indicate a personal interest, and a personal interest expressed by a constituent has its influence with a public servant.

It will only require four letters, one to your congressman, one to each of your senators and one to the President — only eight cents worth of postage—to give to those at Washington the benefit of your views.

Write, write now, and if one letter is not sufficient, write often.

By acting promptly you may save yourself many dollars in taxation, and what is more you may save your country from the menace of militarism and from the danger of wars which will be provoked by a policy copied from Europe, and based upon the idea that peace can be built only upon fear and threats of force. Do not delay.   W. J. BRYAN.

President's Message Analyzed

I have carefully read the President's message. We are committed to legislation which there and make it less probable that any nation in the near future will desire to colonize Latin America.

The President is unfortunate, also, in his suggestions in regard to taxes. The democrats will not take kindly to the idea of taxing gasoline and automobiles. A few years ago only the rich den be placed on large incomes and inheritances, rather than on the incomes of those who will have to do the fighting if there is any fighting to be done.

The President's plan of taxation is quite sure to arouse opposition among the republicans, whose support is solicited, as well as among the,

---

After Bryan's resignation he conducted, on the stump and through his periodical *The Commoner,* a strident campaign urging the public to protest to Congress against enlargement of the army and navy and against preparedness generally, saying, "This nation does not need burglars' tools unless it intends to make burglary its business."

American Humanity League, American Women of German Descent, German-American Peace Society.

The position Bryan took, and kept urging, combined the attitudes of both pro-Germans and pacifists: Forbid Americans to travel on vessels of belligerents — "Why should an American citizen be permitted to involve his country in war in travelling upon a belligerent ship when he knows that the ship will pass through a danger zone?" Forbid American ships to enter the war zone. Prevent shipment of munitions to the Allies by refusing to permit any ship carrying them, whether American or otherwise, to leave an American port. Resist all movements for preparedness. "Write to your Congressman; write to both your Senators; tell them that this nation does not need burglars' tools unless it intends to make burglary its business; it should not be a pistol-toting nation unless it is going to adopt a pistol-toter's ideas."[12]

As the relations with Germany grew more tense, Bryan grew more violent. The American people, he said after diplomatic relations were broken, "are not willing to send American soldiers across the Atlantic to march under the banners of any European monarch or to die on European soil in settlement of European quarrels. . . . Wire immediately to the President, your Senators, your Congressmen. A few cents now may save many dollars in taxation and possibly a son."

VIII

The news that war had been declared came to Bryan at Albany, Ga., where he was lecturing. He wired the President offering his services as a volunteer in any capacity, stated that "the quickest way to peace is to go straight through supporting the government in all it undertakes no matter how long the war lasts," and retired to his Florida home. Later, he spent the time of the war lecturing up and down the country on ethical and semi-religious topics, excluding all reference to public affairs.

[12] From Bryan's weekly paper, *The Commoner*.

7

HENRY FORD TAKES A HAND AND A SHIP

Earnest American Advocates of Ending the War Set Up an Institution for "Continuous Mediation." Henry Ford Joins the Venture and Charters a Vessel, Officially the *Oscar II*, but Colloquially the "Peace Ship," or the "Ark of Peace." "Out of the Trenches by Christmas." Log of the *Oscar II*.

THE more ardent pacifists took it for granted that the United States would never enter the war — that would be too shocking. Feeling confident about this, some of the more earnest dedicated themselves to bringing the war in Europe to an end.

With this fine altruistic purpose, some of the most high-minded persons in America, led by Doctor David Starr Jordan, head of the American Peace Society, President of Stanford University, and Miss Jane Addams, leading welfare worker, head of Hull House, Chicago, organized what they called an "Emergency Peace Conference," and joined at the Hague an "International Conference of Women" — called impishly by Walter Page the "Palace of Doves" — which should unite with others in carrying on what Miss Addams called "Continuous Mediation."

Their aim, no less, was to labor directly with the heads of the European governments at war. They did labor with them. Miss Addams and some companions called on Foreign Minister von Jagow in Berlin, Foreign Minister Grey in London, and other foreign ministers of the belligerent nations. What they learned is to this day unknown. The canny Colonel House said

Miss Addams "accumulated a wonderful lot of misin-
formation," that the foreign ministers with whom she
talked "were not quite candid with her," and that she
"has a totally wrong impression."[1] Miss Addams, how-

Jane Addams, distinguished American leader in good works, whose "Emergency
Peace Conference" partly inspired Ford to try to "get the boys out of the
trenches by Christmas."

ever, and the women who accompanied her, were sure
that all the heads of states desperately wanted peace,
were only deterred from saying so by fear of "losing
face," and would ardently welcome peace if pressed
upon them from outside.

A sheaf of confidential statements of what the min-

[1] In a letter to Wilson, July 17, 1915.
Colonel House's skepticism about Miss Addams's efforts may have reflected
the depreciation that men are prone to feel about activities of women in public
affairs, common at a time when woman was still a newcomer, and an interloper,
in politics. The Colonel would have been especially subject to this sentiment;
he was elderly, he was an old-fashioned man, and he was a Southerner.

isters of belligerent states were alleged to have said to the peace-making ladies was turned over to a Hungarian woman, Mme. Rosika Schwimmer. Mme. Schwimmer, carrying the alleged statements in what newspapers later referred to as a "little black bag," came to Washington to lay her information before President Wilson and to solicit him to take the steps toward peace which, she asserted, the belligerents would welcome. Wilson was cordial, interested, but noncommittal — he had been warned by Colonel House to be cautious.

While waiting for some action by Wilson, Mme. Schwimmer went about the country delivering lectures in the interest of peace. On a day in early November, 1915, she arrived in Detroit and found the newspapers there excited about something that had occurred the day before in the office of Henry Ford.

II

Ford, from its opening in 1914, had been impatient with the war, often used his advertising space in newspapers to decry the folly of it, gave out interviews to the same effect. On a day in the Fall of 1915 he happened to see in the war news a definite figure and a concrete fact — in the fighting of the preceding twenty-four hours, 20,000 men had been killed.[1a] That struck Ford as shocking, the inhumanity of it, the economic waste. With a manner that implied "This thing has gone on long enough," he strode into the hall outside his

[1a] Miss Jane Addams, who has read the proofs of this chapter, makes the important point that it was not merely the death of 20,000 soldiers in one day that struck Ford with the need for action. On this particular day, 20,000 soldiers were killed "without changing the military situation and without shifting the position of the armies — such killing was a matter of routine, as it were." The hideous stalemate, accompanied by futile slaughter, into which the battle-

office exclaiming something to the effect that he would be willing to spend half his fortune to shorten the war by a single day — Ford had a good deal of practical faith in the power of half his fortune. A reporter of the Detroit *Free Press*, Theodore Delavigne, jumped from his bench and snatched out his pencil. His story, quoting Ford's remark, naturally made the first page of the *Free Press*, was broadcast by the news associations. Immediately Ford was deluged with letters pleading with him to lead the way. Ford, pleased, employed reporter Delavigne to answer the letters, added Delavigne permanently to his staff as secretary and publicity man for matters having to do with peace.

It was in the midst of newspaper excitement about Ford's peace purpose that Mme. Schwimmer arrived in Detroit. She tried to get in touch with Ford. Day after day she was put off by his secretaries; the cordon around Ford had learned to guard him from any who might appeal to his impulsively and erratically enthusiastic nature. Some one told Mme. Schwimmer that Doctor S. S. Marquis, dean of the Episcopal Cathedral of Detroit and spiritual adviser of Mrs. Ford, might help her reach Ford's ear. She saw Marquis, showed him the secret contents of her black bag, to no avail. Then on the evening of November 7 an unknown voice on the telephone (it turned out to be a reporter rather more interested in news than in peace) told her that if she went

---

line fell from time to time was expressed by Edwin Dwight, in *Life,* April 8, 1915, in a verse entitled, ironically, "Victory!"

> Five hundred miles of Germans,
>   Five hundred miles of French,
> And English, Scotch and Irish men
>   All fighting for a trench;
> And when the trench is taken
>   And many thousands slain,
> The losers, with more slaughter,
>   Retake the trench again.

to the main office next morning she could see Ford. It was a time when Ford's innermost secretary, Liebold, happened to be away.

Mme. Schwimmer went. She saw Ford. She stayed to lunch with Ford. It was the psychological moment; he was eager for her persuasions. Next day was even better; Ford approved heartily of the mediation plan and promised not only to support it but to go to Europe himself and take part in it. They added one to their party upon the coincident arrival in the outer office of Louis P. Lochner, agent of the Carnegie Peace Endowment. Ford was on fire. "All we know," he said, "is that the fighting nations are sick of war, that they want to stop, and that they are waiting only for some disinterested party to step in and offer mediation."

III

Ford's impulse was not unique and not necessarily impracticable. Millions of Americans shared it — to stop the war was indeed the prevailing American wish. Many Americans of elevated position were actually active in the purpose in one way or another. Ford differed from them only in his possession of great facilities. He was absolutely sincere — never more so — his action was by no means the gaudy gesture of a money-confident man bent on getting his name into history; whatever Ford's shortcomings, showy display was not among them. Ford may have been over-optimistic, doubtless he underestimated the difficulties of the task he set himself. But who, in view of Ford's record, could place a limit on what it might be possible for him to achieve? Ford, following his own methods, had accomplished the impossible in business. In the field of economics he had evolved and put in practice a new principle — if he could defy the old ways of economics, why not the old ways of statesmanship? Ford's decree of a five-dollar-a-day minimum wage in his factories[2] had blown up the old classical economics and substituted for it a system of his own, which, at the time and for years after, was

Photograph by Underwood & Underwood.

Henry Ford with Mme. Rosika Schwimmer, who largely persuaded Ford to take his expedition on the "Ark of Peace."

looked upon by great numbers of Americans, including many educated and thoughtful, as the closest practicable approach to Utopia on this planet. With this record of successful innovation, perhaps the most important since the beginning of the Industrial Era, and with the moral support of the overwhelming majority of the American people, who looked upon Ford as the evangel of a new and better world, Ford had reason to feel hopeful in his new purpose. The war, in Ford's eyes, was a wholly mad and evil reversion to savagery, needless to

[2] For an account of this event, see Vol. III, "Our Times."

tolerate. For the ways of orthodox diplomacy, state-craft, he had a disdain equal to that in which he held the orthodox economics. He had seen the statesmen fail, ignominiously, disastrously. Ford's own approach to a problem was the antithesis to that of statecraft. He was directness, simplicity, decision, intelligence, originality personified. If buffoons pirouetted across the world stage in 1915, they were not Ford and the half dozen who participated with him in the project of halting the madness of Europe; the buffoons were the rulers and statesmen and diplomats whose inability to maintain peace among civilized nations stood as the most tragic failure in all the annals of humanity.

IV

In a few days Ford went to New York, took a suite at the Biltmore, and moved at once to join a group at the McAlpin in which were Mme. Schwimmer and Miss Addams, together with several other earnest pacifists — "militant pacifists," one might call them — including: Oswald Garrison Villard, editor of the New York *Evening Post* (subsequently editor of a liberal weekly, *The Nation*); Paul Kellogg, editor of an organ of social workers, *The Survey;* Prof. George W. Kirchwey of Columbia University, and Mme. Schwimmer. Mme. Schwimmer remarked that it would be pleasant to have a ship for the delegates. Ford had been a bit lost amid the generalities of their pacifist theories, but "ship" meant something in his line, graphic and tangible: "We'll get one!" he said; immediately he phoned for agents of the steamship lines to come to the hotel.

At about this point the press took up the enterprise

and irrevocably transformed its nature. What was in essence a not necessarily infeasible idea became, in the eyes of the newspapers (and by that token in the eyes of the public), a band-wagon for extravagant hopes, a gro-

The common newspaper attitude toward Ford's expedition was one of extreme satire. In this cartoon by Chamberlain, Ford is pictured as saying to the whole war, "Now you stop!"

—New York Evening Sun.

tesque circus for the delectation of the man in the street. Reporter-secretary Delavigne had toppled the structure in this direction; his last act before following Ford to New York had been to give the Detroit papers a statement in which he said: "We'll get the boys out of the trenches by Christmas"[3] — and this was almost December 1! The newspapers leaped on the phrase. Mme. Schwimmer, having a clearer sense of the ridicule appropriate to such an impossibility, was said to have fainted when she heard it. After that phrase the "Peace Ship" had not the slightest chance for serious credence. It was natural enough that the editorial writers, humorists, cartoonists, and columnists should make Roman holiday;[4] what they had to work on scarcely needed exaggeration — the facts of the succeeding days were sufficiently entertaining to sustain any extravagance of newspaper jeering.

Ford had himself introduced to the group of shipping agents as "Mr. Henry." After they had amply shown they thought a man crazy who wanted to charter a whole steamship, he relished their delighted surprise at finding the demented one was a man amply able to charter a ship, or a fleet. Ford ordered the *Oscar II* of the Scandinavian Line for December 4. Then he summoned a corps of stenographers from the Long Island branch of his company, settled them at the Biltmore, and proceeded to send out invitations for the trip. Among others asked were all Senators and Representatives, all State Governors, and a student-delegate from each university. The sole governor to accept was the one of North Dakota, and since he confessed he was an advocate of military preparedness, one presumes he went for the ride. Ex-Congressman Bartholdt of the German section of St. Louis, likewise unique, accepted the invitation and then withdrew on being told that Ford was pro-Ally.

[3] Some newspapers quoted Ford as using the same phrase: "I hope every mother in the world will bring all the pressure she can in order that the boys can be brought out of the trenches by Christmas."

[4] One wonders, at this distance, if the newspapers were living up to their function in the highest way, when they made this attempt at peace an occasion for ridicule.

Margaret Wilson, the President's daughter, sent regrets.
Jane Addams pleaded illness.[4a] David Starr Jordan declined. William Jennings Bryan said he could be of
greater use remaining at home to oppose large increases
in preparedness expenditure.

Ford, seeking official sanction, went to Washington,
met Wilson, told him a Ford joke,[4b] and came away in
a huff because Wilson declined to give countenance to
the expedition. A cablegram to Rome asked the blessing
of the Pope; that it was addressed to "Pope Pius VII"
— who had died in 983 — is an index of the confusion
that reigned in the Biltmore suite.

If the invited guests showed no hurry in accepting,
volunteers and miscellaneous gate-crashers were innumerable. Ford and his peace secretaries were besieged
night and day. The president of the Anti-Smoking
League considered his theories had a bearing on the
problem and demanded passage. An engaged couple

[4a] Miss Addams objects, justly, to an implication in the words "pleaded illness." When the *Oscar II* sailed she was seriously ill in the Presbyterian
Hospital, Chicago, and was forbidden by her physician to consider a winter
voyage to Northern Europe where normal cold weather was accentuated by
war-time dearth of fuel.

[4b] The "Ford joke" that Ford told Wilson was preserved for posterity by
one who was present, Louis P. Lochner. Lochner represents Ford as saying
that this was the one Ford joke that he himself had made up, among the ten thousand that were current:

"One day I was driving past a cemetery when I noticed a big hole being dug.
I said to the grave-digger, 'What's the matter, are you going to bury a whole
family in the hole?' 'No,' the grave-digger replied, 'this is for one man.'
'Then why so big a hole?' I asked. The old grave-digger scratched his head.
'You see, it's this way: the man who is to be buried in this grave was a queer
fellow; he provided in his will he must be buried in his Ford car, because, he
said, his Ford had always pulled him out of every hole, and he was sure it
would pull him out of the last.'"

In return for the joke, Wilson recited a limerick to Ford. The limerick was
not preserved, but any one who knew Wilson can guess—there was one limerick
that Wilson told everybody:

> For beauty I am not a star,
> There are others more handsome by far,
>   But my face, I don't mind it,
>   For I am behind it—
> It's the fellow in front that I jar.

with a romantic wish to be married at sea were hopeful that the *Oscar II* would provide the opportunity. A woman was enraged that she, who had "torn ten thousand bandages for the Belgians," had not been invited. The author of "I Didn't Raise My Boy to Be a Soldier" was hurt when he found himself outside the list. The Biltmore suite was jammed with star-eyed enthusiasts, as well as cranks, fanatics, butters-in, and joy-riders of all sorts. In the shuffle genuine delegates got mislaid, lost their heads and tempers. So great was the turmoil it was difficult to make out order or purpose. The delegates would tour the neutral capitals; then they would set up a permanent base at the Hague and take over the "Continuous Mediation" project that Miss Addams and her associates had already started. That much became known. But conflicting statements were rife. One day Ford was quoted as saying: "A general strike [of the contending armies] on Christmas Day, that is what we want." The next day brought heated denials, and cablegrams to the warring powers that the expedition had no such purpose. In the British House of Commons, a member said Ford should be notified that his peace mission would be "irritating and unwelcome at this time." The Undersecretary for Foreign Affairs replied that "it would be undignified for the British Government to send any intimation to a lot of ladies and gentlemen who, whatever their merits may be, are of no particular importance." Holland alone among the nations took official notice of the project, an inhospitable notice, declared rather tartly that it would countenance no attempt to set up an anti-war base within its borders; Henry Ford could set up no "Big Bertha"[5] peace-guns on Netherlands soil.

[5] Name given to the biggest gun used in the war, a German one that dropped shells on Paris from a distance of 70 miles; so named for the daughter of the manufacturer, Fräulein Bertha Krupp.

At home, Secretary of State Lansing found it necessary to inform several foreign governments that our government was in no way responsible for the Ford party. Aside from that, there was scant reticence of opinion in this country. John Wanamaker said that Ford had "a mission, a generous heart, and a fat pocket-book, but no

The satirizing of Henry Ford's peace ship was as fierce in this cartoon from London *Punch* as it was in much of the American press.

plan."   Roosevelt thundered that "the movement would not be mischievous, only because it was so ridiculous," and added that it was "a most discreditable thing for this country."[6] Judge Alton B. Parker publicly stigmatized Ford as "a mountebank and a clown."[7] The Middle Western mechanic, albeit a wealthy man, tilting with the Allied and Central Powers, appealed to the country's risibilities — "Tin Lizzie" versus Mars. Said the Boston *Traveler:* "It is not Mr. Ford's purpose to make peace; he will assemble it."

[6] *Independent,* December 13, 1915.   [7] *Current Opinion,* January, 1916.

V

But the skurry and flurry of preparation was mild comedy in comparison with the sailing of the *Oscar II* from Hoboken on the afternoon of December 4, 1915. Fifty-four newspaper and magazine correspondents, three news-reel men, Ford's personal staff of twenty, and sixty-odd delegates (the number is even yet indeterminate) had to be winnowed from a crowd which blackened the ship and the pier. The captain swore he would sail by two, passengers or no passengers; as he watched the proceedings he swore harder. It was a carnival, in the slang of the day, "a scream." A German band alternated with several other providers of musical well-wishing. A young Hebrew stood in the bows and bantered the crowd in Yiddish. The Reverend Doctor Jenkin Lloyd Jones of Chicago offered prayer from the rail amid hoots and yells at his splendid white beard. Bryan came sailing through the mob in his wide hat, to be greeted with cheers.

Presently the tumult died down a little as Thomas Edison, acutely embarrassed, pushed toward the ship — followed by a man in a derby hat and a fur-trimmed coat, on whose "colorless face . . . there was drawn tight the smile of a sick man who didn't quite know what to do about something, but who surrendered himself to the thing he was caught up in."[8] It was the proprietor of the show. An actor, Lloyd Bingham, in beret and windsor tie, waited until Ford stood beside him at the rail, and then led "three cheers for Henry." The noise broke out redoubled. Some one shouted: "Why don't you start?" Bingham called back: "You know it's a Ford!"

[8] Bernard Dailey, an eye-witness; *Forum*, March, 1916.

There was more delay. Berton Braley, commissioned at the last moment as a special correspondent of the United Press, came tearing down to the dock in a taxi with his bride-to-be. Arrangements had been made, as

International News Photograph.

Henry Ford (bareheaded, in coat with fur collar) together with Captain Hempel (with raised cap) on the bridge of the *Oscar II,* as it departed from New York.

with the most of the other correspondents, for Braley to take his wife along, but he hadn't, in the rush, been given time to make her his wife. So he asked the Rev. Jenkin Lloyd Jones to officiate. The Reverend performed the ceremony in the packed saloon, with Ford and Bryan as witnesses. Then it was discovered that Jones had no license to officiate in New Jersey; the captain assured the couple he would marry them again as soon as he was on the high seas, where his jurisdiction began. In the excitement Bryan escaped to the dock, crying out to hecklers that he had *not* kissed the bride!

An hour late, amid a din of steam-whistles, yelling and cheering, and the fanfare of bands, the *Oscar II* drew up the gang-plank and got under way. Some one on board threw roses to the crowd. On the dock, Bryan sat precariously on the end of a pile and shouted his

International News Photograph.

The Scandinavian liner, *Oscar II,* better known as the "Peace Ship."

blessing. A man jumped into the water and tried to swim after the ship, only to be picked up by a tug; he was a spectacular welfare worker of the time who called himself "Mr. Zero." The Peace Ship headed down the Narrows, bearing Ford, Mme. Schwimmer, Lochner, Doctor Marquis (who had come aboard at the last moment), Samuel S. McClure, magazine publisher; Ben B. Lindsey, judge of the Denver Juvenile Court and energetic participant in all good causes — he allowed

As part of the fierce satirizing of Ford's Peace Ship, the "comic strip" figures, "Mutt and Jeff," were represented daily as taking part in Ford's attempt to bring about peace.

—*Fisher in the San Francisco Chronicle.*

no progressive parade to pass without getting on the band wagon; State Senator Helen Ring Robinson of Colorado (the first woman state senator); Mrs. May Wright Sewall (mother of the "Canadian Plan"); Inez Milholland Boissevain — by her maiden name, Inez Milholland, she was known as a militant suffragist and a beautiful woman; the Reverend Doctor Jones, the Reverend Doctor Charles F. Aked of San Francisco, and other "consecrated spirits," engaged in the greatest mission ever before a nation — thus the delegates were described in Ford's letter of invitation. It may or may not have been that in Ford's estimate all the delegates fitted that ecstatic description. In the eyes of the newspaper men, some at least of the delegates were of a sort that caused them to speak of the *Oscar II* as the greatest squirrel cage in history — it contained so many "nuts." There were two vicarious passengers — "Mutt and Jeff" went along; "Bud" Fisher, the cartoonist, sketched them as peace delegates every day in the comic strip that was printed in hundreds of newspapers.

VI

Doubtless a log of the *Oscar II* might have been written, by some of the earnest delegates, possibly Ford or Mme. Schwimmer, which would have seen the journey as a lofty and hopeful enterprise. Most, however, of the narratives that reached the public, then or later, came from sources that were sceptical from the start or soon became disillusioned. The log that follows is skeletonized from the day-by-day narration of an observant student-delegate[9] on board:

On Sunday night, December 5, a long sermon by the Reverend Doctor Aked was transmitted at great ex-

[9] William F. Noble, in *The Midwest Quarterly*, July, 1916.

pense to the mainland (at the time this was the longest wireless message on record).

Monday the newspaper correspondents organized

International News Photograph.

American newspapers as a rule, in text, by cartoon, and by photograph, jeered at the Ford Peace Ship. This photograph pictures two of the peace delegates, Reverend Charles F. Aked and Reverend Jenkin Lloyd Jones (beneath, with beard), achieving exercise on the deck of the *Oscar II* by leap-frog.

themselves into a society whose name was "The Friendly Sons of St. Vitus," whose motto was "skoal," and place of meeting the bar.

Tuesday Publisher McClure delivered a lecture on himself and Europe.

Wednesday a Western Union messenger named Jake, who had "stowed away" in a bathroom, came out of hiding and was given a salaried job by Ford. The Reverend Doctor Aked, thanking Colonel McClure for his speech of the day before, talked from eleven to eleven-thirty P.M., when the lights were put out.

Friday Mr. McClure read aloud to the ship's company the President's preparedness message to Congress of that day (December 10); it drew sparks. Mme. Schwimmer appeared for the first time (Mr. Noble could not tell whether she were thirty-five or sixty) and delivered a clear address to tell the delegates that the papers in her black bag assured the good-will of the belligerent governments toward their mission.

Saturday there was excitement — of a sort inconsistent with the nature of the expedition. At a closed meeting of the delegates the Committee on Resolutions offered a declaration for their signatures which stated: first, that Mme. Schwimmer's speech held the keynote of the expedition; second, that the delegates guaranteed their good faith to Mr. Ford; and third (to the consternation of the audience) that they repudiated flatly President Wilson's plea for preparedness. Sam McClure jumped to his feet: "I cannot sign anything which separates me from my President!" Some one else spoke in the same vein. Lochner cried out: "Anybody who won't sign that resolution has come on a colossal joy-ride!" There was pandemonium in the saloon. Fifty-four correspondents broke in for news, and radioed their papers that there was "mutiny aboard the *Oscar II.*" A near-by ship inquired: "Are you in need of assistance?"

Monday a British war-vessel set a lieutenant and six marines on board; their muskets were fingered curiously by pacifist ladies.

Tuesday the *Oscar II* put in at Kirkwall, Scotland. A

clerk "scooped" the entire body of correspondents by making his escape to shore, against regulations, with an armful of despatches and pictures of the trip.

News sent from the peace ship from day to day jeered at the expedition, asserted that the delegates were quarrelling. Such despatches inspired cartoons like this by Bartholomew in the Minneapolis *Daily News.*

Friday the ship left Kirkwall and the usual ceremony of dinner to the captain took place. Ford gave him a sedan.

Sunday, December 19, the *Oscar II* docked at Chris-

tiania, Norway. Ford was quoted as saying "The landing of the peace pilgrims will be recorded as the most
benevolent thing America ever did."

In Norway there were banquets and speech-making;
a "Who's Who" of the delegates was distributed; Ford
gave $10,000 to the Students' Association for a new
club-house. Most important of all, Ford came down
with a cold. And here Doctor Marquis stepped into the
foreground again, for he worked on Ford, left him pur-
posely secluded and alone for hours, and constantly suggested the bright advantages of home as against a strange
and cold foreign country. On Christmas Day (when
the boys were to have been "out of the trenches") the
delegates were astounded to learn that Ford had left for
America at 4 A.M. the day before.

Some of the delegates resigned at once and went home.
The others elected a Committee of Seven, called themselves the "Neutral Conference for Continuous Mediation" and toured the neutral capitals; intent on making
the name of America "once more respectable,"[10] they
preached the message that America was not a "buzzard
nation . . . feeding too noisily on war profits." But
though the delegation remained in Europe through 1916
it had no faintest effect on the war.

Ford, back within the comfortable cordon of the Ford
Motor Company, was asked what he had really got out
of the peace expedition.[11] "I didn't get much peace,"
he replied. "I learned," he added, "that Russia is going
to be a great market for tractors."

As respects the belligerent governments, the sum and
essence of their views was that Ford was an excellent
manufacturer of automobiles.

[10] Helen Ring Robinson, *Independent*, February 14, 1916.
[11] The question was asked by E. G. Pipp, first editor of the Dearborn *Independent.*—"Henry Ford — Both Sides of Him," E. G. Pipp.

The Ford Peace Expedition had one serious result, directly counter to the purpose with which it started. After its failure, dying down to an echo of gigantic and exhausted laughter, it deprived every other peace movement in the country of force and conviction. The dove of peace had gone forth a Ford and come back a flivver — flivver and peace movement were one, it appeared.   It put pacifists on the defensive against a weapon more deadly to them than guns — laughter.[12]

[12] Miss Addams thinks, with justice, that this judgment is one-sided. While she concedes that the peace movement was subjected to satire as an incident of the Ford expedition, nevertheless the peace movement from the beginning to the end was respected, and success for it was hoped, by much of the best thought of the time, including not a few officials of governments engaged in the war.

8

GERMAN PLOTTING EXPOSED

A Secret Service Operative Has an Authentic Adventure Which for Stark Incredibility Outshines the Most Improbable Exploits of Nick Carter, and Stretches the Long Arm of Coincidence to the Limit of Extraordinariness. A Brief-case Belonging to a German Propagandist, Which the Secret Service Man Purloins, Turns Out to Be a "Veritable Box of Pandora." It Explains the Origin of Numerous Fires in American Munitions Factories and Names the Perpetrators of Other Acts of Violence Designed to Injure the Allies through Crippling American Industry and Shipping. American Feeling Against Germany Grows.

On July 24, 1915 — it was a hot Saturday afternoon — an operative of the government Secret Service, W. H. Houghton, shadowed George Sylvester Viereck, editor of the German-American *Fatherland*, to the headquarters of the Hamburg-American Steamship Line at 45 Broadway, New York City. While Viereck was in the building, Houghton called up the Secret Service office, finding there another operative, Frank Burke. Burke had intended to take the Saturday afternoon off, but some instinct for the game overcoming his zest for a holiday, he joined Houghton.

At three o'clock the two Secret Service men saw Viereck leave the Hamburg-American building, with a companion to whom Viereck paid obvious deference, a distinguished-looking man about six feet tall, weighing about 190 pounds, and about fifty years old, bearing on his ruddy German cheeks the saber marks of student duels. The German and the German-American walked to the Sixth Avenue elevated, entered a train, and sat down together about the middle of the car. One Secret-

Service man, Burke, took a seat immediately behind, Houghton one across the aisle. A regrettable incompleteness in the education of Secret-Service operatives prevented Burke from following the animated conversation in German — but left him free to concentrate his

Photograph by Brown Brothers.

George Sylvester Viereck, one of the leading pro-German propagandists in the United States, editor of the German-American *Fatherland,* and unlucky participant in the episode which enabled America to learn about German plots in the United States.

attention on a large, heavily stuffed brief-case which the German placed on the seat between himself and the side of the car. At the 23d Street Station Viereck (with Houghton following him) got off, leaving the German free to enjoy a Teutonic snooze. At the 50th Street station the German, waking from his doze and discovering that his stopping-place had been reached, dashed to the rear door of the car. Instantly the forgotten brief-case was seized by Burke, who darted with it for the front door. As Burke hurried down the aisle, he observed, out of the corner of his eye, the German in a panic rushing desperately back toward his seat — his speed impeded, for the few seconds Burke needed for success, by an unconscious instrumentality of fate in the person of a fat and elderly woman straphanger. Burke left the car by the front door; the German, after finding his brief-case gone, left by the rear door, and was now between Burke and the stairway leading from the station to the street. Burke, holding the brief-case to his breast, using some waiting passengers as a screen, edged his way to the wall of the station, where, facing the wall and pretending to use it as a shelter from the wind, he went through the motions of lighting a cigar, the process prolonged by the fact that Burke, every time he put a match to the cigar, quietly blew outward till the match flickered and went out. Presently the German rushed down the stairs. Burke, after a few minutes, followed.

The German, panic on his features, was standing some distance out in the street where he could get the best view of persons coming down the steps. Instantly upon seeing Burke and the brief-case, he plunged forward to retrieve it. Burke, moving with more agility than the middle-aged German commanded, dashed to a moving surface car, jumped on the running board, and told the conductor that the man chasing the car was crazy, that he had just a moment before made a scene on the elevated station. The conductor, looking back, found sufficient corroboration in the appearance of the pursuer, and called to the motorman to pass the next corner without stopping. Burke remained on the car for five blocks, then boarded another on a different street, and rode to a drug store where he telephoned his chief, William J. Flynn. Flynn, ordering Burke to remain where he was, drove up in his automobile; and the two, with the brief-case, went to the Secret Service office.

Photograph by Brown Brothers.

Doctor Heinrich E. Albert, whose portfolio, stolen by an American Secret Service operative, revealed that under Doctor Albert's direction some 28 million dollars had been spent by the German government on propaganda and plots in the United States.

The *"STRENG VERTRAULICH"* ("strictly private") marked in large letters on the documents in the brief-case was not as deterring to an American Government employee as it was intended to be to German ones. Indeed Flynn did not understand the phrase nor any of the rest of the mainly German contents, but he grasped enough to cause him to telegraph to his superior,

Secretary of the Treasury William G. McAdoo, who was taking a vacation at North Haven, Me. McAdoo wired Flynn to come at once to North Haven, and the two spent an afternoon and evening examining the documents. After thoughtful consideration McAdoo concluded the best use to make of them would be to expose them, and to Frank I. Cobb, editor of the New York *World*, he presented one of the most sensational serials any newspaper ever published.

From *The World*, America learned that the owner of the brief-case was Doctor Heinrich F. Albert, that Doctor Albert was the head of an intricate system of German "intrigue, conspiracy, and propaganda" — the words are Viereck's — in the United States; that he spent in all some $27,850,000; that Albert with others, including German consuls and officials of the German Embassy at Washington, had conducted espionage and sabotage of a kind and degree so melodramatic as to seem incredible. "Albert's portfolio," wrote the unhappy Viereck twelve years later, "was a veritable box of Pandora; it unloosed every half-hatched plan of the Germans; the inner workings of the propaganda machine were laid bare. . . . The loss of that portfolio was like the loss of the Marne."[1]

II

From the contents of the Albert brief-case, and through many other disclosures from many sources at divers times, America learned, among much else that

---

[1] "Spreading Germs of Hate," George Sylvester Viereck.

Of the capture of Doctor Albert's portfolio there are scores of versions, some attempting to be even more fantastic than the facts. For the purpose of this history I have accepted the account given by William G. McAdoo in "Crowded Years," received by him from one of the Secret Service men, Frank Burke. An account given by another of the principals, George Sylvester Viereck, in "Spreading Germs of Hate," does not differ materially.

HOW GERMANY HAS WORKED IN U. S. TO SHAPE OPINION, BLOCK THE ALLIES AND GET MUNITIONS FOR HERSELF, TOLD IN SECRET AGENTS' LETTERS.

LETTERS MR. VIERECK AND DR. ALBERT WROTE TO EACH OTHER.

Chancellor, Ambassador, Financial Agent and Bankers Chief Figures in Vast Scheme Revealed in Documents Obtained by The World—Fatherland Financed, Author Fox's Expenses Paid, Plans Laid to Buy Press Association and Otherwise Control News of the War.

COST PUT AT $2,000,000 A WEEK;
BERNSTORFF DRAFT $1,100,000.

Big Arms Plant and Powder Works, Which Outwardly Dicker With Allies, Secretly Owned by Germany and Preparing to Deliver Munitions Sept. 1—Edison's Supply of Carbolic Acid Taken Over for Shipment—Plan to Buy Wright Plant Considered—Poisoned Gas Supply of Allies Crippled—Strikes in Munitions Plants Fomented.

Copyright, 1915, by The Press Publishing Co. (The New York World.)
The World to-day begins the publication of a series of

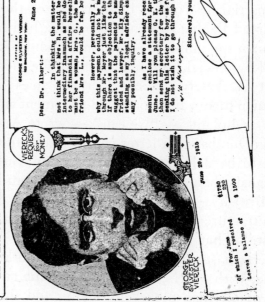

The contents of the stolen portfolio, which revealed German plots in America, were printed in the New York *World*, in which this headline and illustration were printed on August 15, 1915.

was sinister, the explanation of fires, explosions, and similar occurrences which, at the time of happening, had been accepted as accidents or dismissed as mysteries. The various revelations showed:

That agents of the German Government had placed "fire bombs," timed for later explosion, on steamships departing from American ports with food and ammunition for the Allies — in a case involving the steamship *Kirke Oswald* carrying sugar from New York to Marseilles, eight Germans were subsequently prosecuted and imprisoned; that the Military Attaché of the German Embassy at Washington had supplied money and materials to a German spy to go to Buffalo and blow up the Welland Canal; that German agents had conspired to bring about sabotaged fires and other "accidents" in American plants making munitions for the Allies; that the partial destruction by dynamite of the International Railroad Bridge at Vanceboro, Me., had been done by a German spy under the direction of and with money supplied by official representatives of the German Government in America. That German spies provided with German money had conspired to foment strikes in American steel plants — "we can" — wrote Austrian Ambassador Dumba (in a letter confided to James F. J. Archibald to be delivered to the Austrian Government, but revealed when Archibald was taken from his steamer by the British) — "disorganize and hold up for months the manufacture of munitions in Bethlehem and the Middle West." That the managing director of the Hamburg-American steamship office in New York, Doctor Karl Bünz, with others, had expended some two million dollars of German money in buying and shipping coal on vessels that pretended to sail for neutral ports in South America, Africa, or elsewhere, but actually delivered the coal to German cruisers at sea. That German agents had been secret buyers of and contractors for munitions, the artful purpose being to delay work on contracts for the Allies; that German agents had under way plans to corner the American supply of liquid chlorine (used for poison gas) so as to keep it from the Allies, and to ac-

The German destroyer as pictured in *Life*—a German plotter in the United States with a bomb for American industries making war munitions.

quire the Wright Aeroplane Company and its patents. That as an ingenious means of sabotaging the flow of American explosives to the Allies, German agents had created the Bridgeport Projectile Company, purporting to be an ordinary American commercial enterprise, which actually conducted negotiations to sell explosives to the British commission purchasing supplies in America. That Germans had systematically forged passports, to enable German reservists in America to return to Germany, and to enable German spies to enter Allied countries from America. That Germans in the United States had plotted with Hindus to foment revolution in India; that certain American publications and writers were secret recipients of subsidies from the German Government; that Doctor Albert was the secret source of money for the purchase of a New York daily newspaper, *The Mail*, which pretended to be American-owned. That plans were under way to finance motion-pictures having a German bias, to invade the Chautauqua circuit with professional lecturers subsidized to present the German point of view; to organize a movement, which should appear to generate spontaneously in the South, to cut off the supply of cotton from Great Britain; and to organize another movement, similarly designed to seem spontaneously American, to have Congress put an embargo on shipments of munitions to the Allies.

"No agency of publicity or service," said the New York *World*,[2] has been overlooked by the keen intelligence that instigates these plots . . . The German propaganda in the United States has become a political conspiracy against the government and people of the United States. This conspiracy is directed from Berlin and is financed by the German Government. It has been organized with all the amazing thoroughness and efficiency that characterizes all German military activity, and it is as much a part of the German campaign as the operations of armies in the field. The German Government is subsidizing sedition throughout the United States."

For various of which, and other actions, the Ameri-

2 August 16, 1915.

On the left, Johann Bernstorff, German Ambassador to the United States. *On the right,* Constantin Dumba, Austrian Ambassador to the United States.

can Government demanded the recall by Germany of the
military and the naval attachés of the German Embassy
at Washington, Captain Franz von Papen and Captain

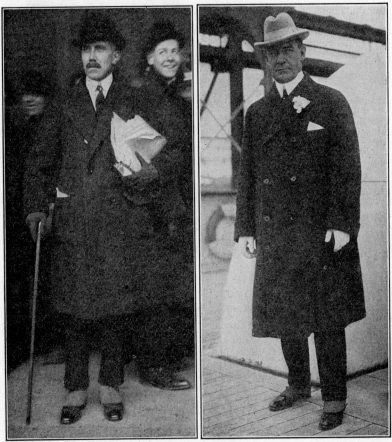

Copyright Paul Thompson.

Captain Franz von Papen (*left*) and Captain Karl von Boy-Ed in New York
en route for Germany after plots and propaganda in which they had participated had been discovered by the American government.

Karl von Boy-ed; and the recall by Austria of its Ambassador, Doctor Constantine Dumba. The last, one felt,
had characteristics consistent with the American pronun-
ciation of his name, and, one suspected, had been manœu-

vred into tasks more risky than the extremely astute German Ambassador, Johann von Bernstorff, cared to take part in.

To Americans at the time, and to readers now unless they reflect as they read, all those German plots and actions in pursuit of plots, being all secret, seemed to have the same degree of sinisterness. Many were as sinister as possible. Some, like the placing of time-bombs in ships bound for sea, put neutral lives in peril. But purchase of munitions by Germans was, apart from the secrecy with which it was done, no more sinister than purchase by the Allies. That the German purpose was not to make use of the munitions, but merely to prevent the Allies from getting them, made no difference. The able and legally well-advised Von Bernstorff was justified in his formal statement that it was his

DR. ALBERT HOLDS HE DID NOT VIOLATE HOSPITALITY OF U.S.

In a Public Statement Following World's Revelations, German Councillor Says He Sought by Acts Only to Overcome Powerful Propaganda of the Allies in America.

DECLARES ENEMY PRESS CAMPAIGN HERE INSPIRED.

Received Letters to Foment Strikes, but Never Even Answered Them—Says His Government Would Buy All Our Ammunition Mills, if Able, to Keep Product Here.

—World, Aug. 20, 1915.

right and duty . . . to place difficulties in the way of the export of war materials to the Allies, either by the purchase of the factories or war material, in spite of the fact that for the present we are not able to make use of these goods. If we possessed the means and opportunity we would buy up every munition factory in the United States.

Similarly, it was no more a crime for German Doctor Bünz to buy and ship coal to German men-of-war than for British Lord Northcliffe to buy and ship fuel for

THE NEW YORK HERALD.

PART II. ••••　　　NEW YORK, SATURDAY, OCTOBER 6, 1917.—BY THE NEW YORK HERALD COMPANY.　　PRICE ONE CENT. {TWO CENTS in Suburbs and 50 miles of New York City. {THREE CENTS in Towns and Environs.

VON BERNSTORFF REVEALED AS ARCH PLOTTER FOR PEACE, WITH BOLO AS ONE OF HIS AGENTS;

British vessels. When the United States authorities sent Doctor Bünz to jail, it was not for the buying and shipping of coal nor for any violation of neutrality, but for making false statements about the destination of the ships he used.

If to the American at the time and to the reader today the distinction is not always clear between actions inherently odious and actions that were mere violation of regulation, so did it seem — in a reverse way — to Germans in America at the time. They saw the Allies permitted to buy and ship munitions freely and without reproach, while Germans were harried in the press and punished in the courts for attempting the same thing — merely because, as they saw it, they were obliged, by Britain's control of the sea, to practise furtiveness.

9

PREPAREDNESS

Ex-President Theodore Roosevelt Demands It, and Reviles President Wilson for Failing to Provide It. Roosevelt Is Charged with Playing Politics. Smallness of the American Army at the Beginning of the World War. A Military Writer Publishes a Book Which Eloquently Pictures America's Need. General Leonard Wood Forthrightly Speaks for a Larger Army, and Is Taken to Task, Very Gently, by the Secretary of War. The Plattsburg Camps.

IN the movement for preparedness the outstanding spokesman was the one man who shared Wilson's elevation in American national life, ex-President Theodore Roosevelt.

For Roosevelt, the War brought revival, not a "comeback" in the colloquial sense, but emergence in a new rôle which included some of the qualities of an Old Testament prophet, a minatory one, thundering reproof and warning, an Ezekiel. His new emergence started from what was perhaps the deepest depth of Roosevelt's mature career. After trying unsuccessfully against Taft for the Republican Presidential nomination in 1912, Roosevelt had organized the Progressive party. When both the Progressives and the Republicans lost to Wilson, Roosevelt was under guilt of having split the Republican party and could hardly hope ever to be taken back by its embittered leaders and members. At the same time he knew — though not all the Progressives shared his expertly sure judgment — that he had not succeeded in creating a new party. He had received many votes, much more than the Republican Taft, and he had carried many States. But it was Roosevelt who had carried them, not the Progressive party. Roosevelt knew this and would gladly have had it otherwise. The test was that only a tiny handful of Progressive candidates had been elected to the Senate or House, or to governorships or other offices. There was no real Progressive party, there was only Roosevelt as a magnetic individual. Roosevelt was wise enough to know that the Progressive party was dead in its borning, yet he was obliged to show a face of cheerful encouragement to his rapt-eyed followers, and to assert and repeat and asseverate that the party would be continued, the cause carried on. When the 1914 elections for Congress and governorships came, Roosevelt, paying his obligations to those who had been for him in 1912, maintaining the fiction that there was still a Progressive party and that it had hope, was obliged to travel through the country campaigning for candidates running on the Progressive ticket who, Roosevelt knew in his heart, could have little chance of winning, Raymond Robbins in Illinois, Albert J. Beveridge in Indiana, James R. Garfield in Ohio, Gifford Pinchot in Pennsylvania. From these trips, from prolonged simulation of a confidence he did not truly entertain, Roosevelt would come back to Oyster Bay weary as he had never been weary before. "I am carrying a dead horse on my shoulders," he would say to friends intimate enough to provide him with the solace of unburdening his mind.

He was unhappy, miserable. He had no Progressive party and the Republican party hated him; he could hardly hope ever again to get a nomination for the Presidency — and in 1914 he was only 56. Publicly and sometimes even to friends, he pretended resignation. "When a leader's day is past, the one service he can do is to step aside." To a friend[1] he wrote that "there is great comfort in no longer being responsible for the

[1] E. A. Van Valkenberg, March 2, 1915.

welfare of [a political] party." But that was not the real feeling in Roosevelt's heart; every instinct of his nature fretted against the position he found himself in — his energy as furious as ever, and no outlet for it.[2] His political career was over and his prestige in non-political affairs, his influence as a public man, was diminished by his political inferiority. "As things are now," he wrote to his son Kermit,[3] "I am utterly out of touch with the American people." "There are," he said,[4] "certain things I can say to small audiences in my writings." Telling a friend that he was engaged in writing an address on "History as Literature," he made a grimace which in effect said, "What a way for me to be using my energy!" — Theodore Roosevelt, who in Henry Adams's phrase was "all act," spending his days pushing a pen across paper in a dim little study at Sagamore Hill! *The Outlook*, which had regarded his joining their staff in 1909 as the most glorious event in their history, now permitted him to learn that the old-line Republicans and old-line conservative New Englanders who composed most of *The Outlook's* circulation were not renewing their subscriptions to a periodical whose staff included a man who had wrecked the Republican party; Roosevelt resigned. Turning to an old man's occupation, he wrote his memoirs, collected his published writings. In his carking sense of being off the stage and nearing old age, he did a naïve and human thing, took an adventurous and dan-

[2] During this period I was editor of *Collier's Weekly* and I arranged that Julian Street should write some articles about Roosevelt, under the title, "The Most Interesting American." When the articles were published as a book, Roosevelt procured a copy, inscribed it to me, and as he handed it to me repeated in words the substance of the inscription, to the effect that this was the nicest thing that had ever happened to him, that it came at a time when he greatly needed it, and that he owed it to me. The words might have passed as a casual exaggeration of thanks, but something in his voice caused me to look closely at him. The emotion in his face was a measure, not of the service I had done, but of his own low spirits, his estimate of his place in the world. The incident was very touching.

[3] February 7, 1915.   [4] To Joseph Bucklin Bishop.

gerous trip into the interior of South America. Returning impaired seriously in health, he was asked by a
friend, with affectionate indignation, "At your age, why
did you do such a thing?" Roosevelt's reply was self-
revealing and self-understanding, and poignant, "I had
just one more chance to be a boy, and I took it."[5]

Throughout Roosevelt's exile from politics and to
some extent from popular favor, his sorrow's crown of
sorrow was that by the same act which had brought him
down, he had contributed to placing in the White House a
man whose conduct of the office distressed Roosevelt
utterly. His distaste for Wilson as President was shared
to one degree or another by the Republicans and most of
his own Progressive following. So long, however, as
Wilson's actions had to do only with domestic matters,
the common dislike of him was not sufficient to overcome the dislike of Republicans and Progressives for
each other. But when the war came, and after Wilson's
attitude toward it developed, there arose among Republicans and Progressives a sense of need for common
leadership in opposition and criticism of the Administration. Roosevelt's was the obvious voice to rally to. Reconciliation came about. Roosevelt and Taft embraced,
publicly; Roosevelt even wrote a letter of apology to
his ancient enemy Foraker, "I realize your absolute
Americanism"; Roosevelt and Root[6] lunched together[7]
— reporters learned about it and it was a public sensation — Leonard Wood, who was present, wrote in his
diary: "Roosevelt and Root seemed to be glad to be to-

        [5] "Roosevelt, the Story of a Friendship," Owen Wister.
        [6] Elihu Root was one of the important Republicans who had become estranged
from Roosevelt at the time Roosevelt split the Republican party in 1912. Root,
after being Roosevelt's Secretary of War and Secretary of State, had presided
over the convention which denied him the 1912 nomination.
        [7] March 31, 1916. Two guests besides those mentioned were Senator Lodge
and Robert Bacon.

gether again, really so; Roosevelt cussed out Wilson, as did Root and Lodge; [it is their] opinion that the country was never so low in standing before." The reconciliation had not progressed far enough in 1916 to bring the Republicans to consider nominating Roosevelt for the Presidency; but after another defeat of the Repub-

Wilson's attitude toward the War and Preparedness led to this cartoon advising Uncle Sam to watch his step.

—*Marcus in the New York Times.*

licans in that year, after realization that Wilson would have another four years in the White House, Republicans and Progressives, every one opposed to Wilson's policies and actions, turned toward Roosevelt as spokesman.

In the very early months of the War, Roosevelt had shared the common impulse toward neutrality. "Only the clearest and most urgent national duty," he wrote in

The Outlook, "would ever justify us in deviating from our rule of neutrality." But in proportion as it was our duty and self-interest to be neutral, so was it the more important we should be able to defend and enforce our neutrality. "When giants are engaged in a death wrestle," he wrote[8] prophetically three weeks after the War began, "as they reel to and fro they are certain to trample on whomever gets in the way." The War was to Roosevelt, therefore, argument for his life-long policy of a strong army and navy. Powerfully he pleaded for preparedness. In time his advocacy of preparedness merged into advocacy of our entering the War on the side of the Allies. In behalf of the double cause Roosevelt carried on against Wilson a crusade that ranged through invective, irony, and loftily solemn warning and appeal.

Because Roosevelt was Wilson's rival, had run against him for the Presidency and been defeated, he was subject to the charge that his advocacy of preparedness, his attacks on Wilson on all counts, were political in motive. That charge served Wilson and the Democrats as a partial protection against Roosevelt's thunderings. It is true that Roosevelt, after he had been in the White House, found it hard to endure seeing another man there, any other man, especially one who, he felt, was filling the office less capably than he himself could have done — and Roosevelt would have felt that way about almost any President. Roosevelt had had this attitude about Taft, whom he had in effect named as his own successor. There was that in Roosevelt's temperament which disliked to sit on the left or to be on the outside.

The force of Roosevelt's attacks on Wilson was further diminished by the public's recent memory of his similar attacks on Taft. Many who recalled and resented

[8] *Outlook*, August 22, 1914.

the fulminations against Taft some five years before, charged that Roosevelt's present attacks on Wilson put him in the category of an habitual scold. He had lost the conservatives among his following by the radicalism of his 1912 proposals; later he had seen some of his Progressive following drift away to Wilson because of Wilson's domestic policies. Consequently Roosevelt, in the early part of his campaign for preparedness, had but little following, and it included some whose adherence did his cause little good. The sum of all was that Roosevelt began his crusade for preparedness from an unfortunate start and under great handicaps.

Wilson knew all this, and because he knew, felt the safer. Wilson ignored Roosevelt. Wilson knew not only how to be subtle with words but how to be subtle with silence. His attitude toward Roosevelt's attacks was one of seeming not to know the attacks or the man existed. Once Wilson said to a friend, "The way to treat an adversary like Roosevelt is to gaze at the stars over his head."

But in truth never was Roosevelt more earnest, more deeply stirred about a cause. His crusade satisfied two passions, his belief in preparedness and his detestation of Wilson.

Roosevelt's hatred of Wilson was not political — certainly not political merely. Roosevelt would have disliked Wilson personally had he never had any controversy with him politically. In practically every detail of temperament and personality, as well as in conceptions about conduct of the country's affairs, Wilson was as near the antithesis of Roosevelt as one man can be of another. "Roosevelt despised Wilson before he ever heard of him — despising his type."[9]

[9] The quotation is from Hermann Hagedorn, in "Leonard Wood, A Biography."

In letter after letter to friends and even to strangers, Roosevelt poured out his detestation; Wilson was:

"the worst President by all odds since Buchanan, with the possible exception of Andrew Johnson; I am simply unable to understand how the American people can tolerate Wilson. . . ." "Wilson and Bryan are the very worst men we have ever had in their positions. . . ."[10] "I abhor Wilson"[11] . . . "the common type of quality in Wilson, he has the regular professional cultivation and is a trained elocutionist, but at heart he is neither a gentleman nor a real man. . . ."[12] "In time Wilson will be the most damned man in America since the days of Buchanan and Andrew Johnson. . . ." [13] "Nothing is more sickening than the continual praise of Wilson's English, of Wilson's style; he is a true logothete, a real sophist, and he firmly believes, and has no inconsiderable effect in making our people believe, that elocution is an admirable substitute for or an improvement on action. . . ."[14] "I am sick at heart over the actions of Wilson and Bryan. . . ."[15] "He [Wilson] has trailed the honor of the United States in the dust."[16] "For Heaven's sake never allude to Wilson as an idealist or altruist; he is a doctrinaire when he can be so with safety to his personal ambition and he is always utterly and coldly selfish;[17] he hasn't a touch of idealism in him; he is a silly doctrinaire at all times and an utterly selfish and cold-blooded politician always."[18]

And, naïvely, in a letter to Rudyard Kipling, "I do not believe I have spoken intemperately!"[19]

[10] Various letters to Henry Cabot Lodge.
[11] Letter to Kermit Roosevelt, February 7, 1915.
[12] Letter to Mark Sullivan, February 19, 1915.
[13] Conversation written down by John J. Leary, Jr.
[14] Letter to Owen Wister, June 23, 1915.
[15] Letter to Sir George Otto Trevelyan, February 6, 1915.
[16] To Joseph Bucklin Bishop, immediately after the *Lusitania* sinking.
[17] Roosevelt could see in Wilson, whether as man or statesman, no good quality. In the Summer of 1916, lunching with Roosevelt at Sagamore Hill, I repeated gossip from Washington to the effect that Wilson, then a widower for about a year, was wearing brighter raiment, his socks matching his tie, orchids on his desk, in short that Wilson was about to marry again. I added that some of Wilson's friends were concerned lest marriage during a Presidential campaign might in some subtle way injure his chances. Roosevelt, absorbed by the news, focussed his eyes inward for a moment of intent cerebration and said, "No, Wilson won't marry while the campaign is on; he is too cold-blooded to let his emotions overcome his self-interest."
[18] Letter to Ogden Reid, January 1, 1919.
[19] The exclamation point is the author's.

Publicly, Roosevelt's denunciation of Wilson was hardly less mordant than in his private letters and conversations, though in his public writings and addresses he put his condemnation not so much on the ground of Wilson's personal traits as on the public issues involved. Mainly these were at all times preparedness and, as our

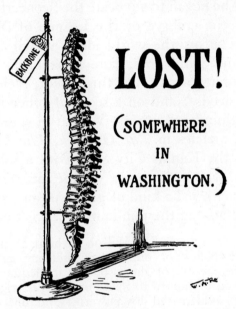

The demand that Wilson accept preparedness was expressed in violent cartoons.
— *Rogers in the New York Herald.*

relations with Germany grew more tense, demand that Wilson should make war.

In these public attacks, personal dislike or political motive played little part. Roosevelt was solemnly sure that Wilson was leading the United States, and later the world, in a direction that must end in disillusion and tragedy. Of all the axioms of personal and national conduct that Roosevelt held to be imperative, perhaps the basic one was that neither a man nor a nation should ever hold out words, whether of promise or of threat, unless it is certain the words both can be and will be translated into action — some early experience or other must have taught Roosevelt that as an ineradicable lesson; he came back to it in a thousand conversations, speeches, and public writings. And a deep trait of prophetic understanding told Roosevelt that Wilson, especially after he began to advocate the "concert of powers" which was the embryo of the League of Nations, was holding up before the world ideals which could not be fulfilled, and which therefore must bring disappointment and bitterness. On this count, "elocution not backed by deeds," and on a score of other indictments, Roosevelt thundered against Wilson in speeches, public statements, articles in *The Outlook, The Metropolitan Magazine*, the Kansas City *Star*, with a solemnity and earnestness which, in spite of the occasional caustic harshness, achieved a kind of grandeur and set Roosevelt on a height among the public men of his time:

No man can support Mr. Wilson without at the same time supporting a policy of criminal inefficiency as regards the United States Navy, of short-sighted inadequacy as regards the Army, and of failure to insist on our just rights when we are ourselves maltreated by powerful and unscrupulous nations. . . . [Wilson was] the popular pacifist hero . . . [Wilson had the support of the] professional pacifists, the flubdubs and the mollycoddles . . . [Pacifists] preach the utter flabbiness and feebleness, moral and physical, which inevitably breeds cowardice. . . . [Wilson's appeal for peace[20] in December, 1916, was] a combination of glib sophistry and feeble sham amicability.

Mr. Wilson now dwells at Shadow Lawn.[21] There should be shadows enough at Shadow Lawn, the shadows of men, women and children who have risen from the ooze of the ocean bottom and from graves in foreign lands; the shadows of the helpless whom Mr. Wilson did not dare protect lest he might have to face danger; the shadows of babies gasping pitifully as they sank under the waves. . . . Those are the shadows proper for

[20] See Chapter 12.
[21] Wilson's summer home at Deal, N. J., in 1916.

Shadow Lawn; the shadows of deeds that were never done, the shadows of lofty words that were followed by no lofty action. . . .

II

The military strength of the United States on the day the Great War broke out consisted of:

	Officers	Men
Regular Army	3,441	77,363
Organized Militia	8,323	119,087
Totals	11,764	196,450

And that was absolutely all. Indeed, that is much more than all. To consider the Organized Militia, improperly styled the National Guard, as effective "military strength" was to assume they would all respond to a call to arms, "in other words, upon a miracle."[22] It involved an assumption that such of the Organized Militia as should take arms would be, at once, effective soldiers. Effective soldiers! All the training required of such militia — required but not always enforced — consisted of 24 drills a year, including a summer camp.

Not only that. The 92,710 officers and men authorized for the Regular Army were not all effective "military strength" in the sense of being available to defend the United States or act as a mobile army. Nearly half were in, and were needed in, the Philippines, Hawaii, Panama Canal Zone, Porto Rico, China, and Alaska. The total of regular troops within the United States was 2,577 officers and 50,445 men. Of these, in turn, nearly half were needed to man the Coast Artillery defenses. The total "mobile army" in the United States was 24,602 — smaller than at any time since the Civil War.

It was a good little army. British and German military attachés said they "had never seen a finer body of

[22] "The Military Unpreparedness of the United States," Frederick L. Huidekoper.

troops, superior discipline, less intoxication, or such perfect sanitary arrangements in camps."[23] But it was very small. The regiments were almost skeletons, scarcely more than half their war strength — a company of infantry, which should have a war strength of 150, had 65; a troop of cavalry had 71, as against a war strength of 100; a battery of artillery, 133, as against 190.

III

Among those who were disturbed by the slightness of the American military establishment, and among the smaller number of those who had the will and capacity to put hand to the plough of remedy, was a military writer, Frederick Louis Huidekoper, who had been preaching national preparedness since 1906. Huidekoper, during the early months of the War, had been in France, England, and Germany. Returning to America, toward the end of 1914, he helped found the National Security League, a preparedness organization destined to have much influence. Then he wrote, under high pressure, within five months, "The Military Unpreparedness of the United States." Many a man might have satisfied his emotion with a stirring pamphlet; Huidekoper wrote an exhaustive history, covering all the wars America had fought, from colonial times on, with emphasis on the price he said we had paid in blood and treasure for lack of preparedness — "Adequate preparation for war has never yet in history been made after the beginning of hostilities, without unnecessary slaughter, unjustifiable expense and national peril."

The book was encyclopædic, buttressed with citations of chapter and verse, 556 pages of text followed by 163 pages of confirmatory references. There were — ad-

[23] They were speaking of the 2d Division as mobilized at Texas City and Galveston in 1913.

mirable ratio of fact to exhortation — 23 chapters of formal history, and one of admonitory conclusion, entitled "The Land Forces of the United States as They Ought to Be Organized." Opening with Kipling's description of the spirit of the American:

> . . . illogical, elate
> He greets th' embarrassed gods, nor fears
> To shake the iron hand of Fate
> Or match with Destiny for beers —

Huidekoper drove home his thesis: "The American people have not yet realized that a man with a uniform on his back and a musket in his hands is not a dependable soldier," and closed with emphasis on what he felt was imperatively needed — action, action at once. "Go, sir, gallop," he quoted from Napoleon's order to Colbert, "you can ask me for anything you like except time." And from Lord Brougham:

> Lose not the opportunity; by the forelock take
> That subtle power of never-halting Time,
> Lest the mere moment's putting off should make
> Mischance almost as grave as Crime.

Huidekoper's book had the spirit of the old Roman omen of impending fate, thunder on the left. Many read it. And as can be the way with good books, the spirit of it spread out through newspaper and other channels, prompting emotion like that in the New York *Tribune*[24] which recognized in it "a high, a humane, a holy purpose."

IV

In the organized movement for preparedness the man of action was General Leonard Wood. By far the out-

[24] November 13, 1915.

standing figure in the Army, Wood had had a brilliant career, had filled the Army's most responsible posts — in Cuba as Military Governor, in Washington as Chief of Staff, in the Philippines as Governor-General. Before the country his standing depended only slightly on his army record; in any career Wood's force of personality

Leonard Wood.

would have given him the position he had as a leading figure of his generation.

When the war broke out in Europe, Wood was in active service as Commander of the Department of the East, with headquarters at Governors Island in New York Harbor. The post had no exceptional importance in a military sense, but — because the metropolitan newspapers, news agencies, and other springs and levers of public opinion were only a stone's throw away — it was ideal for promoting the cause to which Wood now dedicated himself.

Wood had already, in 1913, using our faint military stirrings about Mexico as a stimulus, started in a tiny way summer training camps for college students, one at Gettysburg, Pa., having 159 young men from 61 institutions. Additional camps were established the following year at Burlington, Vt., Asheville, N. C., and Ludington, Mich. The training, lasting five weeks, conferred upon the exceptionally intelligent type of young man who attended some understanding of arms in the practical sense some touch of the spirit of responsibility for national defense. Most important, from General Wood's point of view, the camps sent missionaries of preparedness into schools and colleges.

Wood, from the opening day of the war in Europe, believed that we should be drawn in, felt we "could not avert it by good intentions, nor protect ourselves by exhortation."[25]

The United States [Wood wrote in a letter] is to-day exactly in the position Harvard would be if she had about one good football player weighing about 110 pounds and another substitute perhaps turning the scales at 120 pounds, but rather poorly trained, the first representing the Army and the second the Militia. They know they have got a game ahead with a first-class team trained to the hour and with at least five men for every position. No one knows when the game is coming off, but we know it is coming some day, and what is worse, we know we are not getting ready for it. . . . I think you and all of us should do everything possible to wake up the sleeping public, for I assure you that the position is one whose gravity cannot be overestimated.[26]

Moved by that feeling, Wood made speeches, gave interviews, inspired books and magazine articles, talked at public and private dinners. He was not in the faint-

25 "Leonard Wood," Hermann Hagedorn.
26 "Leonard Wood," Hermann Hagedorn.

est sense an orator — in his qualities as a whole Wood was as distant from the plumed-knight, Henry-of-Navarre, "once-more-unto-the-breach" type of leader, as the sighting and firing of a modern siege gun is distant from a horse-back sabre charge. But Wood had the quality which need only be called bigness, magnitude of personality. He was the type to whom, when they have sincerity, average men instinctively pay deference.

Presently, success of Wood and others, and resulting public uneasiness about the small size of our army, brought frowning attention from President Wilson, who, in his message to Congress in December, 1914, declared: "We shall not alter our attitude toward the question of national defense because some amongst us are nervous and excited. . . ."[27] ("Nervous and excited," incidentally, was about the most impossible state of mind that the imperturbable Wood could be imagined as falling into.)

Difference between the Commander-in-Chief of the Army, and the best-known soldier in the Army, about national military policy, was a serious matter. Eager pacifists told Wilson he should take disciplinary notice. Wood's actions were "most unsuitable," wrote George Foster Peabody, in a letter to Colonel House, meant, of course, for Wilson's eyes: Wood was "reflecting upon the President. . . . I hope he may be promptly called down." Secretary of War Garrison, in his heart sympathetic to Wood and to preparedness, sent a letter officially classified as an admonition, but tactfully phrased, written in the Secretary's own hand, otherwise designed not to hurt much. Because, in the preparedness campaign, Wood was backed up by Theodore Roosevelt, and because both were old friends and Republicans, Wood's differences with the Administration could be charged

[27] Address to Congress, December 8, 1914.

by the suspicious with having partisan implications. It was on this ground, partially, that Secretary of War Garrison put his tactful rebuke: "There was clearly an attempt in certain quarters [Garrison said], to thrust

A cartoon which, putting Roosevelt's criticism of the Wilson administration into a form easy for any one to understand, cast ridicule on Wilson's early opposition to preparedness.

— *Wilson in Post Intelligencer, Seattle.*

the question of the national defense into partisan politics. . . . It would be wise for Wood, for the present, to decline all public expression."[28]

Wood abated little of his activity, kept up his speech-

28 The quotation is from a paraphrase of Garrison's letter made by Wood's biographer, Hermann Hagedorn.

making to universities, chambers of commerce, any gathering that was appropriate. Preparedness organizations sprang up. One university after another adopted military training. Samuel Gompers conferred with Wood about a summer training camp for labor. Wood became patron saint, guide, and inspiration of the National Security League, the American Defense Society, and the American Legion, Inc.[29] The American Legion, Inc., inspired by Wood and endorsed by Theodore Roosevelt, "proposed to establish an unofficial reserve enrolling men of military age who had had military training or possessed peculiar qualifications which might be turned to use in case of war — automobile drivers, telegraph and telephone operators, bridge-builders, mechanics of all sorts; in time of peace a list, and nothing more; in time of war a source not impossibly of three or four hundred thousand volunteers. Wood approved the idea 'unofficially' and lent his aide, Captain Gordon Johnson, as military adviser. . . . From the War Department came excited inquiry. The Secretary of War, it seemed, knew nothing about this plan for the organization of a 'reserve army.' Wood had been 'indiscreet.' "

Commotion arose. Suspicion continued on the part of the Administration that the activities of Wood and Roosevelt were political. Wood was called on the carpet, was ordered to evict American Legion, Inc., from the Army Building in New York. Secretary Garrison issued an order — addressed to all officers of the army — but well understood to mean Wood — forbidding the "giving out for publication any interview, statement, discussion or article on the military situation."

Wood with a sardonic touch explained that Roosevelt's only connection with the Legion was "as a volun-

[29] Not to be confused with the later "American Legion," composed of veterans of the Great War, founded in Paris, March, 1919.

teer enrolled for service, and that the Legion was conducting not propaganda but a card index."

Wood, obeying the letter of the order by not "giving

© *Underwood & Underwood.*

Richard Harding Davis at Plattsburg.

out" statements for publication, continued to disobey its spirit, flagrantly. He inspired a "business men's camp" for military training at Plattsburg, N. Y., at which a most incongruous group of some 1200 men touched shoulders in "fours left," "fours right." A former Secretary of State, Robert Bacon, acting as a sergeant, obeyed the orders of his son, a first lieutenant. A distinguished author, Richard Harding Davis, then fifty-one years old, discovered that while shifting equipment from back to shoulder may give alternations of ease to both, the feet remain ignorant of any change. The Mayor of New York, John Purroy Mitchel; his Police Commissioner, Arthur Woods; a leader of the Philadelphia Bar (subsequently United States Senator), George Wharton Pepper; the General Counsel of the United States Steel Corporation, Raynal Cawthorne Bolling; together with male social butterflies from Newport and Bar Harbor and busy bees from Wall Street, were inducted into the esoteric duties of "kitchen police."

To Wood at the Plattsburg camp came a telegram from Roosevelt saying that Roosevelt would make a speech to the "rookies" and that "I request . . . that it be made out of camp, at a time when the men are not on duty," and "if possible the men should be in citizen's clothes." Wood, warned of brimstone, thought it prudent he should edit Roosevelt's speech in advance, and did. That evening, however, several hours after the speech, Roosevelt said to newspaper reporters the things which he had omitted from his speech, to the effect, chiefly, that "standing by the President" was a fetish that could be overworshipped. The country, right or wrong, yes; but not the President — let men stand by him when he was right, against him when he was wrong. "To treat elocution as a substitute for action," so Roosevelt's statement to the press concluded, "to rely upon high-sounding words unbacked by deeds, is proof of a mind that dwells only in the realm of shadow and of shame."

This denunciation Roosevelt supplemented with an improvised metaphor, inspired by a friendly Airedale terrier which, feeling regret on bumping into Roosevelt, rolled over on his back, his paws ingratiatingly limp in the air. "That is a very nice dog," said Roose-

International News Photograph.

A machine gun squad at drill in a Preparedness camp at Lansdowne, Penna.

velt in hearing of the reporters. "I like him — his present attitude is strictly one of neutrality."[30]

Sensation in the newspapers. More commotion in Washington. The Secretary of War, under impulsion from the White House, sent Wood a sharp rebuke: "There must not be any opportunity given at Plattsburg or any other similar camp for any such unfortunate consequences [as Roosevelt's statement]." Wood replied: "Your telegram received and the policies laid down will be strictly adhered to." Wood, frustrated,

[30] New York *Tribune*, August 26, 1915.

found momentary satisfaction in a cutting quip. When a newspaper man told him that Luther Burbank had announced himself as an opponent of all military preparedness, he became contemplative. "Isn't he the man who developed spineless cactus?"

One would like to say that the Plattsburg camp, and the other results of Wood's campaign, contributed as much to our military strength as they did to the zest of life in America during 1915 and 1916; but the training for five weeks of a few hundred men, many of them middle-aged, was but as a drop in the bucket to an army which, when war came, had to muster four million. As influence, however, as stimulus to sentiment for preparedness, the Plattsburg camps and the "Plattsburg idea" were important. They, with other influences, increased preparedness sentiment to a point where it was politically dangerous for Wilson to fail to take account of it.

Photograph © International News.

A class in field telegraphy at the Women's National Service School Camp near Washington, D. C., 1916.

10

WILSON CHANGES, A LITTLE.

While Privately Sympathetic to the Allies, Publicly He Clings to Neutrality. He Evolves a Plan in Which He Should, Later On, Have the Rôle of Peacemaker Extraordinary. The Sentiment of the Country Swings to Preparedness, and Wilson Swings with It, His Change Causing Displeasure to Roosevelt, Who Reproaches Him for Using "Weasel Words" and Calls Him a "Logothete."

WE come now — at roughly the time when the war had been under way about a year — to the second stage in the evolution of Wilson's mind. It was an extremely able mind, and the evolution of it was the most important one fact in the war, in the making of peace, and for an indefinite period following. To understand the evolution of Woodrow Wilson's mind is as important as to understand the military strategy of Foch.

As between the Allies and Germany, the second stage of Wilson's evolution represented no change — on this point there never was any change. From the beginning, Wilson was strongly pro-Ally, strongly anti-German. "I found him," Colonel House wrote,[1] "as unsympathetic with the German attitude as is the balance of the country." He would never, he told Tumulty,[2] "take any action to embarrass England when she is fighting for her life and the life of the world. . . . England is fighting our fight." When Brand Whitlock, officially neutral because Minister to Belgium, told Wilson, "in my heart there is no such thing as neutrality, I am heart and soul for the Allies," Wilson replied, "so am I, no decent man could be anything else."

[1] Diary, August 30, 1914.
[2] "Woodrow Wilson as I Knew Him," Joseph Tumulty.

With this permanent attitude went a collateral condition. Wilson carefully restrained himself from giving
expression to his personal partisanship (except to such
intimates as House and Tumulty). For this there was
the obvious motive of keeping officially neutral. There
was, however, another motive: To remain neutral was
essential for a later rôle for which Wilson had begun to
cast himself, the rôle of peacemaker. "Peacemaker" is
much too narrow a word to describe the part for which
Wilson began to envisage himself. This part of the evolution of Wilson's mind, however, came later.[3] For the
present, about the middle of 1915, let us say merely that
Wilson was a partisan of the Allies, but that he held himself neutral, partly because of his official position and
more because of the intention that had begun to germi-
nate in his mind.

There was another condition. Wilson was determined
that the United States should never[4] enter the war. He
did not believe America should enter, and he did not
expect that America would. His partisanship for the
Allied cause never brought him to the impulse to have
America join them. The neutrality he steadily adhered
to arose not only from ordinary motives; uninterrupted
neutrality on the part of himself and on the part of
America was essential to the rôle for which, in his innermost soul, he had begun to reach out. That America
should not take any part was a fixed condition with him.
When, later, entry was forced upon him by the Germans

[3] Feb. 22, 1916, Colonel House, acting with Wilson's authority, signed a memorandum with British Foreign Minister Grey providing for the summoning of a
peace conclave by Wilson, and containing the proviso that if the Allies accepted,
and Germany declined, "the United States would *probably* [the word was inserted
later by Wilson] enter the war against Germany." At about the same time, Wilson held meetings with Democratic leaders — the "Sunrise Conference" — to discuss, according to hearsay gossip, America's joining the Allies. These events
have been misinterpreted ; actually, they were merely details in Wilson's plan for
a peace brought about by him, but without America's becoming a belligerent.
[4] "Newton D. Baker, America at War," Frederick Palmer.

he was utterly surprised, angry, and also dismayed, because participation in the war would endanger the rôle he looked forward to for himself and for America. This, however, is a detail of a later evolution of his mind, and is dealt with in a later chapter. As of 1915, Wilson was a determined neutral.

II

About preparedness, Wilson was less unbending. On that, his mind was, in his own words, "open and to let." Preparedness or non-preparedness would make no material difference in the rôle which he had begun to envisage for America and himself. On preparedness, he could afford to be expedient and was ready to be. Preparedness that would go so far as to bring peril of actually involving us in war with Germany — that Wilson would resist and resent and thwart. Once he saw in the Baltimore *Sun* an item saying "It is understood that the General Staff [of the Army] is preparing a plan in the event of war with Germany." Sending for Assistant Secretary of War Breckenridge, Wilson directed him to find out if this was true and "if proved true to relieve at once every officer of the General Staff and order him out of Washington." Breckenridge's investigation carried him to fine, rugged old General Tasker H. Bliss, who pointed out that "the Army War College had studied over and over again plans for war with Germany, England, France, Italy, Japan, and Mexico."[4] Secretary Baker suavely told Wilson it was just a game, the Army called it "war games"; Wilson said he did not think it a very good game. Baker told the Generals to go on with their games — but to avoid letting the public know about them.

[4] "Newton D. Baker, America at War," Frederick Palmer.

Preparedness aimed directly toward war with Germany, Wilson would not have — that would have interfered with his larger purpose. But preparedness which

Wilson's veering around to preparedness, after long opposing it, was pleasing to the public. The artist here pictures Uncle Sam in a smiling mood as Wilson starts to play the song now popular, "Johnny Get Your Gun."

— *Marcus in the New York Times.*

seemed inspired by and appropriate to our difficulties with Mexico, now recurrent for some three years; or preparedness having the color of precaution against the state of the world in general — that would not interfere with the program that had begun to crystallize in Wilson's mind. If a considerable section of public opinion demanded a limited preparedness, Wilson was tolerantly willing to go as far as seemed necessary to keep his hold on the people — and also willing, one surmises, to regard himself as the head of a political party, with a duty to keep his party in power by taking account of currents of popular emotion. Personally he did not like the notion of a large military establishment, but if a formidable public opinion favored preparedness, he could yield without impairing the project that had become his chief aspiration.

He "investigated and weighed public opinion in and outside Congress."[5] For assaying the national mood, he had one extraordinarily able adviser, his secretary, Joseph Tumulty. Wilson, having himself a distaste for talking with men, relied upon Tumulty for contact with Congress and with party leaders, for information about the drift of the press, for insight about popular emotion.[6]

Great as was the weight Tumulty had, he could never move Wilson toward any gesture that might lead to war

[5] Thomas W. Gregory, Attorney-General in Woodrow Wilson's Cabinet, in the New York *Times*, January 25, 1925.

[6] "The success of Woodrow Wilson's first administration may be attributed in no small measure to the . . . political sagacity of his private secretary, Joseph P. Tumulty. Nobody in the entire eight years kept in closer touch with editorial opinion. He watched the upward and downward curve of administration popularity with all the concentration that a banker studies the rise and fall of the markets."—"The True Story of Woodrow Wilson," David Lawrence.

Not only did Wilson depend on Tumulty for information about the drift of editorial opinion; he relied on Tumulty also to influence the press, to make public opinion what Wilson wanted it to be, an art at which Tumulty was shrewd: "You will know," Wilson once wrote in a memorandum to Tumulty, "how to create the impression on the minds of the newspaper men that I regard it [an agitation for a coalition cabinet after we entered the war] as merely a partisan effort to hamper and embarrass the administration."

"Tumulty was able to set the stage for an address by the President or for the announcement of some other important action, hinting a few days in advance, revealing bit by bit, with all the arts known to the practical publicity expert, divulged with an idea to headlines and conspicuous display."—"The True Story of Woodrow Wilson," David Lawrence.

with Germany. When Tumulty warned him that people felt "there was in him a heartlessness and an indifference to the deep tragedy of the *Lusitania*," Wilson said

Paul Thompson Photograph.

President Wilson and his Secretary, Joseph Tumulty.

coldly, "Tumulty, it would be much wiser for us not to dwell too much upon these matters."

But toward advice from Tumulty about preparedness, Wilson was amiable. As Tumulty observed preparedness sentiment rise, he induced Wilson to take his first advanced stand,[7] and wrote out some passages which Wilson used in the speech in which he reversed his position.[8]

Underwood & Underwood Photograph.

President Wilson marching at the head of a Preparedness Parade in Washington.

When Tumulty observed preparedness sentiment rising

[7] Tumulty, urging preparedness as a concession to public emotion, was successful with Wilson. Colonel House, urging preparedness on principle, as a step toward intervening, toward going to war with Germany, could never move Wilson. Over and over, House persisted. "I have urged him from the beginning," House wrote, "that this country prepare for eventualities. It should have been started the day war was declared in Europe. . . . The United States might have changed the course of history had we armed to the teeth at the beginning of the war and waited for the proper opportunity to intervene. Wilson did not," Colonel House summed up years later, "seem to see the difference between our having a great military establishment and no preparation at all."

[8] At the 50th anniversary dinner of the Manhattan Club, New York, November 4, 1915.

still further, observed it becoming a Republican partisan issue, and when he saw preparedness parades taking place in city after city, Tumulty, on the principle of "count 'em carefully and if they seem to have a majority join 'em," inquired when there would be one in Washington — and arranged that Wilson should march at the head of it.[9] "By getting into the 'front line,' " Tumulty observed in satisfaction over the device he had suggested, "the President had cleverly outwitted his enemies and took command of the forces in the country demanding preparedness."

III

By the meeting of Congress in December, 1915, Wilson was willing to go so far as to recommend an increase in the standing army to 141,843 rank and file, and a reserve force of 400,000 volunteers, to be built up by giving two months' training a year for three years. "So much," Wilson said, "by way of preparation for defense seems to me absolutely imperative now."[10] This was, on Wilson's part, a middle ground. The ardent preparedness leaders wanted to adopt General Wood's plan for universal, compulsory, military training of all young men between 18 and 22 for two months a year for four years. Congress, as it turned out, was unwilling to go even so far as Wilson advocated. At all times, until war actually came, the majority sentiment of Congress was against preparedness, or reluctantly assented to a smaller preparedness than even Wilson thought desirable.

Wilson, to bring pressure on Congress, made a tour through the country. At the opening speech, New York,

[9] "Woodrow Wilson as I Knew Him," Joseph P. Tumulty.
[10] "This program involved a very marked change of mind on his part."— "Eight Years with Wilson's Cabinet," David F. Houston.

January 27, 1916, he was candid in announcing his change of step. He admitted that a year before he had told Congress that "this question of military prepared-

At the time Wilson got around to accepting a policy of partial preparedness.
—*Webster in the New York Globe.*

ness was not a pressing question." "But," he went on, "more than a year has gone by since then and I would be ashamed if I had not learned something in fourteen months. The minute I stop changing my mind, with the change of all the circumstances of the world, I will be a back number."

On the tour, he spoke for preparedness, and as audiences cheered him increasingly, so did he talk with in-

creasing force; by the time he reached St. Louis he advocated "a great navy second to none in the world." But
never did he say anything that would compromise his
inner and primary determination to avoid war with Germany. Always his plea for preparedness was coupled
with an equally strong affirmation of determination to
remain at peace. With his extraordinary skill in phrasing
he carefully tied the two purposes into the same sentence: "This country should prepare herself, not for war
. . . but for adequate national defense."[11]

He said, we must "be ready . . . upon the shortest
possible notice; I do not know what a single day may
bring forth"[12] — but he also said, "It is . . . a more
desirable thing that all Americans should draw together
for the successful prosecution of peace."[13] He said,
"We are daily treading amongst the most intricate dangers"[14] — but he also said, "You may count upon my
heart and resolution to keep you out of the war."[15] He
said he was asking for "the force by which the authority
and right of the United States are to be maintained and
asserted"[16] — but he also said, "If there is one passion
more deep-seated than another in the hearts of our fellow countrymen, it is the passion for peace; I myself
share to the bottom of my heart that love of peace."[17]
He said, "There is danger to our national life"[18] — but
he also said, "I pledge you my word that, God helping
me I will keep this nation out of war if it is possible."[19]

The balanced impression that he strove successfully
to maintain he put in consecutive sentences at Cleveland:
"You have laid upon me this double obligation: 'We are

[11] Pittsburgh, January 29, 1916.
[12] Cleveland, January 29, 1916.   [13] New York, January 27, 1916.
[14] Cleveland, January 29, 1916.   [15] Cleveland, January 29, 1916.
[16] Kansas City, February 2, 1916. [17] New York, January 27, 1916.
[18] Des Moines, February 1, 1916.   [19] Milwaukee, January 31, 1916.

relying upon you, Mr. President, to keep us out of this war; but we are relying upon you, Mr. President, to keep the honor of the nation unstained.' "

A newspaper correspondent who accompanied Wilson

Wilson, after opposing preparedness and describing America as "too proud to fight," now reverses himself and aims his guns against his own former words.

— *Robert Carter in the New York Evening Sun.*

on the tour, David Lawrence, very friendly to the President and very intelligent, was obliged to record that "inconsistencies and contradictions appeared in Mr. Wilson's speeches."[20]

There was another commentator. Theodore Roosevelt's permanent hostility to Wilson now had reason to

[20] "The True Story of Woodrow Wilson," David Lawrence.

be accentuated, for Wilson, in embracing preparedness, was stealing Roosevelt's and the Republicans' political raiment. Roosevelt was a highly intelligent person, but his intelligence never quite grasped the whole of Wilson's adroitness with words, or, so far as Roosevelt did grasp it, he was enraged by it. Once, Roosevelt, provoked to fury by reading one of Wilson's speeches, called him a "Byzantine logothete." Newspaper explanation of the mystic epithet went only far enough to let readers understand vaguely, and not too accurately, that "logos" was a Greek term meaning "word," and that Roosevelt considered Wilson to be a man who did wicked things with words.

After the close of Wilson's preparedness tour, Roosevelt erupted:

In the fourteen months from December 8, 1914, to February 10, 1916, there were fifteen messages, letters, and speeches of President Wilson's which I have read. [We can be sure Roosevelt read them!] In those fifteen messages, letters, and speeches President Wilson took 41 different positions about preparedness and the measures necessary to secure it; and each of these 41 positions contradicted from 1 to 6 of the others. In many of the speeches, the weasel words of one portion took all the meaning out of the words used in another portion, and those latter words themselves had a weasel significance as regards yet other words. He argued for preparedness and against preparedness.

If Roosevelt could not understand Wilson, the public did. Wilson knew the mass mind deals less with argument than with feeling. He was intent not on syllogistic argument, but on making an impression. And the public got precisely the impression Wilson meant it should get.

It is true Wilson used words adroitly; no other statesman in the world had his skill. More than that, he used ideas adroitly. For his art he had much need. He was looking forward to an immense enterprise, and he was obliged to be always "shifting his pace, like an expert boxer, to match the dexterity of the most cleverly adroit diplomats in Europe."[21] Wilson knew from his ambassadors and other agents abroad, the kaleidoscopic changes constantly taking place in the European situa-

International News Photograph.

President Wilson speaking, from the rear of his train, on behalf of Preparedness at Waukegan, Ill., in February, 1916.

tion, and was always adjusting himself to it. He had determined, when the right time should come, to take hold of it, dominate it, and bend it to an idealistic purpose he had conceived. To accomplish this purpose, it was desirable that America should not enter the war. And it was imperative, of course, that Wilson should

21 The quoted words are from "Wilson the Unknown," by Wells Wells (a pseudonym).

still be President when the war should come toward an end. To be re-elected in 1916, it was expedient that he should guardedly endorse preparedness, and otherwise

Too many cooks threaten to spoil the preparedness broth. Wilson, recently converted, still differs from Roosevelt, while Bryan, Congress, and Uncle Sam make diverse comments.

—*De Ball in the Chicago Post.*

take account of the varied and shifting currents of feeling in America. He was obliged to be for preparedness and also against going to war. He was obliged to be for preparedness far enough to avoid wholly alienating the moderate believers in preparedness, but not far enough to alienate those who feared preparedness might take us into the war. To manage all that took some art with words, but by no means so much as Wilson possessed. To Wilson it was easy. He was destined to have occasion, before the War ended, to show what he could really do with words.

Meanwhile it was imperative he be re-elected.

LITTLE BOY BLUE

"'Now, don't you go till I come,' he said,
'And don't you make any noise!'
So toddling off to his trundle bed,
He dreamt of the pretty toys."

A cartoonist's picturization of the nascent public interest in preparedness.

— *Life, September, 1915.*

11

"HE KEPT US OUT OF WAR"

The Campaign of 1916. Wilson Retains the Presidency, Though by So Slight a Margin That for Three Days the Result Is in Doubt. How a Californian Named Hiram W. Johnson Brought It About That One Whom He Little Liked, Woodrow Wilson, Should Be President from 1917 to 1921; and How That Incident Influenced History.

WILSON, facing in the Spring of 1916 the problem of renomination and re-election, realized like every one else that the issue would be the war, and the attitude of America toward the war.

That he would be renominated at the Democratic National Convention went without saying. The matters to which he must give care were the platform, and the keynote to be struck in the convention and by Wilson in his campaign. Wilson dominated the convention utterly. He had a private telephone from the White House to the convention hall, sent Secretary of War Baker to be his spokesman, and kept in contact constantly.

The convention received its keynote from a loyal, warm-hearted devotee of Wilson, Governor Martin Glynn of New York. He was ill and reluctant but Wilson urged him to the task. Glynn's Irish traits of sentiment and eloquence put into words of moving vividness the record Wilson wished emphasized:

This policy may not satisfy . . . the fire-eater or the swashbuckler but it does satisfy the mothers of the land at whose hearth and fireside no jingoistic war has placed an empty chair. It does satisfy the daughters of the land from whom bluster and brag have sent no loving brother to the dissolution of the grave.[1]

[1] Proceedings, Democratic National Convention, 1916.

Turning to give some placation to another group, Glynn continued:

It does satisfy the fathers of this land and the sons of this land who will fight for our flag and die for our flag when Reason primes the rifle, when Honor draws the sword, when Justice breathes a blessing on the standards they uphold.

The neutrality theme, "the saving of neutral life, the freedom of the seas," was further emphasized by the permanent chairman, Senator Ollie James of Kentucky, an elephant of a man with a booming voice:

. . . without orphaning a single American child, without widowing a single American wife, without firing a single gun, without the shedding of a single drop of blood, he [Wilson] has wrung from the most militant spirit that ever brooded above a battlefield an acknowledgment of American rights and an agreement to American demands.[2]

By assuming that a convention audience hot physically and emotionally would not distinguish between a "peacemaker" and a "peace preserver," James was able to evoke Christ as an endorser of Wilson's record: "I can see the accusing picture of Christ on the battlefield, with the dead and dying all around him, with the screams of shrapnel and the roll of cannon, and I can hear the Master say to Woodrow Wilson, 'Blessed are the peacemakers, for they shall be called the children of God.' "

Both James and Glynn, as well as Wilson himself during the subsequent campaign, and all the Cabinet members and official party spokesmen, were careful to use the past tense, "He *kept* us out of war." They may have anticipated, perhaps shrewdly expected, as a detail of campaign psychology, that the grammatically undiscriminating public would not distinguish so carefully between the tense of past record and that of future

[2] Proceedings, Democratic National Convention, 1916.

promise, between the literal wording of the speeches and the atmosphere of them. "He kept us out of war" became the slogan of the campaign,[3] as potent for its future implication as for its past record. The careful emphasis on the past tense by the official speakers at the convention was neutralized, however, and yet the desired public impression was accentuated, by one who was no longer in the cabinet, and was now in the convention unofficially. William Jennings Bryan, present as a newspaper reporter, introduced by Ollie James as "America's Greatest Democrat," told the convention that "I agree with the American people in thanking God we have a President who has kept — *who will keep* — us out of war."

Another aspect of the war that the convention and the platform must, or at least ought to, take account of was the hyphenated vote. When on this point the convention showed a disposition to "pussyfoot," Tumulty, always alert, sent a memorandum to Wilson to "urge you as strongly as I can" to have the platform "meet these things in a manly, aggressive, militant fashion." Wilson sent a telegram to Baker. The platform, in a turgid paragraph which did not use the word "German-American" nevertheless "condemn[ed] all alliances and combinations of individuals in this country of whatever nationality or descent who agree and conspire together for the purpose of embarrassing or weakening the government or of improperly influencing or coercing our public representatives in dealing or negotiating with any foreign power."

During the campaign, when a fire-eating pro-Ger-

[3] "There is no question that the slogan 'He kept us out of war' was one of the determining factors in Wilson's favor in that election." — "Political Education of Woodrow Wilson," James Kerney.

man, himself belonging to the Irish group, Jeremiah O'Leary, wrote an offensive letter to Wilson, Wilson made a public reply: "I would feel deeply mortified to

A New York *Times* cartoon on the hyphenated vote which both sides were wary of.

have you or anybody like you vote for me; since you have access to many disloyal Americans and I haven't, I will ask you to convey this message to them." That scornful rebuke, wrote one of Wilson's biographers, "made the front-page of every newspaper and thrilled the country."[3a]

To a committee of students arranging an anti-military

3a "The Political Education of Woodrow Wilson," James Kerney.

demonstration in New York, Wilson wrote:[4] "The whole spirit and principle of militarism is abominable to me." A last-hour appeal addressed by the Democratic campaign management to the workers of America said: "You are working, not fighting; alive and happy, not cannon fodder. . . . If you want war, vote for Hughes. If you want peace with honor and continued prosperity, vote for Wilson."

Toward the end of the campaign, Wilson, taking a master's hand, practised a Gettysburg manœuvre of dialectic against the Republicans:

We must draw the conclusion, [he said,[5]] that if the Republican party is put in power at the coming election, our foreign policy will be radically changed. They say all our present policy is wrong. If it is wrong and they are men of conscience, they must change it; and if they are going to change it, in what direction are they going to change it? There is only one choice as against peace and that is war. A very great body of the supporters of that party outspokenly declare that they want war, so that the certain prospect of the success of the Republican party is that we shall be drawn, in one form or another, into the embroilments of the European war.

That is, Wilson said: Elect the Republicans and you will be in the war; elect me and you will be kept out. As debate, as campaign strategy, it was superb. It placed Hughes and the Republicans in a dilemma and kept them there. But in doing that Wilson "unquestionably promised the nation there would be no war, While he did not expressly pledge it, his words are open to no other interpretation, and the election was clearly won on that issue."[6] Wilson, it is not too much to say, by implication, committed himself to a promise, a literal contract — elect me and you will be kept out of war.

He was elected, very narrowly. Election night he

[4] September 30, 1916.   [5] September 30, 1916, at Shadow Lawn.
[6] "The Unknown Wilson," Wells Wells.

President Wilson's re-election promised the continuation of the hum of industry.
—Godwin in the Pittsburgh Dispatch.

went to bed believing he had lost.[7] The doubt lasted three days. The electoral score was, Wilson 277, Hughes 254.

II

After any close election, it is common, and often fallacious, to ascribe credit (or blame as the point of view

[7] It was Wilson's intention, if he lost, to bring about the immediate induction of the successful candidate into the Presidency. The ingenious plan had been suggested to him by Colonel House. The successive steps in it would be: Have

may be) to some particular group of votes close in number to the margin by which the winner has a majority. Wilson's victory, of course, came to him by virtue of each and all of the thirty-one States he carried. But the margin by which Wilson won and Hughes lost was twelve electoral votes — to win required 266 and Hughes had but 254; and it happened that one State which Wilson carried had just that number of electoral votes, and one over. For this, and other reasons more convincing, California stood out with a conspicuousness which to Democrats was admirable, to Republicans odious, and on the part of everybody now gave rise to acrimonious discussion.

California had been regarded as a strongly and safely Republican State. In the last preceding Presidential contest between Republicans and Democrats, 1908, Republicans had carried it by 2 to 1. In the campaign just closed, the Republicans had counted on California almost as surely as upon Pennsylvania or Maine. Now the figures cried out for explanation: Hughes had lost the State to Wilson by the narrow margin of 3773 — but the Republican candidate for United States Senator, Hiram W. Johnson, had carried the State by an enormous majority, 296,815.

From every Republican politician and organ throughout the nation came angry inquiry, pointed at Johnson, "How come?" Within California, the Republican Los Angeles *Times*, bitter enemy of Johnson, did not ask any question but gave an answer, saying, in great headlines: "Johnson is blamed for treachery . . . How Johnson's perfidy beat Hughes . . . Hughes was se-

---

Vice-President Marshall resign; have Secretary of State Lansing resign; then appoint the successful candidate, Charles E. Hughes, to be Secretary of State; thereafter, Wilson would resign, and Hughes as next in line of statutory succession would step into the Presidency.

cretly traded off for Johnson . . . The Benedict Arnold of California."

The case was not quite that simple. For some six years, California, and the Republican party within Cali-

Attempt of a cartoonist (in the Albany, N. Y., *Knickerbocker Press*) to picture the suspense following the November, 1916, election, when for three days the result was in doubt.

fornia, had been torn by a factional strife peculiarly feudal in its bitterness, with the regular Republicans still in control of the party machinery and the Progressives in growing revolt, led by Hiram Johnson. In the course of this struggle, Johnson, in August, 1916, was running in the Republican primaries, against a regular, for the nomination for United States Senator. In that condition Hughes, campaigning for the Presidency, made a three days' tour of the State. As he crossed the State line he was met, naturally and in accord with custom, by the heads of the regular organization; the regular heads accompanied him throughout his tour, presided and were otherwise conspicuous at his meetings and at luncheons and dinners given him. Hughes could not object; as a Republican and as a lawyer, he knew he must recognize those who held the official places in the regular Republican organization of every State. His only allusion to the California feud he made in the opening of his first California speech: "I come here as the spokesman of the National Republican party; with local differences I have no concern."

At no time during Hughes' tour did he and Johnson meet. Hughes' friends felt that Johnson, who was extremely temperamental, stood off, sulked; Johnson's friends felt that the regulars managing Hughes' tour kept Hughes from seeing Johnson. Johnson took the position he could not call on Hughes without a direct, personal invitation. For some hours the two were under the same roof, at a hotel in Long Beach. Hughes did not know Johnson was in the hotel, and therefore must be exculpated from slight to Johnson. "Johnson knew that Hughes was in the hotel," but—the question of courtesy was so intricate as to be expressable only in a highly involved sentence, "Johnson did not know that Hughes did not know that he, Johnson, was in the hotel."

In the angry recriminations that arose after it was recognized that the incident had lost the Presidency for the Republicans, Johnson was able to produce, in defense of himself, newspaper headlines describing speeches he had made during the campaign, "Vast Throng Cheers Wildly as Johnson Lauds Hughes." However much the outcome was due to Johnson's tem-

perament (peculiarly liable to see slight and resent it);
however much of it was due to actions of Johnson's
followers whom Johnson could not control, the incident,
normally a local teapot tempest, achieves high importance when we realize how different history would have

Photograph by Brown Bros.

Senator Hiram Johnson, whose re-election to the Senate on the Republican ticket
in 1916, at the same time that the State's Presidential vote went to Wilson,
started an acrimonious debate between the liberal and conservative divisions
of the Republican party.

been, not only in America but in the world, had Charles
E. Hughes defeated Woodrow Wilson for the Presidency.

Hiram Johnson was for a full generation a colorful
figure in American public life, at times a not unim-
portant one. Once he was the Vice-Presidential candidate on a major ticket, the Progressive, in 1912; twice

he tried for the Republican Presidential nomination. Once (at the Republican National Convention of 1920) the friends of Philander C. Knox proposed to Johnson that he throw his strength to Knox for the Presidential nomination, taking the Vice-Presidential nomination for himself. The proposal was accompanied by a suggestion, as cynical as politics can often be, that Knox had a heart disease and would not live out the term. Johnson angrily showed the tempters out of the room; he would have the Presidential nomination or nothing; "they are trying to put a heart-beat between me and the White House," he said. In the same convention, another tender of the Vice-Presidential nomination was made him, by Warren Harding; again Johnson angrily refused to take any but the highest honor; had he accepted, Harding's death would have made him President instead of Calvin Coolidge. Johnson was destined to end his career without the Presidency, without a Presidential nomination, but with knowledge, whatever emotion it may have given him, that his important place in history was as the agency which, by defeating Hughes, made Woodrow Wilson President from 1917 to 1921.

12

WILSON UNFOLDS HIS PLAN

Planning to Put an End to the Great War and to Prevent Future Wars, He Finds His Hand Forced by an Offer of Peace from the German Kaiser. Persisting, Wilson Proposes a "Peace Without Victory," and Is Berated for Being an Officious Meddler. First Allusion to an Institution, Still Inchoate, Which Was Destined Very Soon to Cause Much Commotion in the World, the League of Nations.

WILSON, secure in the Presidency for another four years, was now able to proceed with his plan. He had just married a new wife. Personal ambition coincided with the spirit of high adventure in idealism.

There had developed in America, even before the Great War broke out (during the period of militance for peace that had been part of the atmosphere of the Progressive movement), a plan for avoiding all wars called "The League to Enforce Peace." A parallel suggestion had arisen in Europe. This nebulous idea Wilson now took hold of, made it his own, expanded it.

Wilson's plan contemplated that he should act as peace-maker, not only as peace-maker to end this war, but as a super-peace-maker — he would use this war as a war to end all wars, by setting up an organization, a concert of powers (it later came to be called "The League of Nations").

While Wilson reflected, not certain yet about details of his plan, and not certain when would be the right time to put it forward, Germany forced his hand.

II

The Kaiser, December 12, 1916, gave out a statement, addressed to the Allies but made public for the world. Germany had the "military and economic strength . . . to continue the war to the bitter end." But Germany's "aims are not to shatter nor annihilate our adversaries." And so, "prompted by the desire to avoid further bloodshed," Germany and her three part-ner-nations "propose to enter forthwith into peace nego-tiations."

To all the world, Germany's proposal was a surprise; to President Wilson it was surprise coupled with em-barrassment. Now he hurried. On December 18, he addressed identical notes to all the belligerents. His hurry seemed to suggest a fear on his part lest the bel-ligerents make peace on the basis of the Kaiser's tender, before he could get his own broader proposal before the world. As if conscious of this appearance of precipi-tancy, Wilson went out of his way to say that his pro-posal had been inspired independently of the Kaiser's overtures — he had "long had it in mind."

Wilson's proposal contemplated, as parts of one act, first the stopping of this war, and second, the prevention of all future wars:

The President suggests that an early occasion be sought to call out from all the nations now at war an avowal of their respective views as to the terms upon which the war might be concluded, and the arrangements which would be deemed satisfactory as a guarantee against the kindling of any similar conflict in future. . . . In the measures to be taken to secure the future peace of the world, the people and government of the United States are as vitally and as directly interested as the goverments now at war.

It was audacious. Here were the two belligerents giv-ing consideration to a tender by one of them for peace between themselves. The attitude of the whole world was one of devout wish that the peace be consummated, of despairing doubt lest it should not be. And here was Wilson, so to speak, galloping in from the West, holding up the proceedings, demanding to be let in on the making of peace. Reversing the question, familiar in American humor — "Is this a private fight or can any

Germany's proposal of peace while still strong, December 12, 1916, provokes ironic comment from an American cartoonist.

— *Robert Carter in the New York Evening Sun.*

one enter?" — Wilson now did not ask, but affirmed that this must not be a private peace, he and the United States must be allowed to take a hand. Not merely take a hand but manage it.

From another point of view, irritation-provoking to the belligerents, especially to the Allies, here were Wilson and America, who had steadily refused to take part in the fighting, now attempting to take a hand in the peace; not merely take a hand, but dominate it, use the occasion to set up a super-state.

Neither Wilson's proposal nor the Kaiser's came to anything.

To Wilson's proposal, the Germans replied, December 26, in the spirit of their own outstanding tender — they suggested "the speedy assembly on neutral ground of delegates of the warring states." From the Allies the reply to both the Wilson proposal and the German one was "No." To Wilson, January 12, the Allies said in many words, that they desired as much as he the end of this war and the prevention of future ones, but the time had not come to obtain such a peace as they deemed just. To the Kaiser the Allies said, in many sentences of reproach and recrimination, denunciation and defiance, that they refused "to consider a proposal which is empty and insincere."

Peace was off. But Wilson was on his way — and he was a determined man. The purpose that had long germinated in him was now in full flower.

III

Ten days later, January 22, Wilson appeared unexpectedly and dramatically before the Senate with an address meant more for the belligerents in Europe than for the Senate. He had a manner of irritation against the Allies for their rejection of his gesture to end the war, a manner implying "I'll make you." The address he now delivered was meant not only for the belligerents but for the world. He was acting, he said, "on behalf of humanity."

Speaking "for the silent masses of mankind everywhere," he adopted the manner of an outsider addressing, rather imperatively, the two sets of belligerents who were making the world a miserable place to live in. To

Much of the comment stirred up by Wilson's proposal of "Peace Without Victory" was ironic and resentful.

— *Nelson Harding in the Brooklyn Daily Eagle.*

the belligerents, he had the air of saying that this fighting must stop. But, he said, it should stop in a particular way. It must end in a "peace without victory." He admitted "it is not pleasant to say this." But "victory would mean peace forced upon the loser, a victor's terms imposed upon the vanquished." Such a peace "would be accepted in humiliation, under duress"; it "would leave a sting, a bitter memory"; it would "rest upon a quicksand." Therefore, Wilson proposed that the peace should be one "without victory," for "only a peace between equals can last."

If the belligerents were willing to come to this kind of peace, he said, the United States would participate in the making of it. Therefore, he proposed, in order to make the peace permanent and universal, there should be a "definite concert of powers which will make it virtually impossible that any such catastrophe should ever overwhelm us again." In this permanent concert of powers, if created along lines Wilson laid down, the United States would be willing to participate — "it is inconceivable that the United States should play no part in that great enterprise." The United States, he asserted (with what later proved to be too much confidence) would "add their authority and their power to the authority and force of other nations to guarantee peace and justice throughout the world."

(Even though we are interrupting Wilson in the midst of a speech, the historian must ask the reader to put his mind on this passage: The United States would "add their authority and their power to the authority and force of other nations to guarantee peace throughout the world" by "adherence to a League of Peace [Later the League of Nations]." Woodrow Wilson made many speeches that gave direction to history, uttered many phrases that stirred men's hearts and had momentous consequences; among them all none was so pregnant as this — and the thing it gave birth to was a curious changeling, in its early phase an angelic aspiration of idealism, in its subsequent stage the bedevilling source of blasted hopes to the world, and in the United States cause

of the angriest controversy that beset the country since
the Civil War. As one reads today this statement by
Wilson that the United States would unite in a League
of Nations, it stands up to analysis; it was not quite a
promise: "It is inconceivable that the people of the
United States should play no part." But like many of
Wilson's speeches, the atmosphere of it made more impact than the meaning, an aura that suffused the words,
conveyed more to the heart than cold-eyed parsing
conveys to the mind. The world understood this
passage to be a promise that the United States would unite
in a League of Nations. That implication was not only
in the aroma which Wilson, with the extraordinary art
he had in words, managed to inject into the statement.
Wilson was President of the United States, and much of
the world assumed that the President of the United States
had as complete a prerogative to make commitments in
foreign affairs as the heads of most European governments have; they forgot that the President has only the
power to propose treaties and that the Senate has power
of rejection or confirmation. Moreover, Wilson at this
time actually had the extraordinary autocratic powers
conferred on him as an incident of the War; little wonder
if the world assumed these war-time powers included
that of making commitments in foreign affairs. Finally,
it was felt at this stage of the War, that a League of Peace
[League of Nations] would be good; of all in Congress
who listened to Wilson's words this day, and of all
throughout the country who read it, probably it occurred
to very few to question the project Wilson here proposed.
But the hard fact of the Constitution of the United States
was that Wilson had only power to propose, that the Senate had power to refuse ratification; and the hard fact
of circumstance and human nature was that Senators had
as much right to oppose a League of Nations as Wilson

had to propose it. Senators did not oppose at the time; when they did, the opposition brought much turmoil and grief to a world which had raptly considered Wilson's proposal to be a binding undertaking on the part of the United States. ¶ So much by way of interjection from the commentator as Wilson delivers his speech of January 22, 1917.)

Wilson continued: "But it is right . . . that this government should frankly formulate the conditions upon which it would feel justified in asking our people to approve its formal and solemn adherence to a League for Peace. I am here to attempt to state those conditions." And, just as Wilson's "League of Peace" was his first[1] putting forward of what later became the "League of Nations," so did the conditions he now laid down include several of what, epitomized by him later, became the "Fourteen Points":[2] The peace ending this war must be a "peace without victory"; "there should be a united, independent and autonomous Poland"; for "every great people" . . . a direct outlet to the great highways of the sea (the allusion was to Poland's need for a corridor); "freedom of the seas," limitation of armament, self-determination of all nations and peoples.

It is common, when any President makes any speech of unusual moment, for superlatives to spring from many sources, "greatest utterance ever. . . ." Now for once, the superlatives were justified. No one denied that only words ending in "est" could adequately describe Wilson's act; what preceded the "est" depended on the source. An Irish leader, John Dillon, thought it "unquestionably the most remarkable and momen-

[1] The first addressed to the belligerents, but not literally the first; there was vague mention of the same idea, though not of the institution, in a speech Wilson had made before the League to Enforce Peace, at Washington, May 27, 1916.
[2] The "Fourteen Points" are given on pages 447-8.

tous utterance by the ruler of a great power for more than a hundred years." A host of comments substituted for remarkable, preposterous; and for momentous, impudent. Some compared the speech to Don

Wilson's early peace proposal (Dec. 18, 1916) was regarded in Germany as an unwelcome intrusion.

Quixote, others to the prophecies of Isaiah. Fully half the comment included the word Utopia. The London *Daily Mail*, holding itself in as much restraint as it could achieve — for the war was still on and Wilson was an important person — wondered "whether he spoke as head of an American university or as chief magistrate of a flesh-and-blood republic." Both sets of belligerents were shocked — jointly by "peace without victory," separately by items in Wilson's formula, Britain by "freedom of the seas," Germany by a "united, independent, autonomous Poland."

The Canadian Senate considered a resolution, that "only representatives of nations which have taken part . . . in the present war should participate in negotiations for peace." Much of America recalled that Wilson the preceding November had been elected President of the United States, but could find no record of his having been chosen "President of humanity." There was much of that feeling in America, an appalled concern over the proposal to inject the United States into the very vortex of about all the quarrels in Europe, not merely those presently acute but the historic ones, freedom of Poland, self-determination of all the small peoples who might feel they wanted to be self-determined. In the Senate a resolution was offered that Monday, January 29, be set apart for full discussion of Wilson's proposal, its startling departure from George Washington's "no entangling alliances."

All that, Wilson anticipated and was prepared to handle. He could have done it, too; he knew America's proneness for adventure in idealism, the appetite for emotional and altruistic debauch of a people about to go alcoholically dry. Wilson had worked his plan out in every step, knew that uproar would arise in some sections of American thought, and counted not only on resisting it but on capitalizing it. Had events gone on in the sequence Wilson anticipated, he would have had a thought-out treatment for every step.

This detailed plan, with each future move worked out, was the third stage in the evolution of Wilson's mind. He kept the fundamental part of the previous stages — he would not take part in the war. To the pattern of his plan he now added an intention to take charge

of making the peace, to put himself forward as statesman for all the peoples in the world, including the belligerent ones, and to use his prestige and the prestige of
America, not merely to make peace but to set up a super-
state, a world union of all nations.

France to President Wilson: "What would you say if that were New York?"
A Paris cartoon which expressed the French feeling that Wilson's proposal
of peace was untimely.

—*Forain in Le Figaro, Paris.*

13

GERMANY UNLEASHES THE SUBMARINE

Taking Back Her Formal Promise to Wilson of a Year Before, She Now Announces She Will Use the Submarine "to the Full." As a Concession to America, She Would Permit Us to Send One Vessel a Week to Britain — Provided It Were Painted Like a Zebra, or, as John Bach McMaster Put It, "Like a Barber Pole"; and Provided We Would Submit to Other Conditions Which Were as Harsh as Those Imposed by a Conqueror upon a Weak and Vanquished Nation. Picture of a President at a Time When He Is Being Pushed toward Taking His Country into War. Wilson Proposes to Congress That American Merchant Ships Be Armed for Protection Against U-boats, but Is Defied by a "Little Group of Willful Men" in the Senate. The Imperial German Government Makes a Blunder Which Excels the Remarkable Record of Ineptness It Had Already Made. The Zimmermann Letter — Its Publication Draws Public Support to Wilson's Course. Germany Proposes to Hand Texas and Arizona Back to Mexico. Wilson Dismisses the German Ambassaor. War becomes Inevitable.

EIGHT days after Wilson had startled the world with his peace address to the Senate, while the contrapuntal discord of plaudit and execration was still crescendo, German Ambassador von Bernstorff, on January 31, 1917, delivered to the State Department, and the State Department delivered to Wilson, a note from Germany. Germany would begin, on February 1, absolutely unrestricted submarine warfare: "All sea traffic will be stopped with every available weapon and without further notice."

II

The German note announced that Germany "has so far not made unrestricted use of the weapon she possesses in her submarines," but that now she proposes to use them to "the full."

Germany would now "forcibly prevent" any vessel of the United States (or of any other nation) from going to England except — and the exception was what made

The Kaiser presents Uncle Sam with a pass good for one trip of one ship per week to England.

— *Rogers in the N. Y. Herald.*

the announcement peculiarly intolerable, it would have been less offensive had the embargo been absolute: The United States would be permitted to send one passenger vessel once each week to England provided:

(*a*)[1] It must go to the port of Falmouth and nowhere else.
(*b*) It must arrive at Falmouth on a Sunday.

[1] The rules laid down by Germany are here lettered in an order different from that in the German announcement.

(c) It must leave Falmouth on a Wednesday.

(d) It must travel by a specified course "via the Scilly Islands and a point 50° North, 20° West."

(e) It must be "marked in the following way . . . on hull and superstructure three vertical stripes one meter wide each, painted alternately white and red; each mast to show a large flag checkered white and red, and the stern the American national flag."

(f) The United States must guarantee that the ship carry no contraband (according to German contraband list).

That limitation, dictated by the German Government, of what America might do upon the sea, is stark enough. It calls for no amplification; but there is some adornment in the paraphrase of it made at the time by the venerable historian of the American people:[1a]

Our country had now received its orders. Once each week *one* passenger steamship, striped like a barber's pole, and flying at each masthead a flag resembling a kitchen tablecloth, might leave *one* port of the United States, and making its way along a prescribed course, enter a specified port in England on a Sabbath day, or be sunk without warning. Had the German armies been in possession of every foot of our soil from the Atlantic to the Pacific, these orders could not have been more tyrannical. No "Avis," no "Proclamation," no "Ordre" signed by von Bissing, or von der Goltz, or von Bülow and pasted on the walls of Brussels, or Liège, was written more in the spirit of the conqueror.

Wilson was utterly shocked. As he read the German defi, the flight of swift emotions across his features was observed by Tumulty — "first blank amazement, then incredulity, then gravity and sternness, a sudden greyness of color . . ."

All that, Wilson had supposed, was safely behind him. Nine months before by a triumph in diplomatic dialects he had manœuvred Germany, through his *Lusitania* notes, into agreeing not to sink except in accord with international law; for nine months, there had been no

[1a] John Bach McMaster.

unlawful sinking. That condition, suspension of unlawful sinkings, was essential to Wilson's plan to make peace as a neutral. The situation in which he had been proceeding to enforce peace as a neutral dictating to both belligerents was now shattered.

III

HOUSE HOLDS WILSON'S HAND

"In great governmental crises of this sort, the public have no conception of what is happening on the stage behind the curtain. If the actors and the scenery could be viewed, as a tragedy like this is being prepared, it would be a revelation." —*Colonel House's Diary, February* 1, 1917.

The same day that Wilson received the German note, January 31, Colonel House in New York read of it in the newspapers.

House, knowing Wilson well and feeling Wilson would need him, took the midnight train to Washington. Going directly to the White House he found Wilson not up yet. Wilson appeared after breakfast, and

we were together continuously until after two o'clock.... The President was sad and depressed; I did not succeed at any time during the day in lifting him into a better frame of mind. The President said he felt as if the world had suddenly reversed itself, that after going from East to West it had begun to go from West to East, and that he could not get his balance. Wilson was insistent that he would not allow it [Germany's defiance] to lead to war if it could possibly be avoided. We sat listlessly. The President nervously arranged his books and walked up and down the floor. We were listlessly killing time. We had finished the discussion within half an hour and there was nothing further to say. Mrs. Wilson spoke of golf and asked whether I thought it would look badly if the President went on the links. I thought the American people would feel that he should not do anything so trivial at such a time. The President at last suggested that we play a game of pool [at which both the elderly men were absurdly inadept.] [2]

2 "Intimate Papers of Colonel House."

IV

A President may be sad, depressed; but inexorable time, imperious events, will not wait for the mood to lift. The next day, Saturday, February 3, was the regu-

Photograph by Underwood & Underwood.

President Wilson and Colonel House during the period of their great intimacy. The mourning band on Wilson's sleeve is for his first wife.

lar day for Cabinet meeting. The members came realizing "that we might be facing the most momentous issue in our experience and in the history of the nation."[3] As Wilson entered, his manner, the droop of his shoulders, the tired flatness of his voice as he spoke to them, caused the more sensitive to look at him closely. His opening

[3] "Eight Years with Wilson's Cabinet," David Franklin Houston.

remark was startling. He "asked what should be done — 'Shall I break off diplomatic relations with Ger-

Wilson's Cabinet at the time America entered the war.

Rear row left to right, Secretary of the Navy Daniels, Secretary of Labor Wilson, Secretary of War Baker, Attorney-General Gregory, Secretary of the Interior Lane. *Front row left to right,* Secretary of Commerce Redfield, Secretary of State Lansing, Secretary of Agriculture Houston, President Wilson, Secretary of the Treasury McAdoo, Postmaster-General Burleson.

many?' "[4] Before any one could make the reply that tugged at the lips of each, Wilson went on:

He would say frankly that, if he felt that, in order to keep the white race or part of it strong to meet the yellow race —

[4] "Eight Years with Wilson's Cabinet," David Franklin Houston.

Japan, for instance in alliance with Russia dominating China — it was wise to do nothing, he would do nothing, and would submit to anything and any imputation of weakness or cowardice.[5]

Several began to speak. McAdoo was for prompt action, we must act or swallow our brave words. Baker was much impressed with the President's long look ahead, as was Daniels. Burleson thought we should make good our warning to Germany.

The President remarked that all these expressions were the result of a natural impulse but they did not aid him greatly.

Finally, Houston spoke. Physically, Houston was a strong, slow-moving Percheron horse; intellectually the same plus the precision of a watch, the clarity of a searchlight — one of the ablest Americans of his generation. Insight he had, too, a gift of perceptiveness about other men's moods. This moved him now to address himself directly and pointedly to what Wilson had said about doing nothing:

We must start from where we are and take the next right step. Nothing worse can ever befall us than what Germany proposes and no greater insult can be offered to any people. If we acquiesce we ought not to pose as a nation or as a free people. We ought to invite the Kaiser to set up as our permanent dictator. I have heard of nothing which Japan stands for which I would not prefer. If we are capable of submitting, Japan or anybody else who would take us ought to have us. We would not be worth saving. . . . I am for asserting our rights, for standing with the Allies, for doing our part.[6]

Fretfully, almost pitiably, Wilson replied: "Very well, that does not reach far enough. What is the proposal? What is the concrete suggestion? What shall I propose? I must go to Congress. What shall I say?"

[5] This is a paraphrase of what Wilson said, as written down after the Cabinet meeting by Secretary of Agriculture Houston.
[6] "Eight Years with Wilson's Cabinet," David Franklin Houston.

Vigorously Houston told him: "Sever diplomatic relations and let come what will. [Then] tell Congress what you have done. Say that you propose to protect American lives and rights."

The following day,[6a] Wilson went before Congress:

I think you will agree with me [Wilson said,] that this government has no alternative consistent with the dignity and honor of the United States. . . . . I have therefore directed the Secretary of State to announce to his Excellency the German Ambassador, that all diplomatic relations between the United States and the German Empire are severed and to hand to His Excellency his passports.

Wilson's address to Congress was at two in the afternoon. Within a few minutes afterward, passports and note of dismissal were handed to Von Bernstorff. The German consuls scattered over the United States and their families were summoned to Washington and, on February 14, the Ambassador and his party, 149 persons, sailed from New York on a Danish vessel.

V

Bernstorff was dismissed, the familiar formula, "sever diplomatic relations," was fulfilled. But what next? Germany was going ahead with her unrestricted sinkings, would presumably sink a vessel of ours sooner or later. Our merchant ships were afraid to sail, unless the government would give them arms and gun crews, make them, in the technical phrase, "armed merchant vessels."

There was question whether the President could do this without specific authority from Congress. Wilson

[6a] February 3, 1917.

was indecisive about asking Congress or acting himself, was plainly reluctant to go on in the course that circumstances inexorably summoned him to. At three successive Cabinet meetings, February 6, 9, and 13, and even at subsequent ones, Wilson was unwilling to go as far as most of the Cabinet urged him. McAdoo was emphatic in pressing Wilson to arm the merchant ships, "Congress or no Congress — action, prompt action was demanded — it was no time for hesitation."[7]

McAdoo's emphatic manner and language nettled Wilson. He reproached McAdoo (and also Lane) bitterly, charged them with "appealing to the spirit of the *code duello*." He recited cautious advice that had been given him by a visitor, Governor McCall of Massachusetts, who had warned him to "go slow, the people approved delay for careful consideration, they did not wish precipitate action."

Houston felt the President should be bucked up, gave him a lecture on the need of action, conclusive action. "We could not afford to let Germany intimidate us, or cut England off and crush France — we would be the next. Germany would be the mistress of the world, and her arrogance and ruthlessness would know no bounds."

Yes, replied Wilson, but what, precisely what, should we do? Houston told him: "Go to Congress and go as soon as possible." Ask for authority to arm our merchant ships.

VI

February 26, Wilson went before Congress. He was not, he said, "proposing or contemplating war or any steps that may lead to war." He was merely requesting that Congress give him "the means and authority to

---

[7] "Eight Years with Wilson's Cabinet," David Franklin Houston.

safeguard in practice the rights of a great people, to supply our merchant ships with defensive arms should that become necessary, and with the means of using them, and to employ any other instrumentalities or methods" necessary to protect our ships and people in their rightful pursuits on the sea.

From painting by Marshall, May 31, 1917. Courtesy of the Navy Department.

Sinking of U. S. S. *President Lincoln.*

She was one of the two vessels of the cruiser and transport service to be sunk by submarines. All but 26 aboard her were saved.

In response to Wilson's request a bill was at once introduced authorizing the President to supply arms, ammunition and the means of using them to American merchant ships, and to appropriate for the purpose $100,000,000. Congress proceeded, somewhat leisurely, to debate the measure. There was real opposition. Sentiment against going to war, or doing what might precipitate war, was still strong. There was doubt whether Congress would give Wilson the authority to arm merchant ships.

VII

GERMANY PROPOSES TO GIVE TEXAS BACK TO MEXICO.

On February 24, Wilson, still not sure he could carry Congress and the country into war — indeed, on the contrary, he was quite doubtful whether he could get from Congress even authorization to arm merchant vessels — received a message from Ambassador Page in London. Page said that the British Secret Service had intercepted and decoded a message sent by an Under Secretary of the German Ministry of Foreign Affairs, Alfred Zimmermann, to the German Minister to Mexico. The message read:

We intend to begin on the first of February unrestricted submarine warfare. We shall endeavor in spite of this to keep the United States of America neutral. In the event of this not succeeding, we make Mexico a proposal of alliance on the following basis: make war together, make peace together, generous financial support and an understanding on our part that Mexico is to reconquer her lost territory in Texas, New Mexico, and Arizona. The settlement in detail is left to you. You will inform the President [that is, President Carranza of Mexico] of the above most secretly as soon as the outbreak of war with the United States of America is certain.

To Wilson — as to every one else when it became public — this instruction by the German Government to its ambassador in Mexico seemed so fantastic as to justify suspicion that it might be a hoax. Certainly it was likely that the public would think it must be a hoax. The State Department spent several days verifying the message and getting the original German text — "*Einverstandnis unsererseits dass Mexico in Texas, New Mexico, Arizona früher verlorenes Gebiet zurück erobert.*"

Thus buttressed, Wilson, on February 28, permitted

the Associated Press to print the message. The Senate, astounded, passed a resolution asking the President if the message as published in the newspapers was correct. The President, through the Secretary of State, replied: "I have the honor to state that the government is in pos-

© *Press Publishing Co.*
Germany promising Texas to Mexico.
— *Cassel in the N. Y. Evening World.*

session of evidence which establishes that the note referred to is authentic." Next day came further verification in the shape of an admission volunteered by Zimmermann, that he had sent the note. Naïvely, Zimmermann emphasized that "the instructions were only to be carried out after declaration of war by America" — an explanation doing more credit to Zimmermann's legalism and morals than to his intelligence.

VIII

Stimulated by the Zimmermann note, the Lower House of Congress passed by 403 to 13 the bill for arming merchant ships. In the Senate, opposition was

kept up by 11 Senators, led by LaFollette.[8] With the
end of the session three days away, they filibustered.
(They had the double motive of wanting an extra session
and of opposition to the armed ship resolution.)

Photograph by International News.

Senator Stone of Missouri surrounded by newspaper men following a conference
on the bill for arming American merchant ships.

Early in the morning of March 3 with adjournment
only a few hours away, 75 out of the 96 members ·of
the Senate, angry at the recalcitrant 11, signed a protest:

The undersigned United States Senators favor the passage
of Senate Bill 8322, to authorize the President of the United
States to arm American merchant vessels. . . . Under the

8 The others were:
Democrats: Stone of Missouri; O'Gorman of New York; Kirby of Arkansas;
Lane of Oregon; and Vardaman of Mississippi.
Republicans: Norris of Nebraska; Cummins of Iowa; Gronna of North
Dakota; Clapp of Minnesota; and Works of California.

rules of the Senate, allowing unlimited debate, it now appears to be impossible to obtain a vote prior to noon, March 4, 1917, when the session of Congress expires. We desire this statement entered in the record to establish the fact that the Senate favors the legislation and would pass it if a vote could be obtained.

In a way, the incident was a godsend to Wilson, gave him opportunity for an emotional catharsis. The anger he was not yet ready to express fully against Germany he poured out on the 11 recalcitrant Senators, inventing a phrase that became famous, "a little group of willful men":

In the immediate presence of a crisis unparalleled in the history of the country, . . . Congress has been unable to act either to safeguard the country or to vindicate the elementary rights of its citizens. More than 500 of the 531 members of the two Houses were ready and anxious to act. But the Senate was unable to act because a little group of willful men, representing no opinion but their own, had determined that it should not. [They] have rendered the great government of the United States helpless and contemptible.[9]

The session adjourned with the armed ship resolution not yet passed. But Wilson had seen that Congress and the country favored the proposal. He asked the Attorney-General whether he had power to arm merchant ships without specific authorization by Congress. The Attorney-General — an office which usually finds it legal for a President to do what a President wants to do — told Wilson he had the power. Wilson directed that guns and gunners be placed on merchant ships, and an announcement was made on March 9 that this would be done.

[9] The incident, and Wilson's angry denunciation, had one important effect. Under the pressure of public opinion, on March 8, 1917, the Senate — which never in the whole course of its existence had laid any restraint on the length of debate — adopted a rule providing that whenever two-thirds of the Senate wish a measure brought to a vote, they may so express themselves, and thereafter each Senator may debate the measure not more than one hour. Thus cloture, of a very limited sort, came to the Senate.

IX

By about this time, early March, 1917, Wilson was clear-minded again and confident, knew once more what he wanted to do. His distraction over receiving Germany's announcement of unrestricted submarine warfare had not been timorousness — there was nothing of that in Wilson. His depression and nervousness had been due to the utter disruption of his plan to enter the situation as a neutral and from that vantage-point press down upon the belligerents — not only the belligerents but the world — the kind of peace he had planned. Prospect of going to war, as such, disturbed him some. But taking up the rôle of belligerent put him out of the rôle he had formerly conceived for himself. Since he must fight at all he must fight on to victory. That meant there could not now be the "peace without victory" which had been fundamental in his plan. That mishap to his grandiose plan was the sufficient cause of his distraction and hesitancy throughout February, 1917.

That, and one other cause. Wilson must now modify his plan fundamentally. That is, he must perforce modify his rôle of neutral, though not his plan. Abandonment of his plan he never considered. But change his own rôle he must. He must now be a belligerent against Germany, and in that rôle instead of neutral, must work out the achievement of his plan. The situation involved considerable adjustment within his own mind, and that adjustment, the gestation of his modified plan, was a contributing cause of his February of distraction. There was in Wilson much of the creative artist, and creativeness, pregnance with modification of his plan, was now under way.

In the modification forced upon him, he must now:

(*a*) Take America into the war — and that was not

easy, though Wilson had no doubt he could do it; (*b*) in co-operation with the Allies, crush Germans arms — he had no doubt about that either (though he might have if he had had at this time the information he later received about the success of submarine sinkings); and (*c*) make peace and set up a League of Nations according to his original plan.

That program, arrived at about early March, 1917, constituted the fourth stage in the evolution of Wilson's mind.

Fighting Germany was the new factor. To that, how best to do it, how best to fight Germany and beat Germany thoroughly but at the same time impair himself least for his rôle at the peace-table — upon these and collateral considerations, Wilson now bent his powerful and flexible mind.

14

WAR

Resumption, by Germany, of Unrestricted Submarine Warfare, Resulting in the Sinking of Three Unarmed American Ships, Provides Wilson with a Casus Belli. He Convokes an Extra Session of Congress. Wilson's War Message, Delivered by Him Personally Before an Assembled House and Senate, Gives Rise to a Lofty Emotion. Wilson's Supreme Talent with Words. He Drives a Wedge of Them, Like an Armored Tank, Between the German People and Their Rulers. Wilson's Ideas the Equivalent of Armies.

On March 9, 1917, Wilson, with his plan clear in his mind once more, his vigor renewed, summoned a special session of Congress to meet April 16.

A few days later came news of an overt act by Germany. Three overt acts. Three American vessels — American built, American manned, American owned — the *City of Memphis*, the *Illinois*, and the *Vigilancia* were sunk by U-boats. Dramatically, Wilson advanced by two weeks the special session of Congress; it would meet, he now announced, April 2, "to receive a communication concerning grave matters."

II

To every person present, from members of the Cabinet and Justices of the Supreme Court in the front row, to observers in the remote seats in the gallery, that evening was the most-to-be-remembered of their lives. Years later McAdoo, with a touch of poetry moving even his active and practical mind, recalled, as a detail that stood out in his memory, "the pouring rain, a soft fragrant rain of early spring; the illuminated dome of the Capitol stood in solemn splendor against the dark wet sky."

David F. Houston recalled the tenseness of the occasion, the escort of cavalry who accompanied the President to the Capitol to protect him from possible annoyance by pacifists who had tried to bank themselves around

Photograph by Clinedinst.

Edward D. White, Chief Justice of the Supreme Court.

the approaches to the building. In the hall of the House of Representatives the Supreme Court occupied the most forward seats, chairs placed for this occasion in front of the rostrum in a half-circle, with Chief Justice White in the middle, the remaining Justices to either side of him. Back of the Supreme Court was the Cabinet and back of the Cabinet the diplomats, among them Spring-Rice of Great Britain and Jusserand of France, expectant and happy. In an atmosphere of tense quiet the President began. Secretary Houston "found myself watching Chief Justice White. When the President said 'The present German submarine warfare is a warfare against mankind,' White gave a vigorous nod. He repeated it when the President added, 'It is a war against all nations, the challenge is to all mankind.' When the President said, 'There is one choice we cannot make, we are incapable of making: we will not choose the path of submission,' White, without waiting to hear the rest of the sentence, sprang to his feet, his action a cue for the entire Senate. His face worked almost convulsively. Great tears rolled down his cheeks. From that moment to the end he was vigorously applauding everything."[1]

III

Wilson's Art with Words, His Power with Ideas.

For the task, complex and delicate, that he faced in this speech, Wilson had the best mind in the modern world — and I can think of none better in history.

Wilson knew words, his armory of them was more full and varied than any military arsenal's store of guns and ammunition. No man ever more fully exemplified the adage that the pen is mightier than the sword; and never was the saying more fully proved than by Wilson in this war. Wilson had words that were the equivalent of ten-inch guns, others the equivalent of lances, not omitting yet others that were the equivalent of submarine torpedoes, poison-gas, and tear-bombs. He knew how to choose one word for its driving force, another for an aura of sentiment to excite emotion, another to

[1] Quoted and paraphrased from "Eight Years in Wilson's Cabinet," David Franklin Houston.

Photograph by Underwood & Underwood.

President Wilson delivering his war message to Congress April 2, 1917.

explode like a star-shell and throw light on a situation. Wilson knew not only the meaning of a word, but its aroma, the emotional associations it would summon up. He could think in syllogisms — none better; but he could also think in pictures, and talk in pictures, ideographs. When choosing a word to describe the League of Nations, Wilson dismissed "compact" or "federation" or "alliance," and picked "covenant" — he knew well the moving effect that word would have in the minds of millions of Americans, of the sort whose support Wilson most desired, Americans having Wilson's own association with "covenant" as a religious term.

Wilson knew more than words, he knew clusters of words. He had ideas, did his thinking in terms of ideas, and knew how to transmit his idea from his own mind to the minds of his hearers or readers — with such modifications as Wilson meant the hearers should have. Further than that, and most important in Wilson's art, he knew how to choose words which would suffuse his ideas with emotion.

I once said it must be that Wilson writes his speeches by a formula: he writes out the sense of his speech; that completed he then picks up a salt-cellar containing the word "heart," and sprinkles the manuscript, and another salt-cellar containing a store of "rights," and sprinkles again, and others containing "hold dear's," and similar emotion-provoking, atmosphere-creating words.

That, while much too crude a way of describing a process so refined and intricate, was not inaccurate as a description of the finished product of Wilson's speeches. He knew how to compose what would at once parse for the logicians and at the same time achieve the picture he desired to set up in the minds of the crowd, whose intellectual processes are not those of logic, but rather of vague impressions. Wilson, at the time when he was not yet for preparedness, said that we should not be "thrown off our balance by a war with which we have nothing to do, whose causes cannot touch us. . . ."[2] That sentence will stand up to analysis by the logicians; it is literally true the *causes* of the war could not touch us. But we may assume Wilson knew pretty well that the country, the crowd, would think Wilson had said the *war* could not touch us — and therefore would be content with Wilson's resistance to preparedness.

When, subsequently, Wilson was for preparedness, and when he switched from neutrality to belligerency, and when he switched from the volunteer to the conscription way of raising America's army — after several such switches his critics and adversaries made peevish remarks. Theodore Roosevelt charged him with using "weasel words,"[3] said that "on almost every question President Wilson has occupied at least two almost diametrically opposite positions." James M. Beck declared that Wilson had been "both an extreme conservative and an extreme radical." A jeering quip said that "men when they followed Wilson, complained that they met him coming back." There was much truth in it. But Wilson knew what he was doing. If he made a turning, it was because the forward path had made a turning. That happens not rarely. To change horses crossing a stream is a familiar simile; but sometimes men change streams without changing horses.

Men who do not understand an art, especially a technique of combat or rivalry, are prone to be suspicious of those who are adept in it; they think of the process as some kind of magic, and therefore to be disapproved.

[2] Address to Congress, December 8, 1914.
[3] Homely American figure of speech for words which suck the meat from words ahead of them; the analogy arises from the weasel's habit of sucking eggs.

Men who use words as bludgeons are often disturbed, made distrustful by those who use words as rapiers. Blunt Grover Cleveland, after some encounters with Wilson, called him "intellectually dishonest." But Cleveland was more fair and more accurate when, as Wilson was running for President with an issue he slo-ganized as "The New Freedom," Cleveland said: "Sounds fine — wonder what it means." Wilson was not using that battle-cry primarily for its meaning; what he was seeking in that particular phrase was atmosphere, the evocation of emotion. He knew how the average man would be moved by those words — and he won the election. Once, Wilson himself, speaking of the art of dialectic that can be picked up by long experience, in a university faculty, paid tribute to the skill of college politicians compared with political politicians. The political politician, Wilson said, "always follows the same rules," consequently, "you always know what he is going to do." But "a college politician should not be mentioned in the same breath; he is shrewd — you never know what he is going to do, and I have been dealing with him for the past thirty years. He has the gift of speech and can make black look like white. . . ."[4]

No doubt Wilson knew how to "make black look like white" — but if he did he was too intelligent to attempt it. What Wilson knew was that things are rarely either all white or all black — nine times out of ten the truth is a mixture of both, gray. And what Wilson could do with words was to achieve the grayness (or whatever other color he desired). Roosevelt said that Wilson's sentences were "deliberately involved," and they were, just that. Wilson knew what qualifying word to insert, and where to insert it, so as to make on the hearer or reader the precise impression Wilson intended. And if

[4] "The True Story of Woodrow Wilson," David Lawrence.

the qualifying word which reduces inaccurate "black" to accurate "gray," the qualifying word used to achieve an exact picture — if such words are "weasel words," let Theodore Roosevelt call them that and make the best of it. The fact is, in all the combats, intellectual, literary, and political, in which Wilson and Roosevelt engaged, Wilson did not come out second best.

Rarely in any polemic combat did Wilson come out second best. Knowing the art of dialectic fencing, he knew you are not called on to reply to more than your opponent asserts, that you must not broaden the issue and therefore expose yourself. If a debater, because he has less skill in dialectics, or through ignorance of facts, makes the issue narrow to his own disadvantage, the respondent is not called upon to present him with advantage by broadening the issue. During the 1916 campaign, Senator Henry Cabot Lodge charged that Wilson's early *Lusitania* note had been qualified with a hint that Germany need not take it too seriously. Lodge had got hold, in an incomplete way, of the fact that Bryan had composed and that Wilson had been on the verge of signing a "supplementary note" softening the original. Had Lodge known all the facts (see Ch. 6 of this history) he could, in the fever of the campaign, have damaged Wilson seriously. But Wilson was able to reply, "No postscript or amendment of the *Lusitania* note was ever contemplated by me." Wilson's safeguard lay in the words "by me." Wilson added, "The public is in possession of everything that was said to Germany." That was true, and was sufficient to rebut Lodge's charge — but it was a fact that Wilson, on Bryan's suggestion, had been about to sign a supplementary note. Had Lodge "worded his accusation in a slightly different fashion, it would have been impossible to deny."[4a]

4a Quoted from "The True Story of Woodrow Wilson," David Lawrence.

To say that Wilson was superbly a man of skill in words[4b] is not to demean him. The common assumption that words are the antithesis to deeds, that words exclude deeds, is quite wrong. Wilson was a master of words — and during some four years Wilson's words inspired more deeds than any other force then moving the world. Wilson's words took some twenty-two million Americans to register for war, and sent some two million of them to France. Wilson's words — but the tale of what Wilson's words and ideas inspired is the history of America's participation in the war, and thereafter for some years the history of the whole world. Roosevelt, hating Wilson, baffled and irritated by Wilson's subtlety with words, said that "Mr. Wilson has been President when the urgent need of the nation has been for action; he has met the need purely by elocution." But in due course Wilson's elocution took America into the war, inspired millions of men to fight, and moved the world as no other man of his time.

"Wilson had a first-class mind in the beginning. He tempered it until it became a tool of absolute precision with an ever-cutting edge. . . . Essentially, he had become a master of thinking processes; not merely of the purely meditative process, but of decisive, incisive method, as well. He so comprehended the formulæ of abstract logic that they became instant and unerring tests of every proposition he encountered. In this development of his intellect, words became more than mere symbols of ideas; in his thinking, they represented also the groups of ideas which the words connoted. He be-

[4b] "The simple, factual, colorless [truth is] that Mr. Wilson deals in words, spends his time, his life, with words; is what he is, and does what he does, by the instrumentality of words. What he has accomplished — and his has been a wonderful record of accomplishment — has been accomplished through statement, argument, appeal. His scepter is his — pen; his sword is his — tongue; his realm is that of — Words." — "The Story of a Style," William Bayard Hale.

came, in fact, a connoisseur of words and an adept in *double-entendre*."[5]

Double-entendre, not in the common sense, but in the sense that every word or phrase has at least two connotations (as I am here saying "double-entendre" has). Wilson knew them all, knew the varying ways in which words would strike the ears of different listeners, the differing emotions they would evoke. All that he knew, and this knowledge, with other qualities, made him the master dialectician of the age. Made him more than that. Wilson's command of ideas and the expression of ideas, his exercise of them in the speech he now delivered, made him the master strategist of the war. The testimony comes from, among others, Ludendorff: "While Germany's armies were victorious in the field of battle, she failed in the fight of intellects against the enemy peoples."

IV

Wilson's War Speech

What had caused Wilson's speech of two months before (to the Senate proposing to dictate peace to both belligerents and set up a League of Nations[5a]) to be described in superlatives, was mainly the sensational quality of his proposal, the audacity of it. The speech he now made, calling on Congress to declare war against Germany, better deserved the superlatives. It was great in many ways, had several different arts compressed into it; was obliged to include several different purposes, including the not too easy task of taking America into the war, which involved persuading or otherwise moving an only half-willing Congress and country. The speech

[5] The quoted passage is from "Wilson the Unknown," by Wells Wells (a pseudonym).
[5a] See Chapter 12.

contained many phrases destined to become historic:
"vessels ruthlessly sent to the bottom without warning
and without thought of help or mercy for those on
board" . . . "reckless lack of compassion or of principle" . . . "It is a war against all nations" . . . "The
challenge is to all mankind" . . . "the rights and lib-
erties of small nations" . . . "The world must be made
safe for democracy."

v

The outstanding quality of Wilson's war speech was a
new and subtle feature of his plan as a whole, which he
now injected.

He would, as a master detail of strategy, military no
less than dialectic, drive a wedge between the German
Government and the German people. Actually he
would, though adroitly yet no less forcefully — and as
it turned out, successfully — solicit the German people
and German army to turn against their government.[6]
Holding out amity toward the German people (as distinguished from their government) would at once help
Wilson win the war, and later cause the demoralized
Germany which Wilson envisaged, to be sympathetic to
his plan for a League of Nations.

It was, as an agency for victory and for Wilson's
larger purpose, superb strategy; from the point of view
of the enemy it was outrageous, the sort of thing that
often caused Wilson's adversaries in politics, national or
college, to charge him with polemic *diablerie*.

In his speech, in his very first allusion, he spoke of
the enemy he was about to fight as "the Government of

[6] In the original draft of the speech, Wilson put his solicitation in plain words.
"Until the German people have a government we can trust." This phrase,
House persuaded Wilson to omit, House thinking "it looked too much like in-
citing revolution."—"Intimate Papers of Colonel House."

the German Empire." America's purpose would be "to bring the Government of the German Empire to terms and" — here, as the concluding clause of his sentence, he used words which he knew would sound well to the war-sick part of the German population — "and end the war."

Having dropped this verbal depth-bomb he receded, dealt for several paragraphs with other matters. With little dialectic forays he came back from time to time to his subtle purpose, dropped phrases like "Prussian autocracy," "dynasties," "rulers," "autocratic govern-

New York Tribune

First to Last — the Truth: News · Editorials · Advertisements

5,706   (Copyright 1917— The Tribune Ass'n.)   TUESDAY, APRIL 3, 1917

The President Calls for War Without Hate

ments." What he proposed to fight against was "autocratic governments backed by organized force which is controlled wholly by their will, not by the will of their people."

In a passage thoroughly Wilsonian, serving his purpose of stirring America to fight by citing German plots, intrigues, and crimes committed within the United States, he cunningly served his other purpose by adding that these crimes were committed only by the German Government — "their source lay, not in any hostile feeling or purpose of the German people who were, no doubt, ignorant of them."

In due course he became explicit, drove the wedge like a military tank between Kaiser and people, held out the olive branch in plain sight before the German people:

We have no quarrel with the German people. We have no feeling towards them but one of sympathy and friendship. It was not upon their impulse that their government acted in entering this war.... [The war was] provoked and waged in the interest of dynasties accustomed to use their fellow-men as pawns and tools.... We are, let me say again, the sincere friends of the German people.

Wilson forging the sword with which he was going to do battle.
— *Morris, in Puck.*

Holding out concrete assurance, he told the German people that, "We seek no indemnities . . . no material compensation; we desire no conquest, no dominion. We have no selfish ends to serve. . . ."

Finally, with magnificent combination of subtlety and audacity, he held out solicitation to the German people to turn from the Kaiser to Wilson himself, no less! Alluding to his major purpose, a League of Nations, a "concert for peace," the "ultimate peace of the world," he promised "the liberation of [all] peoples, the German peoples included."

But the masterpiece of Wilsonian art lay quite unnoticed in the concluding four words of his speech. Departing from overt allusion to Germany, dealing with the decision America must make, the path America must follow, he built up an eloquent, moving peroration, ending: "God helping her, she can do no other."

Probably not one of a hundred of his American hearers recognized that paraphrase of Martin Luther's declaration, immortal to every German Lutheran, "Ich kann nicht anders" (I can do no other). And Germans, in America as well as Germany, who felt the sentimental pull of it, did not recognize the Wilsonian art cf it.[7]

[7] There is a distant similarity between this ending of Wilson's speech, and the ending William Jennings Bryan contrived for his Cross of Gold speech. Both used the same device, both achieved a religious flavor and both did it by indirection. Bryan, using the technique more crudely than Wilson, managed to evoke religious associations, not by quoting the Bible directly but by paraphrasing it. "You shall not press down upon the brow of labor this crown of thorns, you shall not crucify mankind upon a cross of gold." Both Bryan and Wilson had art with words; but Bryan's was to Wilson's as a meat-axe is to a stiletto.

V

Against hostile armies, Germany had prepared well; soldier for soldier she was at all times superior. She was now to face a foe who fought with ideas. Ideas more dynamically explosive, more subversive to the German military machine than all the shells the Allies ever fired.

15

CONSCRIPTION

Realization Comes, Belatedly, That a Declaration of War
Against Germany Means That Some One Must Shoulder
a Rifle. American Traditions and Sentiment Are for a
Voluntary Force, but Wilson, Siding with the Army Chiefs,
Decides for Conscription. To Bring the Country to Ac-
cept the Draft Wilson and Baker Prepare Shrewd Plans.

VAGUELY, but only vaguely as yet, America realized
that war on Germany involved something more grim
than the thrill of hearing the declaration. Somebody
must fight the war. A number of young men would be
glad to — about the proportion that in any war would
volunteer, the adventurous, the romantic, those who
found their ordinary life dull, those having associations
they would be glad to get away from, those without
jobs, those who preferred the routine of military life
above the self-responsibility of civil life — in any country in any time there is always a ratio who will volunteer
in any war. In America at this time the proportion to
volunteer would be smaller than normal, for nearly three
years of watching the Western front had brought realization that war under modern conditions meant hard-
ship, dirt and death,[1] and very little glamour or romance.
As for economic motive, there was none; every man in
America who wanted a job could have one, and at high
wages — America was furiously busy turning out munitions for the Allies. Moreover, of those who would
normally volunteer, a considerable proportion had already gone forward. A few, the most dashing, had gone

[1] "By 1917 the glory had passed from war. Young men saw soldiering as a
cruel duty rather than as a sport."—"Newton D. Baker, America at War," by
Frederick Palmer.

early in the war to Canada, and managed to get into the fighting. Many had enlisted in our own Regular Army or Navy or National Guard in the moderate expansion which Congress had authorized at Wilson's request a year before. Those volunteer enlistments had been slow.

Photograph by Underwood & Underwood.

Americans living in Paris, in the early days of the war, organized a volunteer regiment to fight with the French. The photograph shows recruits off to camp.

It was not likely that a call for volunteers to fight Germany would bring numbers adequate for this major war. There must be conscription, but art would be needed to lead the country to accept it, an art with which both President Wilson and Secretary Baker were exceptionally endowed.

II

Wilson personally did not like conscription, he preferred the spirit of volunteering. In his early discussions of preparedness he had emphasized the volunteer system, and his faith in it:

I have been asked by questioning friends, whether I thought a sufficient number of men would volunteer for the training or not. Why, if they did not, it is not the America that you and I know; something has happened. If they did not do it, I should be ashamed of America. I am sorry for the skeptics who believe that the response would not be tremendous; not grudging, but overflowing in its abundant strength.[2]

Not only had Wilson been, by temperament and conviction, personally unsympathetic to conscription. He knew that America as a whole did not like it — indeed it never occurred to the masses of the country that conscription would be attempted. Conscription, in the American mind, was associated with autocracy. Never in any war of ours had conscription been suggested at the outset; only once had it been tried at all, and when, after two years of the Civil War, an attempt had been made to draft, rioting mobs in New York had sacked the provost marshal's office, burned and smashed the wheels and lists and the other paraphernalia for taking Americans to war against their wills. In this war, not only would there be the usual American repugnance; further, 13 per cent of our people were of German birth or descent, and a considerable percentage more were of peoples embraced in the Austrian Empire. In the war in Europe so far, the precedent we most respected had been against conscription — Britain had relied on volunteers for the first eighteen months, her government unwilling or afraid to attempt conscription.

All this Wilson knew. But Germany had flouted him and America; he had a high purpose in which, since Germany had forced him to it, crushing of German

2 From Wilson's preparedness speech at Chicago, January 31, 1916. Wilson was speaking of a volunteer system for building up the regular army through two months of training each year for three years.

Leslie's Weekly.

The fact that an attempt at a draft during the Civil War had led to riots in New York caused Secretary of War Baker and President Wilson and the Army heads to be apprehensive and to be careful in the methods they used to bring about conscription for the Great War.

The 1917 Draft begins. Men waiting to register in down-town New York. Our Allies in the war were astonished at the speed and orderliness with which America's draft army was raised.

arms was now the first and indispensable step. Wilson could be hard; "like most reformers," said Doctor Charles W. Eliot, "Wilson had a fierce and unlovely side."

III

Wilson's decision to conscript America was made before he called on Congress to declare war, and more than two months before Congress passed the Act that legalized the draft. By agreement,[3] kept secret, of Wilson, Secretary of War Baker, and Judge Advocate General (later Provost-Marshal) Enoch H. Crowder, the colossal machinery for enforcing the draft was set up and made ready long before the country knew[4] there would be a draft — while, indeed, the country continued to take it for granted that only the volunteer system would be used.

Anticipating that the country would be shocked, that it might refuse to submit to conscription, a procedure was devised that would be least offensive to the people, that would indeed give the process to some extent the color of volunteering. The direct act of taking young men from their homes would not be done by army officers in uniform; the process would be carried out by civilians, so far as possible by neighbors of the conscripted man. "Instead of having soldiers . . . ride the country side going from door to door and listing men of

[3] The genealogy of the Draft Act, according to Frederick Palmer's biography of Newton D. Baker, began with recommendations by Generals Leonard Wood and Hugh Scott, the latter Chief of Staff during the period preceding our entry into the Great War. These recommendations convinced Baker. Baker took the recommendations to Wilson and, with these and his own arguments, convinced Wilson. The bill was written by conferences in which the participants were Generals Scott, Tasker H. Bliss, Crowder, McCain, and other army officers— "Newton D. Baker, America at War," by Frederick Palmer.

[4] "Six weeks before the enactment of the Selective Service bill, the plans for its execution had been formulated in minute detail." Provost-Marshal Enoch H. Crowder in "The Spirit of Selective Service."

draft age"[5] the draft would be made to appear "like going to the polls to vote."[5] The order, so soon as, and if, Congress should pass the Act, would be that all men of draft age register at the place in the local precinct where it was their custom to vote. Out of those thus

© *Underwood & Underwood.*

General Enoch H. Crowder.

registered — it would be all of draft age — local civilian officials would pick the ones to be turned over to the army for service, would say who was exempt, who must go. The process would be one, not of the army walking into the draftee's home, but of civilian officials, mainly neighbors, delivering the draftee to the army. It would be supervised by civilian sheriffs and governors, officials holding their offices by popular vote. But the draftee would reach the army just as surely as if the army had come and taken him.

[5] "Newton D. Baker, America at War," Frederick Palmer.

This depriving the draft of the appearance of compulsion, but at the same time getting the advantage of compulsion, is attributed to Secretary of War Baker.[6] Baker, like Wilson, knew the importance of appearances, had much of Wilson's skill with words. Both had exceptional understanding of the art of causing popular psychology to be what they wished it to be.

In the same spirit, it was decided to have the draft machinery ready to start in motion the day when Congress should pass the act. Setting up of the immense mechanism would consume two months — and two months between public knowledge of the intention to draft, and actual drafting, might provide time for resistance to generate.

Baker, before Congress had passed the Draft Act, before it had appropriated the money for what he was about to do — indeed with care to prevent Congress from knowing — Baker, acting through General Crowder and he through Major Hugh S. Johnson, arranged with the head of the Government Printing Office, to print secretly the more than ten million blanks that would be required to put the draft in effect when and if Congress should enact it. To the Public Printer, secrecy was easy; it was an ordinary incident of his duty in printing advance copies of Presidents' messages and Supreme Court decisions. He went ahead with printing the blanks, wrapping and sealing them. He "did not realize how much space the millions of forms would occupy; the corridors were so full he had to find storage elsewhere; the local Washington postmaster now became a conspirator; soon the cellar of the city post office was stacked to the ceiling. Still no word of the operation reached the public or Congress."[7]

[6] By his friendly biographer, Frederick Palmer.
[7] Quoted from "Newton D. Baker, America at War," by Frederick Palmer.

Then Baker, April 23, wrote a confidential letter to every State governor: "The President desires [not directs[8]] that I bring to your attention the following con-

Newton D. Baker, Secretary of War, from the official portrait preserved in the War Department.

siderations which he is not at present ready to give to the press. . . ."

In the letter Baker explained to the governors the secret preparations being made for the draft, and asked them to be ready to co-operate, so soon as Congress should pass this Act. "Then all the sheriffs of the

[8] This precision in words, subtlety in psychology, was at once Bakerian and Wilsonian.

land were taken into confidence; to each was mailed his quota of blanks, accompanied by a slip saying that it was a matter of urgent government secrecy that there be no mention of their existence until the word of release came from Washington."[9] Every sheriff kept the secret.[10] After the sheriffs, the men chosen to compose the local draft boards were secretly notified and "eagerly awaited the signal."[11]

IV

All this was before Congress had passed the Draft Act, before it was certain they would. The opposition was strong; Congress knew the country would not like the draft, and Congress reflected the country. Wilson, in his request for the Act, used words designed to rob it, in appearance, of some of its unpalatability: "The necessary men will be secured . . . by volunteering as at present, until . . . a resort to a selective draft is desirable." Congressmen who were friends of the measure sought further camouflage. Representative Richard Olney of Massachusetts observed that "the words 'draft' and 'conscription' are rather unpopular," and suggested the wording of the bill be altered to say, "personal obligation to service." Congressman John Q. Tilson of Connecticut asked Baker if there was not "something to be said in favor of accepting a system, volunteering, that is known to be bad, inefficacious and inadequate, rather than to create the effect which might be created by a very unpopular measure."

In the public debate on the floor of House and Senate,

[9] Quoted from "Newton D. Baker, America at War," by Frederick Palmer.

[10] Major Hugh Johnson, later Brigadier-General retired, recalled in 1933 that in all this immense, widespread and essentially sensational enterprise, only one newspaper, a Philadelphia one, learned of what was going on.

[11] Quoted from "Newton D. Baker, America at War," by Frederick Palmer.

opponents of the draft used the harshest words: "Prussianize America" . . . "destroy democracy at home

The dispute as to whether the war should be carried on by the volunteer system or by universal conscription was pictured by J. N. Darling in the Des Moines *Register,* April 11, 1917. With irritation he pictures Congress as a volunteer fireman throwing the children (sound measures) out the window while carefully carrying the feather bed down the ladder.

while fighting for it abroad" . . . "a sulky, unwilling, indifferent army" . . . "abject or involuntary servitude" . . . "un-American" . . . "conscription makes the term 'sovereign citizen' irony" . . . "conscription is another name for slavery" . . . "rioting all over the United States will add more joy to the German heart." Champ Clark, Democratic Speaker of the House, said: "I protest with all my heart and mind and soul against having the slur of being a conscript placed upon the men of Missouri; in the estimation of Missourians there is precious little difference between a conscript and a convict."[12]

Chairman Dent of the House Military Affairs Committee declined to introduce the draft bill; a majority of the committee were opposed to it. Wilson, sending for the House leaders, informed them that he would not "yield an inch of any essential part of the programme for raising an army by conscription." A Congressman friend of Provost-Marshal Crowder warned him, "Your name will become the most odious in America." Senator Reed of Missouri said to Baker, "You will have the streets of our American cities running red with blood on Registration day." But Baker knew his art and went on with his plan for robbing the draft of its unpalatability.

The bill passed and was signed by the President May 18. "The singularly brief act delegated to the President more power than any of his predecessors had been granted over the lives and destinies of their fellow-citizens."[13]

V

Meanwhile, May 1, sixteen days before Congress acted, Baker, carrying out his project of making the draft seem what he conceived[14] it, rather than what the

---

[12] *Congressional Record,* April 25, 1917.

[13] Quoted from "Newton D. Baker, America at War," by Frederick Palmer.

[14] Baker made a distinction between conscription practised by some other countries and conscription practised by the United States. "Militarism," he wrote, "is . . . the designation given to a selfish or ambitious political system which uses arms as a means of accomplishing its objects. The mobilization and arming of a democracy in defense of the principles on which it is founded, and in vindication of the common rights of man, is an entirely different thing."

BACZNOŚĆ!

REGISTRACYA WE WTOREK, 5. CZERWCA

Każdy mezczyzna od roku 21. do 31. roku zycia czy obywatel czy nie obywatel stanow Zjedno czonych, musi sie dac wpisac do registru w swojej wardzie, we wtorek, 5. czerwca.

Registracya we nie przemus- za do sluzby wojskowej, do sluzby wojskowej tylko pozem- usza sie obywateli stanow Zjednoczonych.

ATTENTION

Register Tuesday, June 5th

On Tuesday, June 5th, every male between the ages of 21 years and 31 years, whether a citizen of the United States or not a citizen of the United States, must register at the nearest voting place in his ward.

Registration does not mean liability to military service un- less you are a citizen of the United States or have taken out first citizen papers.

ATTENZIONE

Il giorno della registrazione avrá luogo il giorno 5 corrente mese ogni Uomo della etá di 21 a 31 anni cittadino o non cittadino sono obbligato a registrarsi al piú vicino quar- tiere di registrazione.

Registrare non significa servizio militare, Seprima non si é cittadino Americano, o almeno abbia la prima carta.

REGISTRIEREN SIE DIENSTAGD 5. JUNI

Dienstag, den 5. Juni, muss jeder Mann zwischen den Jahren 21 und 31 registrieren, ob er ein Bürger der Vereinig- ten Staaten ist oder nicht. Dies muss man in der Wahl- bude tun, die in seiner Ward ist.

Dies bedeutet nicht, dass man Soldat fuer den Krieg werden muss, nur dann muss man dienen man ein Bürger der Vereinigten Staaten ist oder seine ersten Papiere heraus- genommen hat.

Kein Deutscher ist gezwun- gen, Soldat zu werden.

The official notices of registration were printed not only in English but in prac- tically all the foreign languages used by immigrant groups in the United States.

public felt it to be, described to Wilson some of his plans:

I am exceedingly anxious to have the registration and selection by draft . . . conducted under such circumstances as to create a strong patriotic feeling and relieve as far as possible the prejudice which remains to some extent in the popular mind against the draft. With this end in view, I am using a vast number of agencies throughout the country to make the day of registration a festival and patriotic occasion. Several Governors and some mayors of cities are entering already heartily into this plan, and the Chamber of Commerce of the United States is taking it up through its affiliated bodies.

"As a part of this programme," Baker added, to Wilson, "I am anxious to have you issue a proclamation when you sign the bill, and I submit herewith a draft for your revision."

The proclamation, written by Baker, modified slightly by Wilson and then signed, was shrewdly designed to create an intended atmosphere. As published in many papers it was captioned "Call to Arms" and surrounded with a border of American flags. Its paragraphs began with "**Whereas,**" and "**Now, Therefore,**" and "**In Witness Whereof,**" in the Gothic type associated with religion and legal documents. Wilson's phrases were carefully composed to bear out the lofty atmosphere:

Now, Therefore, I, Woodrow Wilson, President of the United States, do proclaim and give notice to all persons . . . and I do charge . . . the day here named is the time upon which all shall present themselves. . . . It is essential that the day be approached in thoughtful apprehension of its significance and that we accord to it the honor and the meaning that it deserves. . . . Carried in all our hearts as a great day of patriotic devotion and obligation, when the duty shall lie upon every man to see to it that the name of every male person of the designated ages is written on these lists of honor. . . .

In Witness Whereof, I have hereunto set my hand and caused the seal of the United States to be affixed. Done at the City of Washington this 18th day of May in the year of our Lord one thousand nine hundred and seventeen, and of the in-

U. S. Army Signal Corps Photograph.

The drafted men were made heroes over night. This photograph pictures a banquet given in Seattle for draftees just before their departure for Camp Lewis.

dependence of the United States of America the one hundred and forty-first.

By the President: WOODROW WILSON.

That proclamation brought the war home to America — literally "home," for it was to the homes that its meaning went.

Within the aura of lofty phrasing, the grim fact that every one sought and many disliked to find, was that on June 5, 1917, between 7 A.M. and 7 P.M. every American male between the ages of 21 and 30 (inclusive)[15] must register; and the registration was surrender of their persons to the government. So far as they and their families were dismayed or sullen, expression of individ-

Another plan gone wrong! The success of the draft registration.
— *Marcus, in The Times, July, 1917.*

ual feeling was kept down by the success of Wilson and Baker in "turning of registration day into a joyous pilgrimage. . . . The sweep of public opinion smothered

[15] By two subsequent acts the age limit was extended to take in all between 18 and 45.

critical questioning. The cozening glove concealed the reminder of the steel gauntlet to enforce the penalty for failure to register."[16] Beneath the lofty phrases designed to evoke a national spirit of patriotic exaltation, lay iron words informing the individual that the penalty of fleeing from the draft was imprisonment for one year.

But if the youth, taking his way to the registration place along the mountain roads of West Virginia or the city streets of New York, had any sullenness, it was dissipated in most cases by finding shortly that Baker's art had made him, unexpectedly, a hero. Presently, under the influence of the national spirit, he began to believe it. Speeches from the mayor, the clergyman, and the Chamber of Commerce head; congratulations by star-eyed committees of women, more intimate attentions from young girls, turned most of the draftees to feeling the war would be a grand adventure.[17]

[16] Quoted from "Newton D. Baker, America at War," by Frederick Palmer.

[17] The method by which the draft was brought about, this use of immense organized propaganda by government to make the public mind receptive to what the government planned to do, coupled with elaborate, secret, advance preparation of a mechanism which should put the draft in effect, without delay that might permit opposition to generate—this was a new thing in America. Essentially it was a process of causing the mass of the public to move in a direction in which the government wished them to go, a direction which the public, if left alone, would not take. The technique included, as a principle or as a condition that arose in practice, exercise of pressure by the majority to compel the minority to conform. In the case of the draft, any who attempted dissent were called "slackers," and subjected to odium by the public as well as to formal punishment by the government.

The device, starting with the draft, was used, with variations, again and again during the war, in drives to sell "Liberty Bonds," in compulsion of business to conform to regulations laid down by the War Industries Board, in requirement of dealers in food to follow regulations laid down by the Food Administration.

The close of the war brought an end to the use of organized propaganda by the government to bring about mass movements. For some fifteen years it lapsed. In 1933, the technique was revived to cause the country to accept a new relation between government and business, called the National Recovery Act. (Abbreviated to N. R. A., and symbolized by a Blue Eagle.) On this occasion, as during the war, the process included compulsion exercised by the majority upon the minority. The majority who accepted N. R. A. agreed to exclude from their patronage the minority who did not. The technique of N. R. A. in 1933 was a duplicate of that of conscription in 1917. The General Johnson who administered N. R. A. in 1933 was the same man who as Major Johnson had managed preparation for the draft in 1917.

16

"YOU'RE IN THE ARMY NOW"

Which in Some Respects Was Like a Reaping-Machine,
Gleaning from the Whole Country, from Every Family,
All the Males Between 21 and 31. And Which, in Its Later
Operations, Was Like a Threshing-Machine, Winnowing the
Wheat from the Chaff. Some Grains Which Escaped, and
Some Others Which Became Entangled in the Machine.
Together with a Picture of Life in the Cantonments. And
Also Some Statistics about Slackers, Including an Enter-
taining Narrative about the Arch-Slacker of All. The
"Conscientious Objectors," the Attitude of the Government
Toward Them, and What Happened to One of Them.

WILSON's proclamation had set June 5, 1917, as Registration Day. Baker's wide-flung, high-powered propaganda campaign to make the day a "festival and patriotic
occasion . . ."[1] had succeeded in stirring up a national
sentiment which dispelled or intimidated any remaining
reluctance to accept the draft. To the polling places went
nearly 10,000,000 young men, the very heart of the
country's vitality, a cross-section of its variety — ore-
passers in Ashtabula, lumbermen in Bangor, cow-punch-
ers in Cheyenne, cotton-farmers in Dallas, miners in
Leadville, shoe-workers in Lynn, sophomores in New
Haven, grocery-clerks in Syracuse, apple-growers in
Walla-Walla, city boys from Third Avenue, country boys
from Main Street and Bear Notch, youths white, black,
and of alien birth, every type and condition of man between twenty-one and thirty-one to be found in the country. Each set down the data required of him: his name,
address, age, physical features, occupation, and reason, if

[1] See Chapter 15.

Registering in a district where many of the registrants were Chinese born.

any, for claim of exemption.[2] Each received the small green card certifying his registration. Without disturbance anywhere, almost one male out of every five in the country had shown his readiness to be tested for the Army.

Now from these 10,000,000 men the Government wanted 687,000 soldiers at once. This quota must be chosen from among those physically fit and without need of exemption. The Provost-Marshal decided upon a lot-

[2] Exemptions provided in the First Draft were: officers and men in the Army, Navy, and Marine Corps; officers of National and State governments; county and municipal officers not replaceable by appointment; subjects of Germany and all other aliens without first citizenship papers; ministers and theological students; pilots and mariners; employees of armories, arsenals, Navy Yards, and the Postal service; felons; *bona fide* members of religious sects whose creeds forbade war; and men with genuine dependents.—First Report of the Provost-Marshal General, December 20, 1917.

tery as the fairest method. It worked in this way: the names on the registration list of each of the 4500 Local Boards had been numbered serially beginning with 1; hence a single lottery to draw as many numbers as there were men in the largest list of any Local Board (this was found to be 10,500) would determine the order of liability among the men on every list in the country.

Then, at Washington on the morning of July 20, 1917, a distinguished group of officials, Senators, Representatives, and high Army officers gathered in the public-hearing room of the Senate Office Building around a large glass bowl containing 10,500 black capsules with numbered slips inside. Rarely has human eye been so privileged to see fate engaged in concrete functioning, the gods of the machine in operation. The gods, for once, made a formal ceremony of their distribution of destinies. Secretary of War Baker was to draw out the first capsule. Senator George Chamberlain[3] of Oregon, next in hierarchical order, was to draw the second, Representative S. Hubert Dent[4] of Alabama the third, Senator Warren[5] of Wyoming the fourth, and so on through a long list of minor gods.

At 9:49 A.M. Secretary of War Baker, blindfolded, put in his hand and drew out a capsule — it was number 258. Flash powder boomed, cameras clicked, reporters sprang for the door. By telephone and telegraph the number "258" sped over the country to waiting newspaper presses, to stock tickers, to crowds standing before the bulletin boards of Draft offices. In each of 4500 local villages and precincts man number 258 was chosen

---

[3] Chairman of the Senate Committee on Military Affairs.

[4] Chairman of the House Committee on Military Affairs.

[5] Francis E. Warren, ranking Republican member of the Senate Committee on Military Affairs.

to fight — he had now to go to camp or show cause why he should be exempt.

The lottery went on until after two the following morning; one blindfolded man took out the capsules, three tellers verified the number, and six tallymen re-

Photograph from U. S. Army Signal Corps.

Secretary of War Baker drawing the first number of the draft lottery.

corded the list, one on a large blackboard which was photographed and reproduced on front pages everywhere. That day there was more excitement throughout the country than on the day of declaring war, for the lottery told each registrant how close he was to battle. War in general had become war personally.

Immediately the local Draft Boards swung into action. White post-cards summoned men for physical examination; thousands of doctors tapped chests, scratched abdomens with a wooden stick, commanded "Say 'ah' ", and culled out the myopia, dipsomania, barbers' itch, flat feet, and such other marks of the less-than-perfect man as the Surgeon General directed. In the national average about 70% qualified physically. Then the men who had passed

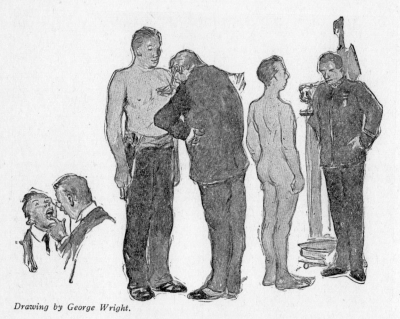

Drawing by George Wright.

Physical examination of promising types.

this test were given seven days in which to file claim of exemption; if this was approved by the Local Board or by an appeal authority, out went a white post-card; if this was not approved a green post-card gave final notice of selection for service. When a Local Board had filled its quota and received word to collect its "draftees" the men selected were given orders by pink post-card to report for entrainment. The red tape, even if indispensable, was almost overwhelming; there were printed forms of a thousand kinds: claims and certificates of exemption, affidavits for every type of claim, notices of classification,

Order of Induction into Military Service of the United States.

THE PRESIDENT OF THE UNITED STATES,

To *William E.*   *O'Shea*
    (Christian name.)   (Surname.)

Order Number *434 D*   Serial Number *1658*

Greeting: *Having submitted yourself to a local board composed of your neighbors for the purpose of determining the place and time in which you can best serve the United States in the present emergency, you are hereby notified that you have now been selected for immediate military service.*

You will, therefore, report to the local board named below
at *509 Und Bldg NC*   , at *10 A* m.,
      (Place of reporting.)   (Hour of reporting.)
on the *8th* day of *Nov.*, 19 *18*,
for military duty.

From and after the day and hour just named you will be a soldier in the military service of the United States.

_____

Member of Local Board for _____

Report to Local Board for   Major U. S. Army
Director of the Draft in the
District of Columbia

Date *11/7/18*

(The term "military service" shall be held to include naval service, including service in the Marine Corps, except where such construction would be unreasonable.—Sec. 1, S. S. R.)
P. M. G. O. FORM 1028. (See Sec. 157, S. S. R.)   3—5115

summonses, discharges, and quota and report sheets; every step in regard to every man was told him by form, filed in the local office by form, reported by form to the Adjutant General of the State and to the Provost-Marshal in Washington — ten million young Americans became men whose fates, and much of the details of their daily actions, were determined by colored cards dealt out by the government at Washington. The work was done with surprising speed. By the end of July, one of the men bearing the number 258, the first selected, had already been examined, inducted, and had reported for duty at Washington Barracks. Working night and day, the Boards heard and disposed of a million cases in one month, and by September 1 they had provided more "draftees" than the Army could take. By December 15, 516,000 men had been sent to camp.

Throughout the process human incidents were first page news, revealing glimpses of the ten million stories that lay beneath the Draft. . . . A man in Mississippi wired Secretary of War Baker: "Thanks for drawing 258 — that's me!"[6] . . . A peanut concessionaire at the Polo Grounds in New York, also number 258, declared before admiring reporters that he'd never smoked nor drank in his life, was ready and fit to go.[7] . . . On a single day, July 31, in the New York Municipal Marriage Chapel 164 marriages had been performed by early afternoon — the usual daily average was 15 or 16. The Provost-Marshal's office, taking notice of the extraordinary activity in the marriage market, burst the boom, phoning from Washington that marriage was of itself no ground for exemption, that evasion of the Draft was a misdemeanor. Reporters, questioning those in the queue, found that 39 out of 50 prospective bridegrooms had been summoned in the Draft, and that 35 out of 50 of the prospective brides were self-supporting, which led a United States Marshal to "forbid the banns" of all men with registration cards. The deputy clerk thought it rather a pity — he had got the ceremony down to sixty

[6] *Literary Digest,* August 4, 1917.   [7] New York *Tribune,* July 21, 1917.

seconds[8] . . . In two Oklahoma counties, bands of ten-ant-farmers, negroes, and Indians rioted, protesting the Draft. Sheriffs chased them into the hills.[9] Small disturbances occurred among some mountaineers in North Carolina and Georgia, who didn't really know what the Draft was about. When it was explained they came back at once (joining the "Wildcat Division" destined to be officially credited with breaking the Hindenburg line).[10] . . . A town in Maine called 72 men for examination; 68 were physically fit. In search for draft dodgers, New York police went into ball parks, pool rooms, and bathing beaches demanding registration cards. . . . A Dallas father, queried as to why we should send our boys to fight in a foreign land, replied: "I'd rather have my son go to heaven in France than to hell in America!"

II

It is one thing to call half a million men to the colors; it is quite another to care for them after you get them there, especially to provide shelter, food, and clothing. Since the existing Army posts were wholly inadequate for this new citizen force already mustered, let alone that projected, housing became the immediate problem. It was planned to set up sixteen camps under canvas in the South and to build sixteen semi-permanent cantonments in the North; each camp and cantonment must have a capacity of forty to fifty thousand men.

As a construction job it was prodigious. Consider that a regiment of infantry of 3500 men required 22 barracks buildings —frame structures 43 feet wide, 140 feet long, two stories high — each accommodating 150 men; and 6 officers' quarters for the 200 officers, 2 store houses, 1

8 New York *Tribune*, August 1, 1917.   9 *Literary Digest,* August 18, 1917.
10 Final report of the Provost-Marshal General, July 15, 1919.

infirmary, and 28 lavatories with hot and cold showers.[11]
To multiples of all this, since a cantonment held from ten
to fourteen regiments, add the construction of a division
headquarters, quartermaster depot, kitchens[12], laundry,
recreation facilities, post exchange (retail store for the
soldiers run by the Army), and a base hospital of 1000
beds. A typical cantonment, then, for 40,000 men
meant 1200 buildings on a camp-site of 5000 to 11,000
acres, rifle range and drill grounds of 2000 acres, lighting, sewer and water supply, and 25 miles of hard-sur-
faced road.

And sixteen such cantonments (plus sixteen camps of
the same capacity, but using tents instead of barracks)
had to be built from scratch in two months' time. The
construction was authorized in May, 1917; the last site
secured on July 6. By September 8 — after a rivalry to
be 80% complete on that day had been won by Camp
Taylor, Kentucky, with a score of 79.4% — the cantonments accommodated 430,000 men, soon increased to
770,000. The camps held 684,000 more.[13] Further-
more, special schools for the Artillery, Aviation, Chemi-
cal Warfare, Engineers, and Tank Corps, along with
proving and testing grounds, and large embarkation
camps at New York and Newport News, were built for
300,000 men. The work was done by private contractors
under the Construction Division of the Quartermaster
Corps. Twelve trains a day of fifty cars each brought in
the materials; 50,000 carpenters and 150,000 other

[11] Report of the Secretary of War, 1917.
[12] Each cantonment had around 350 kitchens. High-pressure steam cooking
was used—a vegetable cooker could prepare 35 gallons in 15 minutes. Machines
sliced meat at the rate of 40 slices a minute, chopped 240 pounds of meat or
vegetables an hour, sliced and stacked 200 slices of bread a minute, peeled 800
pounds of potatoes an hour; washed, sterilized and dried 10,000 dishes an hour.
The bakeries in all the camps could turn out 2,000,000 one-pound loaves of bread
a day, the refrigerators 4,000,000 pounds of ice a day. "America's Munitions,
1917-1918," Benedict Crowell, Assistant Secretary of War.
[13] "The War with Germany, a Statistical Study," Col. Leonard P. Ayres.

workmen labored incessantly, using 2,000,000,000 eight-
penny nails, stringing 5500 miles of wire, and laying
down enough roofing to cover the island of Manhattan,
Atlantic City, and one square mile over. The cantonments
alone required 450,000,000 board feet of lumber, 140,-
000 wooden doors, 54,000 toilet bowls, and 721,000 cots.

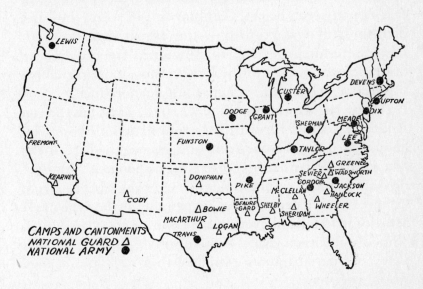

At both Camp Travis, Texas, and Camp Taylor, Kentucky, a standard barracks building was erected in an hour
and a half. At the latter camp barracks were built which
had been standing timber in a Mississippi forest one week
before.[14] Each cantonment cost an average of $8,000,-
000 — each camp $1,900,000; the maximum profit al-
lowed a contractor was 3%.

As a construction project it was second only to the
Panama Canal, but whereas the Canal had cost $375,-
000,000 over ten years, the Army housing cost seven-
tenths as much in three months. Quarters had been built
for more men than the total population of Philadelphia.

14 New York *Tribune*, August 5, 1917.

Already the Army was spending over $1,000,000 an hour.

III

The first Draft seemed sufficient, in early 1918; during the first thirteen months of the War less than a million men had been called. But the great spring drive of Germany soon began, Cambrai fell in May, the First British Army was crushed — the urgent demand from overseas resulted in more-than-doubled troop deliveries in France, and Class I of the Draft (those most available) was nearly exhausted. There must be more men.

A new registration on June 5, 1918,[15] and another on August 24 called forward for examination all boys who had reached twenty-one years of age since the date of the first Draft a year before. 912,564 responded. And yet this new crop was not enough. On August 31, 1918, Congress took a decisive step, expanding by law the draft age-limits to take in every male from 18 to 45 inclusive. The President set aside September 12 as Registration Day. Actuarial figures estimated that 12,800,000 men would register.

But this late Draft did not have the fresh appeal of the early one. The country had been at war a year and a half, excitement had staled, in every town in the land were homes in mourning; moreover, the age-limits cut on the one hand into mere boys, on the other into older men who were settled in responsibilities. As a result of these drags on willingness, the Government felt the gravest fears for the success of this final draft. It met the difficulty by a propaganda and publicity campaign of a magnitude never seen before or since in this country. During seven days prior to registration day, 30,000 Four-Minute men talked; 4000 daily papers and 14,000

---

[15] On May 17 General Crowder's office promulgated the "work or fight" order. A man must enlist or work in an industry directly contributing to the war.

minor ones printed news stories and advertisements put out by the Government; several hundred cartoonists put into patriotism-provoking pictures ideas supplied by the Government; all Army and Navy bands played in public places in cities throughout the country.[16] As a result, 13,395,706 men registered, nearly half a million more than statistics said there were.

All told, the Draft listed 23,908,576 men (325,445 more in the territories). That was 44% of the total male population. Our man-power equalled that of England and France combined, plus almost half again as much.[17] The Draft yielded 6,373,414 men available for service; of these, 2,702,687 were accepted into the Army.[18] This was the wheat winnowed by the threshing-machine.

IV

In every town and village in America, from Eastport, Maine, to Coronado Beach, Calif., occurred an event almost as standardized as an army uniform.

The train drew in. On the station platform were the

[16] A more extended summary of the propaganda carried on by the government to stimulate the final registration, September 12, 1918, would recite that the government issued 63 news stories and advertisements to 4000 daily papers, and bulletins to 150 farm weeklies, 500 trade papers, 1400 foreign language papers in 14 languages, and 14,000 minor newspapers. It sent bulletins to 15,000 manufacturers, 17,000 labor unions, 25,000 Chambers of Commerce, 8000 Ad clubs and 8000 Rotary clubs, 125,000 ministers, priests and rabbis, 3500 branches of the Y.M.C.A., 9000 libraries, 32,000 banks, 60,000 general stores, 50,000 drug stores, 55,000 station agents and 56,000 postmasters. It placed large signs in 350 cities, scattered 35,000 window posters and 50,000 car cards throughout 550 cities, sent 100,000 bulletins to local committees of the Red Cross, and distributed by mail to all rural free delivery and star routes more than 7,000,000 leaflets. Ideas were furnished to several hundred newspaper cartoonists; films announcing the date were prepared for exhibition in 17,000 movie houses; some 30,000 Four-Minute Men spoke in public places and all mayors were told to give the day patriotic emphasis. A striking fact about this huge agitation is that it cost the government just $20,000—all the rest was donated upon the government's request. —Second Report of the Provost-Marshal General, Dec. 20, 1918.

[17] "The War With Germany, a Statistical Study," Leonard P. Ayres. The whole Selective Service process cost over $30,000,000, or $1.26 for each man registered, $11.34 for each man accepted.

[18] Final Report of the Provost-Marshal General.

draftees, wearing their civilian clothes for a time which would be the last for many months, in some cases the last forever. Accompanying them were wives and mothers whom they kissed good-by, sweethearts, friends and acquaintances with whom they exchanged farewells half gay half solemn — the emotion of the whole scene was of the sort that is delicately balanced between smile and tear. The local band played patriotic airs, rather avoiding the music of parting[19] such as "Auld Lang Syne." In country villages in the North the airs included many Civil War ones, particularly "Marching Through Georgia"; in the South, where that would not do, there was "The Bonnie Blue Flag" — and everywhere, always, "Dixie." As the engine bell rang, they picked up their suitcases and the pies and cakes and doughnuts pressed upon them by the Red Cross Committee or the Ladies' Aid, and climbed into day coaches decorated with flags, bunting, and huge signs which read: "We're off to lick the Kaiser!" or other facetious expression of exalted purpose. Camp was the next stop.

V

Cantonment Life

The whistle blew, the band played a last tune, the crowd increased its shouting, the train pulled its length

[19] In one local entrainment I happened to see (at Peru, Ind., in April, 1918) there was a feature which I think was not common, and was very poignant. Among those who came to see the draftees off was the local post of the Grand Army of the Republic, a tottering handful of very old men come to give a blessing to their grandsons, grandsons destined to substitute, in the newer generation's experiences, Belleau Wood for Gettysburg, St. Mihiel for Bloody Angle. The Civil War veterans wore their army uniforms, and evidently had been at pains to get together what was left of the fife and drum corps that had played them off to war some fifty years before. Now once more it played "Rally 'Round the Flag, Boys," to old men who could no longer rally. As one watched them saying good-by to the younger men, one wondered how much the furtive tears in their eyes were for their own long-gone youth, how much for the fates that might await their grandsons.

Photograph from U. S. Army Signal Corps.

Above: Their first army clothes. *Below:* Two-day Rookies at Camp Meade, Md.

of flags and bunting, its freight of "draftees," suitcases, pies, and cakes, out of the station.

Then the men sat back. It had begun; they were on their way. Each man squared his shoulders, thought what he would do to the first Boche he met. Only when in the exaltation of celebration some one started to pass a bottle did they discover another side to this adventure; a tall man, one of their own number, stepped up with "Cut it out! You're in the Army!" He was the "draft leader" — order and discipline began at the first turn of the engine's wheels. Yet they were still heroic, glorious. Cheers floating in the window at every village they passed told them so, benevolent ladies who boarded the train at every stop to distribute candy and cigarettes made it plain. The men felt like veterans, already victorious, glory already achieved, until the train drew up at its last stop and they saw olive-drab step forward to meet them. The Army in the flesh was something new to each man.

There followed bewildering events: loud-spoken orders, getting on trucks or buses, getting off before an expanse of bare wooden buildings; more orders, officers at tables inside demanding Draft cards, other cards to be filled out, a doctor's curious thumping on their chests once again (those who failed in the camp physical examination were returned home at once), standing in weary yet jocose line while the sergeant rummaged through piles of olive-drab and flung out coats and breeches. Not until he emerged into sunlight, a service hat over one eye, his arms filled with strange-looking apparel, could the "draftee" catch his breath. He was no longer miner, bookkeeper, grocery-clerk; he was, in one of the most familiar cantonment phrases, epitome of all that was different from civil life — he was "in the Army now."

The cantonment day began, as days everywhere com-

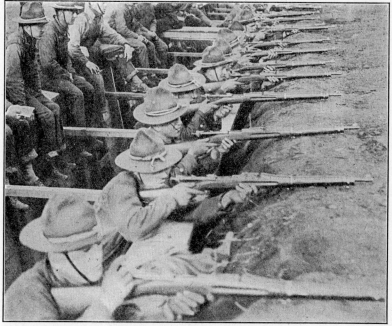

Above: Non-commissioned officers training at Camp Hancock, Ga. *Below:*
In the firing trench at Camp McClellan, Ala.

monly do, with getting up in the morning, and about that there was a remarkable army song written by a sergeant at Camp Upton, who was named Irving Berlin, and who, preceding his army life and after, was America's greatest contemporary composer of popular songs. Berlin's civilian life would never have given him the materials with which to compose this song. It "could only have been written by one who knew what it was to hate a bugler."[20]

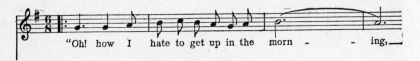

"Oh! how I hate to get up in the morn - - ing,

"Oh! How I hate to get up in the morning,
Oh! How I'd love to remain in bed;
For the hardest blow of all
Is to hear the bugler call —
'You've got to get up,
You've got to get up,
You've got to get up this morning!'
Some day I'm going to murder the bugler,
Some day they're going to find him dead;
I'll amputate his reveille
And step upon it heavily,
And spend the rest of my life in bed!"[21]

Little wonder that song delighted the rookie. It stated plainly his opinion of the one large, inescapable and never-to-be-forgotten fact of Army life — that the bugle blew at 5:45 in the morning. Loud and clear in the dawn it shrilled:

I can't get 'em up,
I can't get 'em up,
I can't get 'em up in the morning;

[20] The quotation is from Alexander Woollcott who considers "Oh How I Hate to Get Up in the Morning," the best American contribution to the music that arose during the war, the most likely to live and be taken up and carried along the roads toward the front by the soldiers of future wars.

[21] Reproduced by permission of copyright owners, Waterson, Berlin & Snyder Co.

I can't get 'em up,
I can't get 'em up,
I can't get 'em up at all;
Corp'rals worse than privates,
Sergeants worse than corp'rals,
Lieutenants worse than the sergeants,
And the Capt'ns worst of all ![22]

Mess at the Pelham Bay Naval Station.

Only those who had come from farms thought this was
an easy rising; to the rest it loomed sign and token of the
immediate strangeness of the Army's ways.

Fifteen minutes[23] after first call the men "stood rev-

[22] In this account of cantonment life, traditional paraphrases of several Army
bugle calls are given in their proper places.
[23] This timing of a "Rookie's School-day" is taken from the *Camp Dix News*
of September 15, 1917.

eille," assembled in line before their barracks to answer the roll. Mess call sounded for breakfast at 6:20:

> Soup-y, soup-y, soup,
> Without a single bean;
> Pork-y, pork-y, pork,
> Without a streak of lean;
> Cof-fee, cof-fee, cof-fee,
> The weakest ever seen!

At 6:45 came sick call; men who felt that they ought to have a doctor's attention reported to the orderly room.

> Come and get your quinine, come and get your pills;
> Come and get your quinine, come and get your pills!

If the regiment were Cavalry or Field Artillery, the stable call was given at 7.

> Come all who are able and go to the stable
> And water your horses and give them some corn,
> For if you don't do it the colonel will know it
> And then you will rue it as sure as you're born!

Otherwise the men returned to quarters to "police up" by making their beds and arranging their kits.

They assembled at 7:30 for the start of the day's serious work. Thereafter for four hours the men were drilled in the intricate technique of the soldier.[24] Mess call

---

[24] All camps received a schedule for sixteen weeks of preliminary training, calling for 40 hours a week. The first week was distributed in hours as follows: School of the Soldier (manual of arms), 6; School of the Squad (formation drill), 10; setting-up exercises and recruit instructions, 6; issue of clothing and equipment, 4; care of uniform and equipment, 4; military discipline and courtesy, 2; orders for sentinels, 2; personal hygiene and care of the feet, 2; Articles of War; lecture—Obligations and Rights of the Soldier, 1; besides 2 hours of inspection. The second week made these changes: rifle sighting and aiming, 4; rifle nomenclature and care, 2; bayonet drill, 3; making pack and tent-pitching, 2; running, 1½; lecture—Why We Are at War, 1; etc. The third week, these: rifle aiming and trigger-squeeze, 12; first aid, 1; etc., and the fourth week, these: gas warfare, 1; grenades and bombs, 1; etc., etc.—*The Camp Dodger*, Camp Dodge, Iowa, October 5, 1917.

British officers (261) and non-commissioned officers (226) and French officers (286) came over to assist in this training.

The equipment of one Infantryman ready for service in France comprised $101.21 worth of clothing, bedding, and tent; $7.73 worth of issue food, eating utensils, and pack; and $47.36 worth of arms—totaling $156.30.—*The Camp Dodger.*

sounded dinner at 12 noon — for once the bugle fell upon willing ears.   At 1 came another assembly call for more

ABC's of the Manual of Arms, Camp Devens, Mass.

drill or fatigue duty (general labor), which lasted until 5.   Assembly for retreat occurred at 5:25 — the men in formation presented arms, the band played the national anthem, and the flag came down (it had gone up at 7:30 A.M.).   Mess call for supper[25] came at 5:45.   A last as-

[25] Army food came in for much reviling by the soldiers at the time, as was natural enough. But many a man revised his estimate afterward.

Consider that the men were fed on allowance of $39\frac{7}{10}$ cents a day per man! A

sembly was often gathered at 7 for an hour and a half of
school — lectures and theoretical instruction; but this
was sometimes omitted. A man then had free time until
the call to quarters at 9:45, and at 10 came lights out and
Taps. If he had never in his adult life gone to bed at
10 before, he was ready to sleep now.

In almost every camp weekly newspapers, some of
them as large as metropolitan papers, with circula-

---

wise chef saved on week-days to give an extra-good menu on Sunday. Here is an
example from *The Camp Dix News,* September 29, 1917: a company chef fed
212 men three meals at a total cost of $48—23c per man provided this "common
menu":

> *Breakfast:* Boiled rice and milk
> Fried bacon   Fried potatoes
> Hot muffins
> Bread and butter   Coffe or milk

> *Dinner:* Puree of bean soup   Croutons
> Roast beef
> Sweet potatoes   Stewed kidney beans
> Tapioca pudding
> Bread and butter   Coffee or milk

> *Supper:*   Meat and potato pie
> Hot biscuits
> Fresh apple-sauce
> Bread and butter   Coffee or milk

So on Sunday his accumulated savings enabled him to set out this menu:

> *Breakfast:*   Scrambled eggs
> Fried bacon   French toast
> Cottage fried potatoes
> Bread and butter   Coffee or milk

> *Dinner:*   Vegetable soup
> Soft roast beef
> Mashed potatoes   Creamed peas
> Bread and butter
> Stewed peaches   Chocolate cake
> Coffee or milk

> *Supper:*   Beef-steak pie
> Browned potatoes   Sliced tomatoes
> Rice pudding
> Bread and butter   Coffee or milk

Above: Teaching a group of depot engineers how to pick up and carry a wounded man, at Camp Grant, Ill. *Below:* Machine gun training at Camp Devens, Mass.

tions of tens of thousands, recorded for posterity innumerable sidelights of life in the cantonments. Their pages were gay, gusty, vigorous, vibrating to the spirits of a constituency of 40,000 young soldiers.

Front-page news was the completion of a row of barracks or a sewer trench, sick-leave for the chaplain, the life-sentence of a deserter, the progress of a Liberty Loan (in one, Camp Dodge by itself subscribed $1,500,000), the item that 2,000 soldiers wanted to join a correspondence club and write to girls. Editorials blasted away at the slacker and the pro-German, spoke a word for the importance of the salute, declared Camp Taylor or Meade or Upton, as the case was, to be the garden of the patriotic universe. Cartoons and humorous columns, often by professionals, played eternally on the rookie vs. the officer, and other awkwardnesses:

> *Rookie on Sentry-Post:* "Who goes there?"
> *Voice:* "Captain Throgmorton."
> *Rookie:* "Put 'er there, cap! I'm Private Cheese!"

Or, after the same preliminaries:

> *Rookie:* "Gee, you're a lucky guy! I'm only a private!"

Other incidents of camp life made "inside fillers": Too many girls are phoning the Adjutant's office and asking the clerk to tell Bill or Henry to meet them at the drugstore at seven. . . . Tables at both officers' and soldiers' messes are concentrating on French conversation to prepare for Paree. . . . Small khaki-bound Bibles distributed to all men. . . . Many a stalwart with a blue beard, who didn't know what a thimble was, has learned to take out his "housewife kit" and mend socks. . . . On Thanksgiving Day every man gets a pound of turkey and a pound of cranberry sauce. . . . So keen is the feeling against waste that a major on seeing a soldier throw away

Above: Army nurses receiving gas instruction at Camp Kearney, Calif. Entering the gas chamber. *Below:* Camouflage produced what appears to be, looked at from above, the carcass of a horse. Actually it is a listening post for an army engineer.

a half-smoked cigarette, taught him to appreciate its value by ordering him to bury it in a hole ten feet deep.

Always a strong note was optimism, sometimes a bit forced. A headline stated that only 11 out of every 1000 men are killed in action. A famous syllogism, heard by every recruit, was "Don't Worry, Boys!"[26]

If the War doesn't end next month, of two things one is certain: Either you will be sent across the big pond or you will stay on this side.

If you stay at home there is no need to worry. If you go across, of two thngs one is certain: Either you will be put on the firing line or kept behind the lines.

If you are behind the lines there is no need to worry. If you are at the front, of two things one is certain: Either you are resting in a safe place or you're exposed to danger.

If you are resting in a safe place there is no need to worry. If you are exposed to danger, of two things one is certain: Either you're wounded or not wounded.

If you are not wounded there is no need to worry. If you are wounded, of two things one is certain: Either you're wounded seriously or you're wounded slightly.

If you are wounded slightly there is no need to worry. If you are wounded seriously, of two things one is certain: Either you recover or you don't.

If you recover there is no need to worry. If you don't recover you can't worry.

The Army meant another way of life, and a new language arose to express and picture it. By reviving old terms, by borrowing or inventing new ones, the soldier formed a special and racy vocabulary which he spoke with professional flair. The list which follows has no claim to completeness; it merely shows the flavor and range. Most of these terms and definitions are quoted verbatim from cantonment sources:

African golf: Shooting crap, playing dice. From a predilection for the sport shown by negro troops, a predilection, how-

[26] *The Camp Dodger,* September 28, 1917.

ever, not distinguishable from that evinced by the white. Pay-day night every company had its big game; the winners met later at the regimental finals. Although there was a military penalty for this indulgence, the danger to those playing lay largely in the fact that the interrupting officer confiscated for the company fund (entertainment and athletic supplies) all the money on the blanket.

Aggie: The Adjutant General. Chiefly officer slang.

Army game: The "old Army Game," hoary with age and tradition, is "to pass the buck."

AT CAMP UPTON

Frueh, the cartoonist, was at Camp Upton, New York, and from there sent these sketches to the New York *World*.

"*A. W. O. L.:*[27] Absent without leave. Said of a man who believes that nine days at home is worth six months' pay."

"*B. P.:*[27] Buck private. A government employee of the next grade above civilian who usually believes that it is his function to avoid all responsibility and to do as little work as possible."

Brass hat: A term borrowed from the British Tommies — hence its use showed that you'd been on the other side. It meant officers of the Staff, from the amount of gilt on their caps.

Buddy: The common, generic, epithetic, and appellative term for soldier. Taken over into civilian use by hitch-hikers and pan-handlers.

Bully-beef: See Monkey-meat.

Canned-willy: See Monkey-meat.

C. M.: Court-Martial. See Jaggie.

C. O.: 1. Commanding Officer; the "old man."
　　　　2. Conscientious objector.

Cootie: A flea or louse.

"Dogey-dog:"[27] The guard-house. It is the soldier's residence for a time after committing some breach of military etiquette. The only branch of the service to which he is not continually trying to get a transfer."

Dough-boy: A private soldier. Not invented in 1917; it was common during the Civil War.

"Drilling:"[27] This consists of going out on a field and doing something you already know."

"Fall in:"[27] The most hated command of them all. It means throwing away your cigarette and getting into formation."

"Fall out:"[27] A command heard even by the deaf. It means break ranks. You will not be wanted again for possibly fifteen minutes."

Fritz: See Heinie.

Front and centre: The command to step out of rank and come forward. It usually denoted trouble ahead.

"F. T. D.:"[27] Feeding the dog. The supposed occupation of a soldier who is killing time."

"G. O. K.:"[27] God only knows. An abbreviation used by English physicians at dressing stations to indicate that they have not had time to make a satisfactory diagnosis." (Adopted as a universal expression of resignation tc the mysterious ways of those in command.)

Gold bricking: Malingering. Pretending you have sciatica when what troubles you is homesickness or hangover.

Gold fish: Tinned salmon.

Ground squirrel: A man in the Aviation Corps whose duties do not require him to fly.

G. S. W.: Gun-shot wound.

Heinie: Any German soldier.

Jaggie: The Judge Advocate General. Chiefly officer slang. The soldier wanted only to avoid all business with him; he handles the C. M.'s. (See *supra.*)

"K. P.:"[27] Kitchen Police. A soldier who sets tables in the mess hall, washes and wipes dishes, and eats the extra ice-cream on Sunday. See also S. O. L."

Monkey-meat: The regular Army ration of canned beef.

Like Bully-beef, it is an importation from the British Tommies. Canned-willy is native-born.

"*M. P.*:[27] Military police. An organization which exists chiefly for the purpose of changing A. W. O. L. into S. O. L. [See *supra* and *infra*.]"

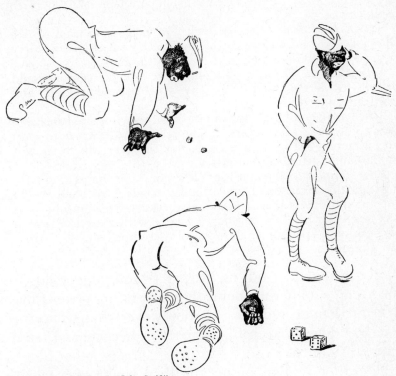

From *Singing Soldiers,* by *John J. Niles*

Crap Shooting Charlie.

"*O. D.*:[27] 1. Olive drab. The color of an Army shirt before it is worn over six weeks or sent to the laundry." 2. Officer of the Day. An inquisitive person who is sure to come around whenever anything irregular is going on.

"*Right dress*:[27] When this command is given, every man puts his left hand on his hip, looks to the right, and jabs the man on his left with his elbow — getting much enjoyment out of same. It is no fun for the man at the left end of the line, because he has no one to jab."

[27] Certain of these items are taken verbatim from *The Trouble Buster,* a weekly published at U. S. General Hospital No. 2, Ft. McHenry, Baltimore, Md.

Rookie: A new and raw soldier.

"*S. C. D.*:[27] Surgeon's certificate of disability. The paper received by the soldier who is unfit for service when he is discharged by the Army."

"*Shave-tails*:[27] Newly commissioned second-lieutenants who haven't got used to the fact yet. They can be spotted three blocks away."

"*S. O. L.*:[27] Soldier out of luck. An expression used of one who is late for mess, has lost his hat-cord, or been given thirty days' confinement to the post for shooting crap."

Somewhere in France: The only date-line the censor would permit for letters sent from any spot between Dover and Bordeaux.

"*War-baby:* A child, legitimate or otherwise, sired in haste by a soldier." (The term was adopted in Wall Street to indicate a factory, producing material for the War, which showed sudden and spectacular profits.)

Your number: The phrase "It's got your number on it" suggests the fatalism of the soldier; a bullet or shell would not hit him unless it was intended specially for him, unless it was marked with "his number." Every soldier carried around his neck on a string a small metal disk stamped with his Army serial number.

Yet in spite of "fall in," "K. P.," and "dogey-dog," the average soldier undoubtedly had a rather better time in camp than in civil life. Certainly everything conceivable was done to keep him entertained, contented, and happy.

A million soldiers meant a million young men taken out of their homes; at the very entrance of America into the War the Army realized this side of the problem and set up the Commission on Training Camp Activities to provide, as well as it could, normal relations of life, "to rationalize the bewildering environments of a war camp."[28] The Commission dealt with all sides of a soldier's recreation.[29] It erected 34 Liberty Theatres in as

[28] Report of the Secretary of War, 1917. The chairman of the C. T. C. A. was Raymond B. Fosdick, brother of Rev. Harry E. Fosdick.

[29] Even the illicit. It waged a strenuous campaign at keeping boot-leggers and "red light" districts properly distant from camp. Every camp had its venereal prophylactic station. Treatments were voluntary, but if a soldier incurred disease without reporting for treatment he faced a severe penalty.

We're in the Army Now.
Mail time at Spartansburg, and every man his own tailor and barber.

many camps; each had a capacity of from two to ten thousand men, and showed current movies every night as well as plays and vaudeville performances. (Vaudeville and actors' associations donated their services to the Army,

Depositing money with the Y. M. C. A. secretary at Camp MacArthur, Waco, Texas.

both here and abroad, with fine liberality). It supplied dramatic managers for amateur theatricals. It appointed 44 athletic directors, 30 boxing instructors and 53 song leaders to oversee these activities in the camps; they had many assistants. And it provided full equipment for all activities and sports — except the favorite, "African golf."

Above: Y. M. C. A. hut in one of the camps. *Below:* Class in English for non-English speaking soldiers 126th Machine Gun Company, Camp MacArthur, Waco, Texas.

All the efforts of the C. T. C. A. to fill the soldier's free hours seemed but little more than a drop in the bucket compared with the semi-private enterprises which came forward. Every benevolent association in the country, apparently, found some facet of a soldier's life to aid and comfort. The Red Cross went further than supplying lint bandages and crutches; it built club-houses, put on vaudeville shows, gave Christmas parties. The Y. M. C. A. had secretaries in every camp to carry out its varied program; at Camp Dodge alone, ten buildings bore the red triangle on circle, international insignia of the "Y" — each with fireplace, piano, phonograph, movie projector, complete sets of athletic goods, 1000 books, current magazines, home-town papers, easy chairs and writing-desks, free note-paper, postal facilities, and sitting-rooms for visiting ladies. The Knights of Columbus[30] (National Catholic War Council) and the Jewish Welfare Board provided similar facilities. The Salvation Army, the Y. W. C. A., and the Travelers' Aid also helped at the camps; the American Library Association collected books and magazines,[31] the Playground Associa-

---

[30] A story which came back from overseas is worth repeating as a relevant sidelight: Kelly was a good soldier, a good Catholic. He had been in the trenches for some weeks when a leave order came, but he didn't have any money. So he wrote to God:

Dear Lord,
You know I've served hard up here, and now I've got leave to go to Paris. But my pockets are empty as a pig's ear. Send me $100, please. You won't miss it, Lord, and I need it. Yours, etc.

He mailed the letter. In due course it reached the censor, whose office, by chance, was in a Y. M. C. A. building. The censor showed the curious letter to the "Y" secretary. The latter knew Kelly and knew he was a good soldier, so he passed the hat, gathered $50, and sent it to Kelly without comment in a Y. M. C. A. envelope.

The day after, another letter from Kelly turned up on the censor's desk:

Dear Lord,
Thanks for that $50. May your shadow never grow less! But next time, Lord, send it by the K. C.'s.—those "Y" boys copped half.

[31] For some months during the War the Government made a drive to collect used magazines. Every national magazine bore a notice on its cover—"Put a

tion of America organized adjacent communities with respect to recreation for the men.

If the drilling, the sentry duty, the regularity of reveille and K. P. grew monotonous for the soldier, this was so completely balanced by baseball, football, boxing

Boxing match in the "Y" auditorium at Camp Devens, Massachusetts.

bouts and track meets, William Farnum and Mary Miles Minter on the screen, Elsie Janis and Harry Lauder in the flesh, pool-tables, song-fests, phonograph records, *Life* and *Judge*, ice-cream sodas and cigarettes that he could almost forget he was a soldier in a war-camp.

1c stamp on this and hand it to your postman; it will reach our soldiers and sailors oversea, A. S. Burleson, Postmaster General." So great was the response that hundreds of tons of magazines piled up at Hoboken, without any room in transports for shipment. Embarrassed by plethora, the Government called off the drive.—"As They Passed Through the Port," Major-General David C. Shanks.

It did not, for a while, even seem that war was serious business.

VI

With the iron, stern and sharp,
Comes the playing on the harp.

"It is just as essential," said General Leonard Wood, seriously or casually — perhaps apocryphally — "that a soldier know how to sing as that he should carry a rifle and know how to shoot it." Probably the General did not really say "know how to sing." The "knowing how" was neither essential nor universal. But the singing was universal. In cantonment, literally every one sang, whether it were a lone tenor in a barrack-lined street lifting his voice in "Good-bye Broadway, Hello France" and "Dearest, my heart is dreaming, dreaming of you," or ten thousand soldiers led by a divisional song leader shouting "Men of Harlech" on the drill ground of an evening.

The C. T. C. A., in its multifarious concern for cantonment diversion, put out a little khaki-bound song-book; with the slightly pedantic spirit the C. T. C. A. had, it chose its songs mainly from among the accepted, the familiar, and the official; there were hymns, and the patriotic songs of the United States, the national anthems of Britain, France, Belgium, and Italy; there were the well-known Scotch, English, and American negro airs, and a selection of American popular songs that had attained the status of quasi-permanence, "On the Banks of the Wabash," "Little Grey Home in the West," "Dear Old Pal of Mine." These the soldiers sang, but mainly at semi-formal occasions under the direction of the C. T. C. A. or Y. M. C. A. song leaders. In somewhat the same spirit were sung the so-to-speak songs of soldiering as a profession, the "Field Artillery Song" — "And the cais-

sons go rolling along"; and the "Coast Artillery Song,"
sung to "The Son of a Gambolier":

Oh, they said the Coast Artillery would never go to war,
And all that they were fit for was to hang around the shore—

Drawn by Captain John W. Thomason, Jr.

The Marine Corps hymn.

But when in France they needed men to shoot the tens and
      twelves,
Why, they cabled to the President to send our loyal selves.

Then it's home, boys, home — it's home that we would be,
It's home, boys, home, when the nation shall be free;
We're in this war until it ends, and Germany will see
That the end of all the Kaiser's hopes is the Coast Artillery.

And the famous Marine Hymn:

From the halls of Montezuma to the shores of Tripoli,
We fight our country's battles on the land and on the sea.

First to fight for right and freedom and to keep our honor clean
We are proud to claim the title of United States Marine.

But those were the almost formal songs of soldiering. Much more spontaneous and rather more characteristic of the citizen army were many songs[32] that were being sung by everybody at the time and were brought into camp by the draftees; and some other songs that sprang up in the cantonments, and yet others that came back from the front. These composed a gorgeous galaxy, gay and appealing at the time, glamorous to recall. Some have faded, almost disappeared; some still live in gatherings of men on Saturday night and are revived at meetings of veterans. To anybody old enough to remember the war, they evoke a time when the pulse of life was strong.

The stammering song "K-K-K-Katy, beautiful Katy," popular before we entered the war, gave rise to many soldier parodies, among them an expression of harsh opinion about "K.P.," "Kitchen police":

> K-K-K-K. P.,
> Dirty old K. P.,
> That's the only Army job that I abhor;
> When the m-moon shines over the guard-house,
> I'll be mopping up the k-k-k-kitchen floor!
> C-C-C-Cootie,
> Horrible cootie,
> You're the only b-b-b-bug that I abhor;
> When the m-moon shines over the bunkhouse,
> I will scratch my b-b-b-back until it's sore!

America's earliest war was recalled, somewhat irreverently, in

> Liberty Bell, it's time to ring again . . .
> Tho' you're old and there's a crack in you,
> Don't forget Old Glory's backin' you . . . [33]

[32] Some who have read this chapter in manuscript or proof complain of the failure to include many songs of war-time held in vivid and glamorous memory: "Madelon," "Sambre et Meuse," "I Paid a Dime to See."

[33] Reproduced by permission of copyright owners, Shapiro, Bernstein & Co.

Inevitably France's patron saint, pronounced "Jona Vark," was celebrated in popular song:

Joan of Arc, Joan of Arc,
Do your eyes from the skies see the foe? . . .

A not too serious apprehension about the effect of mar-

K. P. at Camp Grant, Ill.

tial experiences on the distribution of population was expressed in:

How 'ya gonna keep 'em down on the farm, after they've seen
    Paree?
How 'ya gonna keep 'em away from Broadway,
Jazzin' a-roun', and paintin' the town?[34]

Among songs indigenous to the encampments, the camp song from Ft. Niagara, N. Y., words and music ascribed to Private Hogan, stands a minor classic; the

[34] Reproduced by permission of copyright owners, Waterson, Berlin & Snyder.

cryptic and gay "Good-morning, Mr. Zip, Zip, Zip!"
was sung from the Presidio to the Front Line.

> Good-morning, Mr. Zip, Zip, Zip,
>   With your hair cut just as short as mine!
> Good-morning, Mr. Zip, Zip, Zip,
>   You're cert'nly lookin' fine!
> Ashes to ashes and dust to dust,
> If the Camels don't get you the Fatimas must;
> Good-morning, Mr. Zip, Zip, Zip,
>   With your hair cut just as short as,
>   Your hair cut just as short as,
>   Your hair cut just as short as —
>   Mine![35]

The soldiers bade the folks at home keep their courage up in

> Keep the home-fires burning, while your hearts are yearning;
> Though your lads are far away, they dream of home.

Then they turned around and sang a like message of cheerful fortitude to themselves. The English "Pack Up Your Troubles in Your Old Kit Bag, and Smile, Smile, Smile" was adopted by the American dough-boys without a blink at its alien "lucifer" for match and "fag" for cigarette. More native, more homely and pungent, was "The Last Long Mile," the Plattsburg Marching Song in 1917:[36]

> Oh, they put me in the Army and they handed me a pack,
> They took away my nice new clothes and dolled me up in kack;
> They marched me twenty miles a day to fit me for the war —
> I didn't mind the first nineteen but the last one made me sore:

[35] Reproduced by permission of copyright owner, Leo Feist, Inc.
[36] Reproduced by permission of copyright owner, Henry W. Savage, Inc.

Knights of Columbus canteen.

Oh it's not the pack that you carry on your back,
Nor the Springfield on your shoulder,
Nor the five-inch crust of khaki-colored dust
That makes you feel your legs are growing older;
And it's not the hike on the hard turn-pike
That wipes away your smile,
Nor the socks of sister's that raise the blooming blisters —
It's the last long mile!

"Long Boy," the picture of the country lad going off to battle the German army, tickled every one's risibili-ties:[37]

> Good-bye, Ma! Good-bye, Pa!
> Good-bye, Mule, with yer old hee-haw!
> I may not know what this war's about,
> But you bet, by gosh, I'll soon find out;
> An' O my sweetheart, don't you fear,
> I'll bring you a King for a souvenir,

[37] Reproduced by permission of copyright owners, Shapiro, Bernstein & Co.

I'll git you a Turk an' a Kaiser too —
An' that's about all one feller can do!

Earliest of the war songs was "Tipperary"; it was widely sung in America from the time, late in 1914, when despatches from the front said it was the marching song of the first British Expeditionary Force:

It's a long way to Tipperary; it's a long way to go;
It's a long way to Tipperary, to the sweetest girl I know!
Good-bye, Piccadilly, farewell, Leicester Square,
It's a long, long way to Tipperary,
But my heart's right there.[38]

A soldier's glimpse of "No Man's Land,"[39] was in Lieutenant Rice's

Keep your head down, Fritzie boy,
Keep your head down, Fritzie boy —
Late last night by the star-shell light
We saw you, we saw you,
You were mending your barb-wire
When we opened rapid fire —
If you want to see your father
    In your Fatherland,
Keep your head down, Fritzie boy

But the soldiers' song of songs was "Mademoiselle

[38] Reproduced by permission of copyright owners, Chappell and Company, Ltd.
[39] Reproduced by permission of copyright owner, Leo Feist, Inc.

from Armentieres," sometimes called "Hinky Dinky, Parley-Vous." It became the folk-song of the army. It was sung in the trenches; in places of recreation behind the lines it was universal; among soldiers on leave in Paris it was decidedly more familiar than the "Marseillaise"; it came to America with returning veterans and, with its flavor of the front, eclipsed in popularity the familiar American tunes. Literally every soldier sang it; and years after the war, veterans moved to song found expression for every mood, solitary or gregarious, in one or another of the countless narratives of the charms and the adventures of the maid — if she was a maid — from Armentieres. She was, to each soldier, what each soldier dreamed her to be. Any one seeking to reconstruct a coherent history of the lady from the thousands of versified accounts of her would be obliged to give up. A version of the song that was somewhere fairly near to its origin pictured Mademoiselle as one who spent her days working in a laundry and her high-spirited evenings in a café frequented by American doughboys:

> Oh, Mademoiselle from Armentieres, parley-vous?
> Oh, Mademoiselle from Armentieres, parley-vous?
> Oh, Mademoiselle from Armentieres
> Will you wash a soldier's underwear?
> Hinky Dinky, parley-vous?

More probable, whether more authentic or not, was the version which pictured Mademoiselle as a bar-maid:

> Mademoiselle from Armentieres
> Won't you bring me a bottle of beer?

One version pictured Mademoiselle as aged and acid:

> Mademoiselle from Armentieres
> She hasn't been kissed in forty year.

That slander must have originated with some doughboy in a pique of disappointment or jealousy; by the evidence of hundreds of other versions, Mademoiselle was distinctly kissable, and rich in experience. She had, in one version or another, every experience of every girl since Eve.

Not only did "Mademoiselle from Armentieres" recite the innumerable adventures of the heroine. The tune was a vehicle for the telling of any story, the expression of any opinion:

Oh, the Medical Corps, they held the lines; parley-vous?
Oh, the Medical Corps, they held the lines; parley-vous?
Oh, the Medical Corps, they held the lines
With C. C. pills and iodine.
Hinky Dinky, parley-vous?

Oh, the General got the Croix de Guerre; parley-vous?
Oh, the General got the Croix de Guerre; parley-vous?
Oh, the General got the Croix de Guerre,
But the son-of-a-gun was never there!
Hinky Dinky, parley-vous?

O, the French they are a funny race,
They swipe your francs
And lie to your face . . .

The little marine he grew and grew,
And now he's hugging and kissing 'em too . .

Froggie, have you a daughter fine?
Fit for a marine, just out of the line . . .

O, oui, I have a daughter fine,
But not for a Yankee just out of the line . . .[40]

Of all the American war songs, the two that divided top honors alike among soldiers and civilians were "Over There" and "The Long, Long Trail." The latter, with its gentle melancholy and suggestion of distant adven-

[40] The dots may be accepted by the reader as representing elisions, adopted here for economy of space; or they may be understood to indicate expurgations. Distinctly, most distinctly, much that was sung to the tune of "Mademoiselle from Armentieres" would not bear printing in a book intended for universal reading.

Drawn by Captain John W. Thomason, Jr.

Mad - em - o' - elle from Ar - men - tieres par - - lez
vous.... Mad - em - ois - elle from Ar - men - tieres
par - - lez vous..... Mad - em - ois - elle from
Ar - men - tiers. She has - n't been kissed in for - ty
years. Hink - y dink - y par - lez vous.........

ture, provided almost perfect solace to the mood of the
soldier contemplating service:

> There's a long, long trail a-winding
> Into the land of my dreams,
> Where the nightingales are singing
> And a white moon beams;
> There's a long, long night of waiting
> Until my dreams all come true;
> Till the day when I'll be going down
> That long, long trail with you.[41]

"Over There,"[42] partly because of its high-spirited,

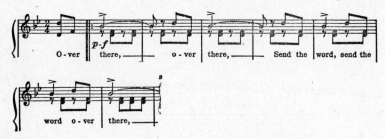

quick-stepping imperativeness, and even more because of
its simple bugle melody, had the effect of a recruiting
song:

Over there, over there. Send the word, send the word over there,
That the Yanks are coming, the Yanks are coming, the drums
    rum-tumming everywhere.
So prepare, say a pray'r. Send the word, send the word to beware,
We'll be over, we're coming over, and we won't come back till
    it's over over there.

[41] Reproduced by permission of copyright owners, M. Witmark & Sons.
[42] Written by George M. Cohan, playwright and actor. Reproduced by permission of copyright owner, Leo Feist, Inc.

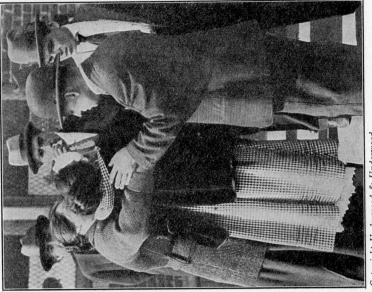

Heartaches and cheers at parting.

VII

The training in the cantonments hewed to its purpose. In due course, out of ten ports, 2,086,000 soldiers[43] sailed for France.

In late 1917, transports were taking 50,000 men a month. By early 1918, after interned German liners had been pressed into service, the rate rose steeply; May saw 245,000 men shipped across, July 306,000 — more than 10,000 a day. By July 1 the first million men had reached France, the second million landed before the end of October.[44] It was an over-water troop movement far greater than any in history.

What had permitted this transportation of two million men across three thousand miles of ocean in so short a time was, of course, an immense production and conscription of ships.[45] Even so, 49% of our soldiers had to be carried in British bottoms. Further, due credit must be given to the rapidity of "turnabouts" — the time between the day when a ship with cargo aboard sets sail, and the day, after it has crossed, discharged cargo, returned and taken on another, when it is ready to sail again. In 1917 the average "turnabout" of a troopship was 52 days, in 1918 it fell to 35.[46]

In spite of the vulnerability of so thick a traffic, only 200,000 tons of transports were lost — 142,000 tons of this by torpedoes. No troopship was lost on an eastern voyage, with one exception, the *Tuscania,* torpedoed off

---

[43] Figures used in this section are taken from Ayres, *supra.*

[44] The full momentum of America's participation had only begun to show itself by Armistice Day. True, 42 divisions (27,000 men and 1000 officers each) had been sent overseas, 12 were well under way in training, 4 were being organized; but plans were in progress to set 80 divisions in France by July, 1919, and 100 by the end of the year.

[45] For an account of America's ship building effort, see Chapter 19.

[46] The *Leviathan* (formerly the German *Vaterland*) and the *Mount Vernon* (the *Kronprinzessen Cecilie*), under convoy which necessarily meant some im-

the Irish coast, with the loss of 100 out of the 2000 troops she was transporting to France.

The division, any division, was still drilling in camp after five, six, seven months.[47] Then one day the rumor spread from barrack to barrack like wildfire: "Tomorrow

The spirit of the ten million.

we move!" Every man's heart lifted and beat quicker; here was real war at last.

Orders multiplied. The division packed. Perhaps the men, with full equipment, boarded a train at night and woke up next morning at the embarkation camp behind Hoboken. Transports were ready in the Hudson, or

---

pediment, averaged "turnabouts" of 27 days. This was faster than the best commercial practice. Two American ships, the *Northern Pacific* and the *Great Northern,* averaged under convoy 26 and 25 days respectively, and each had done a "turnabout" in 19 days.

[47] The average experience of the 1,400,000 men who fought in France comprised six months in training on this side, two months overseas before entering the line, one month thereafter in a quiet sector.

across the bay in Brooklyn,[48] and the troops marched aboard. Fantastic with camouflage, the ship moved down the bay and met other transports; together they headed toward open sea. Somewhere in the Atlantic they would pick up their convoy of gray, rake-lined destroyers.

Ten days on a transport was misery. The men crowded

Red Cross canteen workers served coffee any hour of the day or night to troops en route.

into the hold, where bunks jammed to the ceiling; when the ship rose, swayed and fell, sea-sickness became contagious, epidemic, the quarters almost unbearable. Officers forbade smoking on deck, ordered all lights covered. There was nothing to do but shoot craps or play poker,

[48] Some soldiers who had never laid eyes on salt water before looked eagerly for France at the end of this ferry-trip.—Maj. Gen. Shanks, *supra*. General Shanks was in command of the Hoboken Port of Embarkation, from which 1,777,109 soldiers sailed.

until, entering the war-zone, one could look for submarines — every piece of driftwood, every breaking
wave, became a periscope. Perhaps, one morning, dough-

Photograph by U. S. Army Signal Corps.

Just a few of America's ten million.

boys lined the rail to watch the white wake of a torpedo
slide by the stern and see the destroyers, belching smoke,
dash in to drop a depth bomb. In the geyser of foam
which boomed up were scraps of metal, and oil spread on

the water. The stands cheered as if Ty Cobb had stolen home.

At dusk they met another convoy, homeward bound. "Hospital ships," said some one, and men talked late in

So This Is Paris!

the night about wounds, death, and battle, and reckoned up their chances until the serg' shouted from the hatch, "Stow it down there!" Next morning early there was a fog and then, suddenly, before them, around them, lay high rocky islands on the gray sea. The gray clot on the hillside ahead, growing clearer moment by moment, was Brest.

It was all a thrilling experience, to be remembered and told to grandchildren. A few, for differing motives, chose to miss it or ignore its spirit — the "slackers" and the "conscientious objectors."

VIII

The Slackers and the Narrative of the Super-Slacker of All

It was the kind of house which barkers in rubber-neck wagons point out: "On yer left's the pal-a-tial res'dence of —!" Back from the corner of Wynnefield Avenue and 52nd Street in Philadelphia, it towered over rich-looking lawns in secure complacency. But any neighbor in Overbrook could have punctured the illusion. For when, on a cold dawn in early January, 1920 (more than a year after the War had ended), several operatives from the Department of Justice pounded at the front door, a stout, middle-aged woman standing in the hall was ready; she screamed, "What do you want? You can't come in here!" and waved a revolver angrily. With professional strategy they kept her busy at her post and came in the back.

The man they were looking for was hiding under a small window seat, his head among pillows. He surrendered readily enough. They slung an Army overcoat over his shoulders, and he said, "I'm glad the chase is over; this coat feels good." Yelling and booing, a crowd outside pushed toward the prisoner, forced the officers to commandeer a car to get him away. When its driver learned the identity of this pale, black-mustached young man, he was so overjoyed at helping that he gave $500 to the officers out of hand.[49] Almost any newspaper reader in the country would have done the same if he could, for Grover Cleveland Bergdoll, notorious draft evader, had been captured at last after a search of a year and a half which had turned the country almost upside down. He was taken away to be tried by court-martial,

[49] *American Legion Weekly,* March 26, 1920.

and his mother was fined $279 for pointing fire-arms.

The Bergdolls were a wealthy brewing family. Grover, during his 'teens, had been given $5000 a year to experiment with airships.[50] Later he turned to automobiles and drove them furiously through Philadelphia

Photographs by Underwood & Underwood.

Grover Cleveland Bergdoll and his mother.

suburbs, with such resultant friction with law that for some years he had had to hire a man to ease his burden of appearing in numerous courts. "Might makes right with him," opined the Merion Town Council of his disregard for traffic regulations. With his brother Erwin, he was engaged in the inventing and small manufacture of automobile parts when the First Draft came along, and at the age of twenty-four he registered and claimed exemption because of his business and because he owned a

[50] These facts are taken from the original record of the General Court-Martial, No. 137698, at the Judge Advocate General's Office, Washington.

farm. Exemption was not granted. In July, 1918, Local
Board 32 mailed him a questionnaire which he failed to
return. The Local Board reported his delinquency to the
Adjutant General of Pennsylvania, who thereupon sent
Bergdoll the dread white post-card, Form 1014, ordering
him to report by 1 P.M. on August 8, or be thereafter
in the military service of the United States and subject to
military law.

But Bergdoll had disappeared. Defiant and bragging
post-cards, mailed by friends in cities where he certainly
was not, sent government agents chasing from one corner
of the country to another. Sheriffs and constables barred
country roads and searched automobiles; city police cast
out their "drag-nets." Excited by slacker hysteria in general and spurred on by newspaper headlines about Bergdoll in particular, watchful citizens thought they saw
him in every dark corner. His old habit of speeding
caused him to be arrested and fined in Peoria, Ill.; ab-
sent-mindedly he gave his right name, which, strangely
enough, was not recognized. In Milwaukee a closer
squeak occurred when he came back to a garage for his
car and found "Bergdoll — Phila." chalked on it — the
warning allowed him a get-away. A nation-wide man-
hunt, backed by the Army, the Department of Justice,
and all the police in the country, failed to capture him
until January 7, 1920, seventeen months after his disappearance and fourteen months after the Armistice.
The search had extended into Mexico and Canada. Bergdoll, when caught, said he never left the country. For a
year and a half he and a companion had lived under false
names at a hotel in Hagerstown, Md. Five times he made
flying visits home.

Even behind bars, Bergdoll was almost as slippery as
before capture. The wealth which had helped him to
play tag with the authorities for so long now hurried to

his defense. Mrs. Bergdoll had given up the thin claim to a felon's exemption based on a three-months' jail sentence Grover had once incurred for speeding, but she hired astute lawyers and gave them *carte blanche* and blank checks. Yet in spite of an attempted habeas corpus proceedings in New York, and in spite of a plea of insanity which a medical board disallowed (Bergdoll as a child used to have fits of jumping up and down in bed and "making faces"), the Army kept hold of him and tried him for desertion at Governors Island, N. Y., March 4, 1920, under the 58th Article of War. A general court-martial[51] of eleven officers found him guilty, and he was sentenced "to be dishonorably discharged from the service" —the formal phrase has an ironic ring, considering the energy, ingenuity and nerve Bergdoll had expended in trying to keep out of this service — and he was committed to the Disciplinary Barracks at Ft. Jay, N. Y., for five years at hard labor. The press proceeded to give loud cheers that the super-slacker had met with his deserts.[52]

And still, in the face of this apparent simplification, the case grew more complicated. This is not the place to survey the lines of influence which ramified behind Bergdoll: Suffice it that in April Judge John W. Westcott, a prominent Democrat of New Jersey and the man who had twice nominated Wilson for the presidency, was asked to secure a lawyer for Bergdoll; suffice that the lawyer thus employed for the renewed effort of Bergdoll to go free was a former Army officer, who had been Acting Judge Advocate General when the desertion was committed; suffice it that in May this lawyer secured from the

[51] A court-martial is a board made up of at least five officers, empowered to try all soldiers in its jurisdiction for violations of the Articles of War. These last are a body of 121 articles enacted by Congress to govern the Army.

[52] Brother Erwin had likewise evaded service, but was still at large; he gave himself up on July 22. The notoriety was too much for two elder brothers of the Bergdolls, who had their names legally changed to free themselves from bad odor.

War Department a certain order in regard to Bergdoll. In itself the order was a wholly commonplace practice; in the light of what followed it became sensational. For from the Secretary of War or from the Adjutant General (the real authority is impossible to trace) Bergdoll's lawyer procured an order releasing Bergdoll under armed guard from Ft. Jay on three days' parole, not to visit dying relatives, etc., as Army practice allowed — but to find a "pot of gold." Bergdoll claimed that while hiding in Hagerstown he had secreted a metal box containing $105,000 in gold in a mountain hiding-place known only to himself; it was this he wanted to retrieve.

The order was carried out. On May 20, 1920, Bergdoll and two armed sergeants got into his chauffeur-driven car and headed south. By accident, as they were passing through Philadelphia the car balked and stopped; the chauffeur could do nothing with it. By accident, Bergdoll discovered that his house stood just around the corner. He invited the sergeants to spend the night there while the car was being repaired. The next afternoon found Bergdoll seated in the second-floor living-room of his home entertaining the two guards by reciting Shakespeare. History does not disclose his selection — could it have been? —

> Once more into the breach, dear friends, once more. . . .
> In peace there's nothing so becomes a man
> As modest stillness and humility:
> But when the blast of war blows in our ears,
> Then imitate the action of the tiger. . . .
> Be copy now to men of grosser blood
> And teach them how to war.

The telephone rang in the next room. Bergdoll got up nonchalantly and went to answer it. After a few minutes the guards grew curious and started to look for him, with increasing panic and no success.

Bergdoll has not been seen again in the United States to this day.

The furore at this escape was tremendous. Press and public called aloud for an investigation; day by day the papers chattered developments, screamed innuendo of scandal. Morning papers[53] reported Secretary of War Baker had given permission for Bergdoll's parole; evening papers denied it. Mrs. Bergdoll threw up her hands and exclaimed, "He is one foolish boy!" The reward for Bergdoll's capture, begun with the regulation Army bounty of $50, swelled by $2000 from Bergdoll's lawyer and $500 from *The American Legion Weekly*, stood at a total of $4075. A Philadelphia Grand Jury indicted nine persons, censured three others. The Army ordered a court-martial of the commandant of Ft. Jay and the two beguiled sergeants—all three were acquitted. A committee of Congress investigated, divided into two groups, and returned majority and minority reports — the former finding the Army culpable, the latter blaming only Bergdoll's civilian friends and relatives.

At last came concrete information about Bergdoll. For months newspapers had reported him heading toward Mexico, Cuba, South America, Japan, and way-points south, east, north, and west. Actually, his car had taken him and a companion to Montreal; they went to Winnipeg where they secured false passports, then moved east again, and sailed for Scotland and finally Germany. American newspapers of November 3, 1920, printed authentic word of Bergdoll's presence in Germany, where he was being treated like a hero; and declared that if he should enter the American-occupied territory about Coblenz he would be arrested. In January, 1921, two mem-

[53] May 22, 1920.

bers of the Army's Criminal Investigation Department, with more zeal than prudence, tried to kidnap Bergdoll from Eberbach. The town was not in occupied territory — the detectives were nearly torn to pieces by a mob, and were saved by the German police only to be tried for attempted manslaughter. Maj. Gen. Henry T. Allen, in command of the American forces at Coblenz, apologized to the German Government.[54]

That is as far as the story need go. If Bergdoll ever returns to United States custody he must serve four years and ten months of his unexpired term, and must face trial for another desertion and for escape from confinement. The man who ran away twice is still running after fourteen years.

Bergdoll was but one of 337,649 deserters from the Draft — the percentage of those inducted into service, 11%, was pretty high. Of these, 163,738 were apprehended and dealt with before July 15, 1919.[55] About 13,000 were later eliminated from the status of deserters for one reason or another, leaving about 160,000 men — the grains which escaped the machine completely. This list, *via gloriæ* of the slacker, was later published formally in the newspapers.

IX

The Conscientious Objector, Including the Story, with a Happy Ending, of One of the Most Sincere

In the eyes of the War Department, Private Richard Stierheim also stood a deserter. But no man can say he

[54] Our Government would have no grounds for requesting the extradition of Bergdoll, since no American treaty provides that political offenders, including military refugees, be extradited. America has harbored many aliens wanted by their own countries on this score.

[55] War Department Information Section, May 18, 1921.

"ran away." His whole running was toward the penalty demanded by the irreducible conflict between the Army and his private conscience — the dilemma of the true conscientious objector. Turning to Stierheim's story from that of Bergdoll is like laying down the depressing farces of Molière and taking up the pages of Bunyan — it is Mr. Christian being tried by a 20th century court-martial in France.

Stierheim had been brought up a Catholic, but after the age of fifteen he attended church chiefly to sing in the choir. He was working in the Sparrows Point Shipyard, Baltimore, when he was drafted and sent overseas as a private in Company D, 315th Infantry. On September 14, 1918, while his company moving into the front passed through Brocourt Woods, he walked quietly away and disappeared until he was arrested at Cerbère on the Spanish border on September 22. A court-martial of eight officers convened at Thillombois on October 21 to try him for desertion in the face of the enemy.

Stierheim pleaded guilty, even when warned by the Court that by this plea he freely admitted "all the essential elements of the crime,"[56] and chose to testify under oath for himself. He didn't believe in war. When he was drafted the Local Board refused his plea of exemption on this ground and inducted him into service. Although his division, the 79th, went to France, the torture to his conscience did not abate; twice he deserted, simply in order to be court-martialled and thus resolve his inner conflict, but each time they returned him to his company. And so, at the last chance before he would be called upon to kill, he had deserted again. By walking and by hopping freight-cars he travelled toward Spain, because he thought if he were once interned there the Army could

[56] This and following quotations are taken from the original record of the General Court-Martial, No. 124728, Judge Advocate General's Office, Washington.

not fail to court-martial him after the War. All this the Court learned.

Question of the Court: "What were your motives in leaving the company?"

Stierheim: "The whole trouble — if I wouldn't I would be in a position where I would have done something the last few minutes of my life I had no reason for and lose the better part of eternal life. It was nothing left for me to do but leave. They didn't see fit to do anything else with me so I ended it myself."

Court: "Tell the Court what your beliefs are about killing other men."

Stierheim: "I believe in God; I believe He is supreme, above all things; I believe He placed me in this world to serve Him. He laid down Ten Commandments which we are supposed to keep. If I take the authority from any other person to break the Commandments, it shows I believe they are higher than God. When the country got into war and since the army had to be killing one another, I could see nothing else but the country's laws are higher than the laws of God, and instead of dying for the laws of the country I choose to die for the laws of God. I knew what it was when I left and know what will have to answer for it — so I left, that is all. I don't claim to be perfect. There was only One Man perfect."

Court: "Is there anything more you want to say?"

Steirheim: "That by going up to the front and being killed I didn't see how I could stand up on Judgment Day and say I died fighting for God Almighty. I wasn't keeping his commandments at the time, I was serving the country at the time, and I don't doubt what He would say — you were serving your country instead of Me, that it is up to you to take the penalty."

The court-martial sentenced him "to be shot to death with musketry." But that was what Stierheim wanted.

Now a court-martial cannot execute its judgment without higher authority. While the record of the trial lay before General Pershing, Stierheim was returned to his company as a prisoner. The company moved into the front. And from the night of November 3 until the Armistice, he conducted himself in such a way that a captain and a lieutenant wrote to the Commanding General of the Division, the C. G. wrote to the Commander-in-

Chief, the C.-in-C. wrote to the Adjutant General of the Army in Washington, the A. G. wrote to the Judge Advocate General, the J. A. G. wrote to the Secretary of War, and the Secretary wrote to the President, with this result of Pershing's own recommendation:

In the foregoing case of Private Richard L. Stierheim (1813987), Company D, 315th Infantry, the sentence is confirmed. In view, however, of Private Stierheim's meritorious service and conspicuous gallantry under fire occurring subsequently to the date of his trial, the sentence is remitted. During the attack of his regiment against Hill No. 378, north of Verdun, France, commencing on November 3, 1918, Private Stierheim who had been taken to the front as a prisoner with his company volunteered to go out into "No Man's Land" at night to rescue wounded men. Unassisted he rescued six wounded men under machine-gun fire, carrying in one man who had been shot six times and could not move. Thereafter for eight or nine days until the signing of the Armistice he voluntarily worked as a litter-bearer carrying wounded men under intense shell fire, showing the utmost indifference to danger and courage and devotion to duty of an unusual character. Private Stierheim will be released from confinement and restored to duty [non-combatant service].

(signed)   WOODROW WILSON.

The White House,
   8 April, 1919.

The conscientious objector is no modern problem; Mark Antony exempted Jews from military service because they would not bear arms on the Sabbath, Gibbon mentions the summary fate of two Roman objectors in the third century, Napoleon during his campaigns allowed Mennonites to serve as hospital workers. But the Army in 1918, with no more precedent than the contemporary practice of Great Britain and Canada, did recognize and treat seriously one class of objector who in earlier wars had received no hearing.

There are two classes of conscientious objectors. The first is easy to attend to, easy to dismiss. By the Draft those members of a religious sect which disenjoined war were declared exempt — an affidavit, and the case was ready for decision; the Boards granted 56,830 claims of exemption to members of such religious bodies as the Quakers, Mennonites, Plymouth Brethren, Dunkards, and Molokans, and others even less familiar.

But the more troublesome problem, albeit numerically

Fellow workers. there is only one thing for workers in America to do. and that is REFUSE TO SERVE IN THE ARMY. REFUSE AT ANY COST TO KILL OR BE KILLED FOR THE GAIN OF PROFIT-TAKERS.

OUR FIGHT IS WITH THOSE WHO ROB US OF THE CHANCE TO LIVE A DECENT LIFE. THOSE PEOPLE ARE ALL HERE IN THE UNITED STATES. FIGHT THEM. LET US UNDER NO CIRCUMSTANCES SUBMIT TO CONSCRIPTION. BETTER DIE AS FREE MEN. THAN KILL OR BE KILLED. OR EVEN TO LIVE, AS SLAVES.

DOWN WITH CONSCRIPTION! RESIST! RESIST! RESIST!

ANARCHISTS COMMUNISTS.

Rare Book Room, New York Public Library.

Anarchists Communists in 1917 published this appeal to "Liberty Loving People" in an effort to defeat the draft.

negligible, was that of the sincere individual objector; his private scruples gripped him just as strongly as the creed of a sect. Pages and pages were written about this type of man, painting him all black or all white — he was a "villain and coward," he was a "saint of a new order." The kernel of this eternal argument lies in two classical quotations; Socrates, speaking as the voice of "The Laws" to Crito, stated the view against the objector: "Having brought you into the world, and nurtured and educated you, and given you . . . a share in every good that we [The Laws] had to give, we proclaim . . . the right to every Athenian that if he does not like us

. . . he may go where he pleases . . . but if he still remains, he has entered into an implied contract that he will do as we command him." Opposed to that is the ideal contained in Marcus Aurelius's words: "He says, 'Dear city of Cecrops'; wilt thou not say, 'Dear City of God'?"

An Executive Order of March 20, 1918, recognized this type of objector with "other conscientious scruples," and arranged for him as well as for the religious objector to engage in non-combatant service. Such men were segregated by themselves in the camps under a "tactful and considerate officer," as the Order commanded, pending judgment on their cases. In June the Secretary of War set up a Board of Inquiry[57] which began travelling from camp to camp all over the country to examine these objectors in personal interviews and determine their sincerity. By December 24, some 2100 men had been interrogated; of these, 478 were recommended for non-combatant service, some 1500 for furloughs to farm and industrial work, and only 122 were assigned to military service because their claim was found insincere. Without examination by the Board, about 1300 other objectors accepted non-combatant service voluntarily; of those more purist in theory or more stubborn, 371 were tried by court-martial (usually for disobedience to orders) and sentenced to an average of ten years' confinement. All told, some 3900 men were recognized by the Army as individual conscientious objectors. The Board of Inquiry was a costly and tedious procedure, but it assured a large measure of justice to these comparatively few grains caught in the threshing machine.

[57] The Board was composed of a major from the J. A. G. D. as chairman; Julian W. Mack, Judge of the U. S. Circuit Court of Appeals, and Harlan F. Stone, Dean of the Columbia University Law School (later Justice of the Supreme Court). The officer on the Board was ordered over-seas in August, to be succeeded by Maj. Walter G. Kellogg, J. A. G. D., whose book, "The Conscientious Objector," 1919, furnished much of the material here used.

17

WILSON ORGANIZES FOR WAR

The Process Consisting, to a Large Degree, of Delegating Functions to Others, While Wilson Reserved His Own Time and Vitality for the Cerebration of Ideas. Wilson's Principal War Captains. To Be at His Best, Wilson Needed Men About Him Whose Personalities Geared Comfortably into His Own, and He Was Fortunate in Having, for Three of the Principal War Functions, Men Whose Power Depended on, and Whose Success Flowed from, Possession of Personal Qualities Which Wilson Found Sympathetic.

WILSON, with the war upon him, retired further into himself.[1] Not in the sense of refuge or brooding, but rather that he might function the better. He visualized the war as one of ideas, he was the principal source of ideas on the Allied side, and he guarded the delicate mechanism of mood and mentality of which his ideas were the fruit.

Always Wilson had shunned company in the miscellaneous sense, welcomed only that which in peculiar and refined ways was kin to his spirit. Partly because of frailness of physical strength, slenderness of his stores of nervous vitality, he had always been fretted by men whose minds or personalities did not happen to possess the particular combination of qualities[1a] that was sym-

[1] "Mr. Wilson's regard for his time became an actual obsession; everything and everybody were excluded that did not bear upon his task."— George Creel.

"Wilson took personal command of the government. He isolated himself still further, remaining much in his private apartments and seeing few people." — "The Political Education of Woodrow Wilson," James Kerney.

[1a] "In such cases — and there were many — he had a way of retiring within himself, there was no 'rise' to him, no sparkle of humor and fancy. [Such] callers would go away with the conviction that they had met a modern impersonation of Jonathan Edwards. Although his personality was sensitive, vibrant, and high strung, he was able to make his countenance a perfect mask. . . . I had the rare privilege of seeing him in intimate relations as a member of his family. I

pathetic to his own. In contact with crudeness, or blatancy, or assertiveness, or exuberance, or pomposity, Wilson's own spirit shrivelled. Even harmless banality, of a sort that to robuster men might have been amusing, was to Wilson a harsh nettle from which he shrank. Once he said to me that of all the experiences the Presidency required of him, the most fretting was to be told something he already knew — "it sends me to bed sick." So slight an irritation as lack of precision in words used by a caller set him on edge: his son-in-law, Secretary of the Treasury McAdoo, used the phrase "under the circumstances"; Wilson, achieving pedagogical patience with some effort, explained the Latin derivation; "circum" meaning "around" and "stare" meaning to stand; hence, McAdoo should say "in the circumstances."

The springs of Wilson's spirit flowed freely only in the company of persons having just the right traits of

---

knew his mental habits, I saw clearly the general pattern of his thought and life. But in another sense I hardly knew him at all. There were wide and fertile reaches of his spirit that were closed to me." — William G. McAdoo, son-in law of Wilson and Secretary of the Treasury, in "Crowded Years."

"Wilson was sensitive, shy, reserved. There were intimacies to which he would not admit the public. These were inhibitions resulting from temperament. He could only with difficulty attempt to reveal himself. With only a few men did he seem to be at real ease. The difficulty Wilson had in freely meeting people, aside from his temperament, was reinforced by a certain philosophy he entertained, by the stress under which he worked, and by his physical state. On account of the fact that he was never over robust and that the demands on him were terrific, he felt it imperative to limit his social contacts to the minimum." — David F. Houston, Member of Wilson's cabinet (Agriculture and Treasury), in "Eight Years With Wilson's Cabinet."

"Mr. Wilson's delicately attuned mind is acutely pained at hearing a statement of fact or opinion which he knows to be wrong or feels to be wrong. He does not have those abundant reserves of nervous energy which enable other men under similar circumstances to be merely amused and to look bland. He has neither the physical nor the nervous strength for rough-and-ready give and take. . . . The President regards his mind as a machine with just so much capacity for just so much output during the twenty-four hours; and if you let the machine tear around on all kinds of trivial subjects, the serious output it can turn out in the course of a day is to that degree reduced. I have often thought that the President must have been made aware in early life that he has a limited quantity of nervous force in his reservoir and must have made up his mind to pay it out only in such quantities and to such ends as will afford the maximum return." — Mark Sullivan, in *Collier's Weekly,* January 31, 1920.

mind and personality. Included among the traits he needed in those about him was femininity; he liked to have women near him, and the men whom he liked had to have feminine traits. Femininity, but by no means lack of masculinity. Many of the men whom Wilson liked best, from whom he got most cheer and refreshment, such as Tumulty, were the most robust of males; but they had to have also sensitiveness, instinctive delicacy, insight, perceptiveness, qualities which in Tumulty's case were supplied by his deeply Celtic temperament.

It was fortunate for Wilson and the country that for the conduct of essential activities of the war, he found, or there gravitated to him, at least three men who in their personalities combined temperaments tuned to his own, together with high executive capacity for the tasks Wilson gave them.

One was Newton D. Baker, Secretary of War; Baker could always smooth the quirks out of Wilson's spiritual commotions — once when Wilson, angry, was about to write a letter "bawling out" a Cabinet member, Franklin K. Lane, Baker suggested: "Let me take on that quarrel; a row between two Cabinet members is no harm but a row between a Cabinet member and the President would be bad." Another was Bernard M. Baruch, extraordinarily endowed with energy and decisiveness coupled with intuition and considerateness — upon Baruch's entering the room, the barometer of Wilson's spirit, if previously disturbed, would subside a degree or so toward serenity. A third, utterly different from Baruch and Baker, but sharing with them, in his own way, the capacity to make Wilson comfortable, was George Creel; Creel's appeal for Wilson lay in his robustious vitality, from which Wilson could absorb some for his own habitually depleted stores; Creel was entertaining; sometimes he was entertaining when he did not try to be — the furies of his indignation, the mordancy of his denunciations amused Wilson rather more than they convinced him; and Creel was superbly entertaining when

Wide World Photograph.

Bernard M. Baruch.

he tried to be, was one of the best story-tellers in Washington, had gifts for humorous and accurate characterization of the exalted characters who came and went, had an art of mimicry as great as that which Wilson himself practised when in moods of humor and intimacy.[2]

There were several others who through one trait or another had for Wilson the same peace-conferring quality — Colonel House, as well as Tumulty; but these did

[2] The rôles Wilson occasionally assumed as mimic included those of a slow-minded haw-haw Englishman, a drunken man with thick-tongued speech and wobbly gait, and several living characters, including his son-in-law, Secretary of the Treasury McAdoo.

not have executive responsibility. And there were others in executive positions whom Wilson liked, or at least found not irritating, Secretary Daniels of the Navy, for example. But Baker, Baruch, and Creel were at once *simpatico* to Wilson and had charge of the three most important channels through which Wilson fought the

Photograph by Brown Bros.

Secretary of the Navy Josephus Daniels.

war. Baker in charge of the army, Baruch as head of industrial mobilization, and Creel in charge of the dissemination of ideas were the three tines of Wilson's fighting trident. There was the navy, but a navy could do little against a German navy which refused to come out and fight; moreover, the American navy could only be the small brother of the British one. There was the Secretary of State, but Wilson wrote all his own state papers. By the nature of this war, and especially in the way in which Wilson conceived it and directed it, the three principal agencies were Baker as Secretary of War, Baruch as Chairman of the War Industries Board, Creel as chairman of the idea-disseminating, emotion-rousing function that went with the Committee of Public Information.

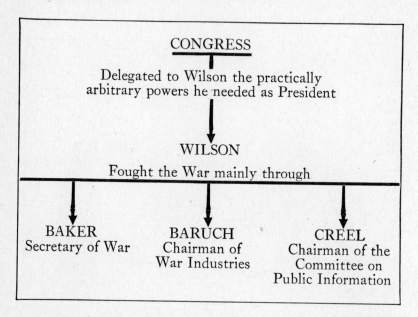

CONGRESS

Delegated to Wilson the practically arbitrary powers he needed as President

WILSON

Fought the War mainly through

BAKER	BARUCH	CREEL
Secretary of War	Chairman of War Industries	Chairman of the Committee on Public Information

Baker was able, fertile with ideas, subtle and eloquent in expression, had more than adequate talent for administration, knew when to delegate authority and when to keep it himself; when he sent Pershing abroad he told him he would give him but two orders, one to go and one to return; when subordinates were troubled by the necessity of ordering army supplies before Congress had appropriated the money, Baker insisted on taking that responsibility, and the risk of Congressional censure, squarely on his own shoulders — "that is what a Secretary of War is for," he said. But fine as was Baker's ability, adequate as was his performance, his adaptability to the job he had was less essential than that of Baruch to mobilizing industry and Creel to conducting the war of ideas, because both these functions were new in this war. Baker had the precedents of a long line of men who had filled his office back to Stanton of the Civil War, precedents teaching sometimes what to do, sometimes what not to

Photographs by U. S. Army Signal Corps.

"Two fine old Romans."

General Tasker H. Bliss.   Major-General Hugh L. Scott.

do; and had Baker been less than able, the War Department could have been adequately conducted through no more than accepting the advice of the two fine old Romans who served Baker successively as Chiefs of Staff, Generals Hugh Scott and Tasker H. Bliss, splendid examples of the type that the army system frequently brings to the top. For the rôles that Baruch and Creel had, however, there was no permanent staff and no precedent; Baruch mobilizing industry and Creel mobilizing emotion and ideas had to embark on uncharted seas.

18

THE "CONFLICT OF SMOKESTACKS"

The Industrial Resources of the Country Are Mobilized for War by the Council of National Defense and by Some Collateral Organizations. When Need Arises for More Compact Solidarity in this Area of War, Wilson Asks for and Receives from Congress Autocratic Power Over Industry. To Achieve Unity of Operation, Wilson Makes Bernard M. Baruch Head of the War Industries Board, with Almost Literally Unlimited Authority.

It was Baker himself who observed[1] that modern warfare demanded a vast deal more than the sling that was enough for David, that in this war the making of the sling, the preparing of the missile, was a process that reached back from the front all the way to every factory, farm, and mine in the country. That realization, shared by everybody, conceded how much more the United States must now do besides the drafting, training, transporting, and arming soldiers that was Baker's function as Secretary of War. The "much more" be-became the function of Baruch.[1a]

[1] "War is no longer Samson with his shield and spear and sword, and David with his sling; . . . it is the conflict of smokestacks now, the combat of the driving wheel and the engine." — Secretary of War Newton D. Baker, to a conference of trade publication editors, May 25, 1917.

"The European War has brought into sharp relief the fact that under modern conditions a great war involves . . . such an organization of the industrial and commercial, financial and social resources of the nation as will enable them to be mobilized both to support the military arm and to continue the life of the nation during the struggle." — Secretary of War Baker, in a memorandum for President Wilson, April 7, 1916.

"Modern wars are not won by mere numbers. . . . They are won by the scientific conduct of war, the scientific application of industrial forces." — Woodrow Wilson.

"The outcome depends upon . . . the skilful and unified use of the nation's entire social and industrial no less than military power." — Theodore Roosevelt.

[1a] Long before Baruch was given command, however, most of the work of mobilization had been done, and well done, by a Council of National Defense, and by some collateral organizations. What Baruch supplied, during the closing half of the War, was unity of command, and the decision and prompt effectiveness which could be achieved only with unity of command.

II

In the early winter months of 1918, complaint rolled up to Washington about conduct of the war. "There is a pervading fear," said the New York *Times*,[2] "[about] administrative incapacity." Part of it was the natural

Secretary of War Newton D. Baker was savagely lampooned by George Harvey's *Weekly*. In this case Secretary Baker was represented as replying unctuously to criticism of his conduct of the War Department: "The situation is entirely satisfactory."

anxiety of the public whose sons had been drafted; part was Republican partisanship. Part came from Theodore Roosevelt — it is difficult to say how much was sincere alarm and how much was equally sincere personal irritation at seeing Wilson filling an office which Roosevelt felt would be better filled by himself — "Wilson sitting in my chair" was a phrase the impish attributed to Roosevelt. Part of the criticism was personal animus

[2] January 14, 1918.

against Wilson and Baker — Colonel George Harvey, Wilson's early sponsor, now his bitter enemy, had started a little sheet called *Harvey's Weekly* of which the spirit was to crucify Wilson and "break Baker." Harvey's paper called Baker "Newtie Cootie," a "chattering ex-Pacifist," said Baker was seated "on top of a pyramid of confusion which he has jumbled together and called a war machine." Others said "We need a butcher, not a Baker."

That some of the criticism was sincere is proved by one who became the principal spokesman of it. Senator George E. Chamberlain of Oregon was a Democrat, therefore free from imputation of unsympathetic partisanship. He was Chairman of the Senate Committee on Military Affairs, therefore had peculiar right to speak and to have weight given to his words. Chamberlain was a man of considerable quality; the friendly biographer of Baker[2a] felt obliged to concede, that "in the present crisis, Chamberlain occupied the position of a leader who has broken party bonds for patriotism's sake."

Chamberlain's Committee on Military Affairs summoned Baker for an examination that lasted three days of four to six hours each. On January 18, Chamberlain, as principal speaker at a public luncheon in New York under the auspices of the National Security League, declared: "The military establishment of America has broken down. . . . It has almost ceased functioning. I speak not as a Democrat but as an American."

In the audience, Theodore Roosevelt sprang to his feet, led the applause. Nineteen hundred persons cheered Chamberlain's courage, expressed dismay and indignation over his charges. The following week, an informal council of protest was set up at Washington; Theodore

[2a] Frederick Palmer.

Roosevelt held a court of indignation at the house of his daughter, wife of Congressman Nicholas Longworth. The demand was in part for a coalition Cabinet, an assembly of the country's best brains to manage the war—

"THE SKIPPER DREW A WHIFF FROM HIS PIPE AND A SCORNFUL LAUGH LAUGHED HE"

"Ding" in the New York *Tribune* drew upon a school boy classic for his inspiration in this cartoon, showing Wilson defiantly facing the storm beating upon his Secretary of War.

the British, with the authority of experience, were quoted as saying, "We wonder if you have all the big men whom you might bring together in your government." In part, the demand was for unified management of supplies. Herbert Hoover was mentioned as a possibility.

Wilson was disturbed, of course. Bringing to bear on this domestic situation the Napoleonic talent he had for strategy in the world of ideas, he instructed Tumulty to manœuvre into the press disapproval of the notion of a coalition cabinet. Then, he said, in effect, by action, "since more efficient administration is demanded, I will show how to attain it, and I will take responsibility for it." He wrote out a bill conferring on himself practically unlimited power to organize and direct the country's resources. He gave the bill to Democratic Senate leader Martin of Virginia to introduce. Martin, reading the measure, startled by the extent of the powers granted, declined to introduce it. It was sponsored by Senator Overman of North Carolina. With some modification, it was passed; since there had been clamor for greater efficiency, there could hardly be refusal to grant it in the form the President proposed it. With the powers in his hand, Wilson summoned Bernard M. Baruch, in effect delegated to him the power to co-ordinate and command the country's resources. Management of the Army of course remained with Baker.

III

The job of Bernard M. Baruch, as Chairman of the War Industries Board, was, to express it in one figure of speech, to operate the whole United States as a single factory dominated by one management, with the relation of the departments to each other worked out as smoothly as in Henry Ford's factory; to achieve as co-ordinated a production of material for war as Ford achieved for automobiles. By another figure, the job was to bring the whole industrial structure of the United States into one organism, similar to the human body, with materials flowing along the arteries, veins, and capillaries in quantities and at a speed regulated and adjusted by a single intelligence.

The "single intelligence" was Baruch, except that Baruch, in the exercise of the many-sided wisdom he possessed, realized that no one intelligence could possibly be enough, and to put away from himself and from the job all notion of autocracy, in fact or in spirit. The men with whom Baruch surrounded himself were an élite of industry. Not that he merely turned to a blue book of business and drafted a list of men who had already come to the top — that would have brought him, for the present purpose, not a few stuffed shirts. Rather he carefully selected men who at once had experience in their fields, together with flexibility of mind, imagination, force, and the qualities of temperament that commended them for a unique, enormous, and intricate job.

IV

There had been, even before we entered the war, vague realization that preparedness on our part must include preparedness in the industrial sense. Out of that early conception grew, as early as 1915, a non-governmental "Committee on Industrial Preparedness," set up by the United States Chamber of Commerce, and also a "Preparedness Committee of the Naval Consulting Board." Out of those, and some other pioneer organizations, grew in 1916 an official "Council of National Defense,"[3] consisting of six Cabinet officers, the Secretaries of War, Navy, Interior, Agriculture, Commerce and Labor, together with an "Advisory Commission" of civilians. Presently, since Cabinet members in those hectic days had more than enough to do in their respective departments, the Advisory Commission, which was the tail,

[3] Set up by Act of Congress, August 29, 1916.

had to wag the dog. This Advisory Commission included some of the country's most eminent business leaders, especially ones familiar with organization of industry on a nation-wide scale, such as Walter S. Gifford of the American Telephone and Telegraph Company; Julius Rosenwald, head of a mail-order house of national scope, Sears-Roebuck; Daniel Willard, head of the Baltimore & Ohio Railroad. The Advisory Commission and the Council of National Defense did a job for which there was literally no precedent, except what they could learn from the experience of other countries already in the War, chiefly Britain. Functioning primarily as "a body of thinkers and directors of research, compilers of data and makers of inventory,"[3a] the Commission set up 184,000 local councils in the States, counties, and smaller communities of the country which, from the beginning of the War to the end, "transmitted to the people the needs of the government and reflected back to Washington the moods of the people."[3a] A women's committee of the Council kept touch with some four million women. As the country got deeper into the war, and the need for organization of industry became more imperative, the Advisory Commission, mainly civilian heads of industry acquainted with sound administrative practice, seeking the indispensable ideal of "central authority and decisive information," recommended, and the official Council of cabinet members voted, in willing abdication, to establish a "War Industries Board,"[4] to be made up largely of civilians familiar with industry. Those two overlapping organizations, composed mainly of the same men, the Council of Na-

[3a] The quotation is from Grosvenor B. Clarkson, Secretary of the Council.

[4] Two books authoritative, thorough, dealing with the work of the War Industries Board, are "Industrial America in the World War," by Grosvenor B. Clarkson, and "How America Went to War — The Giant Hand," by Benedict Crowell and Robert Forrest Wilson.

tional Defense and the War Industries Board, carried on the industrial side of the War during the first eleven months. One of the members was Bernard M. Baruch, and when the need arose for greater solidarity of command, Wilson, on March 4, 1918, wrote a letter to Baruch, appointing him chairman of the War Industries Board, and delegating to him, centralizing in him, much of the power that Congress had given to Wilson.

V

"The functions," Wilson wrote in the letter which was a charter of authority to Baruch, included:

"The creation of new facilities and . . . opening up of new sources of supply.

"The conversion of existing facilities. . . .

"The determination, whenever necessary, of priorities of production and of delivery. . . .

"The making of purchases for the Allies. . . ."

Which meant, in practice, that Baruch was to take control[5] of American industry.

As Baruch exercised the function, "control," so far as that word implies dictatorial authority, was too strong. Yet the power of control was there; so far as it was not put baldly into the franchise Wilson gave Baruch, it lay in the personal relation Wilson had with Baruch. Wilson trusted Baruch absolutely, had perfect confidence in his wisdom, and — what was important in the case of Wilson — he was fond of Baruch personally, liked to have Baruch near him. All this, known at once to Washington, and presently known to every head of industry in the country, gave Baruch supreme power.

[5] "As to the control of American business, it became absolute. There was no freedom of individual enterprise. The control was autocratic, as powerful as any which ever reigned in the Russia of the Romanoffs." — From "How America Went to War — The Giant Hand," Crowell and Wilson.

The power in the crude sense, the statutory power to compel, which Congress had given Wilson and Wilson now transferred to Baruch, was never — I think literally never — used. It was Baruch's pride, and the pride of the men he drew round him, to make a "stunt" of getting the results without using the power.[6] In the technic of administration as they understood it and practised it in their private callings, it was confession of ineptness to be obliged to exert arbitrary authority, to say "you must," — they would be a little shamed if any one knew of their doing anything that way. What seemed to them to be the true test of expertness as executives was to achieve their purposes by reason, argument, persuasiveness, understanding of the personalities of the heads of private industries over whom they now had, in effect, command. But the power was always there, and they considered it imperative that the power should be at their hands. They called it "the big stick behind the closet door" — the "pistol in the hip pocket" — but their zest was to keep the pistol concealed, the closet door locked. If ever tension approached the need of threat, the threat took the form not of reaching for the statutory stick, not of an arbitrary "got to," but rather of a gentle insinuation that the Board might bring the recalcitrant to the attention of public opinion, particularly the public opinion of his home community. But that happened only rarely. Far more than on statutory au-

[6] One of Baruch's men, charged with the duty of enforcing "priorities" (prior claims on material, transportation, etc.) against startled and unwilling business men, was a Texan named Edwin B. Parker, by profession a lawyer, by nature a diplomat. "Urbanity, a temper as hard to ruffle as his sense of humor was easy to stir, deliberate and measured in speech, moderation in phrase and nicety in enunciation. Courteous toward another man's ideas even though they conflicted with his own — in sum a personality disarming to the angry, encouraging to the timid, soothing to the ruffled, and confidence-inspiring to the distressful — and above all a supreme belief in the integrity and necessity of his own work — these were the endowments of the priorities commissioner."—"How America Went to War — the Giant Hand," Benedict Crowell and Robert Forrest Wilson.

thority or any form of threat, each of Baruch's aides, skilfully chosen for his experience, got his essential and invincible power from knowing more about the matter in hand than the manufacturer he dealt with. Once I was with Baruch's chief[7] of the Steel Division when he was preparing to discuss prices with the head of the United States Steel Corporation. Replogle could not talk for chuckling. He had before him figures dealing with costs, and as a steel manufacturer himself, as one a little closer to the mills and hearths than the head of the larger corporation could be, Replogle knew more about costs than his caller. The confidence with which Replogle knew what would be a fair price for the government to pay enabled him to carry on the argument with more of eye-twinkling than of table-banging.

Among them, Baruch's men knew all the tricks of every trade. They had had varied experiences as engineers and executives accustomed to being summoned from one industry to another wherever there was pressing need to get things done. They knew figures and studied figures as a tiger knows the tracks of game. For the most part they were the sort that was described by the slang of the day as "Indians," a wild lot in a way. They knew nothing and cared nothing for rule, form or ceremony. One day the Italian Ambassador came into the office of the head of Baruch's production division, Alexander Legge, who had begun life as a Wyoming cowboy and was now in his private capacity general manager of the International Harvester Co. The Italian Ambassador made his entry in a manner that is fitting to Italian ambassadors. If he was surprised when he was greeted with "Hello, sunny Italy! What can we do for sunny Italy today?" — if he was surprised, I say, he was too good an Italian ambassador to let his surprise be seen.

[7] J. Leonard Replogle.

Moreover he could recognize simple friendliness and good-will when he saw it. He asked for some coal. "Sure!" said Legge, "anything Italy wants Italy's got to have"; and he got his coal and got it without red tape, which was the thing he wanted and the thing that Baruch's men were past-masters at doing.

The organization Baruch set up included Divisions of "Requirements," "Finished Products," "Facilities," "Priorities," together with a "Price-Fixing Committee." Beneath these and six other administrative divisions were more than a score of divisions and sections dealing with Chemicals, Explosives, Steel, Textiles, Hide and Leather, Building Materials, and so on through the entire gamut of industry. The War Industries Board had control, potential at all times, actual when they chose to use it, over everything from steel billets to carpet tacks, from pig iron to corsets. And when they decided that the 8000 tons of steel per annum used in corsets was just so much subtracted from that for cannon, they ordered discontinuance of corset manufacture, at the same time giving the makers the opportunity to use their plants to make masks and belts for the army medical corps. That was part of the Industries Board's art, at once of emollience to business men and service for the war: manufacturers could not consume materials and labor for products not essential to the national life — but they were always shown how to convert their factories to war uses. Women's waist factories made signal flags, radiator manufacturers turned to making big guns, automobile body builders made airplane parts, gear plants made gun-sights, piano factories made airplane wings.

There were cases, of course, in which conversion from peace-time industry to war-time could not conveniently be made. Some materials, and labor at all times, were scarce. If they were needed for war work, non-war

work had to be given up. When "Priorities Circular
No. 21" substantially put a veto on non-war building
construction (because of the need for war buildings,
ships, and shipyards), indignation rolled up to Baruch's
office in a cyclonic storm. Senator Calder of New York
complained that the order "prevents the construction of
a barn, a silo, or even a private dwelling-house." The
War Industries Board tactfully backed down to the extent of announcing that if a prospective barn-builder or
other user of materials could get a certificate of necessity from a committee of his neighbors, the War Industries Board would consider the application. The Reverend "Billy" Sunday complained that he was forbidden
to build the "tabernacles" in which he conducted his
meetings. Explanation from the War Industries Board,
combining as always, reason, persuasion, and urbanity,
brought from Mr. Sunday a hearty telegram:

Winona Lake, Indiana,
1918, September 17, p.m. 10.20.

Edwin B. Parker,
War Industries Priorities Committee,
Washington, D. C.

Your kind letter received. I thoroughly understand and
sympathize with you in your position. I gladly comply with
your wishes regarding building of tabernacles and will carefully explain so there will be no misunderstanding on the part
of the public.

W. A. SUNDAY.

VI

One practice of the War Industries Board had a permanent effect on American business, indeed on our fundamental social system, accelerated the tendency toward
uniformity which was rapidly becoming a feature of
American life. Since labor was scarce, whatever would
reduce labor was sought. The Conservation Division[8] of

[8] Headed by A. W. Shaw of Chicago.

the War Industries Board dedicated itself, with enormous ingenuity, to elimination of waste. Manufacturers of plows were persuaded to reduce their 376 different sizes to 76. 232 kinds of buggy wheels were reduced to 4. Manufacturers of typewriter-ribbon were persuaded that 150 different colors was an unnecessarily broad spectrum; 5 standardized colors were substituted. Cutting out unnecessary adornments from pocket knives reduced the number of styles from 6,000 to 100, saving not only much labor but steel that was needed in France. 287 styles and sizes of auto tires were reduced to 9. Colors of shoes were reduced to 3, black, white, and tan; and length of uppers was reduced that there might be more leather for soldiers' shoes. "Baby carriages were standardized, the vanity was stripped from coffins; brass, bronze, and copper caskets were taboo, the sizes and styles of steel ones curtailed." By similar simplifications labor and material for war were saved in the manufacture of bicycles, clocks, furniture, dress-goods, almost everything.

But these comparative trivialities give a too small-faceted picture of what the War Industries Board was, and of American industry under the Board's co-ordinating control. One could visualize it, the stream of materials, minutely intricate in detail, massive in the aggregate, which from the finished shell on the front, ran back to the ultimate mines and factories in which they were produced: a trickle of copper from a Utah mine brought into conjunction with another trickle of manganese from Georgia, and other trickles of chemicals and metals coming through arteries and capillaries from a score of widely separated sources; the flow of each, and their junction-points regulated as nearly watch-like as was attainable by Baruch and his aides at Washington.

In the hot little cubicles of emergency war buildings they never compared either the hard work or their dollar-a-year from the government with the comfort and large incomes of their private callings. They enjoyed it hugely. The judgment of Grosvenor Clarkson[9] was not extreme: "It was undoubtedly the greatest gathering of able business men into a single public enterprise

Photograph by U. S. Army Signal Corps.

Women workers placing powder in shells in a munition plant.

necessitating energetic and continuous effort by each and all that this country and indeed the world has ever known."

For their talent as a group, much was due to the fact that Baruch selected them; for their success, much was due to the radiations that came to them from Baruch's personality. He had made a fortune as a Wall Street speculator. The fortune gave him independence; the

[9] Author of "Industrial America in the World War."

manner of his making it — by the exercise of his individual judgment, without association with any banking group, or with any industry — gave him freedom to
deal with all industries and all bankers impartially; "he
had no past favors to reward, no future benefits to cul-

© Underwood & Underwood.

Making shells in an ammunition factory at Bethlehem, Pa.

tivate." That sounds as if he were grim, puritanical.
Actually he was gay, humorous, gallant, fond of company, boyish, simple — except when circumstances gave
him occasion to draw on his incredible resources of subtlety. His quick insight into human beings told him
instantly whom to cajole, to whom to be father-like and
patient, with whom to be firm; his blue eyes — their
normal softness and variety of expression suggested an
artist as much as a business man — could become cold
steel toward a manufacturer who tried to profiteer. Between him and his associates on the War Industries

Board there was an intimacy and informality like that of a college fraternity. They were all unusual, all had salient personalities; and there was a quality about them that made the sum of them, when they were together, greater than the arithmetical addition of each to each. They understood each other by intuition, resolved themselves into team-work by instinct, generated high spirits

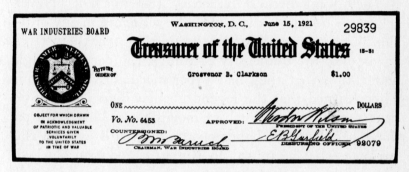

Check to a "Dollar-A-Year Man."

The payee of this, Grosvenor B. Clarkson, was Executive Director of the Council of National Defense. The check is signed by Woodrow Wilson, and in this case countersigned by B. M. Baruch, Chairman of the War Industries Board. A United States statute, for some reason, prohibited accepting services without pay—hence the "Dollar-A-Year." Those who gave all their time and their high talent to the government during the war on this basis included most of the country's leading business men, such as Charles M. Schwab; Alexander Legge, head of the International Harvester Co.; Robert S. Lovett, head of the Union Pacific Ry.; Samuel M. Vauclain, head of the Baldwin Locomotive Works. A complete roster would be a Blue Ribbon list of American industry.

both in accomplishment at their work and in the gay camaraderie which, at Baruch's home in the evening, was the chief reward of their labors.

When their task was finally done, they performed one last and exalted service. When the armistice came, or as quickly thereafter as each could cut off the tag-ends of his war-work, they went home — stopping at the Treasury to get the check for $1 which they would frame for their homes and pass on to their children. They had

had no taste for bureaucracy, and their experience with power and with Washington had infected them with none. Every war-time control, regulation, priority or other form of rule was tossed in the waste basket. American business went back to its basis of individuality as completely as if it had never been interrupted.[7]

They went home. But they remembered. Never again was life quite the same. Never again in any ordinary business or walk of life could they feel themselves geared into the immensity of things, the pace, the high momentum that they had experienced in Washington. They learned that the legend about Cincinnatus, to be true, should be modified. Cincinnatus, in his farm on the Tiber, kept his hands on the plow, his eyes on the furrow — but he mused on Rome, as about an old love never to be recaptured.

[7] But, 14 years later, the wartime regimentation of America was revived, and revived along lines identical with those that had been developed in the war. One of Baruch's subordinates was George N. Peek, another was Major (later General) Hugh L. Johnson — Johnson having become a member of Baruch's organization after he had conducted the operation of the Draft (see Ch. 15). When, in 1933, during the administration of Franklin D. Roosevelt, it was determined to again mobilize American industry, Peek was put in charge of agriculture and Johnson in charge of the remainder of industry. Both men in their new rôles practised with very little change the methods they had learned during the War. This result, fourteen years later, constituted perhaps the most important consequence of the Great War in America.

19

"THE BRIDGE TO FRANCE"

The Sinking of Allied and American Shipping by German
Submarines Goes on at a Pace which Means Defeat for
the Allies. To Meet the Emergency the United States
Creates Vast Ship-building Plants, and the American Navy
Collaborates with That of Britain. New Anti-Submarine
Weapons Are Devised and the Danger Is Averted.

HARDLY had we entered the war when the British told
us of a terrifying condition. That is, they told our government — carefully they, and subsequently we, concealed it for the time being from the public.

The German policy of unrestricted submarine warfare was succeeding. In the first month of unrestriction,
February, 1917, they had sunk 536,000 tons; in the
second month, 603,000 tons. It was estimated that in
April, the month of our entrance, the sinkage would
reach 900,000 tons.[1] And the number of submarines
was increasing, their cruising range extending.

The submarine warfare was succeeding, and success
by the submarines meant that Germany was winning the
war, winning it with the steady deadliness of slow, inexorable strangulation.[2] For the rate at which the sub-

[1] These figures are from "Newton D. Baker," by Frederick Palmer. Edward
N. Hurley, wartime chairman of the United States Shipping Board, in "The
Bridge to France," gives the number of "deadweight tons" actually sunk by
German submarines during April, 1917, as 1,250,000. In all figures in this field
there is a discrepancy between deadweight tons and gross tons. American
tonnage is reckoned in deadweight, British in gross.

[2] "Ships are being sunk faster than they can be replaced by the building
facilities of the world. This means simply that the enemy is winning the war.
There is no mystery about that. The submarines are rapidly cutting the Allies'
lines of communication. When they are cut or sufficiently interfered with, we
must accept the enemy's terms."—Message from American Naval Headquarters
in London to American Ambassador Walter H. Page, June 25, 1917. Printed
by Admiral Wm. S. Sims in "These Eventful Years."

marines were sinking tonnage was *more than twice the rate at which new tonnage was being built.*

During 1917, the submarine destroyed 6,618,623 tons. During the same year, Great Britain's entire new building was but 1,163,474 tons. The next largest builder was ourselves; we turned out about 1,000,000 tons. Except these two, no country was doing enough ship-building to count in such totals. All the other Allies, France, Italy, Japan, and in addition all the neutrals, Norway, Holland, Spain — all told, produced only

U-BOATS SINKING 1,600,000 TONS A MONTH, NEARLY THRICE THE WORLD'S PRODUCTION; DEFEAT THREATENS IF LOSS IS NOT REDUCED

18 British Ships Week's Toll in U-Boat Zone; No Gain Shown Since Beginning of July | APPEAL FOR AID FROM US

New York Times, July 19, 1917.

539,871 tons.[3] All the building by all the Allied countries and by all the neutral countries, by all the world outside of Germany and Austria, was but 2,703,345 tons — less than half what the submarines destroyed.

But the case was really worse than that. To the sinkings must be added the ships which the submarines incapacitated, which were towed limping to port, and often turned out to be more or less total loss; and the ships put out of commission through the normal operation of accident or other misadventure — this source of loss was greater than during peace times, for ships were badly manned, ran without lights, and in the emergencies of war took big chances; and finally the loss of service due to the slowness of operation forced upon ships

[3] From Mark Sullivan's "Wake Up, America," published in April, 1918.

by guarding against the submarine, the waiting for convoys, the low speed entailed when every ship must wait upon the slowest in the convoy, the inability to use some ports, the congestion of others — an American official[4] told a Senate Committee that under normal conditions a ship "ought to make a round trip to Europe in three weeks, but now that the congestion is so great it takes from 50 to 60 days." The sum of all — delays, normal accidents, submarine injuries, submarine sinkings — was that practical paralysis of Allied shipping was in sight — in sight of the alarmed governments but not of the public.

The custodian of the facts about submarine sinkings was the British Admiralty. They published once a week the number of ships sunk by German submarines, eight or ten or twenty or as the case might be. Always the British announcements described the size of the sunk ships in the same phrase, as "of over 1600 tons." To the average man, carrying vaguely in his mind the weight of some remembered great liner, 30,000 tons or so, the phrase "over 1600 tons" seemed soothing. But the British Admiralty knew, and our Shipping Board soon learned, that "over 1600" meant actually on the average "over 5000," that in a week in which the submarines sank 20 ships they sank about 150,000 tons — and that this was much more than twice the quantity of new tonnage built in all the world during the same week.

The theory upon which the British Admiralty, in their weekly public statements, minimized the loss of ships by the phrase "of over 1600 tons" was that it would help destroy German morale; that a submarine commander could not know the size of a ship he sank, having as a rule only one brief look at her through his periscope; that the figures given out by the British

4 Edward F. Carry, Director of the Emergency Fleet Corporation.

would be the first knowledge by the submarine captain of the degree of his success, and that making the figures at once indefinite and low would tend to discourage the submarine commanders, the German Navy, and the German Government.

One may surmise, however, that part at least of the motive of the British Admiralty was not to destroy German morale but to preserve their own. The deadliness of the submarine sinkings to Britain as an island nation might have terrified the stoutest British heart. Shipping was, Lloyd George said, Britain's "jugular vein."

It was not merely that as in every war ships as communications were vital; not merely that as Napoleon put it, "the secret of war is the secret of communications"; not merely that as Fourse[5] put it: "It is an axiom that no army in the field can exist for a long time in an efficient condition unless it has safe communications with its base." It was not merely that as Clausewitz put it, "The lines of communication . . . are to be considered as so many great vital arteries."

It was not merely that. In this war the principal contender on the side of the Allies, Britain, was an island, dependent on ships for food for its civilian population, for its very life. And Britain was now in danger of literal starvation. On April 27, 1917, Ambassador Walter H. Page reported confidentially to President Wilson that the food in the British Isles was not more than enough to feed the civil population for six weeks or two months.[6] It was seriously apprehended that by November Britain might be compelled to surrender by lack of food.

II

Three years before, at the opening of the war in

5 "Lines of Communication in War."
6 "Crowded Years," William G. McAdoo.

1914, the Australian Government had bought or contracted for all the wheat crop of that country. Then it bought some twenty-one ships to carry the wheat to Europe. But the submarine had its way with those ships, and by the time we entered the war not more than four or five were left. Meantime the wheat had been piling up along the Australian docks and railroads. They put some of it in sacks, made walls of the sacked wheat, and poured the rest within the walls. Along the railroads in the interior of Australia there were great bins of wheat ten or twenty feet high and wide, and more than ten miles long. Soon mice appeared. They gnawed through the bags, and the hempen walls collapsed. Under such favorable conditions, the mice multiplied until they became a plague. The Government of Australia put its shoulder to the perfectly serious business of fighting mice. It had special ways of catching them, and crews of men with specially constructed incinerators. Night after night they burned five to ten tons of mice in a single night. But the mice continued to increase. On the soil of Australia, for a few days, man's age-long contest with the forces of nature became an acute pitched battle. Man won a respite only when some mysterious law of nature brought a plague upon the mice, a disease described as a sort of soft ringworm. Then the mice, fleeing from the infection, deserted the wheat piles and ravaged the fields, so that the new crop of Australian wheat was only a fraction of what normally it ought to be.

Meantime, men who had been trying to salvage the piled-up wheat were infected by the disease whose germs had been left in the wheat by the departing mice. From the workmen the infection spread to families and neighbors. There in Australia — about as far away from the battle-fields as one could get and remain on this earth

— was a sort of huge cancer, a direct result of the war —
more specifically a direct result of the famine in ships,
a direct result of the submarine.[7]

III

Rescue from the situation depended on America.
Britain could not increase her building; her man-power
was at the front; her elderly and her young, and much
of her woman-power, was in her munitions plants, and
must remain there. France was much the same. Such
neutral nations as were equipped for much ship-building, Norway, Holland, Spain, had but limited man-
power, and had other uses for it.

America's entrance into the war increased the need
for shipping. If already the tonnage of the world was
under strain to carry enough food to the Allies, enough
munitions to their armies, now there must be more shipping to carry American soldiers to France, and to carry
the food and munitions our soldiers would require. A
solid highway from America to France would hardly be
enough — the "Bridge to France" was what Chairman
Edward N. Hurley called the need which the United
States Shipping Board must meet.

We were ill-equipped. Shipping had not been, since
the days of wooden clippers, an American trade; neither
in shipping nor in ship-building had it been possible for
America to compete against the cheaper labor and long
traditions of other nations. Little more than 10 per cent
of our water-borne foreign commerce (measured in dollars) was carried in American bottoms.

We had little plant to start with, and we were now

[7] This story was told me at the time by an official of the Australian Government who had come to Washington for liaison purposes. Further than that,
I never verified it. I thought at the time it was a situation which some writer
with adequate talent, and leisure to get the details, could make into a narrative
equal to some of Poe's or De Quincey's.

beset, in degree, with the same embarrassment as Britain and France. All our man-power between 21 and 30 had been registered for the draft, and most of those physically able would be taken. And this would be subtracted

WILL TURN 'EM OUT BY THE MILE.

—By De Mar.

Among the greatest of war-time needs was ships to carry supplies to Europe. This cartoon is an artist's conception of how, with mass production, America would meet the emergency.

— *Cartoon by De Mar in Philadelphia Record.*

from a man-power already feverishly busy making supplies for the Allies, and now required to increase its output to meet the added needs of supplies for our own army.

One of our first steps was to elevate work in shipyards into the equivalent of service under arms — men thus employed were exempted from the draft or given "deferred classification." Families having shipyard workers were given service flags, like those for soldiers and sailors. With slogan and poster we made the ship-

Photograph by Underwood & Underwood.
Edward N. Hurley, Chairman of the Shipping Board.

yard worker a hero of the day. To stir him to pride in exertion and facilitate his work, mass meetings were called; an official of the United States Chamber of Commerce[8] went about the country holding meetings near shipyards and urging that, to supplement crowded street-cars, private owners of automobiles should carry shipyard employees to and from their work. A journalist[9] of the day, dwelling upon suggestions for making the need vivid, for creating the spirit of emergency and hurry, wondered "would this situation reach our hearts if we should send couriers throughout the country like

[8] Edward A. Filene.   [9] Mark Sullivan in "Wake Up, America."

Paul Revere, calling out 'two to one; two to one' [the ratio by which we were losing the race]; if we should have the police in the cities warn each home just as he would give warning of fire or of flood; if we should adopt a code for all our bells and whistles and gongs,

ON THE JOB FOR VICTORY
UNITED STATES SHIPPING BOARD   EMERGENCY FLEET CORPORATION

A Shipping Board poster designed to attract workers to the shipyards.

and sound them as we do when fire threatens. The menace is not less great, only the nature of it is such that it appears distant, scattered."

IV

Ultimately we managed it. By organization, eked out by many examples of individual inspiration and inventiveness, we assembled about everything that would float, and set to building new ships in ways that had occurred to no naval architect since Noah. Two San Francisco business men, stimulated mainly by the current emotion and by the spirit of adventure, employing not a naval architect but one who designed houses, made an experiment in concrete ships. The one sample they turned out they named, significantly, the *Faith*; it was satisfactory under some conditions, made several voyages — but ten years after the war was a derelict without salvage

Photograph by Underwood & Underwood.

Palo Alto, one of the largest of the concrete ships, with a displacement of 7500 tons, under construction. The ship was launched sideways at the Government Island Shipyard, Oakland, Calif.

value. Equally daring in innovation but more successful in execution were the "fabricated" ships. Up to that time, the whole of a ship had been built in its yard, each individual plate and strut bent and shaped to its individual complex use. To some engineers, stimulated by the stress of the time, it occurred that ships might be adapted to mass production, that standardized parts could be made in distant steel works, as the parts of bridges and automobiles are, and merely assembled at the yards. It worked; fabrication was the method used at the government's biggest war-time yard; toward the end, 85 per

© *International Film Service.*

When war was declared, crews aboard many German ships damaged them to prevent further use. Under the supervision of the U. S. Shipping Board, repairs were made and the ships pressed into service.

cent of the hulls of ships and much of their other parts were made in distant steel-works.

The government commandeered every ship being built for private ownership in every American shipyard, 431 in all; requisitioned every American steel cargo carrier (of over 2500 tons) afloat, took possession of the

German ships which had been interned in American
ports at the outbreak of the war in 1914, chartered or
commandeered (in some cases by "right of Angary")
neutral ships in our ports, bought ships under construc-

Photograph by U. S. Army Signal Corps.
A ship launching at Mare Island, California.

tion in neutral countries, gave contracts for ships to neutral yards.

We commandeered ships that had been designed and
built for the smooth waters of the Great Lakes, refitted
them for ocean service, and brought them to the seaboard — 12 that were too large to pass through the
Welland Canal were bisected amidships, the parts sealed

by water-tight bulkheads, the sections taken through the Canal, and rejoined in dry dock. We built enormous new yards, expanded what existing ones we had. The little Virginia city of Newport News expanded in a year from a population of 30,000 to 60,000, the growth

Launching of the U. S. S. *Accoma.*
As fast as one vessel was launched, the keel of another was laid.

attended by trying problems of extending water-mains, sewers, and gas-pipes. A dreary, marshy island in the Delaware River, "Hog Island," was turned into 846 acres of compact shipyard, by far the biggest in the world, with 250 buildings, 80 miles of railroad tracks, 20 locomotives, 34,049 male employees, 50 ways upon which 50 ships could be built at once while 28 more were being fitted out at the piers — the central telephone at Hog Island did the business of a city of 140,000.

By the Armistice we had increased the number of our shipyard workers from 50,000 to 350,000; had practically completed 341 shipyards with a total of 1284 launching-ways, more than twice the capacity of all the rest of the world. We built steel ships, fabricated ships,

Submarine chasers alongside floating hangar at Pensacola, Fla.

wooden ships, composite ships of steel and wood, concrete ships; the rule was, take a chance, build any kind of a ship that might be expected to last long enough to make one successful round-trip. We launched 95 ships on one day, July 4, 1918, making the deed feed the day as a substitute for less useful forms of celebration. The Shipping Board built and delivered in 1918, 533 ships of 3,030,406 tons. It was not enough. Half of the American soldiers were carried to France in British ships.   But what in part defeated Germany was the psychological effect of the formidableness of our effort, realization that the submarine could not keep America out of the war, that we could send a huge army to France and maintain it there.

Also, gradually, the submarine was checked, by addition of the American Navy to Britain's, by escorting merchant ships with convoys of naval vessels, by aggressive warfare against the submarines with destroyers and with other devices designed to detect them.   Gradually the submarines diminished in effectiveness: from February 1, 1917, to August 1, 1917, they destroyed an average of 640,000 tons per month; from August 1, 1917, to February 1, 1918, it was an average of 300,-000 tons a month; from February 1, 1918, to the Armistice, the average was 200,000 tons a month.[10]

[10] Admiral William S. Sims, "These Eventful Years."

20

"FOOD WILL WIN THE WAR"

For Food Administrator Wilson Finds the Obvious Choice in One Who Had Had Experience in Feeding Belgium. Story of the Rise of a Man Who, Publicly Unknown when the War Broke Out, Became, in a British Judgment, a "Weary Titan," "the Biggest Man Who Has Emerged on the Allied Side During the War." America Gives and Works and Knits for Belgium. Wheatless Mondays and Meatless Tuesdays and Porkless Thursdays. War-time Eminence of the American Hog, Especially the Female of the Species.

To organize the country's food supply, Wilson's choice was predestined.

Herbert Hoover may be termed a benevolent casualty of the war; caught up in it by accident, a young mining engineer comparatively unknown outside his profession, he came out at the end "the biggest man who has emerged on the Allied side during the war."[1] The rise of such a figure, its combination of quality in the man with adventitious circumstance, is always a fascinating aspect of history.

On August 1, 1914, the only persons who had ever heard of Herbert Hoover were the members of his profession, the alumni of Stanford University, and a small

[1] The quotation is from the London *Nation*. The New York *World* (September 2, 1919) added: "It is a place unique in history that Mr. Hoover has won; he has made that place for himself without reward either of goods or titles by . . . simply seeing the thing that needed to be done and saying, 'Come, let us do it.' "

It is a striking fact that the Great War produced, in America certainly, no outstanding military or naval hero. No fighting man became, in the popular imagination, a hero and symbol; there was no equivalent of Grant or Sherman or Sheridan or Farragut, whose Civil War fame lasted for more than a generation. There was no soldier about whom songs were written, no one who symbolized the glory of war. The only romantic figure, the only American who rose to national eminence as a result of the Great War (Wilson, of course, had achieved his eminence before) had functioned as a civilian, mainly as an organizer of food supply and of humanitarian activities.

number of personal acquaintances. During the first few days of August, however, some thousands of Americans had occasion to become familiar with his name, learn his quality and become beneficiaries of the helpfulness that was his strongest instinct. They had been, some seventy thousand of them, travelling in Europe. Suddenly the paralysis of civilization that war brings left them stranded. In dining-rooms throughout the war zone, hotel waiters disappeared in an hour with explanation reduced to a word, "mobilization," "call to the colors"; trains were diverted between stations to become troop carriers, travellers' cheques became scraps of paper, boundaries between countries became impassable walls. By one device or another most of the stranded managed to reach London, but the relief which came with being in a country where English was spoken was more than offset by discovery that practically no trans-Atlantic boats were available — ships had grimmer business now.

In London, the refugees crowded about the American Embassy. Ambassador Page, harassed, busy with a hundred heavy tasks, looked desperately about for some American — he must be one acquainted with London — who could help him take care of the distressed travellers. He noticed, among the Americans resident in London who had instinctively come forward to help, a quiet, almost shy, boyish-looking man whose efficiency was in proportion to his inconspicuousness. Page asked him to take responsibility, and there resulted a news despatch from London to New York which was the first mention of Herbert Hoover as in any sense a public or important figure:

Another who did admirable relief work was Herbert C. Hoover, a California mining man, who opened an office of his own in the American Consulate and advanced sums of $25 or more in coin to over 300 Americans who had nothing but paper money. He declares he will continue to do so till his stock is exhausted.[2]

The grateful Page, his own appreciation the symbol of that of thousands of the distressed Americans, was able, a few months later, to write to President Wilson a letter which remained in Wilson's memory three years afterward.

. . . Life is worth more, too, for knowing Hoover. . . . He's a simple, modest, energetic man who began his career in California and will end it in Heaven; and he doesn't want anybody's thanks.[3] . . . Hoover himself gave $5,000 for helping stranded Americans and he goes to the trains to meet them, while the war has stopped his big business and his big income; this is a sample of the noble American end of the story.[4]

II

By early September, 1914, Hoover, through infinite resourcefulness, had found ways for the last of the stranded Americans to get home and had begun to make arrangements to come himself. "His private affairs had been disorganized, he had already sent his family home and his one ambition was to get on the first ship sailing for the United States."[5] Hoover was destined to learn, however, that the true rule of life runs contrary to the accepted one, that one good turn leads to a request for

[2] From the New York *Times,* August 6, 1914, reprinted in the same paper 19 years later with a comment which added: "He did not stop till he had fed millions in Belgium and later in all the suffering countries of Europe. The record of that service, as of the activities of the American Red Cross and the Near East Relief, and other such agencies, runs as a golden line of mercy through all the dark pages of the war."

In the same issue of *The Times,* August 6, 1914, Mrs. Hoover is mentioned as helping stranded American women.

[3] American Ambassador Walter H. Page at London to President Wilson in Washington, January 12, 1915. "Life and Letters of Walter H. Page."

[4] The latter part of the passage is from a letter from Page to Edward M. House, September 22, 1914.

[5] The quotation is from Burton J. Hendrick, "Life and Letters of Walter H. Page."

another, that one responsibility accepted and lived up to
leads to an ascending series of heavier ones. About the
time Hoover was ready to sail for home, there appeared
in London from Belgium some persons who told Page of
a condition "immediately alarming: Brussels had only
food enough to feed the people for 36 hours; after that,
unless help was forthcoming, the greatest distress would
set in."[6] Germany's armies, sweeping westward through
almost the whole of Belgium and a segment of northern
France, had left behind a population of approximately
ten million, three-quarters of them Belgians. The region, being predominantly industrial — Belgium normally imported 80 per cent of its food — quickly was
face-to-face with famine. At the beginning of the war
food stocks in stores and warehouses were no more than
enough to supply the needs of the populace for a month;
part of these supplies the invading armies expropriated.
Belgian merchants, when they tried to secure new stocks,
found themselves frustrated by conditions largely the
normal consequences of war, but in their maleficence
seeming a diabolic plot for the extinction of the millions imprisoned behind the German lines. Attempts to
get food from Holland met with refusal: the Dutch
anticipated a food shortage in their own country; besides
Holland was already feeding 700,000 Belgian refugees
who had escaped across the border. Appeals to Germany
met with the reply that Germany had no more than
enough food for herself, that it was a physical impossibility to spare any supplies at all. Belgium literally could
not be fed, either from within her own borders or by
imports from her normal sources of supply. "The suffering in the coming winter," said King Albert in a plea
for help, "will be terrible, but the burden we must bear
will be lightened if my people can be spared the pangs

6 "Life and Letters of Walter H. Page," Burton J. Hendrick.

of hunger, with its frightful consequences of disease and violence."[7]

The cry for help focussed upon Page in London, as representative of the richest neutral country. Again Page turned to Hoover. To Hoover the appeal was a personal crisis; this, he realized, would be no emergency of a few weeks; it would be for the duration of the war. He was obliged to think of his own business affairs; having made enough money to retire, he had intended to devote himself to social and educational projects associated with his university, of which he was a trustee; now, if he abandoned his business affairs, it might become necessary for him to earn his independence anew. A friend[8] who was a guest at his house observed him silent, preoccupied; there was a night of walking the floor. The next morning "Hoover came down to breakfast, we were alone in the dining-room; he bade me good-morning, poured and sweetened his coffee, looked up and said, 'Well, let the fortune go to hell.'" He spent a day winding up his affairs, and notified Page he would take on the Belgian job. Three months later Page was able to write to President Wilson:

"But for Hoover Belgium would now be starved. He's gathering together and transporting and getting distributed $5,000,000 worth of food a month, with a perfect organization of volunteers, chiefly American. He has a fleet of thirty-five ships, flying the Commission's flag — the only flag that all belligerents have entered into an agreement to respect. . . . The surplus food being near exhaustion in the United States and Canada, he has now begun on the Argentine, where the crop is just coming on. I introduced him to the Argentine

[7] The condition of Belgium was once expressed in a vivid simile: "After the burning of Louvain an American correspondent walking along a road near the ruined city saw a child's rag doll that had been run over and crushed by one of the giant gun caissons of the Germans. That doll, he declared, 'was Belgium as he found it after the ruthless invasion.'"

[8] Will Irwin, Stanford classmate of Hoover. The incident is recited in Irwin's "Herbert Hoover, a Reminiscent Biography."

Minister the other day, and the Minister said to me afterwards: 'Somehow I feel like doing what that man asked me to
do.' A stone would weep to hear what Hoover has seen in
Belgium — pitiful beyond all telling."[9]

The Commission for Relief in Belgium was really a

Facsimile of a Belgian Bread-Check

The card is in French and Flemish. The face reads: "No. 6,715. Gratis. City
of Brussels. Department of Public Supplies. Committee No. 1. Street
—. Card issued to the family ——, living at ——, for the daily delivery
of —— portions. To be presented at —— Street. N. B.—Victuals will be
delivered only to the father or mother of a family." The reverse side bears
stamps showing the dates on which rations were issued to the holder. The
original is somewhat larger than this reproduction.

state, an imperium of itself. Its function was triple:
Diplomacy and statesmanship must be exercised continually to get and keep the right to exist. To placate alternately Germany and the Allies, Hoover was constantly
and anxiously back and forth to Berlin, to Paris, to
Brussels, to London. The Allied governments, especially
the British Navy busy with blockading Germany, feared
that food sent into Belgium might fall into the hands

[9] Ambassador Walter H. Page to President Wilson, January 12, 1916.

of the German army, and certainly would relieve Germany from drain on her own food to supply the Belgians; the German government, on the other hand, was at all times on the point of taking the position that permitting food to enter Belgium prolonged the war — to the "*schrecklichkeit*" type of Prussian a literally starving Belgium would be an instrumentality to force peace. A second function of the C. R. B. was to organize at once, in a desperate hurry, a food supply which must come from the ends of the earth, and be enough to feed ten million people — who or what organization had ever before undertaken to feed an entire nation for an indefinite period with imported food? Finally, the Commission must finance itself; it did so in slight part by selling food to affluent Belgians at a price which would permit profit with which to purchase more and better food for those unable to pay, who were about 55 per cent of the whole; the bulk of the support, however, must come through gifts from the benevolent all over the world. When the operations of C. R. B. reached their peak, twenty-five million dollars a month, it was more than the budget of the United States in the Presidency of Grover Cleveland.

In the United States, raising funds and collecting gifts of food and clothing for Belgium was, until we took up arms, the principal direct participation of our people in the war. From practically every village and farm flowed little rills of charity from America's well-to-do to Belgium's starving, even from the comparative poor in America to the desperately poor in Belgium. In Ohio, there were local Belgian relief organizations in 80 out of the State's 88 counties; California had 90 local committees, there were 37 State-wide organizations; the movement expressed itself, among many ingenious ways,

Times Wide World Photograph.

President Herbert Hoover in 1933.

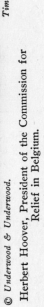

© *Underwood & Underwood.*

Herbert Hoover, President of the Commission for
Relief in Belgium.

in "State food ships" — California sent the *Camino*, Kansas the *Hannah*, loaded with flour contributed by the millers of the State. Catholic children contributed through the Cardinal Gibbons Fund; there was a Dollar Christmas Fund, and a "Belgian Kiddies Limited." The Rocky Mountain Club of New York gave the $500,000

© *Underwood & Underwood.*

John Wanamaker cheering the mercy ship *Thelma* as she sailed for Belgium, loaded with food, clothing, and medical supplies, donated by Mr. Wanamaker. One of America's many efforts to aid the relief work in Belgium.

they had raised to build a new club house. The Rockefeller Foundation sent freighters loaded with flour, beans, and bacon. Shiploads of clothes retrieved from American attics were cleansed, renovated, and distributed — little tots in Liège and Louvain wearing clothes that in their prime had covered and adorned children in Wichita and Des Moines. *The Literary Digest*, Thanksgiving week 1914, organizing a Belgian Flour Fund, asked each reader to "send a barrel of flour, 10 barrels,

50 barrels; we will start the barrels rolling with a contribution of 500; who will match it? Ten ounces of flour a day will keep a soul and body together; a barrel of flour will keep one human being alive a year, the price of one good meal for a family in an American home will keep a Belgian alive for a fortnight, every $5 contribution means a barrel of flour landed in Belgium." *The Digest* printed week after week long lists of those

An illustration used by *The Literary Digest* in its appeal for gifts of flour for Belgium.

who contributed. "Feeding starving Belgium" was for some two years a universal American usage.

III

When America entered the war, management of Belgian relief by an American must perforce end; by the same act Hoover became the obvious man to take on the administration of food which would be a necessary function in war-time America. "Administrator" as the word for it was picked by Hoover; his knowledge of the brevity of official life of European food dictators, as well as his strong instinct for individualism, liberty, and co-operation rather than compulsion, rejected the word "dictator" as well as the minor titles suggested, "controller" and "director."

The job was so to manage the raising and distribution of food crops as not only to feed our own new army and our civilian population, but also to supply much of the food for all the Allied armies and civilian populations. As President Wilson put it, with a vividness of homely phrase Wilson often achieved, America and the Allies, soldiers and civilians alike, were now "eating at the common table." The catering must be accomplished mainly by a country in which much of the man-power on farms would now be diverted to the army and more to ship-building and other essential war-time activities.

At all times, America was the largest producer of meats and cereals (except rice and millet); now the normal dependence of the Allies upon us had been made greater by three years' absorption of their man-power in war. Their need was acute, imperative. Once, late in 1917, English Food Controller Lord Rhondda, hearing the American wheat surplus was exhausted, cabled despondently to America: "We are beaten, the war is over." By care America was able to scrape an extra 20 million bushels from the bottoms of our bins. Again, at the beginning of 1918, Lord Rhondda cabled to Hoover, "Unless you are able to send at least 75 million bushels of wheat over and above what you have sent up to January 1st . . . I cannot take the responsibility of assuring our people that there will be food enough to win the war; imperative necessity compels me to cable you in this blunt way." February 22, 1918, the representatives in America of the three Allied powers, Lord Reading, Ambassador from Great Britain; Count di Cellere, Ambassador from Italy, and André Tardieu, high commissioner from France, united in notifying Hoover: "We feel that every endeavor must be made to ship at least 1,100,000 tons in March. . . . Our excuse for our insistence is the fact, which is well known to you, that a failure to make adequate shipments in March may produce events of incalculable gravity in both Europe and America."

Within this broad process of seeing to it that all the

An important part of America's war effort was to furnish food to the Allies. Fortunately America had adequate crops in 1917 and 1918.

—*Bachelor in the Evening Journal, July, 1917.*

Allies and all America, homes and camps alike, should have ample food, were infinite complexities. Other things being equal, it was desirable that Americans should eat the forms of food that were more perishable and more bulky, those less adapted to shipment across the ocean at a time when shipping was even more scarce than food. Types of food essential for growing children must be set apart for the civilian populations.

Of certain fundamentals, there must be an indispen-

save

1-wheat
use more corn

2-meat
use more fish & beans

3-fats
use just enough

4-sugar
use syrups

and serve
the cause of freedom

U. S. FOOD ADMINISTRATION

A United States Food Administration poster by F. G. Cooper.

sable minimum for all, civilian populations and soldiers alike. One was sugar: America, Hoover said in late 1918, must learn to forego the pleasures of its undeniably sweet tooth, must live up to a voluntarily restricted ration of two pounds per month per person. Another food indispensable to every human being was fats. (Exhaustion of fats had much to do with the break-down of Germany's morale.) Normally, the Allied nations got much of their fats in the form of vegetable oils, from Manchuria; now, scarcity of shipping made that long haul impossible. The need must be met by the American hog — and already the American hog had been reduced in numbers by stimulated sales to the Allies during three years before there was regulation in America.

The American hog became, after America entered the war, an exalted animal, commanding for the moment a rather more intent regard than the lion and the unicorn or the eagle; the hog population was almost as much a concern to government as man-power. It was said of Hoover, after he got under way as Food Administrator, that not only had he counted the hogs in America, not only did he know the weight of each, and the proportion of fat and lean on every porcine rib, not only did he know and keep a discriminating finger on the daily amount of corn fed to each — not only that, the legend said that as to female hogs he knew the dates of their last pregnancies and the probable size of their litters and followed the progress of gestation with as much solicitude as any royal physician ever took the temperature and tapped the abdomen of an expectant queen mother.[10] Such humorous burlesques were not serious exaggeration of the facts of Hoover's grasp on the sources of food for three hundred million people in America and Europe, the intricate channels it must follow to reach them, the delicate manipulation to make it go round. It was at this time that Bernard M. Baruch, then head of an analogous function about metals and other materials, said that of all the men he had ever met, Hoover had the largest capacity for absorbing facts, assembling them into order, deducing the course of action their net suggested, and bringing the

[10] Hoover and his Food Administration were the subject of jests innumerable. One, almost as grisly as funny, and probably apocryphal, was about a family of immigrants in North Dakota who, wishing to ship the body of their dead father back to Norway for burial, encountered a war-time prohibition against all shipping except necessities, but were relieved by an ingenious Food Administration official — Hoover's men were famous for resourcefulness — who, going over the regulations carefully, found the shipment could come within the law if formally labelled "animal fats, not edible."

result about. "To Hoover's brain," Baruch said, "facts are as water to a sponge; they are absorbed into every tiny interstice." Baruch added that on any problem so complex as to demand almost superhuman grasp of detail, he would sooner have Hoover's judgment than that of any other man.

But Hoover must do much more than grasp and organize existing facts. He must bring about change of the facts; bring it about that more of one crop should be raised, less of another; bring it about that America should eat less wheat and more corn. Above all, America must waste less food — not necessarily eat less but waste less. Such modifications of diet and habit could never be enforced upon one hundred and twenty million individuals; it must be accomplished by persuasion on Hoover's part, voluntary action on the part of the people.

As respects manufacturers and dealers, Hoover was given authority by the law, with power to coerce if he chose; all (except those whose business was less than $100,000 a year) were licensed and Hoover could take away the license of any who profiteered or otherwise violated regulations. Very rarely, almost never, did Hoover impose the penalty; his practice with flagrant violators was to exact a contribution to the Red Cross, equivalent of a fine, and let them continue in business on good behavior. Mainly, however, he secured conformity by innumerable conferences with groups of dealers, in which they were shown the need and were moved to co-operate in spontaneous good will.

As for the 105 million American consumers, Hoover reached them with a vast mechanism of organization and vocal and printed urging, designed and expressed in a temper which caused housewives and children and men to feel a glow of pleasure in helping toward a process which Hoover called "food conservation," but which the millions of loyal participants in sacrifice preferred to call "Hooverizing" — the word was used for anything that helped about food, mothers serving no more than was necessary, girls planting gardens, boys working in the fields, children wiping their plates clean. There will be Americans in the year 2000, venerable

Food supplies were eked out by "war gardens" in the cities.

nonagenarians then, who will have forgotten Foch and Joffre, Pershing and von Hindenburg — but will recall a time when their mothers told them, "Chew your food," to please a deity of their childhood, vaguely associated with omnipotence, who was called "Mr. Hoover."

To be economical with food became a vogue with the smart, with the simple and sincere almost a prayerful rite. Hoover's appeals were read out from pulpits and in schools, thrown on the screen in motion-picture houses, printed in newspapers. At all times, before the eyes of all, on poster, placard, and bill-board was kept

the slogan, "Food Will Win the War." In the Topeka
Daily Capital for February 9, 1918, typical issue of any
newspaper at any time during the war, are four separate
articles on the importance of conservation and production
of food-stuffs. The spirit of crusade spread into the
advertising pages; a dealer in meats — whose private interest was to cause the public to buy prodigally — now in
the spirit of the day urged, "Serve Just Enough" and

*"The First Fifty" of Women of Society
Band for Spartain Simplicity in Meals*

Restrictions and regulations having to do with food were obeyed, conscientiously
and enthusiastically, by all classes.
— *New York Herald, May 16, 1917.*

"Use All Left-overs." A baker called attention to his
oatmeal bread, his war buns, and his bran cakes, "all
made under the new government regulations." The
Forbes Milling Co. announced the winners of its "corn-
bread recipe contest." The Royal Bakery invited the
public to "eat Over the Top bread [made partly of bran
and middlings] and do your bit."

Hoover's directions were numerous and specific; a
comprehensive one on January 26, 1918, included, in
the phrases the public came to express them in, wheatless
Mondays and Wednesdays, meatless Tuesdays, porkless
Thursdays and Saturdays, and use of "Victory bread,"

which contained more of the wheat-grain than ordinary white bread. February 11, 1918, he forbade the killing of hens until May 1. March 29, he suspended his meatless order for 30 days. May 26 he proposed a limit of two pounds of meat per person per week. October 12, twelve rules for public eating places were given out, including: no bread until after the first course, only one

The citizen who was suspected of having more than his share of prunes.
A *Life* cartoon on the rationing of food.

kind of meat, one-half ounce of butter per person, no sugar bowl — such sugar as was served was in small cubes, only two pounds of sugar for every ninety meals served.

The spirit in which Hoover asked it led to serious ardor in the carrying out of it, or, with the humorous, gay geniality: "Do not permit your child," said *Life*,[11] "to take a bite or two from an apple and throw the rest away; nowadays even children must be taught to be patriotic to the core." Recalling what it alleged to be the

[11] February 21, 1918.

earliest recorded case of food conservation, *Life* declared that the "handwriting on the wall was a warning from Hoover to Belshazzar to cut out the feast business." Translating Hoover's appeals into rhyme, *Life* printed a burlesque of a polite diner-out thanking his hostess, a war-time "bread and butter letter":

> I cannot thank you for your bread,
> Because there wasn't any,
> Nor any butter, either, though
> Its substitutes were many.
> But your pecan and fig croquettes;
> Your muffins, flour- and eggless;
> Your beef-steak, raised in window-box;
> Your mock duck, wing- and legless;
> Your near-fish, wheedled from oat-meal;
> Your butterine, from apple;
> Your catnip salad, dressed with lard;
> Your porkless, parsnip scrapple
> Composed a menu so conserved
> That Mr. Hoover'd better
> Commend my cheer in sending you
> This meatless, wheatless letter![12]

Expressed more austerely, in statistics of net metric tons, the result of Hoover's food conservation was a multiplication by roughly three of the quantity of food America had shipped to the Allied countries in normal pre-war years. Without that multiplication the Allies could not have fought on, they could not have lived:

	Normal pre-war average	War year 1918–1919
Breadstuffs	3,320,000	10,566,165
Meats and fats	645,000	2,369,630
Sugar (from U. S. and West Indies)	618,000	1,704,523

[12] *Life,* January 31, 1918.

21

A NEW DEVICE IN WAR

Wilson Sets Up a "Committee on Public Information,"
Assuming It Would Be a Perfunctory Institution for Such
Censorship and Propaganda as America Cared to Practise.
But Wilson Puts in Charge of It a Man of Exceptional
Efflorescence, Who Makes It a Remarkable Institution.
George Creel Mobilizes the Oratorical Talent of America
into the Four Minute Men, 75,000 Strong; and Mobilizes
also the Artists and the Authors and the Dramatists and
the College Professors and the Advertising Men.

WILSON, early in the war, while he was still wrangling
with Congress over the War Resolution, while he was
busy organizing the country, while he was rushed with
conferences dealing with man-power, dreadnaughts,
munitions, food supplies, all the matters commonly considered to be of first importance to a nation at war —
while in the midst of all that, Wilson turned aside for a
moment to bring into being an agency which, while classi-
fiable among war activities, bore no remotest resemblance
to the conventional and traditional methods of bringing
an enemy to submission. Indeed, this creation of Wilson, the "Committee on Public Information," was so
different in its function from any war activity ever before engaged in by any country at any time that it may
be regarded as an American contribution to the science
of war.

Secretary of War Baker, speaking[1] in retrospect after
the Armistice, described the purpose and achieved objective of the Committee on Public Information as "the
whole business of *mobilizing the mind of the world*"

[1] At a dinner given George Creel, Chairman of the Committee.

(including, toward the end, the mind of Germany). It was a "fight for the minds of men, for the conquest of their convictions." Generously Baker implied that the fight for men's minds, as carried on by the Committee, had had an equal importance with his own function of overcoming the physical power of the enemy. Considering that the principal ammunition the Committee used was the speeches of Wilson, and considering the part that Wilson's ideas played in winning the war. such allocation of credit was not unreasonable.

Like most institutions, the Committee on Public Information was the shadow of a man; and the man was not Wilson, it was George Creel. Wilson officially initiated it (as a different thing from what it became); Wilson took advantage of it and in his war purposes profited by it greatly. But it was the incredibly efflorescent imagination of George Creel, his fertile ingenuity, his prodigious energy which, beginning with a perfunctory clearing-house for day-to-day information about government activities, developed it into something new in war, new and very formidable.

When we entered the war, the question of censorship came up. Army and Navy urged on Wilson the usual thing, the strict limitations found by the Allies to be necessary. American newspapers felt that a nation three thousand miles from the battle-front need not be so rigid about publishable news. While the controversy was on, George Creel wrote a letter to Wilson. Characteristically Creel had a new conception, proposed an innovation; characteristically also, he expressed it violently, by paradox. No censorship of war news at all, said Creel, except such as the newspapers would voluntarily impose on themselves after receiving explanation of the need. What is wanted, Creel said, is not suppression but expression — "unparalleled openness," a spreading abroad among our own people of information about our activities in the war and especially about our purposes, to the end of arousing a war-emotion, a morale that we did not yet have. It was, as Creel saw it, "a plain publicity proposition, a vast enterprise in salesmanship, the world's greatest adventure in advertising." Such a proposal lay within the field of propaganda; but, Creel told Wilson, let there be no propaganda in the sense in which it was practised by the combatants in Europe, no false claims of victories, no concealment of defeats — in short, no lies of any kind, no lies either to deceive the enemy peoples or to allay the home population.

Wilson, receiving Creel's letter, sent for him, turned the whole nebulous idea of censorship, and of propaganda of whatever sort, over to him.

II

Wilson had known Creel before, during the Presidential campaign of 1916, and had begun to treat him as one of the very small number of men whom Wilson enjoyed having near him. Creel was an enjoyable person. He was indeed two persons. The private George Creel of intimate contacts was a humorous, vigorous, laughing human being, pungent, racy, robust, fervidly temperamental in a way that pleased and amused, one of the best story-tellers of his day; he had a gift of mimicry, especially burlesque mimicry of the pompous and the smug; he enjoyed telling jokes on himself — and he had many experiences lending themselves, in the serenity of afterward, to comic telling; he was fecund with the spirit of comedy, rich in sensitiveness and kindness, likeable to the last degree.

But the instant Creel arose on a public platform or took up his pen, he became a raging reformer, compound of the more berserker qualities of Danton, Marat, and Charlotte Corday. Whatever the ink-stand in front of Creel contained, to his pen it yielded only gall; out on the paper flowed objurgations, denunciations, maledictions, imprecations. As a public speaker he was subject to orators' intoxication in a peculiar form. The disease is not unusual, but with most persons the onset is gradual, does not appear until after half an hour or so of orating. Creel became blind drunk with it the minute he opened his public mouth. He passed into a different personality, became tense, bitter, bellicose, angrily emotional. Once, picking up a newspaper the morning after he had delivered a political speech, the private Creel held wringing hands to his dismayed head. "My God," he exclaimed, "could I have said those things?" He had been a writer on newspapers in Denver and Kansas City, and subsequently on magazines in New York, his writings having the purpose of denouncing divers aspects of the world that seemed to Creel imperfect. Wherever he was, in whatever public rôle, trouble, commotion, angry controversy arose about him as surely as smoke goes upward. To Wilson, one feels sure, it was the humorous, generous George Creel of intimate contact that appealed. To a President, one militant reformer more or less is no treat; but a man may be a Godsend who can tell good stories and "take off" the pompous and the ponderous.

III

Creel started his Committee on Public Information with an advisory, and supervisory, Board of Cabinet Members — that was the usual formula for war-time organizations. He held one meeting with Secretary of State Lansing, Secretary of War Baker, and Secretary of the Navy Daniels. He found the deliberations too dilatory for a young man of spirit and energy, and he never held another meeting. The Committee on Public Infor-

Photograph by U. S. Army Signal Corps.

George Creel.

He "was a humorous, vigorous, laughing human being, pungent, robust, fervidly temperamental."

mation was George Creel — and continued to be George Creel even after it had expanded to a point where some hundred and fifty thousand people were taking part in its incredibly varied and far-flung activities. It was not merely desire for brevity that caused newspapers, Congress, and every one else to speak of it as "the Creel Committee."

At first, with a small staff, he merely gave out news

of the government departments to Washington correspondents, or helped them verify information they picked up. In this stage, Creel and the Committee were little more than a liaison, of the usual type, between Washington correspondents and the government. This was the original conception of the Committee's function.

But Creel was, of all things, expansive; his imagination was literally boundless. Within a week he conceived himself — and lived up to his conception — as having a mission to make America war-conscious. In that enterprise he mobilized under his direction just about every spring or avenue of publicity, imagination, or other attention-compelling activity that there was in America. As the war-spirit spread, persons of many arts or callings were moved to do their bit. When they came to Washington, Creel became the man for them to see.

Creel mobilized the artists. Painters, sculptors, designers, illustrators, and cartoonists, as Creel put it, "rallied to the colors." Under the chairmanship of Charles Dana Gibson, they became what Creel called — military terminology was the order of the day — his "Division of Pictorial Publicity." Commending his subordinates as a good general should, he declared that "no other class or profession excelled them in devotion that took no account of sacrifice or drudgery." "America," Creel exclaimed, "had more posters than any other belligerent, and they were the best." They were, too. Some of the work that Charles Dana Gibson, Harrison Fisher, Montgomery Flagg, Joseph Pennell, and others did under the inspiration of war was among their finest and could bear comparison with the war efforts of French and British artists. Charles Livingston Bull's marine pictures, Howard Chandler Christy's "Win the War — Buy a Bond!" Wallace Morgan's "Feed a Fighter," and other paintings and drawings constituted for many Americans a glamorous recollection of the war years, and will be for the future an authentic record of the high enthusiasm and faith America had at the time.

Creel mobilized the advertising forces of the country

Photograph by U. S. Army Signal Corps.

James Montgomery Flagg drawing a poster as an incident of a drive to get recruits for the Marine Corps, July, 1918.

— press, periodical, street-car, and out-door, including a special species of the advertising genus known as "idea men" — in a vast patriotic campaign which thundered on the consciousness of every person in America who could read or understand a picture. From the walls of subway stations, from bill-boards, from barns along the highways, Creel's artists shouted exhortations for a united front against the enemy — "The Battle of the Fences," he called it.

Creel organized a motion-picture Division to stimulate American interest and morale by showing in every city and village pictures made under the direction of his Committee: "Pershing's Crusaders," "America's Answer," and "Under Four Flags." As time went on this branch of the Committee's work expanded to take in every phase of photography. "Stills" by the thousand were sent out to the newspapers, great quantities of stereopticon slides were made and distributed, scenario departments were formed, comedy films especially adapted to the entertainment of troops were prepared and sent to cantonments.

Creel mobilized the oratorical talent of the country, chiefly amateur, 75,000 voices strong, into an organization called the "Four Minute Men" — the relation was obscure between this designation and the unlimited Minute Men of the Revolutionary War, or perhaps those were only One Minute Men.

Creel's talkers were introduced to the public mainly at motion-picture theatres, where, during the performance, a slide would appear on the curtain saying:

4 MINUTE MEN 4
(Copyright, 1917. Trade-mark).

. . . .
(Insert name of speaker)

**will speak four minutes on a subject
of national importance. He speaks
under the authority of**

THE COMMITTEE ON PUBLIC INFORMATION
GEORGE CREEL, Chairman,
Washington, D. C.

War posters by American artists.

Top left, Liberty Loan poster by Howard Chandler Christy. *Top right*, recruiting poster by Herbert Paus. *Bottom left*, poster drawn by Charles Dana Gibson to glorify workers in ship-yards. *Bottom right*, recruiting poster by James Montgomery Flagg.

From motion-picture theatres the service was expanded to lodge meetings, grange-meetings, schools, churches, synagogues, Sunday schools, sessions of labor unions — it became difficult for half a dozen persons to come together without having a Four Minute Man descend upon them. The supply of talent being generous, the service reached out to lumber camps. "Indian Reservations," Creel wrote in his report, "furnished some of the largest and most enthusiastic audiences."

As one of its functions, the Four Minute Men organization was a mobile army, a flying corps of vocalization and exhortation which could be directed to working up sentiment for whatever happened to be the current "drive" — their aggregate voices turned on as if by a spigot. During May 12 to 21, 1917, their topic was "Universal Service by Selective Draft" — that was when the Draft Act was before Congress, doubtful of passage, and public support was needed. In other periods they were at the service of Red Cross, Food Conservation, Farm and Garden, and other drives. When the Treasury was selling Liberty Bonds, the Four Minute Men were loaned to Secretary McAdoo. McAdoo had President Wilson subscribe for a $50 bond and challenge everybody to match it. Fifty thousand Four Minute Men carried the President's challenge to every community, and, Creel recorded, "the loan took a leap that carried it over the top." Between drives, the Four Minute Men gave standardized talks prepared by Creel's committee, on "Why We Are Fighting," "The Importance of Speed," "Maintaining Morals and Morale," "The Meaning of America," "Where Did You Get Your Facts?" (designed to overcome detrimental rumors).

The derisive sometimes described the Four Minute Men as the "Stentorian Guard," their talks as "patriotic pep." They were, however, very useful, and one of the most picturesque and vivifying features of the time. Those who contributed their voices had pleasure in the work. Pleasure to audiences as a rule was assured by the spirit of the day, by the brevity that was enforced with military rigidity, and by the care exercised to admit only good voices and pleasing personalities to the ranks. Creel gave particular attention to enlisting recruits — chiefly a matter of picking one for service out of ten that volunteered — until he found that trying out the voices of ambitious embryos of William Jennings Bryan and Paul Revere would leave him too little time for other matters. Wilson, when the war ended, took time to tell the Four Minute Men that "each member of your organization, in receiving honorable discharge from the service, may justly feel a glow of proper pride." Creel put his appreciation in a rotund sentence, "An organization unique in world annals, as effective in the battle at home as was the onward rush of Pershing's heroes at St. Mihiel." Creel added some statistics: the 75,000 Four Minute Men had delivered a grand total of 7,555,-190 speeches, to audiences aggregating 314,454,514. And they had elicited from the press, Creel said in concluding satisfaction, 900,000 lines of publicity commending their work.

Creel mobilized the singing voices of the country, prepared a bulletin of songs specially selected to incite patriotism, and appointed a corps of song-leaders to take charge of motion-picture theatre audiences.

Creel mobilized the novelists and dramatists. Booth Tarkington, Mary Roberts Rinehart, Meredith Nicholson, Samuel Hopkins Adams, and many others contributed articles. Ernest Poole, Harvey O'Higgins, and some others gave all their time.

Creel mobilized the historians and college professors.

Drafting Guy Stanton Ford, Professor of History at the University of Minnesota, to be head of a new Division — Creel dripped new Divisions — he set a corps of volunteers at a task which Creel called "popular pamphleteering," writing booklets or commandeering and editing material already in existence. An annotated treatment of President Wilson's first war speech was put out, under the title, "How the War Came to America." Professor Stuart P. Sherman of the University of Illinois wrote "American and Allied Ideals." "America's War Aims and Peace Terms" was compiled by Professor Carl Becker of Cornell; "American Interest in Popular Government Abroad" by Professor Evarts B. Greene of the University of Illinois; a "War Encyclopedia" by Professors Paxson of the University of Wisconsin, Corwin of Princeton, Harding of Indiana University, and some others.

Creel mobilized — but let us cease detail, and merely say Creel assembled leaders of about every group in America whose occupation or function was in the field of imagination, creative art, or publicity. Indeed he did not stop with America. He set up a Division whose function was to bring from France and England speakers whose experiences or ideas might help stimulate American interest in the war. Drafting Rotary Clubs and Chambers of Commerce to serve as impresarios, he sent his foreign speakers throughout the country — an exceptionally pleasing and effective one, Captain Paul Perigord, a French priest who became a private and won fame by heroism at Verdun, made 152 speeches during a 7-months' tour of America. (Creel thought Captain Perigord was the best of all his tens of thousands of speakers, American or foreign.)

The sum of Creel's activity was prodigious. Only one

branch of it lends itself easily to statistical estimate —
the words of his orators were as the winds of the world;
the posters and pictures he put out, as the leaves of the
forest. The number of printed words he inspired and

When Creel was deluging Germany with Wilson's speeches, the German government tried to prevent the speeches from reaching the army or the civilian
population.

— *Knoxville Journal and Tribune.*

distributed reached a point at which, the Government
Printing Office proving unable to keep step with his
imagination, he developed his own machinery for printing and distribution. His own franked envelopes, he
reasoned, with justified faith in the interest he drew to
himself, "were more certain of attracting attention than
the Congressional frank." Of "How the War Came to
America," the printing was 5,428,048; editions for the
foreign-born in Swedish, Polish, Italian, Spanish, Bohemian, and — yes, even Portuguese — brought the

total to 6,775,892. This was the most widely distributed of the pamphlets — it contained Wilson's speech to Congress calling for declaration of war, and Creel's judgment, as well as his personal affection, put emphasis always on circulating Wilson's speeches. Of Wilson's Flag Day address he distributed 6,813,340 copies. Of other pamphlets, booklets, leaflets he circulated a grand total of some sixty million.

IV

By this time, America was sufficiently war-conscious. And, as some carping Congressmen and others thought, sufficiently Creel-conscious.

The virtue of Creel for his job was his exuberance. That so much imagination should be united with austere exactness or caution in statement would be more than could fairly be expected of mortal man. Creel's Committee put out a statement from the War Department that "The first American-built battle-planes are to-day *en route* to the front in France." It was February 21, 1918, nearly a year after our entrance into the war, high time that American planes should be not only *en route* but at the front. Investigation revealed that the plural "battle-planes" were really one; and that "*en route* to the front" meant the lone plane was passing from the factory to an aviation field (in America) for a radiator test. In the same optimistic spirit, Creel's Committee gave out four photographs of airplanes bearing captions which, as Creel himself put it later, were "flamboyant and over-colored." An account written by Creel for publication July 4, 1917, about the trip of the first American transports to France included a description of an attack by German submarines and the repulse of them, which, critics thought, were more in the spirit of July 4 jubilation than was justified by the facts. These and some other episodes made Creel what nature had destined him to be, a storm-centre.

Creel's pugnacity, his gift for biting sarcasm, and a talent he had for epithets at once caustic and accurate, brought him into row after row with Congress; and the rows, exploited in the newspapers almost as much as

Attitude of George Creel, friend of Wilson, toward Congress, as caricatured in the weekly paper conducted by George Harvey.

the battle of the Aisne, were a source of highly diverting entertainment to a war-serious country. Because Creel, naturally, emphasized President Wilson, Republicans accused him of partisanship. Senator Sherman called him a "rake-hell"; Republican leader "Uncle Joe" Cannon said he "ought to be taken by the nape of the neck and the slack of the pants and thrown into space." Once, when Creel was making a speech in New York, some one in the audience, either naïve or with subtly impish intention, asked him "What do you think of the heart of Congress?" Creel, his creative spirit stimulated by the expectant titter in the audience, said, "Oh, it's years since I've been slumming." For this and other insults, Congress considered bringing him to the bar of the House for contempt. Wilson called Creel up to ask solicitously, "I trust you are not worrying over the antics of Congress?" and to say he would take pleasure in standing by his chairman of the Committee on Public Information — that official title for Creel, incidentally, was translated by Congress to "Wilson's press agent."

But Creel was abundantly able to take care of himself. For the moment, to avoid embarrassing Wilson, he was obliged to practise some discretion, and that restraint was perhaps the only irking one of the duties his office entailed. When he could, he hit back. Writing a report of the Committee's work, he observed that "Congress is the one place in the whole United States in which a mouth is above the law; the heavens may fall, the earth be consumed, but the right of a Congressman to lie and defame remains inviolate." Of three of his critics, august Senators, he wrote with magnificently achieved insouciance — his thrusts the more cutting since he was avenging Wilson as much as himself — the three Senators were Wilson's most persistent adversaries in Congress:

Back in 1913 I wrote an article for *Everybody's Magazine* in which I tried to give a fair and dispassionate study of Johnson [Senator Hiram Johnson of California]. It was not a flattering estimate and the abnormal vanity of the man never forgave it. The Johnson wattles swelled and reddened to a state of chronic inflammation as far as I was concerned. . . . As for Reed [Senator James Reed of Missouri] I had known the fellow from the start of his career, and during the ten years in which I lived and wrote in Kansas City there was not a week in which I did not try to hold him up to the contempt and ridicule that were deserved by his character and abilities. . . . I was always inclined to give Senator Lodge [of Massachusetts] the benefit of the doubt, crediting him with ignorance rather than dishonesty. The Lodge mind was like the soil of New England — highly cultivated, but naturally sterile. An exceedingly dull man and a very vain one — deadly combination — his vanity fosters his ignorance by persistent refusal to confess it.

V

Creel's work had deluged America, saturated it, the country was as much war-conscious as it could become. But Creel was an artist, had to an extraordinary degree the floreating quality that dreams huge projects. And Creel was in a position, had a freedom from limitations, such as no artist ever knew. He had access to as much money as his most expansive dream could call for. While Congress had limited his appropriation to $1,250,000 (and in subsequent anger threatened to curtail the amount), Creel could draw on a "President's fund" of $50,000,000 which Wilson had been given to lay out in his discretion. Wilson let Creel have $5,000,000[2] of it.

More than money, Creel had, without cost or at very little, such help as money could never command. All the writers, artists, and other persons of imagination, practically all the country's genius, were on fire to help win the war, and would throw into Creel's projects such talent, inventiveness, fervor, and devotion as probably was never before assembled. Creel's own generous description of his aides was not extravagant, "all that was fine and ardent in the civilian population came at our call."

Finally, Creel had Wilson. Wilson would do about anything Creel suggested, would O. K. anything Creel proposed — Wilson's signature to documents beginning

[2] It should be said that Creel made the film portion of his enterprise partially self-supporting; his work "cost the taxpayers just $4,912,553!" (The exclamation point is Creel's.)

"I hereby create under the jurisdiction of the Committee on Public Information" — was a familiar sight, and, of course, a potent one.

Thus equipped, it occurred to Creel to conquer the world — and this became the activity that made Creel seriously important in the war. His own phrase for what he now undertook was "a world-fight for the verdict of mankind." Including — this was the daring and subsequently decisive part of it — a fight for the minds of the German people. Some of Creel's lieutenants in his Division of Advertising would have called it "selling America to the world," that is, selling America's part in the war, especially America's war aims. And since America's war aims were Woodrow Wilson's ideas, Creel's enterprise became mainly one of "building up" Wilson, causing Wilson's ideas to dominate the mind of the world, including Germany, including even the minds of Germany's armies in the field.

He, with Wilson; Wilson as forger of verbal thunder-bolts, Creel as propagandeer of them; Wilson as Napoleon of ideas, Creel as Marshal Ney of dissemination — the two would conquer the world.

22

WILSON MAKES WAR WITH IDEAS

With an Effectiveness Which Caused a Discriminating Biographer, Years Later, to Say: "No other man has ever so completely proven the power of the spoken word; not only did Wilson's words arouse his own countrymen and animate the flagging spirit of the Allies, but, filtered into Germany and Austria, they shattered the enemy morale; let the unthinking scoff as they may, Wilson's winged words were almost as potent for victory as the nation's sacrifice in blood." [1] Wilson, at the Suggestion of George Creel, Compresses His Ideas into "Fourteen Points" and Creel Projects This Polemic "Shrapnel" Across the Battle-Lines into Germany.

WILSON kept forging the thunderbolts of ideas. Steadily, with ringing blows of dynamic words, in speech after speech, he drove home the wedge which in his early[1a] address to Congress calling for war, he had inserted between the German government and the German people, his strategy of turning the people of Germany against their military masters, against the Kaiser, against their government:

We are not the enemies of the German people and they are not our enemies.[2] . . . This power [which we are fighting] is not the German people; it is the ruthless master of the German people.[3] . . . The ruling classes in Germany.[4] . . . The Imperial government and those whom it is using for their own undoing.[4]

[1] "Wilson the Unknown," Wells Wells (a pseudonym).
[1a] April 2, 1917. See Chapter 14.
[2] Flag Day address, June 14, 1917.
[3] Wilson's reply to the Pope's peace suggestion, August 27, 1917.
[4] June 9, 1917.
The brief phrases and sentences here given are inadequate to convey the force and passion, and subtlety, of the passages and speeches in which Wilson played upon one emotion after the other in the entire gamut of appeal to the German people as against the German government.

... The military masters under whom Germany is bleeding.[5] ...

In an Isaiah-like indictment Wilson denounced

This intolerable Thing. . . . This menace of combined intrigue and force which we now see so clearly as the German power, a Thing without conscience or honor or capacity for covenanted peace, must be crushed.[6]

And promised that

When the German people have spokesmen whose word we can believe, and when those spokesmen are ready in the name of their people.[6] . . . This is a People's War . . . and we are to make the world safe for the peoples who live upon it, the German people themselves included.[7] . . .

Driving the wedge between German people and German government was only part of the strategy Wilson pushed forward with acute intelligence and splendid force. Cunningly he drove another wedge, between Germany and her allies:[7a]

The military masters of Germany who proved also to be the masters of Austria-Hungary.[7] . . . Austria is at their mercy.[7] . . . Austria-Hungary their tool and pawn.[7] . . . They have regarded the smaller states as their natural tools and instruments of domination.[7] . . . Filling the thrones of Balkan states with German princes. . . . Developing sedition and rebellion in India and Egypt, setting their fires in Persia.[7] . . . Binding together racial and political units that could be kept together only by force — Czechs, Magyars, Croats, Serbs, Roumanians, Turks, Armenians.[7] . . . Their purpose is to make all the Slavic peoples, all the free and ambitious nations of the Baltic peninsula . . . subject to their will.[8]

[5] Flag Day address, June 14, 1917.
[6] Message to Congress, December 4, 1917.
[7] Flag Day address, June 14, 1917.
[7a] Carrying out this idea in action, Wilson refrained from declaring war on Austria until after we had been in the War eight months. Against Turkey we never declared war, and we did not even break off diplomatic relations with Bulgaria.
[8] Speech at Baltimore, April 6, 1918.

Flatteringly, he appealed to

the proud states of Bohemia and Hungary, the stout little commonwealths of the Balkans, the indomitable Turks,[9]

Life, Jan. 17, 1918.

Constantly Wilson emphasized that it was the German military masters we were fighting and not the German people.

and seductively held out to them promise of independence:

We shall hope to secure for the peoples of the Balkan peninsula and for the people of the Turkish Empire the right and opportunity to make their own lives safe ... from the dictation of foreign courts.[10]

[9] Flag Day address, June 14, 1917.
[10] Address to Congress, December 4, 1917.

II

Creel Spreads Wilson's Messages

These messages, all of Wilson's speeches, Creel and his Committee of Public Information distributed to the world.

Opening an office in every capital of the world outside the Central Powers, he set up, using the American Government wireless, a daily news service which, translated and relayed, penetrated to newspapers as remote as Arequipa in the Peruvian Andes, and the interior of Asia — three hundred Chinese newspapers were supplied with Creel's war news from America. "For the first time in history," Creel wrote proudly, "the speeches of a national executive were given universal circulation. The official addresses of President Wilson, setting forth the position of America, were put on the wireless always at the very moment of their delivery, and within twenty-four hours were in every language in every country in the world, Teheran getting them as completely as London. Carried in the newspapers initially, they were also printed by the Committee's agents on native presses and circulated by the millions."

The daily news organization was but the beginning and the framework. A Foreign Mail Press Bureau, directed by Ernest Poole, sent out weekly packages of printed material. A volume of Wilson's speeches, translated, "became," Creel reported, "a best seller in China." A translation of one of Wilson's speeches "was adopted as a text-book in a Madrid school." Collateral activities pushed motion pictures of America's war preparation into theatres all over the world, into towns and villages that had never before seen an American film of any kind. Creel's pamphlets were translated into every language, distributed to libraries and schools. Creel's posters, window-cards, and photographs were displayed where such modern devices as window-cards had never been seen before. All over the world, in little Andalusian villages, in tiny mirs in the interior of Russia, in the mountain passes of Italy, Creel's myrmidons and colporteurs, some of them authors of high standing or important newspaper men, carried the American message. Much of it was about all aspects of American life, America's war preparations — but always Wilson's speeches, always translated in full; photographs of Wilson, posters of Wilson. "The Wilson cult," wrote Creel's agent in Spain, "is truly making astonishing progress; newspapers devote innumerable columns to his career, his views, his present actions, personal details." "I have seen," wrote Creel's man in Denmark, "a new understanding of President Wilson come into the minds of the Danes so that they placed him on a plane beside their greatest national heroes; I have known them to cut out the photographs of him sent out by us which appeared in Danish papers and place them in a sort of family shrine."

III

One detail of Creel's carrying the Wilson message to the world directly influenced the course of the world. From an agent Creel had in Russia, Edgar G. Sisson, a newspaper man, came a request to meet a need which a newspaper man would be likely to see. Sisson found it difficult to get Wilson's long speeches translated and distributed in a form that Russians and Germans could easily read. He conceived the notion of a condensation into brief paragraphs, of the sort that the newspaper craft

calls "snappy." "If President Wilson," Sisson cabled to
Creel from St. Petersburg,

'will re-state anti-Imperialistic war aims and democratic
peace requisites of America [in] almost placard paragraphs
I can get it fed into Germany in great quantities in German
translation, and can utilize Russian version potently in army
and elsewhere. Excerpts from previous statements will not
serve. Need this for external evidence that President is thinking of German and Russian common folk in their situation
and talking to them.'[10a]

Creel, newspaper man himself, saw the force of his
assistant's suggestion and took it to Wilson. Wilson consulted Colonel House, and the two boiled Wilson's war
aims and peace terms down into what, within a little
while, was known from Archangel to Patagonia as the
"Fourteen Points."

IV

Wilson's Fourteen Points, Followed by His Four Points

Wilson put his epitomized Fourteen Points into a
speech which he delivered to Congress January 8, 1918,
labelled as a "statement of the War Aims and Peace
Terms of the United States." This was not merely for
Germany; it was for the world. One point or another appealed to practically every small people aspiring to independent nationality, and to every existing nation. The
sum of the Fourteen Points enlisted behind Wilson most
of the opinion or emotion within practically every nation of the world, big or little, Allies or enemy, or
neutral. The Fourteen Points (with Wilson's other
terms) were not merely a peace proposal to the nations
at war; they were directed to the whole world, an appealing charter of a new order, glamorous to all; they

[10a] The text of this cable is printed here as given by Creel in a letter to the
author, August, 1933.

constituted Wilson's promise to the world of what he would cause the peace to be, and the world to become. Within this broad allurement were specific proffers to many nations and peoples; to Russia, promise of non-interference and co-operation in any social experiment she chose to make; to Hungary and other peoples within the Austrian Empire, autonomy; to the Balkan States, independence; to Serbia, access to the sea; to Poland, independence and access to the sea; to Armenia and other peoples under Turkish rule, autonomy:

1. Open covenants of peace, openly arrived at. . . .
2. Absolute freedom of navigation upon the seas. . . .
3. The removal, so far as possible, of all economic barriers and the establishment of an equality of trade conditions among all the nations. . . .
4. Adequate guarantees given and taken that national armaments will be reduced to the lowest points consistent with domestic safety.
5. A free, open-minded, and absolutely impartial adjustment of all colonial claims based upon a strict observance of the principle that in determining all such questions of sovereignty the interests of the populations concerned must have equal weight with the equitable claims of the government whose title is to be determined.
6. The evacuation of all Russian territory and such a settlement of all questions affecting Russia as will secure the best and freest co-operation of the other nations of the world in obtaining for her an unhampered and unembarrassed opportunity for the independent determination of her own political development and national policy. . . .
7. Belgium must be evacuated and restored. . . .
8. All French territory should be freed and the invaded portions restored, and the wrong done to France by Prussia in 1871 in the matter of Alsace-Lorraine . . . should be righted. . . .
9. A readjustment of the frontiers of Italy should be effected along clearly recognizable lines of nationality.
10. The peoples of Austria-Hungary, whose place among the nations we wish to see safeguarded and assured, should be accorded the freest opportunity of autonomous development.
11. Rumania, Serbia, and Montenegro should be evacuated; occupied territories restored; Serbia accorded free and secure access to the sea . . . international guarantees of the political

and economic independence and territorial integrity of the
several Balkan states should be entered into.

12. The Turkish portions of the present Ottoman Empire
should be assured a secure sovereignty, but the other nationalities which are now under Turkish rule should be assured an
undoubted security of life and an absolutely unmolested opportunity of autonomous development, and the Dardanelles
should be permanently opened as a free passage to the ships
and commerce of all nations under international guarantees.

13. An independent Polish state should be erected which
should . . . be assured a free and secure access to the sea. . . .

14. A general association of nations must be formed under
specific covenants for the purpose of affording mutual guarantees of political independence and territorial integrity to great
and small states alike.[11]

Wilson, pleased with this condensation of his war
speeches into a form lending itself to distribution
throughout the world by Creel, wrote and gave out supplementary and overlapping terms, the whole becoming
a complete set of terms for peace between the warring
groups, and in addition, the constitution of a new world
order, a League of Nations. Taking July 4 as the day,
and Washington's tomb at Mount Vernon as the scene,
he laid down a supplementary "Four Points," which,
Wilson said, were

the ends for which the associated peoples of the world are
fighting and which must be conceded before there can be
peace.

The phrase, "for which the associated peoples of the
world are fighting," is important. To what extent the
Allies were bound by these tenders of terms made by
Wilson to Germany, to what extent Wilson had authority or right to speak on behalf of the Allies, or to what
degree the Allies subsequently endorsed Wilson's terms
and thereby became bound by them — all that became
important after Germany accepted the terms.

11 From Wilson's Address to Congress, Stating the War Aims and Peace
Terms of the United States. (Delivered in Joint Session, January 8, 1918.)

Of the Four Points, the first was a restatement and re-emphasis in general terms of the solicitation to the German peoples to get rid of the Kaiser and the Ger-

© *Sun Printing & Publishing Association.*

President Wilson in his study in the White House, March 31, 1918.

man military autocracy. It applied to autocratic governments everywhere:

I. The destruction of every arbitrary power anywhere that can separately, secretly, and of its single choice, disturb the peace of the world; or, if it cannot be presently destroyed, at the least its reduction to virtual impotence.

The second of the Four Points was pregnant because it embodied a portion of the idea which later came to be known (and to cause much commotion) as the "self-determination of small peoples":

II. The settlement of every question, whether of territory, of sovereignty, of economic arrangement, or of political relationship, upon the basis of the free acceptance of that settlement by the people immediately concerned, and not upon the basis of the material interest or advantage of any other nation or people which may desire a different settlement for the sake of its own exterior influence or mastery.

The third of the Four Points was an aspiration toward idealism in international relations:

III. The consent of all nations to be governed in their conduct toward each other by the same principles of honor and of respect for the common law of civilized society that govern the individual citizens of all modern States in their relations with one another. . . .

The fourth of the Four Points was a reaffirmation in part of the crown of Wilson's projected new structure of human society, the League of Nations:

IV. The establishment of an organization of peace which shall make it certain that the combined power of free nations will check every invasion of right. . . .

These peace terms, this proposal for a new world order, Wilson kept restating all through the year. Especially appealing to Germany was a declaration in a speech made September 27, which, without mentioning Germany by name, held out the promise that Germany would be dealt with in a spirit of justice the same as if she were not an enemy:

The impartial justice meted out must involve no discrimination between those to whom we wish to be just and those to whom we do not wish to be just.

Especially important were two conditions Wilson laid

down in an address to Congress February 11, 1918. The first was in effect a direct promise to Germany:

There shall be no annexations, no contributions, no punitive damages.

The second of the conditions laid down in the February 11 speech was, in the mass of discussion in which it later figured, abbreviated to "self-determination." In full it read:

National aspirations must be respected; peoples may now be dominated and governed only by their own consent. "Self-determination" is not a mere phrase; it is an imperative principle of action. . . .

The speech in which "self-determination" was put forward by Wilson was one in which he dealt mainly with peace with Austria. "Self-determination" was likely to appeal powerfully to the small peoples, Bohemians (later Czecho-Slovakians), Hungarians, and other groups having national aspirations, now embraced within the Austrian Empire. Just as Wilson had been driving a wedge between the German people and the German government, so did he by "self-determination" set dynamite beneath the loosely cemented Austrian Empire. The phrase, however, was of universal application; was received as promise of independence by oppressed peoples everywhere, throughout Europe, in Asia and Africa.

v

Creel Undertakes to "Americanize Mitteleuropa"

All these, the Fourteen Points, the Four Points, all the terms and conditions and promises in all Wilson's speeches — all these, as fast as Wilson emitted them, Creel distributed throughout the world. These phrases, these speeches, these assurances, these appeals, this strategy,

were vocal missiles which, as Wilson forged them and
Creel fired them, seeped down among peoples everywhere
and gave rise to hopes of a new world order.

Now Creel, as his greatest enterprise, his most unlimited audacity, proceeded to — as he put it — "Americanize *Mitteleuropa*." To penetrate that ring of steel and
rigid censorship was difficult — indeed could not be done.

Aber das ist nur ein Teil der Geschichte. Wir wissen jetzt genau so
wie wir es gewußt haben, bevor wir am Kriege teilnahmen, daß wir nicht
die Feinde des deutschen Volks sind und daß es nicht unser Feind ist.
Es hat diesen furchtbaren Krieg nicht heraufbeschworen oder ange-
strebt, und es hat auch nicht gewünscht, daß wir in ihn hineingezogen
würden, und wir ahnen dunkel, daß wir für seine Sache genau so wie
für unsere eigene kämpfen und daß es das eines Tages einsehen wird.
Es ist selbst in der Gewalt der finsteren Macht, die jetzt endlich ihre
häßlichen Krallen ausgestreckt und unser Blut gefordert hat. Die
ganze Welt ist im Kriege, weil jene Macht sie gepackt hält und sie die
große Schlacht kämpft, welche entscheiden wird, ob sie unterjocht werden
oder sich frei machen soll.

Example of Creel's methods of conducting propaganda in Germany. This is an
    extract from Wilson's Flag Day address, translated into German and dis-
    tributed by plane over the German lines and among the German civilian
    population. This passage illustrates the wedge that Wilson was constantly
    driving between the German people and the German government: "We are
    not the enemies of the German people and they are not our enemies. We are
    fighting for their cause just as much as for our own, and some day they
    will recognize this. . . ."

The ring must be leaped. Creel must go over it, through
the air. The British already had some mechanical devices for the projection of propaganda into Germany,
a six-inch gun that would carry ten or twelve miles and
scatter several thousand leaflets from each shell; the Italians used rockets carrying 40 or 50 leaflets. For many
months the British, French, and Italians had been using
such devices. They had, however, made no impression
on German civilians or Germany Army. Effectiveness
depended not on the gun but on the ammunition, depended on having the right arguments, the right appeal.

This Creel supplied. Facts about America's war effort, figures and photographs of our troops in training and on their way to France, designed to impress German soldiers with America's military invincibility — that and Wilson's speeches.

Creel's propaganda, dropped in Germany by airplanes, cause Fritz to wonder who was his true friend — Wilson or the Kaiser.

— *Harvey's Weekly, January 26, 1918.*

With pictures and accounts of America's fighting forces, Creel intimidated the Germans; with Wilson's speeches he allured them by the promise of a just peace. "Always the speeches of President Wilson" — the words[12] and the italics are Creel's — "were the spear-

[12] In a letter to the author, July 20, 1933.

head of our attack; we *deluged* Germany with them."
They were printed in German, with care to achieve
German appearance in paper, type, and the fine points
of German diction, the work being done by German
prisoners in France.

Presently there was obvious effect on German morale;
both the German General Staff and the Austrian Government felt obliged to prescribe severe penalties for
civilians or soldiers guilty of picking up, possessing, or
reading "printed lies" against the government. That the
orders were not effective is suggested by the number of
German prisoners who, toward the end of the war, were
found familiar with Wilson's speeches, especially the
promises in his Fourteen Points.

Against missiles of the physical kind, the German
military leaders had provided their soldiers with adequate defenses. But not all the steel helmets and gas
masks in Germany could keep Wilson's words from entering German heads after Creel set to work distributing
them.

About the measure of its effect, we should be hesitant,
naturally, to accept a view coming from Creel himself,
for Creel believed Wilson's speeches to be the all-time
apotheosis of statesmanship; and besides Creel was not
lacking in proper pride in his own work as gunner of the
ammunition Wilson created. It is in the light of Creel's
esteem for himself and ardor for Wilson, that we must
read his judgment:

It was the speeches of Wilson that did the work. It was
easy to mark their progress through the enemy country by
the trail of ferment and disaffection that each one left. . . .
We could actually *feel* the response. What happened to the
Germans was an utter spiritual collapse, a disintegration of
morale both on the firing-line and among the civilian population, and history will say that this was due to the words
of Wilson in even larger degree than to the hammer blows
of Foch.

Creel is not the first who has appealed to future history as a witness not yet in existence. As history begins to emerge, doubtless it will remember there were other factors; that aside from Wilson, there were some generals, Foch and Joffre, French and Haig; that there was a British Navy, that there were some[13] 39 million Allied soldiers, of whom five million gave up their lives; that the millions of tons of ammunition are at least to be given a place with the explosive force of Wilson's speeches. Yet we may assume that account of all this was taken by the most competent of all judges when he said that, "While her armies were victorious in the field, Germany failed in the fight of intellects."[14]   It was Ludendorff who said that.

VI

Creel, at the end of it all, when the truce came, had several experiences. Congress, finding now safe opportunity for revenge, kicked him out of office, indeed destroyed his office, cut off his appropriation, not only terminated his function but left no physical shelter for his records. For months the mass of files and papers was shunted about Washington until Creel, appealing to

[13] The total number of Allied soldiers, British, French, Russian, Italian, American, Belgian, Portuguese, Roumanian, Greek, Montenegrin, Japanese, was 39,-676,864. The total killed was 4,755,992.

[14] "Wilson's 14 Points were the trumpet call which crumbled the ramparts of the central powers; Germany was his Jericho." — George Sylvester Viereck, leading pro-German propagandist, in "Spreading Germs of Hate."

"Wilson's propaganda sapped the ardor of the German people. . . . Let the unthinking scoff as they may, Wilson's winged words were almost as potent for victory as the nation's sacrifice in blood." — "The Unknown Wilson," Wells Wells.

"When the history of the war is finally written, the work of the Creel Bureau will have an honorable place in the record."—"Woodrow Wilson and His Work," William E. Dodd.

The Bulgarian Prime Minister, after the conclusion of the Bulgarian armistice, said: "I consider President Wilson's ideas as great a power in bringing about the defeat of the Central Powers as the force of arms."—New York Times, October 6, 1918.

Wilson, found a haven for them in an unused room of one of the government bureaus. There for years they gathered dust, the documents and ideas that had once vitalized a war, now supplying musty nourishment to the mice and termites who alone had an interest in them.

That to Creel was saddening yet stimulating. It provided opportunity for the combative energy in which he always took pleasure; he could fight back at Congress, speak his opinion of them.

For one other regret he had, there was no surcease. During the heyday of his Committee there had come to his office in Washington an inventor with a new device for carrying leaflets across the enemy lines, a balloon with a range of six hundred miles having a tin container of ten thousand sheets, and a clock attachment which would drop the leaflets — Creel called them his "shrapnel" — one at a time. Creel's Committee supplied money for experiment and development, but, unfeelingly, the Germans surrendered before Creel could put the invention in use. The author of that blow was cold fate, offering no opportunity for Creel to retaliate.

From one aftermath Creel had an unqualified sweet satisfaction. Travelling by motor in a remote, mountainous part of Italy, rain and a burst tire drove him for shelter to a peasant's lonely cabin. Drying himself by the fire, he observed, in a sacred niche on one side of the chimney, a wax figure of the local patron saint. In a corresponding space on the other side was a poster of Woodrow Wilson.

23

OVER HERE

Some Facets of Life in America During the War Years.
"Doing Your Bit." Spy Hysteria. The Espionage Act
Prosecutions, and Some Persecutions. McAdoo, Who, Be-
cause of Ubiquitous Activities, Became, to a Genial Versifier,
"McAdid." Immigration Ceases. Negroes Move North.

FOR the services that were urged upon non-combatants
— women, elderly folks, invalids, and children — by
slogans and appeals from the Food Administration, the
Red Cross, Belgian Relief, the Fuel Administration, and
other organizations, a phrase became current — it was
borrowed from the British — "doing your bit"; one
patriotic lady thought the phrase implied too little, suggested "doing your all." The number and variety of
such organized and sloganized urgings reached a point
where, in an apotheosis of organization, it was proposed
that a "What Can *I* Do? League" (emphasis on the "I")
be organized. Several of the forms of helping to win
the war available to women and girls were enumerated
in verse:[1]

> I have never rolled a bandage,
>   I don't know how to knit, . . .
> But I want to serve my country,
>   I want to do my part.

                    So

> . . . I have hung a flag, a big one, from my window.
> I always wear a small one in my coat,
> When the S.-S. B.[2] is played I stand attention,
> And my sentiments my friends are proud to quote.
> I applaud my brother's plan to go to Plattsburg,

[1] By F. P. A. in the New York *Tribune,* May 2, 1917.
[2] "Star-Spangled Banner."

I read the war news as-sid-*u*-ous-ly.
I always clap and cheer for passing soldiers,
And I have even blown a kiss to two or three of the hand-
somest.

The war, coming at a time when the feminist movement was making an immense surge forward, led to a
vast broadening of the activities in which women took
part. They served as nurses and in the other fields which
tradition had sanctioned. But they also did work that
women had never done before. They became messenger
"boys" for the telegraph companies, operated elevators,
acted as street-car conductors, labored as full-time and
able-bodied operatives in munitions factories, railroad
repair-shops.[3] Girls who in groups worked on farms
were called "farmerettes"; if their handling of hoes and
rakes seemed inexpert, one observed that the uniforms
they wore were attractive. When bureaus in the naval
establishment appealed for clerks and stenographers, but
found there was no appropriation for the hiring of civilians, Secretary Daniels asked: "Is there any law that says
a yeoman must be a man? Then enroll women!" he
ordered. "The uniforms of the Yeomen (F) and the
Marines (F) were nattty and beautiful, were worn with
pride, and are preserved by them as the honorable token
of service."[4] The women "Yeomen" (it was not permitted to call them "Yeomanettes") numbered 11,000; the
women Marines (popularly called "Marinettes") were
269.

"Lick the stamps and lick the Kaiser" was a punning
slogan devised to stimulate sales of War Savings Stamps,
one of the Treasury's methods for raising funds — the

[3] August 15, 1918, Police Commissioner Enright of New York named six
women for regular police duty. In a number of cities women were given places
on police forces depleted by the draft, but were assigned to such tasks as directing traffic and not to ordinary police service.
[4] "Our Navy at War," Josephus Daniels.

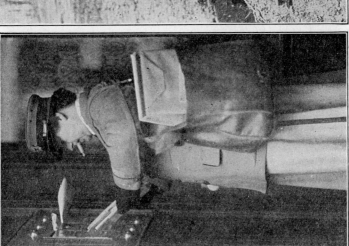

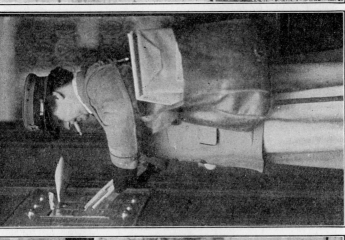

Right: College girls in woman's land army raised crops for Uncle Sam. *Centre:* The first of ten women letter carriers on the job in New York City. *Left:* Washington, D. C.'s first female traffic cop.

When women took over men's jobs.

stamps and some other concomitants of war time were
enshrined in an Omarian quatrain:

> A Book of Thrift Stamps underneath a bough,
> A loaf of Victory Bread, some coffee, sugarless—and thou
> Beside me, knitting in the wilderness,
> Ah, wilderness were Hooverized enow ![5]

Even children were enlisted to help sell war saving certificates and
"thrift" stamps.

Mirroring the country's good-natured acquiescence in
abnegation, were quantities of jokes, puns, verse in every
issue of every magazine and newspaper, which mildly
derided the slogans and regulations and verbotens that
were the price of winning the war:

With meatless, wheatless, eatless days,
Coal indicating heatless days,
The melancholy days have come, yet taxes make us miserless.
An avalanche of less-less days,
Successless days and lessless days,
Just makes us fight with all our might that Germany be Kaiser-
less ![6]

[5] *Life,* May 16, 1918.　　　　　　　[6] *Life,* January 10, 1918.

To stand and look reverent whenever the Star-Spangled Banner was played became a war-time ritual. Failure to conform incurred suspicion of being pro-

—*Briggs in the New York Tribune, Jan. 23, 1918.*

German; always such lapse brought frowns from the audience, sometimes more tangible evidences of disapproval, in the form of missiles, vocal or vegetable. Though all became sufficiently familiar with the music to recognize it and rise, and many carried deference far enough to put the lips through the motions of singing, few learned the words. *Life* printed an apocryphal dialogue:

Suspected Traveller: I tell you I am an American.

French Sergeant: Sing the words of "The Star-Spangled Banner."

Suspected Traveller: I can't.

French Sergeant: Pass, monsieur. You are an American.

[7] March 28, 1918.

II

Unification of the country for promptest possible delivery of the largest quantity of supplies to the front
suggested one-man management of all railroads. Wilson
appointed William G. McAdoo as Director-General
"with an authority as nearly absolute as any power can
be in America."[8] The number of offices and activities
McAdoo already held, Secretary of the Treasury, ex-
officio head of the Federal Reserve Board, director of
Liberty bond drives, Farm Loan banks, soldiers' insurance — including the post of son-in-law to President
Wilson, which led some of the satiric to speak of him as
the "Crown Prince" — all combined to enable him
to entitle the autobiography he subsequently wrote,
"Crowded Years." With his energy went willingness to
let his deeds be known; combination of his function of
Director-General of Railroads with that of head of the
Public Health Service (a bureau of the Treasury Department) enabled him to sign a warning about averting dis-
eases which, posted in the toilet-room of every railroad
car, provided raw material for smoking-room humor.
The impression of expansiveness of McAdoo led a poet[9]
to write, and much of war-time Washington to quote:

> The Who, preeminently Who,
> Is William Gibbs, the McAdoo.
> (Whom I should like to hail but daren't,
> As Royal Prince and Heir Apparent.)
> A man of high intrinsic Worth,
> The Greatest Son-in-Law on Earth —
> With all the burdens thence accruing,
> He's always up and McAdooing.
> From Sun to Star and Star to Sun,
> His work is never McAdone.

8 The quoted words are McAdoo's, "Crowded Years."
9 Arthur Guiterman.

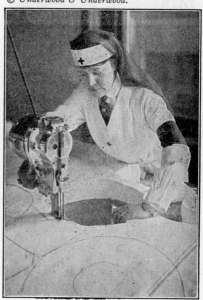

Everywhere and all the time women kept up their share of the work.

Upper left: Miss Ann Orr, a stage star. knitting between times at a rink. *Upper right:* A stenographer puts a pause in dictation to good account. *Lower left:* The Washington, D. C., Canteen Corps serving soldiers. *Lower right:* Two hundred and sixteen patterns were stencilled and cut at one time by Red Cross workers.

He regulates our Circumstances,
Our Buildings, Industries, Finances,
And Railways, while the wires buzz
To tell us what he McAdoes. . . .
I don't believe he ever hid
A single thing he McAdid!
His name appears on Scrip and Tissue,
On bonds of each succeeding issue,
On coupons bright and posters rare,
And every Pullman Bill of Fare.

Specimens of regulations and prohibitions imposed on commerce and manufacture by one or another of the Boards or Commissions sired by the war: the ban on gold and silver for artistic and industrial purposes. . . . The ruling that employers engaged in war work could not advertise for unskilled labor. . . . The fixing of the price of shoes by the War Industries Board (Oct. 2, 1918). . . . The interdiction on the use of platinum in jewelry manufacture (W.I.B. Sept. 30, 1918). . . . Instructions to the automobile manufacturers to convert their plants to 100 per cent war work before January 1, 1919 (W.I.B. Aug. 9, 1918). . . . Government order that automobile tire production be reduced 50 per cent for sixty days after August 1, 1918. . . . Postmaster General Burleson's expropriation of telegraph and telephone wires. . . . Organization of the American Railroad Express Company under Government supervision, by merger of the Adams, American, Wells-Fargo and Southern Express Companies (May 28, 1918). . . . Prices for newsprint paper fixed by the U. S. Trade Commission. . . . Price of aluminum put at a maximum of 32 cents a pound. . . . By Presidential order (Feb. 15, 1918) no commodities could be exported or imported except under special license by the War Trade Board. . . . Production of passenger automobiles cut by government order June 10, 1918, to 25 per cent of previous year's output. . . . Use of coal or fuel oil prohibited on private pleasure yachts, May 29, 1918. . . . 170 silk factories at Paterson, N. J., closed by order of the Federal Fuel Administrator, January 3, 1918. . . . Only

Photographs © Underwood & Underwood.

Left: Peach stones were saved. When reduced to a charcoal powder, they were used to filter the poison out of gas. *Right:* A patriotic marcher in the "Win the War" parade, New York, April, 1918.

bakery products containing at least 20 per cent wheat substitutes was permitted after September 1, 1918, by order of the Food Administration. . . . Sugar allowance, by edict of the U. S. Food Board, was reduced from three to two pounds per person per month, July 26, 1918. . . . The President put stockyards and slaughtering and packing business under Federal license and supervision, June 18, 1918. . . . Balance of the 1917 wheat crop was taken over by the Government May 15, 1918, at $2.20 a bushel. . . . By order of the New England Fuel Administrator, James J. Storrow, business hours were limited to from 9 A.M. to 5 P.M., theatres, bars and all places of amusement were to close at 10 P.M., and all nights but Saturday were to be "lightless." . . .

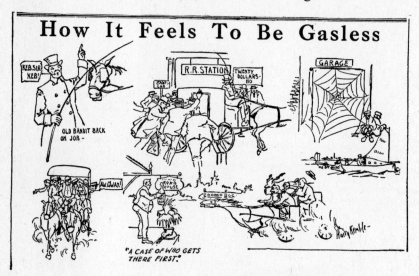

The horse came into his own again on the gasless Sunday.
— *Harry Kemble in the New York Tribune, Sept. 8, 1918*

January 16, 1918, Federal Fuel Administrator Garfield ordered the closing down of manufacturing plants in territory east of Mississippi, January 18 to 22, and for nine subsequent Mondays.[10] . . . March 30, 1918, daylight saving went into effect throughout the United States, in accordance with a Federal law. . . . March

---

[10] Managing Editor Lincoln of the New York *World* called Tumulty, Wilson's secretary, out of bed at midnight. Tumulty asked Wilson, "Has the groundwork been laid for this radical step? Do the people know how much coal we have on hand and what the real shortage is? . . . I greatly fear the consequences upon the morale of the people."

Wilson replied: "This is a tremendous matter and has given me the deepest concern. . . . We must just bow our heads and let the storm beat."

3, 1918, the Federal Food Administrator reduced the meatless days to a beefless and porkless Tuesday. . . . July 16, 1918. Lightless nights were ordered four days each week in New York and northeast Atlantic Coast States; all the rest of the country to be lightless Monday and Tuesday evenings. . . . August 27, 1918, owners of automobiles, motorcycles, and motorboats were asked to refrain from using them on Sundays. . . . November 22, 1918, the lifting of the "lightless nights" ban put New York City's Great White Way in an old-time blaze of illumination.

III

"Under modern conditions of warfare," said James Truslow Adams, "hate becomes almost as essential as ammunition, and hate is manufactured." In our manufacture of verbal schrecklichkeit, clergymen helped much. Doctor Newell Dwight Hillis of Plymouth Church, Brooklyn, contributed a brand: German "soldiers [are] sneaking, snivelling cowards. . . . The Reverend Doctor Henry van Dyke (American Minister to Holland during the war) invented a new epithet for the Kaiser, the "Werewolf of Potsdam," more literary, if less alliterative than the "Beast of Berlin." Doctor Van Dyke would "hang every one who lifts his voice against America's entering the war." Doctor S. Parkes Cadman, pastor of Central Congregational Church, Brooklyn, dealing also in figures of speech, declared that the Lutheran Church in Germany "is not the bride of Christ, but the paramour of Kaiserism." The Reverend W. Bustard stepped out of the pulpit manner long enough to say, succintly, "To hell with the Kaiser!" The gentle, patriarchically bearded Reverend Doctor Lyman Abbott judged the German military organization to be the "most efficient band of brigands the world has ever known."

The Reverend Doctor Billy Sunday, invited to deliver a prayer in the House of Representatives at Washington, began: "Thou knowest, O Lord, that no nation so infamous, vile, greedy, sensuous, bloodthirsty ever disgraced the pages of history."

In the concoction of hate, college professors contributed as generously as clergymen: Doctor Louis Gray, of the University of Nebraska, judged that "The Prussian is a moral imbecile, an arrested development." Doctor Joseph Jastrow, of the University of Wisconsin, was credited with a new literary and scientific term, "Mania Teutonica." Professor William H. Hobbs of the University of Michigan called Germany "the nation which sold itself to the devil." Stuart P. Sherman, then associated with the English department of the University of Illinois, warned the country against "'Prussianism streaming into Anglo-Saxon communities through the forty volumes of Carlyle." Doctor William Roscoe Thayer, historian, poet, biographer of John Hay and Theodore Roosevelt, one-time President of the American Historical Association, wrote "Volleys from a non-Combatant" "to prevent the total pollution of our people by letting loose of the Prussian moral sewers."

One of the most exact-minded persons in the field of American learning, and one of the gentlest of men, Doctor Vernon Kellogg, of Stanford University, later head of the National Institute of Science, contributed an eloquent excoriation of Germany. Doctor Kellogg had reason for emotion; he had been in Belgium as an official of Herbert Hoover's Belgian Relief, and had seen the German at his worst:

Will it be any wonder if, after the war, the people of the world, when they recognize any human being as German, will shrink aside so that they may not touch him as he passes, or will stoop for stones to drive him from their path? . . .

Melancthon Woolsey Stryker, President of Hamilton College, put his emotion into verse:

> The clock has struck! The death-smeared double vulture
> Shall swoop no more adown the insulted skies,
> To spill the venomous bacterial Kultur. . . .[11]

IV

A "spy fever," natural fruit of war-time psychology, given official encouragement by the stringent law against enemy espionage and seditious utterances, set every one to watching out for German agents. The official "Intelligence Section" of the Army was ubiquitous, meticulous. American Ambassadors Walter H. Page from London and William G. Sharp from Paris, coming to Washington in 1916 to report on the progress of the war, were invited to lunch at the Shoreham Hotel with Cabinet Members Lansing, Lane, Baker, Gregory, and Daniels. To Page's distaste, "all the talk [he wrote in a memorandum afterward] was jocular or semi-jocular, and personal — mere cheap chaff; the war was not mentioned; Sharp and I might have come from Bingtown and Jonesville." Subsequent explanation from the cabinet members said they had been warned that hotel waiters might be German spies.

In addition to the Intelligence Section of the Army, civilians were asked to keep their ears and eyes open, report disloyal utterances or suspicious activities. To the amateur detectives, "suspicious activities" became a broad term. One of the functions was to investigate the antecedents and associations of persons of German birth

---

[11] *American Mercury*, June, 1927. Article by Charles Angoff, "The Higher Learning Goes to War." Most of these quotations are from two sources: *American Mercury*, which during the 1920's published a number of articles about the activities of American scholars in the war, and George Sylvester Viereck's "Spreading Germs of Hate."

or associations. Employers were asked to furnish data about employees having German names, and to be responsible for their loyalty.

Those who had authority from the Army Intelligence

RED CROSS BANDAGES POISONED BY SPIES

Startling Plot Reported by Director Staub in Urging Precautions by Philadelphia Workers.

Special to The New York Times.

PHILADELPHIA, March 28.—Albert W. Staub, Director of the Atlantic Division of the American Red Cross, addressing the local Red Cross organization today, said:

"You women of Philadelphia must clean house. Go over the list of your members and make sure of the loyalty of every one. Under no circumstances allow any one in your board rooms unless you know who they are. Keep persons out of the workrooms who have no right to be there.

War hysteria.

—*N. Y. Times, March 29, 1917.*

Section were supplemented by volunteers, even more zealous, even less discriminating, proving once more Carlyle's saying, "Of all forms of government, a government by busybodies is the worst." A lamp kept lighted all night anywhere within sight of the sea was a signal to German submarines. A street conversation in German, or in any language other than English, even a sentence or a word, was likely to bring trouble. It became dangerous to say "Prosit!" or "Auf wiedersehn!"

It was asserted, and in theory was true, that five German spies, taking up points of strategy and acting simultaneously, could paralyze the city of New York: One, placed at the right point, could by bomb or otherwise interrupt the telephone service for days; another the electric light system, another the gas plant, another the water supply. Some ten German agents, acting simultaneously, could stop indefinitely all railroad traffic entering New York, by dynamiting all the railroad bridges over the Harlem River, the Delaware, and the Hudson. This condition was indisputable and was recognized by the government. At each end of every bridge stood, during the war, a soldier. On trains, travellers who sat on the rear platform were asked, on the approach to a bridge, to step inside; it would be easy to drop a bomb that would paralyze a trunk line railroad.

The spectacle of actual danger guarded against gave rise to grotesque mare's nests. It became a hysteria. Whispers predicted, or asserted as actually having happened, armed uprisings in Milwaukee, St. Louis, Cincinnati or other German-American centres. Trifling epidemics of diarrhœa proved that German spies had put germs in the local water supply. An individual illness unduly prolonged was related to the German name of the apothecary who made up the prescription. Failure of a cut in a child's hand to heal quickly was due to germs placed in the court-plaster supplied by German agents. Any interruption of the flow of munitions from a factory was due to a German sabotageur who had tampered with an essential mechanism.

The night before Wilson delivered his speech asking Congress to declare war, he talked with Frank Cobb, editor of the New York *World*: "Once lead this people into war, and they'll forget there was ever such a thing as tolerance; to fight you must be brutal and ruthless, and the spirit of ruthless brutality will enter into the very fibre of our national life, infecting Congress, the courts, the policeman, the man in the street."

The war-time laws against espionage and sedition, passed June 15, 1917, amended May 16, 1918, prescribed penalties for speaking, printing or otherwise expressing contempt for the government or the constitution or the flag or the uniform of the Army or Navy; using language calculated to aid the enemy's cause, using words favoring any country with which the United States was at war, saying or doing anything likely to restrict the sale of United States bonds. The Postmaster General was empowered to deny the mails to any one deemed by him to be violating the act.

Under this law 1532 persons were arrested for disloyal utterances, 65 for threats against the President, 10 for sabotage. William D. Haywood and 94 other members of the I. W. W. (Industrial Workers of the World — translated in current humor to "I Wont' Work"), after a trial lasting 138 days, were sentenced to prison terms. Two prominent Socialists, Eugene V. Debs and Mrs. Rose Pastor Stokes, were convicted and sentenced.

The number charged informally with plotting, or suspected, was legion. After the hysteria died down, a Federal judge, George W. Anderson of Boston, who during the war had been a United States attorney and otherwise in intimate personal association with the men charged with responsibility of discovering, preventing, and punishing pro-German plots, said, "I assert, as my best judgment, that more than 90 per cent of the reported pro-German plots never existed; I think it is time publicity was given to this view." To the same effect, Mrs. Alice Roosevelt Longworth said: "I personally know of not a single case in which anything was proved."[12]

With volunteer spying by Americans on alleged German spies, went volunteer censorship, informal punishment of persons suspected of lack of loyalty. On a street-car in Cleveland a man of foreign appearance was seen angrily to pull from the rack above him a Liberty Bond poster and tear it up. Super-loyal Americans, taking him from the car, handled him roughly. When some one who could speak the alien's language pressed forward, it developed that the man could not read English, and that what had excited his rage was not the words of the poster's appeal to buy Liberty Bonds, but a drawing of the Kaiser which the artist had injected into the poster as a stimulus to patriotic generosity. Search of the man's pockets, revealing two Liberty Bonds, completed his vindication.

The mob spirit emerged in quarters more elevated than a street-car crowd. The Poetry Society of America and the Author's League felt they were demonstrating the superiority of American culture to German, and helping to win the war, by expelling from membership a German-American poet named George Sylvester Viereck. (One should add that Viereck had been pretty offensive as a propagandist for Germany, a panegyrist of the Kaiser.) Opera singers were made to understand that German birth made their voices less musical than they had been accepted as, before the war. Demand was made for removal of the German-born conductor of the most famous orchestra in America, Dr. Karl Muck, and he was taken into custody as an enemy alien. The

[12] It should be made clear that Mrs. Longworth and Judge Anderson are speaking of pro-German plots after we entered the war. Of German plots on American soil before we entered the war, there were many, and they were abundantly proved. (See Chapter 8.)

patriotic mayor of East Orange, N. J., would not permit Fritz Kreisler, outstanding violinist, formerly a lieutenant in the Austrian Army, to play in a concert. Brown University helped to win the war by revoking an honorary degree it had previously conferred on German Ambassador von Bernstorff. In the ranks of business and elsewhere, zealous Americans demonstrated their patriotism by calling for removal of German-born clerks. German-born were not the only victims. Any who failed to share the current hysteria were crucified by it. Two boys in Madison, Wis., one destined to become a Senator, the other a Governor, saw their father, Senator Robert M. LaFollette, burned in effigy.

When Czechoslovakians in America organized, not to help Austria but to incite rebellion against her by their racial brothers at home, they encountered violence. In Iowa and Nebraska, meetings to rally recruits for the Czechoslovakian army were broken up by patriotic Americans whose cause for zeal was their lack of understanding of the Czechoslovakian tongue. In Seward County, Neb., the local council for national defense required all the churches in the district to conduct their services in English except one, for persons at once too old either to be German soldiers or to learn English. German and Scandinavian communities desiring to hold Liberty Loan or Red Cross rallies found it prudent to meet secretly. No distinction was made, the language of Allied and neutral countries being under the ban as well as enemy languages. The Governor of Iowa gave out rules —

First. English should and must be the only medium of instruction in public, private, denominational, or other similar schools.

Second. Conversation in public places, on trains, or over the telephone should be in the English language.

Photograph by U. S. Army Signal Corps.

Photograph © Underwood & Underwood.

Above: Douglas Fairbanks urging a New York throng to buy Liberty Bonds. *Lower left:* Arthur Guy Empey, war hero and author of "Over the Top," aiding a Liberty Bond selling rally. *Lower right:* A character of the day known as "King of the Hoboes," urging a street crowd to buy Liberty Bonds.

Third.   All public addresses should be in the English language.

Fourth.   Let those who cannot speak or understand the English language conduct their religious worship in their homes.

Some lost not only their tolerance but their sense of humor.   The word "sauerkraut" was tabooed as German, but since we did not care to banish so agreeable a food we continued to eat it as "liberty cabbage."   Cincinnati ruled pretzels off the free lunch counters of local saloons.   In some parts of the West the name of a familiar ailment was changed from "German measles" to "liberty measles."   Dachshunds became "liberty pups."

In the crusade one spot stood out: November 5, 1918, citizens of Berlin, N. H., by a vote of 933 to 566, decided that the name of their town was not so humiliating as to demand change.

Associated with the spirit of censorship and suspicion was the spirit of compulsion.   Cruelties practised in Northwestern communities where Germans and Scandinavians were a majority of the citizens, left scars which remain livid to this day, and will remain so for generations to come.   In Ontagamie County, Wisconsin, a farmer, John Derul, was awakened by his wife to find —

"A large number of men on the front porch, pounding and rapping on the door, besides talking in a loud tone of voice. . . . I came downstairs and went to the front door, where they were, and I asked them, who was there! Several answered at once, 'The Council of Defense.' I then asked them, 'What do you want?' and they replied, 'We want you to sign up.' I replied, 'I have done my share.' And they asked me when, and I replied, 'I did my share in the spring.' (That is, I meant to say I had done my share in the Third [Liberty] Loan, when I subscribed to $450 in bonds.)

". . . They all at one time closed in on me, some grabbing my fingers or wrist, others my legs, and several of them were shouting, holding a paper before me, 'Sign up.' I said, 'I will not sign up at this time of night.' Then a man shouted, 'Get the rope!' The first I knew was when the rope was about my

neck and around my body under my arms. Then a man (whom
I recognized) said, 'Boys, you are going too far.' "[13]

V

An athlete of the day, Walter Camp, conducting setting-up exercises, on the lawn of Congressman William
Kent's house to achieve war-time physique for elderly and
adipose Cabinet members. . . . The thrill of the phrase

Foch and Pershing at Pershing's headquarters, Val des Ecoliers,
Chaumont, France.

wrongly attributed to General Pershing in a ceremony
after he arrived at Paris, "Lafayette, we are here" — by
1919, American soldiers, restlessly homesick, kept in
France long after the Armistice, paraphrased it to "La-

[13] *Atlantic Monthly,* January, 1919.

fayette, we are *still* here." . . . The trying emotional experience of Miss Jeannette Rankin of Montana, first woman member of Congress: in the roll-call on the declaration of war, she did not answer, moved nervously in her seat; in a second roll-call to give opportunity for record to any who had come late, all eyes were on the unhappy Congresswoman; finally, in deep unhappiness she rose and said, "I want to stand by my country, but I cannot vote for war." . . . President Wilson's white suit, worn when pressure of war kept him at Washington during the summer; an innovation for Presidents, it started a vogue for males. . . . Wilson's favorite poem "The Happy Warrior" which, the country assumed, was idealization of himself. . . . One of Wilson's favorite limericks; it had an added touch of interest from being recited by a President and a Presbyterian:

> A wondrous bird is the pelican;
> His mouth holds more than his bellican;
> He takes in his beak
> Enough food for a week,
> But I'm darned if I see how the hellican.

The newspaper witticisms about Secretary McAdoo's patched trousers — he wore them ostentatiously to stimulate economy of cloth and labor when we needed all for war purposes; and the other example McAdoo gave, to Liberty Bond salesmen, on a rainy day going from house to house in Washington, ringing door-bells and asking housewives to buy bonds. . . . "Gone west" — for ten American generations the phrase had been one of romance and enterprise for those who went to make careers on the frontier; during the Great War it became a soldier's euphemism for death in France. . . . "Buy a bale" — phrase of despair when cotton was six cents a pound after the war broke out — succeeded by cotton at thirty cents in 1918. . . . "Business as usual," phrase of Couéeian assurance when business was decidedly not as usual, soon after the war began in 1914 — succeeded by wheat at $3.25 a bushel and copper at 30 cents a pound

Photograph © Underwood & Underwood.

Chauncey Olcott, famous at that time as an actor of romantic Irish rôles, singing "My Wild Irish Rose" as an incident of a Liberty Loan Drive.

in 1918. . . . "Spurlos versenkt," "sunk without trace," phrase used incautiously by the German Ambassador to Argentina in advising the German Navy to do a complete job in sinking Argentine ships, and which, after exposure by the British Secret Service, became another count in the world's indictment of German ruthlessness. . . . "Eat plenty, wisely, without waste" —

cautionary second thought of Herbert Hoover, Food Administrator, when over-zealous persons took the appeals for food conservation too seriously, to the detriment of health. . . . "Made in Germany," formerly having connotation suggesting flaxen-haired dolls, small hardware, and similar imports, but now endowed with a new and sinister significance. . . . The "Eagles" of Henry Ford — small and very bouncey submarine chasers turned out at the rate of one a day in the Ford factory in Detroit. . . . "An Atlantic port," censorship's ambiguous phrase, appearing in newspaper despatches telling of troop movements to France; sometimes the intended secrecy was flouted by a bull, "an Atlantic port past the Statue of Liberty." . . . The appeals of the Allies for ships, more ships, and more ships; men, more men, more men; money, more money, more money. . . . "We are fighting with our backs to the wall" — Allied plea for hurry when the Germans were smashing through the British armies in Northern France in the Spring of 1918. . . . "Anti-loafing Bill" — name given to a law enacted in New Jersey to end vagrancy. . . . "Work or fight," order of May 17, 1918.[14] . . . Official commissions and dignitaries from the Allies who came to visit us after we entered the war — they became so numerous we lost track of them a little and Will Rogers said we were "meeting Serbian commissions with Roumanian flags." . . . "Change from debtor to creditor nation" — that phrase for America's altered status was talked about much and learnedly; it was assumed the dollar would take the place of the British pound in international trade. . . . "A navy second to none" — a detail of Wilson's preparedness program; we embarked upon it, but stopped when at the Conference for Limita-

---

[14] Signed by Governor Edge, Feb. 16, 1918. It required that all able-bodied males, 18 to 50, be regularly employed in some useful occupation.

Left: Geraldine Farrar selling a Bond to Secretary Houston in Liberty Loan Drive in Washington. *Centre*: Paderewski, noted Polish pianist, speaks for the Drive at City Hall, New York. *Right*: Mrs. Gerard, wife of the Ex-Ambassador to Germany, selling Bonds.

MISS FARRAR
WILL SELL
BONDS

tion of Armaments in 1922 we agreed with other nations in stabilizing naval armament in a fixed ratio. . . . "Associated Powers," Wilson's careful term for America's relation to the Allies — Wilson wished to preserve a distinction between us and the Allies. . . . Indisposition of some aggressively democratic American soldiers to salute their officers; General Leonard Wood, when two privates simultaneously stooped to tie shoestrings in order to avoid saluting him, explained that the salute is a survival from the days of armor — a knight with his face covered by a visor raised it to show that he was a friend. . . . "Liaison," war-word from the French, used at first for an interpreter between groups of Allies speaking different languages, adopted in American usage to describe any intermediary. . . . Wilson delivering his addresses to Congress in person, revival of a usage obsolete for a hundred years — Roosevelt was said to have exclaimed, "Why didn't I think of that!" . . .

VI

The social and economic effects of the war were deep, far-reaching, and intricate. The active ferment which was at all times the condition of American society was now greatly speeded up. Not only individuals but groups rose or fell. Change in the purchasing power of money (caused largely by expansion of credit as an incident of war-financing and war-time business activity) sent some classes upward in the world, others downward. The rearrangement was visible. The type of person that had composed for a generation almost the exclusive patronage of expensive hotels and of Pullman cars on the railroads was diluted by a class to whom these luxuries were new.

One stratum of the rich were made relatively poorer. Those who lived on the income from mortgages and bonds saw the purchasing power of their dollars go as low as 40 cents. These were the most conservative class of the well-to-do, persons who had inheritances of gilt-edged mortgages: widows, beneficiaries of trust funds,

Photograph © Underwood & Underwood.

Girls loading rattan on freight cars tracked in the Bush Terminal Docks, Brooklyn, New York.

teachers in colleges whose fixed salaries came from endowments — after the war it became necessary to conduct "drives" to increase college endowments and raise faculty salaries. So far as this class were the principal custodians of taste, the possessors and practitioners of learning and of interest in art and the like, their lowered status was unsettling to tradition, played a part in the general overthrowing of accepted standards that came soon after.

Another class of the rich benefited enormously. These were the owners of factories, the participants in active business, the stock-holding class as distinguished from bond-holders, and the land and goods owning class. These benefited by the increased valuation of their properties as expressed in dollars, and benefited extravagantly by the profitable manufacture of munitions and the supplying of goods to meet the needs of a war-paralyzed Europe. "War-millionaires" became a current term for the new rich; "war babies" was a Wall Street term for corporations that became suddenly fat.

In proportion, labor benefited most of all. So great was the war demand for goods, both in America and from Europe, and so restricted the supply of workers due to diversion of man-power to war, that labor could command almost any wage it chose to ask — indeed, what actually happened was not demand by labor but furiously competitive up-bidding by employers. As a rule, sudden ease about money expressed itself in free spending. Arrival of workmen at the factory Monday morning wearing silk shirts, an incident probably over-emphasized in proportion to its novelty, was much talked about by those who held the fixed view that workmen did not know how to handle money. The free spending for luxuries, hitherto commonly bought only by the well-to-do, in turn accelerated the profits of manufacturers.

Scarcity of labor, and therefore elevation of labor's economic status, was accentuated by practically complete cessation of immigration. For the year that ended June 30, 1914, immigration amounted to 1,217,500. With the mobilization in Europe, the number fell to 315,700 in 1915 and continued to fall until less than 20,000 a month entered this country, of whom a large number came from Mexico and the West Indies. Thus the war brought about a result which many Americans had begun to think desirable. As the war came toward an end, and it became apparent that millions of soldiers disbanded in a poverty-stricken Europe would at once flood to fat America, the check on immigration, which war had been, was made statutory; in the early 1920's America adopted

As the European reservist was called to the colors, the negro waiter was called from the South to fill his place.

—*New York Telegram, Aug. 7, 1914.*

a restrictive policy which was the reversal of its practice since the earliest times. The social and economic consequences, and even the ethnic effect, first of immigration and then of its restriction, were so fundamental and so complex as to be almost incalculable.

With cessation of the immigration that had long been the supply of cheap unskilled labor, and with the increased need for such labor, industrialists in the North sent agents into the Southern states. To the negro in the cotton fields and on the levee the labor-agents sang a siren song: undreamed of wages, steady jobs, political equality, no race discrimination, better housing, good schools for the children, free transportation north and frequently money for food while on the way. The song fell on willing ears. A large percentage of the South's negroes were living on hunger wages. The boll weevil was virulent, crops had been bad for several consecutive years. Floods in 1916 had done great damage in Alabama and Mississippi. Many of the plantations paid but 50 to 75 cents a day, and this only when there was work. $1.25 to $2.00 were high wages and went to only a few men in the cotton oil mills and the saw mills. Housing and schools were inferior; "Jim Crow" cars, political inequality — the combination made the negro eager to go — "I'se gwine to live till I die anyhow; I might as well go up No'th." The exodus started. "A negro minister may have all his deacons with him for the mid-week meeting but by Sunday every church officer was likely to be in the North."[15]

The South, complacent at first about the social result of diminution of negro majorities, began to be alarmed by other effects: the disappearance of field hands essential to plantation life, of house servants held in affection, of factory workers indispensable to industry; break-up of a familiar and cherished social order. The Macon *Telegraph* printed a plaintive warning: "Everybody seems to be asleep about what is going on right under our noses — that is, everbody but those farmers who waked up mornings recently to find every negro over twenty-one on their places gone — to Cleveland, to Pittsburgh, to Chicago, to Indianapolis."

Estimates said that 50,000 went North from Georgia, the Commission of Agriculture in Alabama thought that

[15] U. S. Department of Labor Report. From this report, some of the facts here related are taken.

90,000 had gone from their State. In Mississippi, negro insurance companies considered 100,000 a conservative estimate. In the North not all the emigrés were as happy as the labor agents had said the Utopia would be. Jobs there were, and high pay; but the cost of living was

Photograph by U. S. Army Signal Corps.

A war-time smile.

high in proportion and the jobs demanded an application and discipline, a speed and efficiency that the easy-going cotton-field had not asked. Exacting foremen and super-intendents, cogs in vast industrial machines, themselves driven by time-clock and cost-sheet, passed on the pressure to negroes whose natural tempo of life was especially ill-adapted to stand the strain. Political equality there was, but the negro came to question the value of the doubtful privilege of voting in Illinois as against the paternalism of planters who had employed your father before you. The advantages of a steam-heated Harlem flat did not balance the easy comfort of a cotton-field cabin, rent-free or nearly so. Presently the process of adjustment, negro labor coming into competition with

Many of the negroes who had gone to northern cities, after encountering race-riots and other harsh conditions, concluded that the South was a good place for a negro to be.

— *Grover Page in the Louisville Courier Journal.*

white, negroes moving into communities formerly wholly white, lack of a settled and accepted tradition about relations between the races, led to riots in Chicago, Philadelphia, and Washington — there was an especially violent one in East St. Louis, Ill. Some of the negro migrants yielded to the pull of nostalgia for their old homes. Most remained, however, and soon a new generation born in the North made permanent negro colonies, urban equivalents of what the South had called the "black belt," which, among other social and political consequences, resulted in a Chicago district being represented in Congress for several years by a negro.

VII

Of the effects of the war on America, by far the most fundamental was our submission to autocracy in government. Every male between 18 and 45 had been deprived of freedom of his body — for refusing or evading the surrender, 163,738 were apprehended and disciplined, many by jail sentences. Every person had been deprived of freedom of his tongue, no one could utter dissent from the purpose or the method of war — for violating the sedition act, 1597 persons were arrested. Every business man was shorn of dominion over his factory or store, every housewife surrendered control of her table, every farmer was forbidden to sell his wheat except at the price the government fixed. Our institutions, the railroads, the telephones and telegraphs, the coal mines, were taken under government control — the list was complete when, after the war and preceding the Peace Conference, Wilson took control of the trans-Atlantic cables. The prohibition of individual liberty in the interest of the state could hardly be more complete. "In the six months after our entry into the war the United States had been transformed from a highly individualistic system . . . into what was almost a great socialistic state in which the control of the whole industry, life and purpose of the nation was directed from Washington. It was an amazing transformation, for nothing like it had ever been attempted before on any such scale, and the process was wholly antipathetic to our ordinary ways of doing things."[16] It was the greatest

[16] James Truslow Adams in "The Epic of America."

submission by the individual to the state that had occurred in any country at any time. It was an abrupt reversal of the evolution that had been under way for centuries. Since Magna Charta, substantially all political

Stars that were sons.
— *Calvert in "Life," Jan. 24, 1918.*

change had been in the direction of cumulative taking
of power from the state for the benefit of the individual.
Now in six months, in America the state took back, the
individual gave up, what had taken centuries of contest
to win.

It was not merely that we had passed through the experience of enforced submission or voluntary surrender

or both. The results remained with us. Government had learned that we could be led to do it, had learned the technique of bringing the individual to give up his liberty, the cunning of propaganda, the artfulness of slogans, and the other methods for inciting mass solidarity and mass action, for causing majorities to insist on conformance by minorities.

The purpose for which we did this, as described by the one who urged us to it and led us into it was "the destruction of every arbitrary power anywhere," "to make the world safe for democracy," a purpose to save the peoples of all nations, including and especially Germany, from autocratic government;[17] a purpose to have the individualist ideal of society (France) triumph in a struggle against the ideal of regimentation (Germany).

That purpose, reviewed fifteen years later in the light of what had meantime happened in the world, seemed very ironic indeed — Germany and Italy under dictators, Russia under a dictatorship called proletarian but more extreme in its deprivation of individual liberty than any personal dictator or absolute monarch attempted, American industry and social organization in the beginning of what was aimed toward regimentation.

[17] "Liberation of [all] peoples, the German people included, from autocratic governments."—Wilson, address to Congress, April 2, 1917.

24

TRAIL'S END FOR ROOSEVELT

It had been nineteen years since Roosevelt had rallied about him the rough-riding, quick-shooting men of the old West and kindred spirits in the East, to charge up San Juan Hill in the Spanish-American War. Meantime, as President, he had been Commander-in-Chief of the Army and Navy, and that had pleased him rather more than any of his honors or powers. For war had always been to Roosevelt at once a summons to national duty, a call to personal adventure. Since he had grown to manhood he had volunteered to or toward every war or threat of war America had faced; even at threat of Indian outbreak or domestic riot he had been eager:

1886. I have written to Secretary Endicott offering to try to raise some companies of horse riflemen . . . in the event of trouble with Mexico.

1886. [Regarding Haymarket Riots]: My men are Americans through and through . . . I wish I had them with me and a fair show at ten times our number of rioters; my men shoot well and fear very little.

1896. [Regarding Altgeld in 1896]: Remember, sir, I may at any time be called upon to meet the man sword to sword upon the field of battle. When war does come I shall be found at the head of my regiment.

1898. We will have a jim-dandy regiment if we go.

1908. If a war should occur while I am still physically fit, I should certainly try to raise a brigade of cavalry, mounted riflemen, such as those in my regiment ten years ago.

1911. If by any remote chance there should be a serious war then I would wish immediately to raise a division of cavalry. If given a free hand I could render it as formidable a body of horse riflemen, that is, of soldiers such as those of Sheridan, Forest, and Stuart, as has ever been seen.

February, 1917. I have already on file . . . my application to be permitted to raise a Division of Infantry, with a divisional brigade of cavalry, in the event of war (possibly with the permission to make one or two of the brigades of infantry, mounted infantry).[1]

Now, as American participation in the Great War loomed closer and closer, Roosevelt saw once more the chance to charge gloriously. He took it as much for granted that he would be in the war as that he would eat; with equal certainty he assumed he would be among the first to go. As early as the autumn of 1914 the seed of a "Roosevelt Division" had taken root in him. By January, 1915, like a dreaming boy, he was listing the men he would take, young army officers who had come to his attention, older ones who had been companions of his in the Spanish-American War, young civilians who begged to be taken as privates. As information about his project became public, tens of thousands of adventurous youths pleaded for a chance to fight under him; at the peak, applications poured in at the rate of two thousand a day. The "Roosevelt Division" was a reality — lacking only authority to exist.

There was embarrassment, Roosevelt realized — but no impediment, he thought — in the fact that the man who was now Commander-in-Chief of the American Army was the same man whom Roosevelt had called "neither a gentleman nor a real man," a "logothete," a "sophist," a "pacifist," "a trained elocutionist," the man Roosevelt had sneered at as "waging peace." That Wilson should now remember Roosevelt's attacks or regard them as making it impossible for Wilson to give him a fighting part in the War; or that it might be, from the point of view of a President, impracticable to send an ex-President to France — nothing of that kind occurred to Roosevelt. Neither did he take account of other considerations. The Great War was no three-months' ad-

[1] Compiled by Henry F. Pringle in "Theodore Roosevelt, A Biography."

venture like the one with Spain, in which bravery and a gay recklessness could substitute for rigid discipline and specialized training. America in the Spanish War had been amateur; in the Great War she must be professional. Organization was essential, on a vast scale, and there must be planning that would comprehend every unit of America's war effort, make the actions of each subordinate to the purpose of the whole. A great, smoothly working machine was what was demanded.

The day that diplomatic relations with Germany were severed,[2] Roosevelt wrote a letter to Secretary of War Baker: "I have already on file in your Department my application to be permitted to raise a Division of Infantry. If you believe there will be war and a call for volunteers, I respectfully and earnestly request that you notify me at once. I have prepared the skeleton outline of what I have desired the Division to be."

Icily, Baker replied: "No situation has arisen. Your letter will be filed for consideration should occasion arise."

Ignoring the rebuff, or more likely not recognizing it, Roosevelt wrote on February 7 a note that had the manner of a reminder: "In the event of being allowed to raise a division, I should, of course, strain every nerve to have it ready for efficient action at the earliest moment," and he requested that Captain Frank McCoy of the Regular Army be assigned him as divisional Chief of Staff to go over preparations. At the same time he was writing Henry Cabot Lodge: "If Wilson gives me the division I shall serve him with single-minded loyalty."[3]

Baker's answer was specific: "In reply to your patriotic suggestion, I have to state the limitations of the War Department. No action in the direction suggested

---

[2] February 2, 1917.
[3] "Correspondence of Theodore Roosevelt and Henry Cabot Lodge."

by you can be taken without the express sanction of Congress."

For a month Roosevelt fumed. On March 19 he wired Baker that if the War Department would furnish him arms and supplies, he himself raising the rest of the money until Congress would act, he could give his division six weeks' preliminary training at Fort Sill, Okla., and be ready to take it direct to France for intensive training.

Astutely Baker put refusal on the ground of lack of authority in himself: "No additional armies can be raised, no contracts assumed, without the specific authority of Congress. General officers for all volunteer forces are to be drawn from the Regular Army."

It was true that at that time, a few days before the declaration of war, Congress had authorized no new army, no contracts and no war. Yet Baker must have known Congress would — as respects creating and equipping an army, Baker was acting on the assumption that Congress would.

Roosevelt became tart. "I wish respectfully to point out that I am a retired Commander-in-Chief of the United States Army and eligible to any position of command over American troops to which I may be appointed," and he cited his own war record in Cuba and gave three generals as references. Baker replied that "the patriotic spirit of your suggestion is cordially appreciated."

Roosevelt saw that letters were getting him nowhere. He went to Washington. There Baker called on him at the home of his daughter, Mrs. Longworth, and found him surrounded with admirers; the two moved upstairs for a talk, which came to nothing. Baker assured Roosevelt that his request would be — trite euphemism for deferred negation — "carefully considered," but added that war took into account many more problems than those of one individual.[4]

Roosevelt decided he would ask Wilson face to face. "I am going," he said to a friend, "to tell Wilson that if he will give me this division, I will give him my promise never to oppose him politically in any way whatsoever."[5] To another intimate he said with sardonic allusion to presumed political jealousy: "I will promise Wilson that if he will send me to France, I will not come home alive."

April 9, 1917, Roosevelt called at the White House — what reflections must have come to him about the contrast between now and the time when he had occupied it, with supreme power to give orders to and about the Army! Between President and ex-President lay the recollection of Roosevelt's bitter words. But they sat in the Red Room chatting with superficial affability, telling each other those impersonal anecdotes by means of which men avoid the frankness that would be embarrassing. Wilson stated that the General Staff was opposed to the volunteer system. Roosevelt found that Wilson had not understood his request, and explained it at length. They parted with friendly salutations. But outside Roosevelt said:[6] "He promised me nothing definitely. If I talked to another man as he talked to me, it would mean that that man was going to get permission to fight. But I was talking to Mr. Wilson. His words may mean much, they may mean little."

In his heart Roosevelt must have known that the decision was already made and that it was against him. But popular feeling for his division was swelling — on May 7 he announced that in a short while he would have 250,000 men. He pursued Baker with letters — in one

[4] "Theodore Roosevelt, a Biography," Henry F. Pringle.
[5] "Theodore Roosevelt, a Biography," Henry F. Pringle.
[6] To J. J. Leary, Jr.

that covered eighteen typewritten pages he let fly at "officers of the red-tape and pipe-clay school, the pedantry of wooden militarism." But all the time he knew where the current was going. He spoke in Brooklyn on May 8: "I ask only that I be given a chance to render a service which I know I can render, and nine out of ten of those who oppose me do so because they believe I will render it too well.[7] He wrote Owen Wister: "The Administration is playing the dirtiest and smallest politics, I don't think they have the slightest intention of letting me go."[8]

What Wilson would not see was the emotional value of Roosevelt's offer. The French saw it; Clemenceau wrote to Wilson: "At the present moment there is in France one name which sums up the beauty of American intervention —Roosevelt. You are too much of a philosopher to ignore that the influence on the people of great leaders of men often exceeds their personal merits. The name Roosevelt has this legendary force in this country at this time. Our poilus ask, 'Where is Roosevelt?' Send them Roosevelt — it will gladden their hearts." Clemenceau's appeal did not move Wilson.[9]

On May 11 Baker sent to Roosevelt the final refusal. Roosevelt had one other chance, to appeal to the legislative branch over the executive. Through friends in Congress he asked that body to enact in the pending legislation for the draft, permission for Roosevelt to organize his division. After a delay of two weeks caused largely by the importunities of Roosevelt's backers, Congress passed the Draft Act with a clause providing for the optional use of volunteer divisions. A gleam of hope flashed before Roosevelt, wholly extinguished on May 18 when Wilson announced: "It would be very agreeable to me

7 "Theodore Roosevelt and His Time," J. B. Bishop.
8 "Roosevelt, the Story of a Friendship," Owen Wister.
9 Clemenceau's letter was made public May 25.

to pay Mr. Roosevelt this compliment, and the Allies the compliment of sending an ex-President, but this is not the time for compliment or for any action not calculated to contribute to the immediate success of the war." In words directed at the picturesque Rough Rider — one of the very few occasions when Wilson took direct notice of Roosevelt — Wilson added, "The business now in hand is undramatic, practical, and of scientific definiteness and precision."[10] A week later, Roosevelt, in words which rang with both a high patriotism and an angry resentment against Wilson, disbanded his paper division, absolved his volunteers from further connection with the movement.

But he had four sons in training. Their share of the war was his share also. All he himself could do was to spend his utmost strength in stirring the country to action. There was serious lack of war-spirit, some lack of national unity. To stimulating that Roosevelt dedicated himself. He, more than Wilson, became the symbol and spokesman of "force without limit."

As the war went on, family upon family received the form-telegram from the Adjutant-General, saw one name leap out from the casualty lists in the newspapers, sadly hung in a window the gold star that was token of their sacrifice, pitifully inadequate substitute for a living son.

One death there was that gave to every sorrowing mother the comfort of bereavement shared, symbolized death in war as a shining honor. Quentin Roosevelt was the youngest son of the old lion; the country remembered him as a lad in the White House ten years before; glamour went with his name, his youth, and his membership in the new and adventurous branch of arms.

10 "Theodore Roosevelt and His Time," J. B. Bishop.

Flying over the lines in battle against an enemy plane, he was shot down:[11]

> Golden lads and lassies must
> Like chimney-sweepers, come to dust.

The news reached Sagamore Hill on a morning when Roosevelt was departing to make an address at Saratoga.

Photograph © Underwood & Underwood.

Roosevelt with Mayor Mitchel and Charles Evans Hughes reviewing New York's drafted men, September, 1917.

His sister, Corinne Robinson, phoned him at once. "My brother himself came to the telephone," she wrote afterward,[12] "the sound of his voice was as if steel had entered into the tone. I asked him if he would like me to come down to Oyster Bay, and his answer was almost harsh in its rapidity: 'Of course not — I will meet you in Saratoga as arranged. It is more than ever my duty to be there.'"

[11] July, 1918.
[12] "My Brother Theodore Roosevelt," Corinne Roosevelt Robinson.

He went. The entire assemblage, knowing his sorrow, rose to its feet, silently. Roosevelt made his speech as arranged, paused, then added: "I have something I want to say to you with all my heart and soul. Surely in this great crisis when we are making sacrifices, surely when we are demanding such fealty and idealism on the part of the young men sent abroad to die, surely we have the right to expect an equal idealism in life from the men and women who stay at home. I ask you to see that when those who have gone abroad to risk their lives, to give their lives, when those of them who live come home, that they shall come to a nation of which they can be proud."[13]

Firm as he kept himself, strong as he voiced his loyalty to public duty, the world had changed for him, the one irresistible sorrow had pierced the soul that had come unscathed through so many gallant battles. Seeing him that day, Hermann Hagedorn wrote: "The old side of him is gone, the old exuberance, the boy in him has died."[14] No one but his immediate family heard him mention his grief. But James Amos, his colored servant, used to see him holding a book open on his lap, staring off into distance, murmuring, "Poor Quinikins!"[15]

That fall, the public began to hear that Roosevelt's vigor was leaving him; it was like hearing that Gibraltar was melting. The sheer physical exuberance of Roosevelt had been for two generations a kind of national institution, phrases for it, such as "the strenuous life," had passed into the common tongue. In February (1918) he had gone to the hospital for a mild operation, the removal of abscesses, without anæsthetics. After a

[13] "Theodore Roosevelt and His Time," J. B. Bishop.
[14] "Theodore Roosevelt, a Biography," Henry F. Pringle.
[15] "Theodore Roosevelt, Hero to His Valet," James E. Amos.

month he returned to Sagamore Hill seemingly recovered. But he was deaf in one ear; years before, he had been blinded in one eye in a friendly boxing bout.

In May he made a speaking tour of the West, to in-

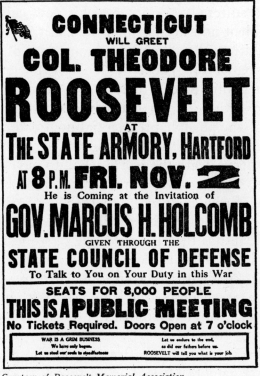

Courtesy of Roosevelt Memorial Association.

spire loyalty for the war.   In September he made another speaking tour through Ohio, Nebraska, and Montana, urging unremitting war upon Germany until unconditional surrender was enforced. October 28 he spoke in New York, and attacked Wilson's plea for a Democratic Congress with such vigor that the ensuing Republican majority in both houses may be partly credited to his words. But he was feeling the first advances of an inflammatory rheumatism, laid to the fever he had incurred in South America four years before. Walking in the fields of Sagamore Hill with Owen Wister one mellow afternoon in Indian summer, he said, "It doesn't matter what the rest is going to be — I have had fun the whole time." On Armistice Day he went to the hospital. He suffered severely, yet his few callers found him confident and keenly interested in the news of the day. Ambition, however, had gone out of him. He wrote to Rider Haggard: "I doubt if I ever again go back into public place; like you, I am not at all sure about the future."[16] To one who asked him what he thought of the possible presidential nomination in 1920, he replied rather sadly: "I am indifferent to the subject; since Quentin's death the world seems to have shut down upon me. If my other boys do not come back, what would the Presidency mean to me? . . . But if I do consent it will be because as President I could accomplish some things that I should like to see accomplished before I die." He had been lying back on his pillows; now he sat suddenly erect and clenched his fist. "And by George, if they take me," he cried, "they will take me without a single modification of the things I have always stood for!"[17]

On Christmas morning, leaving the hospital, he returned to Sagamore Hill. The doctors were confident of his complete recovery. So was he. He was only sixty-one. He sat down to Christmas dinner in the midst of his family, and during the holidays seemed to gain in health. "I feel like a faker," he wrote his sister on December 28, "because my troubles are not to be mentioned in the same breath with yours."[17] On the first day of the new year he wrote to a friend that in all probability he could go devil-fishing with him in Florida on March 1.

[16] "Theodore Roosevelt and His Time," J. B. Bishop.
[17] "Theodore Roosevelt and His Time," J. B. Bishop.

He dictated letters, he wrote editorials for the Kansas City *Star* and *The Metropolitan Magazine*. There was enough pugnacity in him to slash Wilson once more in a letter to the New York *Tribune:* "For Heaven's sake never allude to Wilson as an idealist . . . he hasn't a touch of idealism in him, he is a silly doctrinaire at times and an utterly selfish and cold-blooded politician always."[18] On January 3 he wrote to the president of the American Defense Society: "There must be no sagging back in the fight for Americanism merely because the war is over. There can be no divided allegiance here. We have room for but one flag . . . we have room for but one language . . . we have room for but one soul loyalty, and that is loyalty to the American people."[18] The letter was read aloud at a great mass meeting held by the Society in the New York Hippodrome on January 5.

That evening at Sagamore Hill Roosevelt was finishing the proofs of an editorial. James Amos entered his room about eight, found his face weary. A little later Roosevelt said, "James, don't you think I might go to bed now?" Amos had almost to lift him into bed. About eleven Mrs. Roosevelt kissed him good-night. Roosevelt said, "James, please put out the light." Five hours later as the colored man sat watching by the bedside, the breath of the sleeper hesitated, went on again, paused, quavered, and stopped.[19]

He was buried with the utmost simplicity in the family plot at Oyster Bay. There was, as he had wished, no music, no eulogy. The offer of a military funeral was declined. Climbing up the hill through new fallen snow, some hundred dignitaries from Washington, with fifty children from the local school where he acted

[18] "Theodore Roosevelt and His Time," J. B. Bishop.
[19] "Theodore Roosevelt, Hero to His Valet," James Amos.

Santa Claus, and four hundred close friends watched the plain oak coffin lowered into the grave. In New York City every policeman and every school-child stood still and silent, the wheels of every street-car, subway train, and factory stopped.[20]

The country was stunned. During more than thirty years of national life, Theodore Roosevelt had become as familiar as the sun, his vitality and permanence almost as much taken for granted. At Washington, the House and Senate adjourned for the day; for the first time in its history the Supreme Court adjourned without transacting business; the Navy Department ordered all ships to half-mast their flags; Alfred E. Smith, in his first official proclamation as Governor of New York, ordered all flags in the State to be half-masted; Wilson, in a just and dignified proclamation sent from Italy where he happened to be, ordered the flags of the White House and the Government buildings in Washington at half-mast for thirty days. To the family came messages of sympathy from the heads of all nations, from every one in American public life, from Rough Riders, locomotive engineers, policemen, war mothers, cow-boys, pugilists, small-town politicians, day laborers, priests, little boys.

The words evoked by Roosevelt's death, verse and prose, many elevated, all moving, compose a small segment of American literature. It was noticeable that many made allusion to the death of Valiant-for-Truth in "Pilgrim's Progress": "My sword I shall give to him that may succeed me in my pilgrimage. . . . my marks and scars I carry with me, to be a witness for me; so he passed over, and all the trumpets sounded for him on the other side."

[20] New York *Tribune*, January 9, 1919.

25

GERMANY CRIES "KAMERAD!"

And Wilson Replies with a Note Which a Comedian of
the Day, Will Rogers, Spoke of as "the President's Questionnaire." The German Government, Rapidly Going to
Pieces, Replies to All Wilson's Questions with a Nervous,
Hurried, "Yes." Wilson, by Iteration and Re-iteration,
Fastens the Fourteen Points Firmly into the Terms of Peace
and the Armistice Contract. Wilson at His Best.

A FREQUENT scene of the war, increasingly repeated
lately, which many newspaper accounts and soldiers' letters had made familiar to America, was that of a German soldier dropping his rifle, raising his hands above
his head, advancing toward whatever Allied soldiers
were about to capture him, and crying "Kamerad!" To
the American soldiers who were made participants in the
scene, it was always a little puzzling, uncomfortable. It
did not have the manner of a clean fight to a finish, and
a surrender without reservations, such as Americans were
familiar with in prize-fighting and sports. It seemed
to have a combination of abjectness with something like
cunning, which American soldiers did not understand.
There was something a little shameless in a man calling
you "Comrade" who a moment before had been doing
his best to kill you — the comradeship was suspected of
being decidedly less than half-hearted. You had to stop
fighting the fellow, and you must treat him decently,
but you were not moved to like him, continued a little
suspicious of him.

Something of the same quality was in what the German government now did. First they got rid of their
former Imperial Chancellor, substituting in his place
one not identified with the extreme militaristic party,
Prince Maximilian of Baden, a "moderate," almost a

kind of parlor socialist, supposed to be more appealing to
Wilson. Prince Max, as his first act, on the night of
October 4–5, wrote a note to Wilson and asked the Swiss
government to deliver it:

The German government requests the President of the
United States to take in hand the restoration of peace. . . .
It accepts the program set forth by the President of the
United States in his message to Congress on January 8th[1] and
in his later pronouncements. . . .
To avoid further bloodshed the German government re-
quests the immediate conclusion of an armistice.

England Fixes Her Eyes on President Wilson in His Fencing with Huns

T P O'Connor Likens Him to Professional Athlete Whose
Individual Skill Is Expected to Win Champion
ship for His Team.

— New York Herald, Oct. 31, 1918.

The picture now posed was dramatic. The enemy who
had long been arrogant toward Wilson, a bully toward
the world, now cringing; and Wilson now a Crom-
wellian victor, stern and austere, all the Presbyterian in
him, all the covenanter, all the schoolmaster, coming out
in an attitude which banished exultation but preserved
justice and insisted on completeness of surrender. In this
mood, Wilson's answer consisted mainly of questions,
questions designed to permit no tergiversation, questions
bringing forward to this climax of the struggle the principles Wilson had laid down in the beginning, making
clear and explicit the stipulations Wilson had made from
the start, and had been jeered at for making. Questions

---

[1] The Fourteen Points. See pages 447–8.

which carefully made reference again to the early speeches containing Wilson's terms, and, by use of the word "only," confined the proposed peace to those terms and nothing else. In logic, in style, in adroit and accurate use of words, Wilson's letter, this whole concluding correspondence[2] with Germany, was Wilson at his best:

Does the Imperial Chancellor mean that the Imperial German government accepts the terms laid down by the President . . . on the 8th of January last and in subsequent addresses, and that its object in entering into discussions would be *only*[3] to agree upon the practical details of their application?

The second question in Wilson's note brought forward his distinction between the German people and the German government:

Is the Imperial Chancellor speaking *merely*[3] for the constituted authorities of the Empire who have so far conducted the war? He [President Wilson] deems the answer to this question vital. . . .

As to the asked-for armistice, that would depend upon the consent of the Central Powers immediately to withdraw their forces everywhere from invaded territory.

Germany replying,[4] made a slight yet history-presaging change in official terminology. "The Imperial German government" disappeared from Germany's notes, never to return. It was the "German government" who responded to Wilson's note. The responses were all "yes," a rather nervous and hurried "yes" to everything:

Yes, "its object would be *only*[5] to agree upon practical details" of Wilson's principles. Yes, "the present German government . . . speaks in the name of . . . the German people." Yes, the German government would

---

[2] In truth, the period of this correspondence with Germany, October 8 to 23, 1918, was the climax of Wilson's career. Within a month he was on the descent, physically, intellectually, and in prestige, rapidly.

[3] Italics the author's.   [4] October 12.   [5] Italics are the author's.

evacuate invaded territory as a condition of the armistice.

Wilson, writing back October 14, opened his letter with words which again incorporated his terms, mentioned them once more specifically by date, nailed them firmly into the contract for peace that was being made through the present correspondence: "The unqualified acceptance . . . of the terms laid down by the President of the United States on the 8th of January, 1918, and in his subsequent addresses. . . ." Again and yet again Wilson drove his conditions home, especially one of his conditions, the separation of the German people from the German government. After dealing with details of the proposed armistice Wilson continued with a repetition of his already often repeated solicitation to the German people that they overthrow their former government:

It is necessary, in order that there may be no possibility of misunderstanding, that the President should very solemnly call the attention of the government of Germany to the language and plain intent of one of the terms of peace which the German government has now accepted. It is contained in the address of the President delivered at Mount Vernon on the Fourth of July last. It is as follows:

"The destruction of every arbitrary power anywhere that can separately, secretly, and of its single choice disturb the peace of the world; or, if it cannot be presently destroyed, at lease its reduction to virtual impotency."[6]

The power which has hitherto controlled the German nation is of the sort here described. It is within the choice of the German nation to alter it. The President's words, just quoted, naturally constitute a condition precedent to peace, if peace is to come by the action of the German people themselves.

Replying[7] to that, it was difficult for the German government to avoid being a little ridiculous. The German government assured Wilson that

A new government has been formed in complete accordance with the wishes . . . of the people, based on equal, universal,

6 This was one of the Four Points.   7 October 20.

secret, direct franchise. . . . The question of the President . . .
is therefore answered in a clear, unequivocal manner. . . . The
offer of peace has come from a government which, free from
any arbitrary and irresponsible influence, is supported by
. . . an overwhelming majority of the German people.

Yes, Germany was saying, we are now a democracy just

A popular interpretation of Germany's note.—*New York Evening World.*

like the United States, just what you, Mr. Wilson, want
us to be.

To that, Wilson's reply, his third note, amounted to
saying, "I don't believe you." Wilson realized that he
could now force, completely, the thing he had long
aimed at, the overthrow of the autocratic government,
and there was no reason to stop with the half-way con-

cessions to popular government that the Kaiser and the militarists had made. In his note Wilson began with a preamble designed to drive home again his terms of

A game two could play.

Wilson, as caricatured by German artists angry over his way of making war, was quite as unprepossessing as the likenesses of the Kaiser drawn by American cartoonists.

peace — they had become, in this correspondence, almost like a litany:

Having received the solemn and explicit assurance of the German government that it unreservedly accepts the terms of peace laid down [by the President] on the 8th of January, 1918 . . . and in his subsequent addresses. . . .

Having thus driven home his terms of peace yet once more, Wilson now, with appalling candor, said in effect, the revolution in the German government has not yet gone far enough to suit me. Almost he might have added, the spirit of his note did add — "and I am the schoolmaster around here." His words — they must have struck the Kaiser like doom — were:

The President deems it his duty to say, without any attempt to soften what may seem harsh words, that the nations of the world do not and cannot trust the word of those who have hitherto been the masters of German policy. . . . The United States cannot deal with any but veritable *representatives of the German people* who have been assured of a genuine constitutional standing *as the real rulers of Germany*.[8]

The New York Times.

XVIII. NO. 22,206. ——— NEW YORK, MONDAY, NOVEMBER 11, 1918. TWENTY-FOUR PAGES ——— TWO CENTS

ARMISTICE SIGNED, END OF THE WAR! BERLIN SEIZED BY REVOLUTIONISTS; NEW CHANCELLOR BEGS FOR ORDER; OUSTED KAISER FLEES TO HOLLAND

Then Wilson put forward in plain words his solicitation to the German people to revolt, his invitation to the Kaiser to get out; he put it in terms of reward for the German people for revolution, penalty for failure to revolt:

If it [the United States] must deal with the military masters and the monarchical autocrats of Germany . . . it must demand, not peace negotiations but surrender. Nothing can be gained by leaving this essential thing unsaid.

Germany replied:[9]

The peace negotiations are being conducted by a government of the people, in whose hands rests, both actually and constitutionally, the authority to make decisions. The military powers are also subject to this authority.

Wilson, seeing his terms accepted, seeing also the revolution under way that he had worked for, now consulted with the Allies about granting Germany an armistice.

[8] Italics the author's.   [9] October 27.

The Allies said they were willing — but first they made qualifications as to two of the Fourteen Points. As to Point 2, freedom of the seas, that, the Allies said, "is open to various interpretations. . . . They therefore reserve to themselves complete freedom on this subject when they enter the peace conference." As to Point 7, "invaded portions [of] French territory [to be] restored," the Allies made a serious qualification.

The Allied governments . . . understand that compensation will be made by Germany for all damage done to the civilian population of the Allies and their property by the aggression of Germany by land, by sea, and from the air.

In the desperation for peace to which Germany had now been reduced, and in the excitement that blazed throughout the world, the act of the Allies in making qualifications to Wilson's Fourteen Points, and making them at the moment when Germany was in the act of accepting them, passed unnoticed.[10] All attention was focussed on the substance of Wilson's notes and on the momentous fact that the Allies were willing to grant Germany an armistice, that the war was about to end.

Hurriedly, Germany acted. Just after midnight November 6, out of the void came a wireless message addressed to General Foch. It was from Berlin. It asked General Foch to name a place where German agents could come to receive the terms of the armistice. Within an hour, at 1.25 A.M. November 7, Foch sent a wireless directing the German agents to present themselves at the outposts of the French army on the road from Guise to La Capelle.

[10] For a discussion of the consequences of the Allies' raising qualifications to the Fourteen Points, and of Wilson's failure to resist the qualifications, see Chapter 27.

26

ARMSTICE, FALSE, AND TRUE

In Which a Nation, Fully Aware by This Time of the Cost and Pain of the War, Twice Celebrated Its Finale with No Loss of Freshness, Excitement, and Relief.

In America, expectation of the end of the War had been created by many events reported in the newspapers: on November 3 Austria surrendered to the Italians; in Germany, sailors at Kiel mutinied openly, troops revolted, the line of battle fell back faster and faster — in plain sight of the world, Germany was going to pieces. In America, in every city, town, and village, in every family, in every heart, there was tension, a feeling of emotion tugging to explode.

The detonant came in early afternoon newspapers of November 7, in the shape of shrieking headlines based on a despatch received through United Press from Brest:

```
UNIPRESS  NEWYORK
   PARIS URGENT -- ARMISTICE ALLIES SIGNED
   ELEVEN SMORNING ["cablese" contraction for
   'this morning"] -- HOSTILITIES CEASED TWO
   SAFTERNOON -- SEDAN TAKEN SMORNING BY
   AMERICANS.
                        HOWARD -- SIMMS
```

New York went wild. It happened to be a day of noticeable sunniness and serenity, the heart of lovely Indian summer. To rend that calm, seeming to tear the very atmosphere to rags, came din of sirens, factory and ship whistles, auto horns, and church bells. Universal holiday was assumed and not questioned. Crowds stampeded out of offices and factories. No traffic could move. Confetti and ticker-tape rained from office windows. The crowds resolved themselves into informal processions, people forming arm to arm, no one cared who, no one cared where. A melting, exulting, half-sobbing, half-heart-lifting mood seized upon a whole city. Moist eyes looked out above ineradicable smiles. Here and there the crowds formed little knots. In front of the Sub-Treasury cheers went up for all the Allies. A crowd sang before the Waldorf. At Columbia University, students rushed out of class-rooms, snake-danced on the campus. The Stock Exchange closed at 2:30 instead of 3 — the Curb, per-force, had stopped at 1. Between 1 and 3 the telephone company carried more calls than in any two hours of its

TWELVE PAGES
Postscript
Full Closing Market Reports

The Evening Post

NIGHT FINAL
Postscript
Full Closing Market Reports

FOUNDED 1801.—VOL. 117. NO. 302. NEW YORK, THURSDAY, NOVEMBER 7, 1918. 2 CENTS.

REPORT ARMISTICE SIGNED; CITY IN WILD DEMONSTRATION; STATE DEPARTMENT AT 2:15 P. M. DENIES REPORT; AMERICAN TROOPS IN SEDAN; ENEMY LEAVING GHENT

November 7, 1918.

history. The wave of feeling struck every one as it did the barber in Park Avenue who left a customer half-shaved, folded his razor, and exclaimed to his assistant, "Finish him and then shut up shop. Me? I'm going home to cry with my wife! That's where I'm going!"[1]

After several hours of this came a spirit of disturbing doubt. It came first, and most poignantly, to the offices of the United Press — they had had an exclusive story, the most sensational in modern times, but after it had re-mained exclusive for some four hours they began to feel uncomfortably that it was "too damned exclusive." No other newspapers followed it up. The doubt, spreading from newspaper offices, expressed itself to the crowds in failure of late editions to have further details. At 4 P.M. Secretary of War Baker said he had no word of an armis-

[1] New York *Tribune,* November 8, 1918.

A sky full of paper, parades, horns, and madness.

Wall Street, New York, on Armistice Day.

tice, Secretary of State Lansing said the same. The Associated Press, after labored inquiry, reported that Paris and Washington knew nothing of an armistice. Little by little people looked at each other, realized their delusion. The heart went out of the excitement. Said an editorial in the New York *Tribune* on November 8: ". . . One of the famous fakes of history. . . . A sky full of paper, parades, horns, madness! Well, in America it has been a people's war throughout. The people made it; they fought it. Why shouldn't they go mad at the thought of German surrender if they want to?" The next day, rather wistfully, *The Tribune* headed an editorial "The Thief of Joy" and said, "When the real news of peace arrives shall we have another celebration as good and joyous as those first hours? Hardly, we think. The edge has been taken off."

II

The newspaper despatch that touched off the "false armistice" came from Roy W. Howard, president of the United Press. On that morning, November 7, he had arrived at Brest from Paris. Calling on the commander of the American Naval Forces at Brest, Admiral H. B. Wilson, Howard was shown a despatch just received from the naval aide of the American Embassy in Paris, saying:

Armistice signed this morning at 11 — all hostilities ceased at 2 P.M. today.

Instantly, Howard sent the news in the cable to New York. That a cable of such importance should be passed without verification by the French censor was due to habit; it was the custom that all United Press despatches passing beneath the French censor's eye at Brest had already been O.K.'d at Paris, and the censor did not know this one had originated at Brest.

During the evening frantic inquiries sent to Paris by the authorities at Brest revealed that the despatch received by Admiral Wilson had not been based on fact. Howard sent a cablegram to New York saying the news in his previous despatch could not be confirmed. But the flare had been lit, and was unquenchable until American newspapers the following morning, November 8, carried definite information that the celebration the preceding day had not had the foundation the happy celebrants assumed.

III

The armistice celebration of November 7 had been false, yet only premature. From events reported in every issue of newspapers, everybody knew the end was near: On November 9 the Kaiser abdicated; the Allied battle line pushed forward furiously to less than eighteen miles from German soil. On November 10 revolutionists seized Berlin; the Kaiser crossed into Holland; the French Army, fighting on land it had not seen since 1914, was astride the Belgian border; the British Army had almost reached Germany; Pershing's First and Second Armies advanced on a front of seventy-one miles between Sedan and Moselle. The end could not be long delayed.

In the early hours of November 11, in the still, sleeping town of Emporia, Kans., an editor of the local paper dozed in his office under a lone light.[2] A dog barked far away over corn lands, the street below his window lay silent in shadows. At 2:22 A.M. the telephone startled him; Topeka was calling. What the far voice said shook him broad awake — with husky, excited words he called the Fire Department. Gongs clanged out in the night. A whistle blew and kept on blowing. All over town men

[2] Emporia *Gazette,* November 12, 1918.

and women jumped anxiously from bed and looked out. By 3:30 A.M. fully two hundred people had gathered in Commercial Street. Bonfires spurted up at every corner. When morning came, business was suspended for the day. The judge of the District Court set over every case on the docket and excused the jury. At 10 an impromptu parade started off — the longest and largest in Emporia history — led by a band of thirty pieces, its auto section more than a mile long. "Wild-cat whistles" screeched from fire-trucks, one Ford towed four tin wash-tubs with

GERMANY HAS SURRENDERED;
WORLD WAR ENDED AT 6 A. M.

November 11, 1918.

monstrous racket. An old horse-drawn hack went by labelled "There ain't no Kaiser!" In the heat of the excitement a young man whose parents were on the Isle of Man cabled them, "I'll bet you are happy today — God bless you all!" and his joy did not slacken when the charges came to $10.03. The war was over in Emporia, and in fifty thousand towns and cities from coast to coast.

In Detroit, where Taps had been bugled every day on the City Hall steps at 4 P.M. — the exact hour when Taps sounded in France for "our boys" — last Taps for the War rang out above exultant crowds. In Newport News, soldiers and sailors took riotous possession of the city, wrecking street-cars, raiding restaurants, breaking windows, building bonfires in the street from smashed delivery wagons. There were no casualties. In Atlanta, crowds thronged Five Points, Peachtree, and Whitehall. Cried *The Constitution:* "And somewhere in Holland an old, old man, the greatest criminal the world has ever known, is shivering before the hosts of accusing shapes who point their ghostly fingers and brand him murderer."[3] In Hartford, the greatest celebration in its his-

Courtesy of the Des Moines Register.

Des Moines, Iowa, turned out in costume to parade.

tory included a parade of 10,000, taking two hours to pass the reviewing stand. Some one who preserved a whimsical spirit noticed that of all the celebrants the loudest noise was made by the employees of the Maxim Silencer Company. A butcher's truck bore a stuck pig with one word on it, "Kaiser."[4] In Chicago, Mayor William B. Thompson ordered that all saloons be allowed to remain open. In San Antonio, headlines shrieked "GERMANY GIVES UP!" and cow-boys yipped in

[3] Atlanta *Constitution,* November 12, 1918.
[4] Hartford *Courant,* November 12, 1918.

the street. In Boston, the hundred-and-sixty-year-old State House bell rang out.

In San Francisco, ten minutes after the flash arrived at 1 A.M., huge bonfires laid by the Fire Department were burning on Twin Peaks, Scott's and Telegraph Hill. Later a monster parade moved down Market Street to the Ferry Building and back to the City Hall. This celebration had a strange aspect — every person wore a white cloth over his nose and mouth, protection against an influenza epidemic which raged over the country. The effect touched the height of incongruity, but the spirit was not marred; the Health Office lifted for the day the ban on music and dancing, and Tait's and other restaurants and the Palace and St. Francis hotels were jammed.[5]

In Washington, Wilson gave out his proclamation at 10 A.M. Shortly after 12 he rode down Pennsylvania Avenue amid an immense ovation to address Congress, reviewed the United War Work Campaign parade (scheduled for the day by chance, thereby gaining tenfold significance), altogether appeared five times before jubilant crowds. In the evening forty-nine bonfires lit up the Ellipse between the White House and the Potomac River.[6]

In New York, the first Associated Press flash arrived shortly before 3 A.M. Presses whirred, and newsboys shrieked "Germany surrenders!" to late stragglers in Park Row who shouted, pounded each other on the back, and danced over the street in the dawn.

Lights sprang out on the Statue of Liberty. Air-raid sirens blared. Noise increased, multiplied, travelled along the water-front; ships and tugs tied down their whistles, lit all their lights, ran up flags; sailors tossed calcium-

---

[5] San Francisco *Chronicle,* November 11, 1918.
[6] Washington *Post,* November 12, 1918.

burning flares on the dark water. Munitions factories across the Hudson took up the chorus. Newsboys were crying themselves hoarse as far as the Bronx. Minute by minute the wave of clangor deepened over the city. No one could sleep. Men and women snatched a bite of breakfast, seized noise-makers they'd bought during

Crowds in Washington, D. C., who had fought to obtain newspapers revealing news of the Armistice, gladly hold them up to a news photographer.

Thursday's celebration, and jammed subways and street-cars headed downtown. This, at last, was "the day!"

The early morning sun found Fifth Avenue a solid mass of people, cheering, waving flags, milling about in ecstacy. Autoists, caught in the mob, sounded horns in continuous din, back-fired intentionally with terrific clatter. Trucks carried whole families on holiday, bore clusters of screaming girls who threw confetti and blew kisses to the crowd. Sudden hand-clasps between strangers, women singing arm-in-arm, little boys firing cap-pistols, men weeping unashamed, old women praying by themselves, gay streamers, signs: "I told you so!" and "Where's the Kaiser now?", hat-bands emblazoned: "I'm going to the Kaiser's funeral!" Crowds packed hotels before charwomen had put away their mops; for the first time in the history of the Tenderloin music was played at breakfast, scarcely heard above the roar of the mob outside.

At the City Hall, just as the great flag covering half the south front was unfurled, a dozen men in caps and derbies rushed up the steps with band instruments and played patriotic airs while the crowd sang. Mayor Hylan declared municipal holiday and ordered a parade which got under way an hour later, picking up every one in its course — fashionable ladies jingling cow-bells; street urchins yelling and dancing; stenographers in red, white, and blue paper caps; sailors grinning under the floppy picture-hats of their girls and the girls flaunting sailors' caps. There were autos bursting with vociferous passengers, one-horse carts, farm-wagons full of giggling girls, life-boats mounted on trucks, sight-seeing busses boiling with people. A transparency of the Kaiser bore the flaming legend: "Let him rule in hell!" A truck carried a coffin out of which the Kaiser's effigy was repeatedly hanged as the parade pushed on. Soldiers and sailors waved signs: "No more beans! No more camouflaged coffee! No more monkey stew!" The parade split up, rejoined, grew bulkier and bulkier, had become forty in one when Mayor Hylan reviewed it at Columbus Circle.

Three thousand war-mothers marched on Fifth Avenue. Five thousand ship-builders, having found their plant at Shooter's Island closed for the day, invaded town with work-clothes and tools, holding banners which said: "We are the layers-out who laid the Kaiser out!" Com-

© *International News Photos, Inc.*

Left: A marine caught up and carried by girls during the celebration. *Right:* The crowds at City Hall, New York, with an effigy of the Kaiser which was repeatedly hanged.

mander Booth and Salvation Army lassies paraded — soldiers rushed out from the side-lines to seize her hand, to carry the girls' flags for them.

After lunch the streets were jammed even more thickly. A Salvation Army band on Fifth Avenue played "The Star-Spangled Banner" to crowds which bared heads in sudden silence. The Kaiser was burned in effigy in front of the Public Library. A lieutenant of Scotch Highlanders was picked up, blushing, by four men and carried at the head of a cheering parade a block long. Wounded soldiers from Ellis Island were kissed and petted. A black-eyed Italian girl rode up the Avenue on a white horse, shouting wildly for Italy. Men, tired of saluting flags, threw their hats away. Girls leaned on the arms of French sailors and sang songs in French quickly learned. A green flag with a gold harp on it and a card, "69th," appeared, to be greeted with a sobbing cheer; five officers, English, French, Italian, Japanese, and American, happened to meet under it; they saluted and went off arm-in-arm. A shop-keeper on Forty-second Street soaped on his window: " 'Heaven, Hell or Hoboken by Christmas.' We've got all three. Heaven for us, Hell for the Kaiser, and Hoboken for the boys!" Another achieved a pale jocosity — translated "Deutschland über Alles" as "It's all over with the Dutch." Ten interned Germans being taken from the Battery were rushed by a crowd, saved by a patrol wagon. A Mr. McCabe, a district superintendent of schools in Brooklyn, ventured out in spite of the fact that he possessed a likeness to Wilson; "There's President Wilson!" screamed a woman at Fifth and Forty-second, and a mob surrounded him; newsreel men, against his protests, forced him to pose until he escaped down a subway entrance. Near the "Y" Hut in Bryant Park, a team of soldiers played rough-house football with a team of sailors in the middle of Forty-second Street, holding up the cross-town line fifteen minutes and ignoring the flustered police. Some one pounded jazz on the battered piano in the War Savings Stamps booth in Nassau Street, and all men in uniform found partners and danced. A dachshund with a German flag tied to his tail ran the

© *International News Photos, Inc.*

Allied officers making their way through cheering crowds on Fifth Avenue, New York.

gauntlet of jeers in Union Square, until some one took pity on him and picked him up. At Our Lady of Mercy Chapel in Washington Square South white-coifed nuns raised windows and looked out at the mob, and at the Cathedral at Fifth and Fiftieth a thousand people knelt in hush and prayer. What the gold-star mothers felt that day no one saw, no paper reported.

Toward evening the celebration shifted from Fifth Avenue to Broadway, but not before one last impressive scene took place in front of the Union League Club.

Men bore flags out on the platform, and a crowd packed solid in the Avenue fell silent a moment and then sang, with one voice, the "Doxology." Cheers and songs went up for Belgium, France, England, and America, then cheers for "the old 69th," "the fighting 77th," and the "Rainbow Division," and one last cheer for "the women

Factories stopped in Indianapolis and the workers commandeered trucks and joined the celebration.

who helped." There was hardly a dry eye among tens of thousands.[7]

In-doors, the evening of that day, theatres and hotels echoed with merry-making. Al Jolson at the Winter Garden was called upon a dozen times to repeat his patriotic songs. Marjorie Rambeau, playing at the Republic, had to stop and make a speech. In the Waldorf ball-room, two thousand people wore carnival hats,

[7] Rhapsodized a reporter: "But oh that crowd! In sheer mass and weight and driving power it beat Thursday's all hollow!"—New York *Sun,* November 12, 1918.

carried grotesquely colored parasols, wielded rattles, horns, and whistles, and cheered themselves hoarse at the mention of an Allied nation or hero. Until far after midnight New York celebrated; it was the day of days.

"The day!" In that phrase lay echoes of Prussian

American Red Cross Headquarters, Paris, the week of the Armistice. Statue of Joan of Arc in foreground.

war-lords, of a German dream of "kultur" and world-domination, which the Brooklyn *Eagle* capped neatly in its issue of November 12:

D isaster
E xhaustion
R evolution

T urkey
A ustria
G ermany.

"*The extraordinary story of hopes, ideals, weaknesses, failures, and disappointments, of which the President has been the leading figure and eponymous hero, will interest and perplex mankind as long as history is read and the hearts of the great ones are the subject of curious exploration by the multitude. Was 'Hamlet' mad or feigning; was the President sick or cunning? . . . His story will symbolize and illustrate some of the mingled and mysterious strains in our common nature.*" — "The Peace of Versailles," John Maynard Keynes.

"*It will be as difficult for posterity as for his own generation, to be indifferent. And the strength of the emotion which his name arouses alike in friend and foe, together with the spectacular nature of his career, will always make him a fascinating and intriguing figure to student and historian.*" — "Woodrow Wilson, A Character Study," Robert E. Annin.

27

MISERERE

"'Soaring to the Rarest Heights of Terrestrial Fortune, and There Stricken by the Blindness of Apollo and the Plagues of Egypt." "Samson Blind and Shorn of His Locks." "Posterity Remembers the Mixed Characters of History Who Have a Star and It Fails Them." — "The Messiah."

ONE of the conditions most forgotten in human affairs is that men grow tired, and grow old. Most do we forget it when they are in our daily sight, functioning in their accustomed ways, without superficially apparent change. And if we fail to observe their aging physically, we completely ignore their growing old mentally. Men who vigilantly subject themselves to periodical physical examination, in order that any deterioration of the body may be identified would be startled at a suggestion that there should be analogous examination to discover incipient deterioration of the intellect. Trustees and directors who would be prompt to take account of impaired physical capacity in any official bearing high responsibility, as occasion for relief from duty, neglect to consider that diminished mental capacity may arrive as inexorably, more unnoticeably, and with much greater detriment to ability to perform duty adequately. Heads of institutions whose advancing years show themselves in one form or another of reduced physical vitality are presumed to be unchanged intellectually; if they exhibit eccentricity, the trait is regarded as a harmless crotchet, increasing affection and esteem for them.

Yet years bring change to the brain as to any other organ; the muscles of the mind grow stiff, or lax, or inexact in operation, the same as muscles of the body; men grow senile or undergo other forms of intellectual deterioration. And an impairment too subtle to reveal itself to ordinary observation may nevertheless express itself in serious decline of that balance of qualities which is called judgment. Recognition of this would forestall or modify many a tragedy. Most unhappily, in proportion as the man is highly placed, the tragedies have consequences to many others besides the individual involved.

Wilson continued to be at his best up to the last of his notes to Germany, October 23.[1] His thought was never more exact, his expression never more lucid, his judgment never more clear, his grasp never more comprehensive. That series of notes was the apotheosis of the functioning of Wilson's extraordinarily able mind. If, immediately thereafter, he became less than his best, it is not unusual that this kind of let-down should come at the end of long years of high-strung strain, the climax which Germany's surrender was. And, since Wilson was then sixty-two years of age and had been frail always, it is not surprising that the let-down should go farther than the normal resilience of a younger man would have recovered from.

Beginning about the last week of October, 1918, Wilson made mistake after mistake, made them in fields in which ordinarily his judgment was subtly sure.

On the suggestion of the more political-minded among his advisers, he appealed to the country to elect a Democratic majority to Congress in the election of

[1] Strictly speaking, the last of Wilson's notes to Germany, notifying her the Allies would grant an armistice, was sent November 5, 1918.

November 6, so that he might "be your unembarrassed spokesman at home and abroad." Much of the country felt hurt, saw in the action ingratitude for the united support the nation had given him, saw vanity in it and imperativeness; some of his critics hinted at what the Spanish call *delirio de grandeza*. Especially did they see, in one of the reasons Wilson gave — "A Republican majority would be interpreted on the other side of the water as repudiation of my leadership" — a wish on Wilson's part to dominate the world at the coming Peace Conference. The Republicans denounced his appeal and capitalized it, fomented public distaste for it. The country elected a Republican majority.

Wilson announced[2] that he would go to the Peace Conference in person. To the country that seemed confirmation of the suspicion of egotism. From the point-of-view of Wilson's effectiveness at the Conference, it was generally recognized by those equipped to judge, his presence at Paris would be a serious detriment to the purpose he had most dearly in mind. Wilson sitting across the table from the European statesmen — wiliest of traders and diplomats — would be obliged to answer questions, to make instantaneous decisions, to commit himself.[3] Every person experienced in conferences or in business knew that Wilson would now be obliged to trade, and he was a poor trader — it was contrary to his nature. Wilson's way was to say, at once, openly and

[2] November 18.

[3] "Time and again, at Paris, he came out of the Council of Ten realizing belatedly and freely admitting in private that he had agreed to something too hastily. . . . His advisers sat silently aghast as he bartered away things which they knew were dear to him, in ignorance of the play on the board." — William Allen White, "Woodrow Wilson."

"Your President," said Lord (then Mr. Arthur) Balfour to Owen Wister, during the Paris Peace Conference, "is no match for some of the men he believes to be dealing with him in his own spirit. He cannot grow used to their ways. They take him unawares again and again."

fully, what he considered the right course, and then to stand on that as a principle. To give and take as traders do, and especially to ask in the beginning for more than he expects to get, in order to have something to "trade with" — which is the essence of negotiation — all that was foreign to Wilson's nature. He would not attempt it, and if he should he would be beaten at it. On the other hand, Wilson in Washington, with representatives under his direction at Paris, would be able to preserve the serenity and detachment which, in his case, were peculiarly indispensable requisites for his functioning well. He would have time to think his decisions out. He would be able to continue to appeal to the world from the same high Washington pulpit which had served him so well thus far, would be able to make use of world opinion, which was the fulcrum that had given him his enormous prestige and success. Wilson at Washington, with his emissaries at Paris referring questions back to him for decision, would have been ideal. His going to Paris in person was one of the major mistakes of his career.

Mistake stepped on the heels of mistake. In appointing the full delegation, four besides himself, he ignored the Senate — and the Senate must ratify or reject whatever treaty he would make. He ignored also the party that had just been given a majority in the Senate — the only Republican he named on the delegation was a venerable gentleman who had spent his life in diplomatic posts abroad, Henry White, and if White had been a Republican at the beginning of his career, hardly anybody remembered it. Certainly Republicans, in the Senate and elsewhere, did not regard White as a representative of their party. The other delegates were Wilson's Democratic Secretary of State, Robert Lansing; his

Democratic personal adviser and friend, Colonel House; and a General of the Army, Tasker H. Bliss. There was no Senator. Republicans considered that there was no Republican.

Indeed, much of the public, considering how subordi-

A malicious caricature of Wilson's peace mission to Paris, published in the *Weekly* of George Harvey. From left to right the figures are: Wilson, House, Lansing, White, Bliss, Baruch, Hoover, Creel.

nate the other delegates were, felt there was nobody but Wilson. "There was so much argument about who was to go," said a humorist of the day,[4] "that Wilson says, 'I tell you what, we will split 50–50 — I will go and you fellows can stay.'"

[4] Will Rogers.

Rogers was hardly to be described as a humorist, in the sense that Peter Dunne ("Mr. Dooley") and Samuel L. Clemens ("Mark Twain") were. The qualification of one who lives up to the definition of humorist is that underlying his jesting there is a pattern, a consistent philosophy. Rogers had little of this. He commonly made the joke for the joke's sake; it was on one side of an issue as often as on another; consequently his jests, brought together, reflected no consistent point-of-view about life. Rogers, properly classified, would be a comedian, somewhere between humorist and clown. One felt he had it in him to be humorist wholly, had he been willing to shed the clown.

II

Wilson's departure[5] for Paris, spectacular under any circumstances — it was the first time any President had gone to Europe — was made more conspicuous by the éclat that accompanied it. He sailed on a government ship, the *George Washington*, trailed by another ship carrying more than a hundred newspaper men. Attending Wilson on the *George Washington* was a retinue, including an immense corps of experts, specialists on the problems that would arise in the Peace Conference, not the American problems but the European ones: Professor Charles H. Haskins of Harvard, specialist on Alsace-Lorraine; Professor W. L. Westermann of the University of Wisconsin, specialist on Turkey; Professor Clive Day of Yale, specialist on the Balkans; Professor W. E. Lunt of Haverford, specialist on Northern Italy; Professor Roland B. Dixon of Harvard, specialist on ethnography; and many others, more than a score. It was quite all right, yet it was odd. The Peace Conference's problems of boundaries were not American, they were European; there must be specialists in Europe who knew them well. If Mr. Wilson did not trust the European specialists, or if he intended to overbear them; if indeed he was going to assert his personal will at all about such strictly and minutely European matters as boundaries, it seemed to some a little peremptory, to others a little farcical — the American President and former college professor, accompanied by a score of other college professors, to tell Europe how to trace boundary lines between

---

[5] On this first trip to Europe, Wilson left New York December 4, arrived at Brest December 13. With the work of the Peace Conference partly done, he left Paris February 14, arrived in Boston February 23. He returned again to Europe. With the work of the Peace Conference completed, he left Paris June 28, arrived in New York July 8.

the intricately mingled races of the Tyrol and the Balkans.[6]

Wilson himself, in occasional moments, seemed to think it so. Walking the deck of the *George Washington* with his intimate, George Creel; looking out over the ocean vastness that facilitated detachment and serenity the thought came to Wilson that maybe he had led the world to expect too much of him; that perhaps he had, in the language of a colloquial American story (about a prize-fighter who had, with overconfidence as it turned out, challenged all comers), "taken on too much territory." Creel was explaining to Wilson how by propaganda he had spread Wilson's ideals throughout the world, including and especially, "self-determination" of small peoples. Wilson was appreciative: "It is a great thing you have done." But he was apprehensive: "I am wondering if you have not unconsciously spun a net for me. It is to America [actually to Wilson] that the whole world turns, not only with its wrongs but with its hopes and grievances. . . . These expectations have the quality of terrible urgency. It has been so always. People will endure their tyrants for years, but they tear their deliverers to pieces if a millennium is not created immediately. Yet these ancient wrongs, these present unhappinesses, are not to be remedied in a day or with a wave of the hand. What I seem to see — I hope I am wrong — is a tragedy of disappointment."

Wilson was approaching one of those periods, not in-

[6] "Down the gangplank walked this Yankee knight errant followed by a desperate crew of college professors in horn-rimmed glasses carrying text-books, encyclopædias, maps, charts, graphs, statistics, and all sorts of literary crowbars to pry up the boundaries of Europe and move them around in the interests of justice as seen through the Fourteen Points." — William Allen White, "Woodrow Wilson."

It was said that some of the experts, as a means of determining just where boundary lines should run, were sent to count the names of the various nationals on grave-stones in border-line communities

frequent in his career, when the desirability of the abstract is embarrassed by the impracticability of the concrete. At almost the moment when he was unbosoming his dawning doubts to Creel, when he was coming to apprehend, belatedly, that he might not be able to fulfil the hopes he had excited — at that moment, Secretary of State Lansing, also a passenger on the *George Washington*, was writing in his diary:

The more I think about the President's declaration as to the right of "self-determination," the more convinced I am of the danger of putting such ideas into the minds of certain races. It is bound to be the basis of impossible demands on the Peace Conference. . . . The phrase is simply loaded with dynamite. What a pity it was ever uttered! What misery it will cause!

Wilson had disdain for Lansing, thought him a "legalist"; once Wilson informed Lansing curtly that this was not to be a "lawyer's peace." But practicality was as strong in Lansing as idealism in Wilson.

III

Wilson arrived at Paris and was fêted there — his entry was more that of a conquering hero at the close of a victorious war than in the case of most military leaders. There had hardly been such scenes since Napoleon. "Vive Le President Wilson!" "Vive L'Amerique!" Over the street where the procession passed waved a great banner, "Honor to Wilson the Just."

He was flattered by the great, sought by the humble. Waiting for him, almost standing on the steps of the house he was to occupy, or arriving soon after, were delegations from the little peoples in Europe and Asia who had been stirred by his promise of "self-determination." "Oppressed nationalities" that for centuries had renewed in each generation, persistently though hopelessly, the dream of independence, had during the war taken Wilson's promise in full faith, looked upon him as the deliverer, the redeemer. Now they sent their elders and

© *Underwood & Underwood.*

This sign flashed a welcome to President Wilson on the rue Royale, Paris, on his way from the station.

patriarchs to Paris to thank him, pay homage to him — and to bring home the fulfilment of his promise. One saw them at the house where Wilson stayed, or making their way along the corridors of an ornate Paris hotel, a little dazed, with the manner of "country come to town" or of survivals from ancient times now jostled by the hurly-burly of soldiers and modernness that Paris was: old men wearing curious costumes, from Armenia, from the Ukraine, from Bessarabia, from Dobrudja, from Korea; Swedes asking correction of the "Crime of '64" by restoration of the Aaland Islands; tribal headsmen from little racial pockets in the Caucasus and the Carpathians; chieftains from the Albanians, from the Hedjaz, from Iraq, from the Banat. Wistfully waiting they were, and many others, for Wilson to redress their ancient wrongs, restore their long-lost autonomy, replace obscure dynasties upon long-lost thrones, cause their dying native languages to live again.

One delegation, typical of others, consisted of figures as extraordinary as ever came to Paris: "They were Polish peasants clad in their own home-spun natural wool, red-embroidered, with Cossack caps of shaggy black fur. They had with them a Polish priest, who spoke French, to tell what they wanted. They were from a little pocket settlement of Poles in the mountains of northern Austria, and in the new boundaries they were included in the new nation of the Czecho-Slovaks. They told, and the priest interpreted, how one of them had heard in his mountain home that the American President who was at Paris had said that people should be free, should have a right to determine how and by whom they were to be governed. He wanted to be in Poland, not in Czecho-Slovakia, and so he had set out to walk to Paris to tell the President so. As soon as he got out of his own native mountains he lost his way and turned aside to inquire of a Polish sheep-herder. 'He was a man,' said the priest, 'who knew the stars, and the way to go.' This sheep-herder, when he heard the traveller tell his story, said that he, too, 'wanted to be free' and came along with him to watch the stars and point out the way to go. They walked some hundred miles to Warsaw where their story attracted the attention of a patriotic Polish society, which sent them on to Paris.

And they came down the boulevards straight to the Crillon Hotel to find President Wilson. They actually did find him. I saw them — the peasant and the wise man who knew the stars, and the priest who talked for them — going up the carpeted stairs of the President's house and into his book-walled study. And I could smell the very odour of their thick woven wool garments, redolent of the soil, in that unfamiliar place."[7]

IV

Wilson had arrived in Paris December 13. The Peace Conference would not begin until January 7. Wilson was deluged with pressure to accept honors — and confer them; to be the guest at great celebrations, to visit the crowned heads of the other Allies; Britain, Italy, and Belgium would be hurt if, visiting the French capital, he failed to visit them also.

He resisted pressure to visit the devastated territory because he felt he might be harrowed and thereby stirred into a mood in which it might be less easy for him to maintain a just point-of-view toward Germany. But he reviewed the American Army. He visited King George at Buckingham Palace and made a tour of England, speaking at the Guildhall in London, at Manchester, at Carlisle. He visited Italy, made speeches at Turin and Genoa and Milan and Rome.

Everywhere he was the idol of the masses. "And the common people heard him gladly." "The mass of European peasantry, shopkeepers, and day laborers looked forward to his arrival as men looked in mediæval times to the second coming of Christ."[8] Never since Peter the Hermit had Europe so blindly, so eagerly followed one

[7] Quoted and paraphrased from "What Wilson Did at Paris," by Ray Stannard Baker.
[8] "Woodrow Wilson and His Work," William E. Dodd.

leader. It was a frequent saying during late December, 1918, that Wilson could overturn any government in Europe by an appeal to the people as against their rulers.

In Rome the reception to him, the crowds beneath the windows of the palace where he stayed, the picture of him in every shop-window, quotations from his war speeches on every wall, the cheering thousands who waited six hours to see him pass, recalled Cæsar back from conquering Gaul united with a second Cæsar after rescuing the city from Attila. A story told at Rome among the American newspaper men — not authentic, but more typical of the atmosphere than mere fact could be, as an artist's drawing often reveals more truth than a camera — dealt with two Italian laborers meeting on the street. Said Guido, "What's the news?" Giuseppe replied, "The Pope is very sick." "Ah," said Guido, "that is too bad, I hope he doesn't die; it would be a pity for the Pope to die just now, for *el Presidente* Wilson might appoint a Protestant."

That was apotheosis of Wilson's fame and prestige, of the glamour and power he had come to have in the world. And that was just five days in advance of the opening of the Peace Conference at Paris. Thence on was downward.

V

At Paris, the tragic procession of mistakes resumed. Wilson had already, as an incident of the Armistice, made a fatal error. His Fourteen Points (and also his Four Points and all his program) had been put forward in the war as a tender to Germany, and had been repeated[9] in Wilson's correspondence with Germany

---

[9] In the manner which lawyers call "by reference," or "by incorporation." See Chapter 24.

leading up to the Armistice. By Germany's acceptance, they became a contract. But some of the Allies, who were Wilson's partners in the contract, now raised qualifications to some of the points.

It was by this act and at this point, so far as such a

Photograph by U. S. Army Signal Corps.

Queen Elizabeth, President and Mrs. Wilson, and King Albert, taken at the King's Palace in Brussels, Belgium.

matter can be asserted with definiteness, that the world got off the track. Failure to live up to the Fourteen Points and the other assurances Wilson had held out was the starting-point of much that bedevilled the world for years. To attempt to say what course the world would have taken had Wilson's contract with Germany been lived up to, his assurances to the world carried out, is of course to deal with one of the "ifs" of history. We know that failure to do so led to consequences definitely identifiable and very unhappy.

. The British raised one qualification about Point number II, freedom of the seas. The British and French raised another about Point VIII, the amount of damages (later called "reparations") Germany must pay. Wilson did not resist the qualifications. That was fatal to the contract, fatal to the Fourteen Points, to Wilson's whole program. Wilson had meant the Fourteen Points as a sincere tender to the German people, to be lived up to punctiliously if the Germans should accept them. The Germans had accepted them — but now the Allies began to repudiate them, whittle them away. All along, one judges, some of the Allies' leaders had regarded the Fourteen Points not as Wilson regarded them, not as a sincere tender, but rather as a ruse of war designed to lure the German people to surrender and overthrow their government. The early assent of some Allied leaders to the Fourteen Points had been with their fingers crossed. Now they had a manner of surprise that Wilson should really have meant them.[10]

There is a question how far the Allies had actually assented to Wilson's tenders, to what extent they were bound. They had given no formal, contractual endorsement to Wilson's pronouncements. But if there can be fair question about their being legally bound, there

[10] The Allies, prior to our entrance into the war, had made secret treaties among themselves about territorial and other arrangements to be made when the war should end. In 1915 England, France, and Russia had made promises of Austrian territory to Italy as an incident of drawing her into the war. There was also an agreement about the partition of Turkey and an arrangement with Japan providing for the future of Shantung. These treaties did not become known until the war was ending, some not until the peace conference. They ran counter to Wilson's Fourteen Points and therefore to the Armistice contract of the Allies with Germany. It would have been tenable for Wilson to insist that these secret treaties had been superseded by the Armistice contract; actually, on some points he permitted the secret treaties to be carried out.

can be little about their moral liability. One of the
most authoritative commentators on the series of events
that now began, John Maynard Keynes, admits that
"our [the British and other Allies'] engagements were
in part vaguely expressed, that they were not cast in legal

Underwood & Underwood photograph.

President Wilson surrounded by admirers, at Versailles.

form, that there is no one [that is, no international
tribunal] to enforce them, and that they cannot therefore constitute a 'contract.'" But, Keynes adds, "imagine
with what indignation these same apologists would explode before a similar argument on the lips of a
German."

However that may be, the world assumed that Wilson's program was the Allies' program; took it for
granted that Wilson could carry out his promises. And
whatever may have been the degree to which the Allies
were committed, there could be no question about the

obligation on Wilson to fight for the sanctity of his promises when attempt was made to depart from them. The Wilson of a few weeks before would have stood firm for the letter of the contract, would have rejected indignantly the idea that the Fourteen Points could be modified after Germany had accepted them and had surrendered on the basis of them.

Wilson, the new Wilson that was less than Wilson, made not only the mistake of permitting qualifications by the Allies to the Fourteen Points. Within his own mind he made what was for such a man the most tragic of lapses. He compromised with his own intellect and conscience, said to himself it would do no harm to let the Allies make qualifications to the Fourteen Points, because he would be sure to set up his League of Nations, and that, when in operation, would carry out the Fourteen Points and correct all other errors.[11] The League of Nations, he thought, was the only indispensable thing. More and more he sank deeper and deeper into that pit of his own making, the relaxation of intellect and conscience which said that his other promises did not matter, that he need only stand by his promise of the League of Nations, and the League, when in operation, would make his other promises good.

At Paris, having permitted reservations to one of the Fourteen Points, he compromised on others. Point Number I, "open covenants of peace openly arrived at,"[12] as the world, especially the newspapers, understood it, was dropped overboard when it was decided that the essential sittings of the Peace Conference should be secret. In that decision Wilson participated. It was un-

[11] "President Wilson accepted the defects . . . because of the belief that the League of Nations would be a continuing peace conference revising constantly the mistakes of the treaty. . . . So he staked all to get the League of Nations established." — "The True Story of Woodrow Wilson," David Lawrence.

[12] There is legitimate question whether this first of the Fourteen Points,

fortunate. It enabled the French and British, especially the French, to manipulate the news, and therefore public opinion, by "calculated leakages." Complete publicity would have been an advantage to Wilson; what he wanted would stand the light, what the others intrigued for would not.

By now, Wilson was permitting not only the two variations from the Fourteen Points brought up by the Allies at the time of the Armistice; he was permitting violations of the Armistice contract itself. And that was a real contract.[13] "The nature of the contract between Germany and the Allies resulting from this exchange of documents is plain and unequivocal. The terms of the peace are to be in accordance with the addresses of the President, and the purpose of the Peace Conference is 'to discuss the details of their application.' The circumstances of [this] contract were of an unusually solemn and binding character. . . ."[14]

Wilson's consent to secrecy at the Peace Conference facilitated the further whittling down of the Fourteen Points that Clemenceau and Lloyd George were intent upon. Lloyd George in England, immediately after the Armistice, taking advantage of the war emotion as a means of getting for himself and his party a renewed lease of power, had brought about a general election, in which he promised to "hang the Kaiser," and to "make

---

"open covenants openly arrived at," was really violated by the secrecy of the sessions of the "Big Five" heads of governments. Wilson did not necessarily mean that the world should be present at "the birth-pains of the peace." He wrote in a memorandum for the Senate, "I meant, not that there should be no private discussions of delicate matters, but that no secret agreements should be entered into, and that all international relations should be open, above-board and explicit." — "Woodrow Wilson and World Settlement," Ray Stannard Baker.

13 "The way was pointed out by Woodrow Wilson in the Fourteen Points. It was agreed to by all the Powers of Europe in as solemn a compact as nations ever undertook. And every tragic month since that day has added fresh proof of their supreme folly in breaking this written compact." — New York *World*.

14 The quotation is from John Maynard Keynes, British economist.

Germany pay the whole cost of the war," "pay to the
last farthing." That ran counter to the stipulations of
the Armistice. Similarly, Clemenceau, between the
Armistice and the Peace Conference, announced that
France stood for the old alliances, the old balance of

Underwood & Underwood photograph.

Lloyd George, Orlando, Clemenceau, and Wilson at Versailles, 1919.

power, and the French Chamber of Deputies sustained
him by a vote of 380 to 134. That ran counter to Wilson's Point XIV, "a general association of nations must
be formed," and to Wilson's promise in his speech of
September 27, 1918: "Third — there can be no leagues
or alliances . . . ."

"God," said Clemenceau in a French mot, "gave
us the Ten Commandments; Wilson gives us the Fourteen Points — we shall see."[15] Wilson had promised

[15] In another Gallic subtlety, Clemenceau said that Wilson was a man of
"grande candeur." Americans liked it — the literal translation sounded like a
compliment, great candor; but the French, and all bi-linguals, knew that in
French usage the meaning was something like "stupid simplicity."

peace with justice; Clemenceau was intent on, so a pun of the day put it, "peace with a vengeance."

To some of the attempted invasions of the Fourteen Points or the other ideals he had put forward, Wilson resisted sturdily — for weeks at a time he had his old fire, as well as his old polemic subtlety, his Napoleonic strategy with ideas. But there were other periods when he was very tired. Late in May (1919) "his face looked like death, sometimes one side of it and his eye would twitch painfully";[16] once he was in bed for several days — the man who at that moment was almost the mainspring of a near run-down civilization, upon whom, almost, it depended to keep the world a going concern. Illness sapped his mental vigor. When he did not fight for a resisted point he again drugged himself with the fatal compromise he had made within himself — he would get the League of Nations, and when the League of Nations got under way, it, and he, would rectify any unfortunate concessions he might make now. Was German reparations wrong? Very well, let it go, the League would fix that![16a]

VI

On the 4th of March, one of Wilson's earlier mistakes came back upon him. In the Senate that he had ignored in selecting his Peace Commission, and among the Republicans he had flouted by his appeal for a Democratic Congress, 39 members of the new Senate which on that day came into power — and 39 was more than

[16] Quoted from Ray Stannard Baker's three-volume narrative of the Peace Conference, published in 1922, "Woodrow Wilson and World Settlement." (By 1933 that title seemed ironic.)

[16a] "Overmatched, and disillusioned as to his power to compel a Peace of Justice, he pinned all his faith to the League of Nations. . . . In the success of this project he saw compensation for the defects, and correction of the errors in other portions of the Treaty." — "Woodrow Wilson, A Character Study," Robert E. Annin.

the one-third that could prevent ratification of a treaty — signed a round-robin[17] saying they would have no League of Nations; let Wilson negotiate a simple peace treaty ending the war and come home; if Wilson set up a League of Nations the Senate would not ratify it. That was notice to the world, especially was it notice to Wilson's adversaries in the Peace Conference.

Wilson, in adjusting himself to meet this threat from the Senate, was for a moment the old Wilson.[18] With his familiar skill in dialectics, his Napoleonic instinct for the unexpected in strategy, he tied the Covenant of the League of Nations into the treaty of peace, knotted the two firmly, so that it would be impossible to have a formal ending of the war without adopting the League of Nations. That was able. But at once Wilson lapsed. The fundamental art of such a move is to let it speak

[17] This round-robin was the beginning of the organized fight against the League of Nations. The story of its arising was told by Senator Frank Brandegee of Connecticut to Mark Sullivan, and by him printed in the New York *Evening Post* (October 21, 1921):

"On Sunday morning, March 2, 1919, Senator Brandegee, going to his office in the Senate Office Building, found in his mail a letter from a stranger, a man whose name is lost to the history in which he had a vitally initiating part; all that Brandegee could remember later was that it was on a letterhead which indicated the writer was in the iron and steel business in New York. The stranger pointed out that if Wilson were permitted to continue his present course in Paris without formal protest, the time would go by when he could be forestalled from committing America to membership in a League of Nations.

"Brandegee, impressed, put the letter in his pocket and walked to the home of Senator Lodge, Republican head of the Committee on Foreign Relations. Lodge was equally impressed. The two went to call on Senator Knox. Knox was not at home; they left word for him to dine with them that night at Brandegee's house. The three Senators concluded the best form of protest would be a round-robin. Knox drafted it that night. The following day, in the Senate cloak-room, the three signed it and solicited signatures from other Republicans. The fourth signer was New of Indiana; the fifth, Moses of New Hampshire; the sixth, Wadsworth of New York. In all, thirty-nine signed. Some Democrats were willing to sign, but it was thought best to have only Republicans."

[18] As an additional strategy, he tried at Paris to get the French, British, and others to agree to a modification of the League of Nations which would remove some of the American objections, make it more difficult for the Republican Senators to refuse to ratify. But the others would not accept the modification. Between the Senate at home and the "Big Five" at Paris, Wilson was caught in what baseball slang calls a "squeeze-play."

for itself.   But Wilson talked about it.   While in America for an interval he told a public audience[19] that

When that treaty comes back, gentlemen [in the Senate] will find the Covenant not only in it, but so many threads of the Treaty tied to the Covenant that you cannot dissect the Covenant from the Treaty without destroying the whole vital structure.

As defiance that was dramatic.   But to reveal strategy, to announce motive, as an incident of indulging in the emotion of defiance — that was far from the subtlety and self-control of the Wilson of his best days.   Defiance for defiance's sake begets defiance in the defied.   Wilson's act strengthened the Senators in their determination, brought them sympathy from quarters which otherwise might have remained indifferent.   "Very well, then," said the Senators in effect, "we will prevent ratification of the whole treaty."

Wilson had supposed that to be unthinkable, and his thus supposing was another mistake.   The Senators proceeded to resist the treaty as a whole.   Congress, to bring the state of war technically to an end somehow, felt obliged to pass a simple joint resolution.   Wilson vetoed it as a disgrace to American honor.   The Senators continued to prevent ratification of the treaty and of the League that Wilson had put in it.

VII

By Wilson's defiance of the Republican Senators, they got for their fight against the League a momentum they could hardly have created themselves.   The arrogance of his retort, the rather autocratically devious means by which he proposed to get the League ratified, his attitude of forcing the Senate to accept the League without

[19] In a speech at the Metropolitan Opera House, New York, March 4, 1919, just before sailing back to France.

opportunity for a separate vote upon its merit standing
alone, was perhaps the most serious of Wilson's mistakes — if we can choose among the mistakes that now
came tumbling upon each other. It imperilled the
League; and, as a consequence of former mistakes, if he
lost the League he lost all.

Up to now American opposition to the League had
come mainly from a very small number of intellectuals
and from Republicans in the Senate. That the principal
spokesmen were Republicans, discounted the opposition
in the eyes of the public; the Senate Republicans, the
public assumed, were opposing the League in the spirit
in which they would have been likely to oppose almost
anything coming from Wilson. The masses of the people had taken the League of Nations for granted. Without fully understanding it or trying to look into it, they
vaguely assumed it was good. It had been talked about
off and on for several years, it had the aroma of altruism
that appealed to America; it purported to be a mechanism for permanent peace, and permanent peace was
an American ideal; practically all Americans of the
type that politicians call "church folks" were for it.
Whenever brought forward by Wilson during the war
it had been as a part of America's aims and therefore
worthy. So long as it remained a generalization, or was
kept within limits, most of our accepted leaders had been
for it, such men as President Lowell and ex-President
Eliot of Harvard, Elihu Root, Charles E. Hughes. The
country had seen one unprecedented spectacle that testi-
fied to the League's worthiness, the Democratic President and the only living Republican ex-President, William H. Taft, standing on the same platform to advocate
it.[20] It must be all right.

The only hope the Senate Republicans could have was

[20] At the Metropolitan Opera House, New York, March 4, 1919.

to get the public out of its taken-on-faith state of mind, to cause the public to listen while they explained the League concretely, pointed out the dangers for America which they said were in it. For getting the attention of the people, Wilson's angry defiance was the greatest possible aid — crowds who would not put thought upon an issue attacked by Senators would pay attention to an issue sensationally defended by a President. With the ear of the public thus caught, the Senate Republicans explained that the League was a "super-state," that America in joining it would surrender some of its sovereignty — a cartoon much used after the fight got under way showed a flag pole with the flag of the League of Nations at the top, the Stars and Stripes beneath. Particularly, and effectively, did the Senate Republicans point to Article X which Wilson called the "heart of the covenant," and Article XI:

X. The Members of the League undertake to respect and preserve as against external aggression the territorial integrity and existing political independence of all Members. . . .

XI. . . . Any war or threat of war . . . is hereby declared a matter of concern to the whole League, and the League shall take any action that may be deemed wise and effectual to safeguard the peace of nations. . . .

That, the Republican Senators said, meant that the League would have the right at any time to call on America to send soldiers to take part in any action the League might dictate. It had the effect, so opponents of the League said, of drawing America into war without declaration of war by our own Congress.

That argument was potent. We had just taken part in one European war, and right at this time, our emotion about it was one of distaste. We had begun to pass into a mood, destined later to grow, which altruists described sadly as a "slump in idealism." Our distaste for wars other than our own was made acute by the fact that one contingent of American soldiers were still at Archangel, in Arctic Russia, sent there as an incident of Allied strategy, fighting a nation against which we had not declared war, with whom we had no quarrel.[20a]

This, and other conditions, caused the agitation of the Republican Senators to take hold on the country. Even persons who had been strong for the League were carried into a mood in which they were beginning to doubt. Wilson was obliged to admit to himself that the League was in danger, not only in the Senate but before the country.

VIII

He determined to make a direct appeal to the people, to make speeches from coast to coast. His physician and devoted friend, Admiral Grayson, opposed it, asked Secretary Tumulty to help prevent it, intimated to Tumulty that the President might pay with his life. Mrs. Wilson joined them. She, personal as women are to a greater degree than men, with woman's surer estimate of relative values as between public distinction and private happiness, was "not interested" in the League of Nations nor "in the President of the United States, I am interested in my husband and his health."

Tumulty, feeling that Wilson was "plainly on the verge of a nervous breakdown," asked him, instead of the speechmaking trip, to take a long rest away from Washington. Wilson pushed him aside. "I know I am at the end of my tether," but "the trip is necessary to save the Treaty. . . . No decent man can count his own personal fortunes."

[20a] "We had no interest in the Old World and were more or less resentful at having been dragged into what had started as purely a European quarrel of the old sort. Many of the 2,000,000 soldiers who had been overseas had come back with no love for the Allies and with a wish to be done with Europe." — "The March of Democracy," James Truslow Adams.

Musingly for a moment, and very sadly, Tumulty remembered the Wilson he had first met a dozen years before, "a vigorous, agile, slender man, active and alert, his hair but slightly streaked with gray."

Now he was an old man. As in all men, age brought

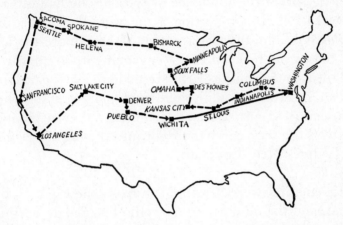

Route of President Wilson's "swing around the circle" in 1919, which he made in an attempt to win popular support for our joining the League of Nations. His speech-making ended with an address before a large and friendly crowd at Pueblo. Just before his special train reached Wichita, Wilson became seriously ill and the remainder of the tour had to be cancelled.

accentuation of his natural qualities. Grimness, determination, was now Wilson's principal motivation. He insisted the trip must be made. Doctor Grayson, solicitous, inserted in the itinerary (which made engagements for some forty speeches[21]) a week of rest in the Grand Canyon of the Colorado. Wilson crossed it out. There must be no suggestion of pleasure in a journey which he regarded as a mission.

He went. Day after day for twenty-two days Doctor Grayson saw continuous brain fag, violent headaches.

[21] Wilson's speech-making tour in behalf of the League of Nations, his last "swing 'round the circle," began September 3, 1919. His opening speech was at Columbus, Ohio, September 4.

At night, in his speeches, Wilson was at times bitter; at Des Moines he called his adversaries "jaundice-eyed bolsheviks of politics." Other times he was despondent, moody, frequently in his speeches "exalted the nobility of death in a great cause . . . From one night to another he forgot the substance of speeches he had already delivered."[21a] In proportion as he was ill, and because he was now old and determined, he was more meticulous than ever to keep every engagement, to appear at each meal in the dining-car, to respond to every call from wayside crowds for additional train-platform speeches. In an excess of an old man's grimness, he even planned to extend the trip, carry the fight into the enemy's country, Lodge's New England.

His enemies were "trailing" him — they spoke of it as that, and the newspapers as well. The Senate enemies of the treaty, collecting a small war fund, hired halls in the territory through which Wilson had just passed; Reed,[22] Borah,[22] Johnson,[22] and others made savage anti-League speeches to the communities to which Wilson had just made his plea — and Wilson, reading accounts in the newspapers, saw that the oppositon was getting larger audiences, evoking more applause and emotion, than himself. At Chicago,[22a] Borah and Johnson, appearing together, had one of the largest audiences the city had ever seen. Johnson, continuing on the trail after Wilson, spoke at St. Louis, Kansas City, Des Moines, Sioux Falls, and farther west. The anti-League Senators were determined, ruthless, relentless; the spirit in which they fought the League and Wilson drew to them desig-

---

[21a] The quotation is from David Lawrence, who accompanied Wilson as a newspaper correspondent.

[22] Senators James A. Reed of Missouri, William E. Borah of Idaho, Hiram W. Johnson of California.

[22a] September 10, 1919.

nations of mordancy, "irreconcilables," "bitter-enders," "battalion of death." Their spirit attracted the crowd. Morning after morning Wilson saw in the newspapers his enemies succeeding, himself waning.

During his speech at Pueblo, Colo., September 25,

© *International News Photos, Inc.*

Senator Hiram Johnson and Medill McCormick, arriving in Chicago Sept. 12, 1917, as they trailed Wilson, arguing against his plea on behalf of the League.

1919, he broke into tears — to so slender a store of nervous stamina had he come. Afterward, during the afternoon, Mrs. Wilson had the train stopped; and, to give him such recreation as was possible, walked with him upon a dusty country road. When he returned to the train, he had a temperature. Doctor Grayson gave him a narcotic.

Late that night (about four o'clock in the morning of September 26), Doctor Grayson knocked at the door of Tumulty's compartment in the sleeping-car, asked him to dress quickly, the President was seriously ill.

In the President's drawing-room Tumulty found Wilson fully dressed. His face was pale, one side of it had fallen. When he tried to talk he could not articulate clearly. Tears running down his face, he said to Tumulty: "My dear boy, this has never happened to me before. I do not know what to do." Tumulty of course proposed to cancel the rest of the trip. Pleadingly, almost childishly, Wilson said: "Don't you see that if you cancel this trip Senator Lodge and his friends will say that I am a quitter and that the Western trip was a failure and the Treaty will be lost?"

Impulsively Tumulty took hold of both his hands: "What difference, Governor,[23] does it make what they say? Nobody in the world will consider you are a quitter, it is your life we must consider." Wilson tried to move nearer to Tumulty to press his argument. "His left arm and leg refused to function."[24]

Tumulty and Grayson announced to the newspaper men that the rest of the trip was off. The train, instead of stopping for the scheduled speech at Wichita, Kans., was switched round the city. With drawn blinds it hurried eastward.

Ten years before, Wilson had stood with a friend, Mrs. Peck, on the Bermuda sands telling her he thought of

---

[23] This title (Governor of New Jersey) had been Wilson's when Tumulty first served him; Tumulty used it to the end.

[24] This is quoted from Tumulty's book "Woodrow Wilson as I Know Him," published 1921. At the time, Tumulty's statement to the press at Wichita, Kans., September 26, 1919, was that the President had "so spent himself without reserve on this trip that it brought on a nervous reaction in his digestive organs." Due to the effort to keep Wilson's condition from the public, the records are diverse about the extent to which Wilson's left side was affected by the breakdown at Pueblo. When he reached Washington he was able to walk the length of the station platform. His affliction became worse and permanent, at the time of the second attack, October 4.

leaving Princeton to enter politics. When he mildly resisted her encouragement but in the end concluded to make the adventure, he had recited, musingly, an anonymous poem he remembered:

> . . . After this life's whim,
> When the heart beats low and the eyes grow dim;
> When the will has forgotten the lifelong aim,
> And the mind can only disgrace its fame. . . .
> For even the purest delight may pall,
> And power must fail, and pride must fall.

IX

The endings of wars, the periods succeeding them, have roughly a common pattern, are attended by the same emotions, including hate. In this lies a parallel between Wilson and Lincoln.

Lincoln during the Civil War promised fairness to the enemy,[25] "with malice toward none, with charity toward all." And as the Civil War ended, Lincoln, to fulfil his promise, proposed generous terms for the South, general amnesty for those who had fought, reconstruction of their state governments by their own people. At once he was reviled by those who insisted on revenge, repression, government of the South as conquered provinces, by force. "Congress rejected Lincoln's policy of peace and mercy."[26] Before the attacks on him reached full momentum, Lincoln had the good fortune to die, five days after the surrender of the Confederates at Appomattox. His death, coming at the peak of his military success and his fame, silenced his enemies, intimidated calumny, made his place in history unassailable.

Wilson, in the Great War, promised fairness to the enemy. When the war ended Wilson, to fulfil his prom-

[25] Second Inaugural.
[26] Quoted from George Fort Milton's "Age of Hate."

ise, tried to form a League of Nations and otherwise
live up to the promises he had held out to the German
people. At once he was reviled and pulled down by those
bent on revenge, the "Hang the Kaiser!" and "Make
'em pay!" partisans in France and Britain, the "unconditional surrender" partisans and "isolationists" in
America.

Wilson, to have shared Lincoln's good fortune, would
have had to die five days after the Armistice ending the
Great War. Had he done so he might have been to-day,
in popular estimation, one with Lincoln.

And had Lincoln lived, as Wilson did, for five years
after the war, probably that part of the parallel, too,
would have been carried out.

There was parallel in their careers but not equality in
the men. Had Wilson been, in nature, as great as Lincoln, his stature in history would have been immeasur-
ably taller, for the scope of Wilson's functioning was
infinitely broader, the stage upon which Wilson acted
was literally the world.

What, then, was Wilson's lack? At what point, and
how, did he fumble? You must not expect the answer
in an epigram. His physical and intellectual deterioration at the end of the long strain of the war had much
to do with it. Aside from that, much of his failure
was predestined.

Turn back in this book to page 32. Read there the
comment made when the war first began in Europe by
a small-town Mid-West newspaper: "We never appreciated so much as now the foresight exercised by our
forefathers in emigrating from Europe"; and on the
same page the view of a newspaper reflecting city
thought, "Citizens of this country will now rise and
tender a hearty vote of thanks to Columbus for hav-

ing discovered America." Had some wise counsellor of President Woodrow Wilson happened to notice that expression of American point of view, had he pasted it on Wilson's desk and urged the President to keep it there for the duration of the war, and never to forget it, in that event Mr. Wilson might have saved himself much suffering, his country much turmoil, the world much disappointment. That an America which in 1914 was universally and profoundly glad of being three thousand miles away from Europe, should by 1918 be willing to enter a tight-bound League of Nations — to assume that was one of the mistakes of Wilson which from 1919 until the end of his life reduced to dust and ashes, bitter in his dying mouth, the triumph he had won by his conduct of America's part in the world war.[26a]

That oversight, that failure to take account of reality, was associated in Wilson's nature with a broader lack. He lived by ideals and words, by words and ideals he perished. With words he inspired millions to ideals; he was not able to translate the ideals into reality. The League of Nations was a noble ideal, but it was more than mortal man could achieve — the world would not be ready for it (as Wilson conceived it) for generations, perhaps centuries.

It had been part of his polemic technique to get assent to a principle, and to refuse to discuss details until the principle was agreed to. Now he had got the world's consent to the League of Nations as a principle, as an abstraction — and when he came to fill in the details, one of them had to be force — and that America would

[26a] "Unfortunately it takes more than vision to make a statesman, and Wilson over-rated both the willingness of his own countrymen and of the world at large to assume the risks of trying to establish a new order in place of the old, while he under-rated the forces of nationalism; he also overestimated his own ability to solve the problem. . . . Wilson did not give sufficient weight to the actualities of the real springs of action in men, and to the strength of historic factors." — "The March of Democracy," James Truslow Adams.

not have. Of all the tragedies that man may bring upon himself, and to those who build their hopes upon him, one of the saddest is to excite expectations which he cannot live up to. When the ideals that Wilson had set up were not realized, as they faded into mist, the world fell into the worst disillusionment the world as a whole had ever had, a universal disease, a sickness of spirit from which almost the whole human race suffered for years.

In familiar thought, the antithesis of words is deeas. But another antithesis of words is things. Wilson all his life had dealt with words, thought in terms of words as distinguished from things. As a child listening to his father in the pulpit he saw the homiletic effect as the end aimed at. As a youth in school and college, winning the debate was the finished achievement. As a teacher he dealt with ideas, handed down principles to minds too immature to subject them to even dialectic test. At no period of his life did he have a career in which he was obliged to put his ideals and theories to the test of trial in the world of things. And the experience of men who function with things — physicists, artisans, business men — is that one theory standing up, out of ten put to concrete test, is a high average of survival.

Wilson came to the point where words, and the ideas they connoted, were the be-all and end-all. If the vision conjured up by a word were good, that was enough.[26b] "Self-determination" as an ideal, no one dis-

[26b] "He had no plan, no scheme, no constructive ideas whatever, for clothing with the flesh of life the commandments which he thundered from the White House." — John Maynard Keynes.

To quote Theodore Roosevelt on Woodrow Wilson is to quote Guelph on Gibbeline, "to view with hateful eyes his rival's conquest." Yet Roosevelt had insight, and his comment on Wilson, though colored with temper, coincides with the quite detached judgment of Keynes and many others: ". . . His [Wilson's] cleverness of style and his entire refusal to face facts, apparently making believe that he really has dismissed and done away with ugly realities whenever he has uttered some pretty phrase about them." — "America and the World War," Theodore Roosevelt.

Once during the Peace Conference when I had written in newspapers some-

sents from. But when Wilson held out the promise of self-determination, he incited among peoples all over the world dreams that no statesman and no Peace Conference could make come true. In little communities throughout Europe and Asia, part of the people, belonging to one race, assumed that self-determination meant their race would dominate that territory; the other part of the people, belonging to a different race, assumed it would be their race that would dominate. To neither did it occur that the promise of self-determination applied to the other race as much as to their own — and that it could not be carried out to both. Both lived as Wilson did during that ecstatic time, in a world of words and of dreams evoked by words. In Poland under Germany before the war, there were Germans who had self-determination and Poles who did not. After the Peace Conference gave self-determination to the Poles, there was then a German minority that lacked it and clamored for it. War was no more distant than it had been during the century when the situation was the reverse.

During the Paris Peace Conference, a group of American newspaper men, resolving themselves into a mock duplicate of the august assemblage across the Seine in the Quai d'Orsay, devoted themselves to applying the principle of self-determination to the facts of the State of California. Peace commissioners representing natives of Iowa now living in southern California argued their right to be supreme in the State, at least

---

thing eloquent in support of one of Wilson's principles, there stormed into my office an elderly gentleman who had spent a vigorous life in a highly active business, Henry B. Joy, then president of the Packard Motor Company. "Principles!" he exclaimed. "You say 'principles,' Wilson says 'principles." When I evolve a new principle I must try it in my business. If I lose my money, I know my principle is wrong. Nine times out of ten I do lose my money. But when Wilson hands down a principle, as a college teacher or a President, he is not required to try it out at his own expense."

in Los Angeles, because of their superiority in numbers to other elements of the population. Native sons argued right based on priority of occupation. A delegation representing Spanish-Americans argued that if priority of occupation had weight, they had been in California before the native sons. A commission from the Indians brought forward proof of still earlier occupation. As against all this, representatives of the Japs pointed to a rate of increase which would presently give them a majority and already entitled them to a share in control.

The sum of all was that a promise of self-determination, if held out to California and taken seriously, would turn that contented commonwealth into a quarrelling Balkans.

The advantage Lincoln had over Wilson lay in the greater concreteness of Lincoln's early experiences, his life-long contact with things — the rails he had split from tough walnut, the scows he had pulled up-stream against Mississippi currents, the strong young frontiersmen he had wrestled with, the lawyers he had been obliged to argue against, the equals he had had to combat, the juries and judges he had been obliged to convince.

X

The rest of Wilson was very sad. In the White House ten days after[27] his break-down at Wichita, he had a second stroke, was found semi-conscious on the bathroom floor. Those about him believed death certain. He could not be shaved; for weeks, lying in bed, he had a scraggly white beard and mustache. He was kept secluded. Only Mrs. Wilson and Doctor Grayson had access to him. Not even Tumulty was admitted, except rarely, and then with Mrs. Wilson standing back of the

[27] October 4, 1919.

head of the bed to put her finger to her lips and shake her head if Tumulty brought up anything likely to excite the President. The wife and physician not knowing what to do about the public aspect of the situation, wondering whether to have the Vice-President take over the government at once, but thinking how terrible that would be to Wilson if he should recover, fearful of letting the public know how ill he was lest that might lead to demand that the Vice-President be inaugurated — all had the result of making a mystery of it, led to frightful gossip and innuendo. On some of the White House windows were bars, put there years before when Theodore Roosevelt's children playing ball broke the glass; the bars were now pointed to with whispers — there was a madman in the White House. In the Senate there was discussion whether the technical condition had not arisen that called for action: "In case of the . . . inability of the President to discharge the duties of said office. . . ." Doctor Grayson was asked if he would certify to the President's disability, he retorted he would not. And if any one else attempted to certify it, Grayson would repudiate it. And Tumulty would unite with him, in avowing that Wilson was not disabled. The Senate buzzed, sent a committee to find out if the President of the United States was capable of carrying on the public business. Ostensibly they put their visit on the ground of a wish to discuss Mexican policy; actually they were, as universal comment at the time put it, a "smelling committee." Mrs. Wilson and Doctor Grayson demurred about admitting them. The leader (a sinister person later publicly discredited), Senator Albert W. Fall[28] of New Mexico, persisted, said it was a matter

[28] As Secretary of the Interior in the Cabinet of President Harding, he was charged with receiving $100,000 from E. L. Doheny and transferring government lands to Doheny's oil company. Convicted, he became the first member of a Cabinet in the country's history to go to jail.

of public importance. On a second trip to inspect, Wilson pulled himself together, exerted what was left of himself to be for a half an hour calm and cogent, even told a joke through his twisted lips. Fall said, "I want you to know, Mr. President, that I am praying for you."

After some months he had, from time to time, periods of improvement, of a sort. In one, he learned that Secretary of State Lansing, during his illness, had been calling meetings of the Cabinet. In a bitter letter, Wilson dismissed[29] him: "Is it true, as I have been told, that during my illness you have frequently called the heads of the Executive Departments into conference?" The dismissal of Lansing aroused strong criticism. "Have I any friends left?" Wilson asked Tumulty. In his invalid chair he would have himself rolled to the window in the rear of Tumulty's office, and Tumulty would tell him — as optimistically as truth would permit — of the course of the League of Nations fight in the Senate. If Tumulty reported a friendly mention of him by some one, he would show emotion, sometimes tears.

To distract him, a motion picture was brought two or three times a week to the White House, and shown privately — the operator, manager of a local Washington cinema house, was instructed to keep his visits secret; Wilson became "as enthusiastic a movie fan as any romantic girl or boy; at times he seemed to live only for the hour each day to see what new picture I had to offer him; he called me his movie doctor."[30] Once George Creel called on him. "At sight of me he gestured pathetically, a tragic sweep of the hand that took in the whole of his helpless, wasted body, and great tears filled his eyes."[31]

[29] February 7, 1920.   [30] Quoted from Robert E. Long.
[31] George Creel, *Saturday Evening Post.*

After some four months he was materially improved. One of the specialists[32] who had been called in declared the President was "organically sound, able-minded, and able-bodied." After some seven months he began occasionally to hold Cabinet meetings. The first was in his

© *Underwood & Underwood.*

President Wilson meeting with his Cabinet for the first time after his illness. He "looked old, worn, and haggard; his jaw tended to drop on one side, his voice was very weak, and strained; it was enough to make one weep."

study.[32a] Secretary Houston observed when he arrived that a White House aide ushered him in and announced his name to the President. "Wilson looked old, worn and

[32] Doctor Hugh Young of Johns Hopkins, February 10, 1920. It may be inferred that Doctor Young went as far in minimizing Wilson's condition as a natural wish for allaying public concern could temper scientific accuracy. In passages in the interview Doctor Young said: "If you think it would quiet uneasiness . . . I shall gladly lay the facts before the public . . . I found him not only organically sound when I visited him last week, but further all the organs were functioning in a normal, perfectly healthy manner. The President's general condition and specifically the slight impairment of his left arm and leg have improved. In October last we diagnosed the President's illness as cerebral thrombosis, which affected his left arm and leg, but at no time was his brain power or the extreme vigor and elasticity of his mental processes in the slightest degree abated."

[32a] April 13, 1920.

haggard; it was enough to make one weep. One of his arms was useless. . . . His jaw tended to drop on one side, his voice was very weak and strained. He put up a brave front and spent several minutes cracking jokes. Then there was a brief silence; it appeared that he would not take the initiative. Some one brought up the railroad situation. Wilson seemed at first to have some difficulty in fixing his mind on what we were discussing. Doctor Grayson looked in at the door several times as if to warn us. . . . Finally Mrs. Wilson came in, looking rather disturbed and suggested we had better go."[32b]

He resumed a fitful and rigid insistence on the League of Nations. Enough of him left to give him authority as Democratic leader, not enough of him left to lead wisely, he refused to consider reservations proposed by the Republicans — the Democrats left to themselves would have accepted the reservations and taken America into the League.[33] At Paris he had compromised with Europe when he ought to have stood firm; now at Wash-

[32b] Secretary of Agriculture (later Treasury) David F. Houston, in "Eight Years with Wilson's Cabinet."

[33] About this statement there may be some doubt. Friends of Wilson claimed that if he accepted any reservations, the opponents of the League would bring forward more; that the proposing of reservations was merely part of the strategy of defeating the League. Wilson's position was that "[material] reservation is nullification," translated by his adversaries as insistence that the covenant must be ratified without so much change as the dotting of an "i," the crossing of a "t."

In the allusions in this chapter to the League of Nations fight in the Senate, the opponents are described as "the Senate Republicans." Actually, the line-up was more complex than is appropriate to explain in full at this point. In both parties were varying shades of position on ratification without reservations, ratification with "interpretive" or "mild" reservations, ratification with qualifying amendments, and no ratification. Roughly, 36 of the Republicans headed by Senator Lodge (and a few Democrats) were for reservations and amendments so material as to be unsatisfactory to the administration Democrats. This was more than the one-third of the Senate, 32 (and one more), which was enough to prevent ratification.

Democratic Senator Gilbert M. Hitchcock of Nebraska, leader of the fight for the League, wrote to the author December 7, 1922: "I shall always believe ratification would have been possible if Wilson's health had not given way; when that tragedy occurred, not even his best friends could exercise any considerable influence on him."

ington, in his illness, he was obstinate against America when he ought to have compromised. To a Democratic dinner[34] he wrote a letter declaring that the coming Presidential election should be a "great and solemn referendum" on the League of Nations. Bryan, half sincerely, half ironically, apologized for him: "Broken down in health by cares and anxieties . . . the Chief Executive has been denied the information essential to sound judgment."

He became more and more irascible; once, without cause, he demanded the resignation of Postmaster General Burleson, and only with difficulty was persuaded to withdraw the peremptory dismissal. To a letter from Colonel House, he made no reply; House wrote again, Wilson did not reply.

With fits of brooding and occasional lapses of memory, were occasional brief periods of bright interest in public matters, of strength pulled together to perform a duty. When it came time to leave the White House, he rode with his successor, Harding, to the Capitol. When Harding, embarrassed, making conversation, told him some irrelevant story about a baby elephant, he broke into tears. At the ceremony, fate had it that his ancient enemy, Lodge, should be the one to announce adjournment of the Senate and ask him the usual formal question: "The Senate and House have completed their work and are prepared to receive any further communications from you." Wilson turned glassy eyes upon him, then looked into space and said: "Senator Lodge, I have no further communication to make. Thank you, good day, Sir!" and stumbled away on his cane. Behind him, as Harding took the Presidential oath, the band played "Hail to the Chief" — to Wilson, recessional.

[34] At Washington, Jackson Day, January 8, 1920.

XII

The final years were spent in a house on "S" Street. Occasionally he went to the theatre, helped to his seat by two doormen; and took rides, people in the streets turning to look with interest amounting to awe, at an old man with a lean, almost weazened face, smiling automatically, keeping the left side of his face averted; the street crowds hurt him, he "shrank from them as from a blow"; when Creel told him the onlookers had "only friendship and devotion in every eye," Wilson replied, " 'No,' and his voice was sad and low, 'just curiosity.' "[35] To the man who had been his last Secretary of State, Bainbridge Colby, he proposed — and of course the proposal was a command — a law firm, "Wilson and Colby," to do an international business. There was an office, the firm name on the door, some letter-heads. Wilson hobbled to the office once; at the end of a year Colby managed to terminate it.

It was terrible, recalled with awful poignance, as if it had been prophetic, the line in the poem he had quoted long ago to Mrs. Peck:

When . . . the mind can only disgrace its fame.

When Tumulty, after a conversation with him, delivered to a Democratic dinner an innocuous message of good will as coming from the great leader, Wilson repudiated it in a public letter that had the effect of a cruel lash. To a pleading request from Tumulty for a chance to explain, Wilson was silent. Reverting to his old interest in limericks he composed one himself, recited it with glee to callers, said he had composed it especially to shock a prim woman friend:

There was a young girl from Missouri
Who took her case to a jury.

[35] George Creel, *Saturday Evening Post*.

She said "car ninety-three
Ran over my knee,"
But the jury said "We're from Missouri."

The man who had composed the Fourteen Points![35a]

If the closing days had terrible tragedy they had dignity also. In age, what comes out is accentuation of native traits. Wilson was a gentleman, Mrs. Wilson a lady. Wilson, out of the White House, received more respect of the right kind than his successor in it. Being an ex-President is difficult under any conditions — to hold, as he cannot help, his personal interest in public affairs yet not embarrass his successor; to lag superfluous on the stage, yet be careful not to interrupt the new star's lines. When the ex-President lives in Washington, the delicacy is increased. Wilson and Mrs. Wilson lived up to the most minute requirement. They achieved what Bacon said was difficult: Men who have held great place and lost it are "impatient of privateness, even in age and sickness, which requires a shadow." Asked how he was occupying himself, Wilson replied: "I am showing President Harding how an ex-President should behave." To solicitations that he write for compensation, he declined. His prestige was not for sale or use. In his days of strength he had carried in his wallet a newspaper copy of Kipling's "If" and was fond of quoting:

If you can meet with triumph and disaster
And treat those two imposters just the same. . . .

Now he was the complete exemplar of the double trial, perhaps the most exalted who had gone through both experiences since Napoleon. His comportment, and

[35a] Some who have read the proof of this chapter think that this sentence, especially the exclamation point, implies greater deterioration of Wilson's intellect than in fact existed. They make the point that Wilson at his best habitually amused himself by composing limericks. But not, I think, any quite so banal as this. It is true there was never anything medically recognizable as impairment of Wilson's mind.

Mrs. Wilson's, was an example of taste that history should make conspicuous. William Allen White said the world "had never seen before so inspiring a spectacle, so triumphant a climax to a bitter tragedy." His mind was at all times clear; his force was the thing that had gone and no amount of rest or care could bring it back. About the world, he thought sanely; it had, he felt, passed into one of those periods in which men's minds are ruled by some world-wide epidemic of sophistry.

Once, pathetically, he made a public appearance. Armistice Day, 1923, was a Sunday. During the afternoon there appeared before Wilson's house a loosely organized parade that had assembled down town, led by a band which divided its program between conventional Sunday hymns and wartime tunes like "Over There." The paraders looking expectantly toward Mr. Wilson's door were chiefly elderly persons of serious countenance, the kind of people who fill the churches; among them were some ex-service men. Senator Carter Glass of Virginia appeared on Wilson's steps. Then the door opened and Wilson came out. He wore a silk hat which he several times raised. Senator Glass read a prepared speech. Wilson listened closely, expressing approval from time to time by a slight nod. His dominant expression at first was one of mellowness. One had the feeling that here was a wise, mellow old man whom one would like to talk with for long hours in his library. When Senator Glass said the League of Nations had been defeated by "a conspiracy of . . . selfish politics," Wilson's eyes for a second seemed not far from tears, his lips trembled. Wilson in his reply, looking toward the ex-service men, said: "I am proud to remember that I had the honor of being the Commander-in-Chief of the most ideal army that was ever thrown together." As his memory and imagination summoned up the picture of that army, of the war he had conducted, of all his high experiences, emotion thrust itself into his features. He was conscious of it and said, "Pardon my emotion." Concluding, he said: "I thank you with all my heart for

© *Harris & Ewing.*

Woodrow Wilson on his 67th birthday, December 28, 1923, when he was presented with the automobile shown in the picture, the gift of a group of admirers.

your kindness." The band, taking this for the end, began "How Firm a Foundation." Wilson, as if moved by the spirit of the hymn, said, "Just one word more. . . . I have seen fools resist Providence before and I have seen their destruction, and it will come upon these again, utter destruction and contempt; that we shall prevail is as sure as that God reigns." In those last words all the mellowness departed wholly from Wilson's face and all the temptation to tears. Now he was not one iota short of the dignity and sternness of an Old-Testament prophet affirming his belief in Jehovah and his reliance on the triumph of his faith.

"Not in all the world," wrote one who saw the scene, "could one have found a more dramatic or impressive ceremony of lofty dignity and moving feeling. It was in the lowering sun of a gentle late autumn afternoon. Throughout it, the maple leaves kept dropping in the windless air. The suggestion of a sombre and pathetic fate attached itself to Mr. Wilson, to the ex-soldiers, and to his lost cause."[36]

To the house on "S" Street came strangers in the spirit of pilgrimage; they stood outside, gazed at the house in awe, as upon a shrine. Democratic leaders of the liberal type, liberals of all kinds from all over the world, came to call on him as on a man who, still living, is ensainted. Wilson, as he grew weaker, had periods of resignation, gentleness. He liked to receive friends who had associations with his youth or had known his parents; liked to talk about his father, the Reverend Joseph Ruggles Wilson; liked to recall old familiar scenes. In his room were mementoes of Princeton; near by him always a Bible, rather more for recollections it conjured up of his youth in a clergyman's family, than for any consolation about his personal future.

Bruised and faded, he clung to his iris, thought of himself as the spiritual leader of a cause only temporarily lost. "From the messages I get," he said to a friend,[37] "I realize that I am everywhere regarded as the foremost leader of liberal thought in the world." But — "I'm helpless, Kerney, this left side is gone." And, as Kerney left, "I hope God will bless you and

36 Mark Sullivan, in the New York *Herald Tribune* and other newspapers, November 12, 1918.
37 James Kerney, October 23, 1923.

© Harris & Ewing.

Wilson just before the beginning of his decline. Taken at
the time of the Paris Conference.

Wide World Photo.

One of the last photographs taken of President Wilson.

your family with good health and every happiness."
That was one of the last callers he had. He died February 3, 1924.

A Presbyterian of simple antecedents, his kin buried in small-town churchyards here and there, himself the owner of a lot he had acquired long ago in the Presbyterian cemetery at Princeton — it was the only real estate he owned — he was buried in a great Episcopal Cathedral still under construction at Washington, in the expectation that his presence might start an American Westminster Abbey.

1914

Henry Ford Makes a Statement to the Newspapers and Immediately Becomes as Universally Known as the Ford Car. A Lawsuit Over the Wright Brothers' Aviation Patents Leads to Several Consequences, One of Them Regrettable. Wireless Communication Makes Epochal Advances. A Great Inventor and Industrialist Dies. Drying Up the Navy — and the Angry Controversy That Followed. Secretary of State Bryan, Filling the Rôle of Conciliator, Is the Target for Harsh Words. The Problem of the Unemployed. Books and Plays of 1914.

January 5. Henry Ford, virtually unknown (at that time) manufacturer of the best known automobile — its trade slogan, "Ford, The Universal Car," was familiar to people everywhere on the globe — gave out a statement to newspapers:

Our firm belief is that the division of earnings between capital and labor is not fair, and that labor is entitled to a greater share. We . . . have, therefore, adopted the plan that no man over twenty-two years of age will receive less than $5 for eight hours' work. We have estimated our earnings for the coming year and are dividing as we go — $10,000,000. It will be in the pay envelope semi-monthly.[1]

Fate of the First Machine That Flew

January 13. Patents held by the Wright brothers, Orville and Wilbur, of Dayton, Ohio, for balancing heavier-than-air flying machines were upheld in the United States Circuit Court of Appeals, as against the claims of Glenn Curtiss, inventor of the Curtiss airplane.

This was an important suit involving valuable patent rights and, of even greater consequence, having a bearing on the allocation of historical credit for invention of

[1] For an account of the extraordinary effect Ford's announcement had on the America of early 1914 see "Our Times," Vol. IV, Ch. 3.

the first flyable airplane. Following an appeal from this decision, Curtiss, in the summer of 1914, obtained from the Smithsonian Museum the airplane which Professor Samuel P. Langley had constructed and attempted to fly, without success, in 1903, and flew it at Hammondsport, N. Y. By some persons, notably the Smithsonian Institution, Curtiss' feat was interpreted as meaning that Langley's machine, which had been completed a few months before the Wrights', was the first of record capable of sustained flight. However, most qualified authorities were not convinced that the Hammondsport trials demonstrated the practicability of the Langley machine, as it was at the time its inventor tried to make it fly, nor did they assent that to Langley belonged the title of primacy in the creation of heavier-than-air aviation. As one commentator put it: "After the Wrights, through experiments carried on over many years, had developed the technique of flying, it became possible for a skilled aviator to fly Langley's old machine or even a barn-door if a powerful engine were attached to it."

A greatly to be deplored result of the Smithsonian's permitting Curtiss to remove Langley's historic plane from the Museum, and conduct experiments with it at a time when he was engaged in litigation with the Wrights, was the decision Orville Wright thereafter made to send his and his brother's earliest plane, the first one to fly, out of the country, to the South Kensington Museum in London.

The First Radio Broadcast

January 28. Wireless communication was established between Germany and the United States. Kaiser Wilhelm sent the first despatch transmitted, a message of greeting to President Wilson.

1914 saw progress also in a companion field of communication — radio telephony. On May 13, the wireless telephone was first used for commercial purposes when the stations in the Wanamaker stores in New York and Philadelphia talked with each other for half an hour. On this day also the first radio broadcast was made, the music from a phonograph being sent by the New York Wanamaker's and picked up by the Philadelphia one.

March 12. George Westinghouse, inventor, died, aged 68. While turbines revolve, incandescent lights burn, and trains run, George Westinghouse will be remembered. Before he was twenty-two years old he had invented the air-brake which made possible high-speed railroad trains (and, later, high-speed heavy-load automobile trucks and busses). His name will always be linked with electric light and power, steam turbines, air springs, and many other advances in the mechanical arts — three hundred patents stood to his credit at the time he died. His mechanical and organizing abilities brought him to the head of corporations using capital by the hundred millions and numbering employees by tens of thousands; yet every workman in his plants knew that "the old man" could take his tools and beat him at his job. He was the first great employer to put in effect the Saturday half-holiday, and he never had a dispute or a strike in forty years. Hard work, justice, and honor were the standards of his life. When he was buried the coffin was carried to the cemetery by eight gray old veterans who had been with him since the shops were started in Turtle Creek Valley, near Pittsburgh. His widow survived him less than three months.

A Tempest in a Wine Bottle

April 5. Secretary of the Navy Josephus Daniels issued an order forbidding the use of alcoholic liquor in the Navy, beginning July 1. Instantly there erupted a din of ridicule and praise, mockery and applause, indignation and approval. No event of the first half of 1914 was so lampooned, or so cartooned. The New York *World* pictured Bryan and Secretary Daniels as pirates making Alcohol walk the plank while a sailor hauled up a banner embellished with the words "Grape Juice." "Naval vessels," joked the *Wall Street Journal*, "will now have no port side."

The approval that was voiced, in newspaper editorials and from pulpits, had for the most part a motif of "uplift," and came from persons who wanted desperately to make America an Eden free of temptation and sin. "If the Navy is to be 'dry'," asked one, "why not the Army also? Whisky is admittedly just as ruinous to soldiers as to sailors." "It may hereafter be embarrassing," another set forth, "to our officers when entertaining those of other services to be able to serve no wine. To our minds, this is far less vital than the removal from our young officers of the temptation to excess. Twenty years hence," continued this editor, not dreaming what was to take place before 1934 arrived, "the wineless man-of-war will seem as much a matter of course as does the man-of-war without grog and the cat-o'-nine-tails."

Had the "dry" proclamation been issued by any other Secretary of the Navy than Josephus Daniels there might have been discussion, but the discussion would have been good-tempered and would have concerned itself mainly with the practical working out of the prohibition, just as had happened a few years earlier when the "canteen" was banished from Army posts. But because the order came from Daniels it was seen as an act of militant social reform having broad implications; and immediately a host of critics arose to assail it. To many Americans, especially those not residing in the South and those not having a farm childhood for a background, Daniels, who had been the editor of a small Southern newspaper before Wilson made him a Cabinet secretary, was a person strongly *non grata*. It was the old story of country versus city, bucolic virtuousness versus urban worldliness. Daniels's myriad of detractors quite unreasonably held for

"DROPPING THE PINT"

Harding in this cartoon, from the Brooklyn *Eagle*, April 7, 1914, harked back to the famous one of William II's dismissal of Bismarck as Chancellor.

him an instinctive and acute dislike (a fact which he recognized and actually took joy in). They disliked everything about him, his broad-brimmed black slouch hat, his perennial low collar and black string tie, his black suits, the upward tilt of the corners of his mouth which for them betokened a sense of personal self-satisfaction grossly disproportionate to the basis on which it

rested.[2] This was emotionalism purely, for Daniels as a
war-time Chief of the Navy displayed the qualities necessary to discharge acceptably the important functions
of his trying office. The New York *World*, speaking for
the point of view of Daniels's critics, became almost incoherent in its vain protests against the action Daniels
had taken:

This command proceeds from one man, and is altogether
arbitrary. It summarily invades the rights of thousands of
American citizens. In an affair of social custom it imposes the
will of one man upon many men. It changes without conference or legislation the qualifications necessary to employment
in an important branch of public service. It is not reformatory.
It is revolutionary. It is a shameful reflection upon the honor
of a noble profession.

No doubt there can be navies without wine, just as there
can be navies without ceremony or culture, but there can be
no navy worthy of the name that is clothed in humiliation.
Under this tyrannous rule we send splendid fleets to sea with
their officers tutored like school boys; chaperoned like school
girls.

Bryan Conciliates Colombia

April 17. Secretary of State Bryan signed a treaty
concerted several weeks before with the government of
the Republic of Colombia, settling the dispute between
the two countries that had arisen in 1903 over the part
the United States under President Theodore Roosevelt
had taken in the secession from Colombia of the then
Colombian province of Panama. The treaty contracted
for a payment to Colombia of $25,000,000 in five equal
annual instalments and contained a virtual apology and
a confession of wrongdoing by the United States:

The government of the United States, desiring to put an

2 In furtherance of Wilson's mandate of "strictest neutrality," Daniels had
issued an order that the British marching tune, "It's a long way to Tipperary,"
should not be sung or played by anybody anywhere in the United States Navy,
whereat Frank Cobb, then editor of *The World*, inquired, "Why should a Navy
that has Josephus Daniels for its Secretary wish to sing?"—Ben Dixon Mac-
Neill, Daniels's secretary, *American Mercury*, July, 1933.

end to all disputes and differences with the Republic of Colombia . . . expresses sincere regret for anything that may have
interrupted or altered the relations of cordial friendship existing long between the two nations.

Every administration since the setting up of the Panama Republic had attempted to reach settlement with Colombia. Secretary Hay made overtures, but when Colombia insisted on arbitration Hay refused on the ground
that arbitration might raise the question of Panama's
right to exist as a sovereign state. Later Secretary Knox
tried to restore cordial relations, offering to make Colombia through indirect methods heavy money pay-
ments, totalling in all more than the $25,000,000
stipulated in the Bryan treaty. Knox's efforts came to
nothing.

Disapproval of the Bryan treaty promptly expressed
itself. Some was partisan, the usual pettifogging fault-
finding with an administration's acts by the opposition.
Some was partisan in a better sense, and on better
grounds. This view held that Bryan as Secretary of State
was in duty bound to take no step which should place the
United States Government in an equivocal light before
the bar of history. Bryan might personally feel that
Theodore Roosevelt's aid to Panama at the time Panama
seceded from Colombia, and his "taking" of the canal,
were reprehensible. But officially, as Secretary of State,
he was inhibited from inweaving his private opinions in
a State paper, especially one so permanent in its nature
as a treaty with another nation. It was held further that
Bryan's "confession" had to do with an event that
was still in controversy and about which there had been
no crystallization of view to the effect that Roosevelt's
course had been, as had been charged, either unethical
or tricky. A large body of opinion felt that Colombia's
greedy and vacillating course, while Roosevelt was ne-

gotiating with her for the Canal strip, had caused to be forfeited any rights she had had to indemnification.

The treaty, when it went before the Senate for approval, was not ratified. Thus matters stood until 1921 when the incoming Republican Senate approved it, after deleting the offending phrases.

A "Bush-League" War

April 9. A whaleboat containing a paymaster and a ship's crew took off from the United States ship *Dolphin*, at anchor in Tampico, Mexico, for the Iturbide bridge landing to obtain supplies. None of the men was armed and the boat carried an American flag at bow and stern. While the supplies were being loaded a force of Mexican Federal troops appeared and placed the Americans under arrest. The party was proceeding up one of the streets leading to the prison when they were met by another group of Mexican soldiers under command of an officer of higher rank than the leader of the arresting party. He immediately ordered the return of the American prisoners to the waterfront, where at the end of an hour and a half they were released and permitted to return to their ship. The release was followed by an apology by the commander of the Mexican troops at Tampico and by an expression of regret by President Huerta. General Hureta explained that martial law obtained at the time at Tampico, and that orders had been issued that no one should be allowed to land at the Iturbide bridge. To the commander of the American naval forces in Mexican waters, Admiral Mayo, the apologies seemed an inadequate reparation for the affront and he demanded that the flag of the United States be saluted with special ceremony by the military commander of the port. This President Huerta declined to permit (April 13), whereupon, on April 14, President Wilson ordered the American fleet to Tampico. Events then followed quick and fast along a course which seemed to be leading straight to war. April 15, President Huerta submitted to the Mexican Senate the American demands for a salute to the flag, and was given a vote of approval for the attitude he had taken. April 18, Huerta was given an ultimatum to salute the American flag by six o'clock of the following evening; the ultimatum was ignored. April 19, President Wilson, in a special message to Congress, appealed for Congress' "approval that I should use the armed forces of the United States in such ways and to such an extent as may be necessary to obtain from General Huerta and his adherents the fullest recognition of the rights and dignity of the United States, even amid the distressing conditions now unhappily obtaining in Mexico." April 20, the United States House of Representatives, by a vote of 337 to 37, approved the President's action; the Senate gave its approval, after an excited debate, April 22. April 21, the port of Vera Cruz was captured by United States marines and sailors, with a loss of four dead and twenty wounded; the number of casualties on the Mexican side was estimated in the hundreds.[3] April 22, Mexican rebel leader Carranza, head of the strongest of several revolutionary groups fighting against Huerta, sent a warning to Secretary Bryan that he would consider the seizure of Vera Cruz an act of hostility against the Mexican nation, and act accordingly, unless the United States withdrew immediately from Mexico. April 24, 3,400 American troops and twelve machine guns left Galveston for Vera Cruz, under General Frederick Funston.

[3] Wilson's decision to take Vera Cruz followed receipt of advices from Admiral Mayo that a German ship with a cargo of war supplies for Huerta would arrive at Vera Cruz on the morning of April 21. It was to prevent delivery of these supplies, which in the event of war would be used against the United States, that Wilson gave his order.

Events as they had developed were not to President Wilson's liking. Years of chaos in Mexico following the revolution that had unseated Porfirio Diaz as President, during which American interests in Mexico had suffered and numbers of American lives had been lost, had not swerved Wilson from the policy of "watchful waiting" he had adopted shortly after assuming the Presidency. He was strongly opposed to war. Yet the events at Tampico and Vera Cruz were driving us into war. Into this situation came an offer of mediation by the so-called "A B C" countries of South America — Argentina, Brazil, and Chile. This at once offered a way out of the Mexican imbroglio that would not involve shameful submission to Huerta's arrogance and that would reassure the countries of South and Central America that their fears of American expansion to the southward were groundless. Wilson promptly accepted the offer. The mediatory commission met and while they were engaged in discussion the crisis dissolved. The American flag was not saluted, as Wilson had demanded, but there was no triumph in this for Huerta, who was forced to resign the Presidency of Mexico on July 15.

General Coxey Marches — Again

April 16. "General" Jacob S. Coxey started from Massillon, Ohio, for Washington, D. C., at the head of an army of unemployed. This march, unlike Coxey's first one of 1894, attracted little publicity and, possibly as a consequence, soon disbanded. During the spring of 1914 unemployment was widespread, and in many communities had reached the stage of an acute problem. Coxey's was but one of many "armies" milling about the country, some of them, like Coxey's, planning to march on the Capital.

The tenor of most of the newspaper stories dealing with the unemployed was markedly in contrast with similar accounts having to do with the same phenomenon during the depression of 1929. Put briefly, the newspapers of 1914 were impatient, almost angry, with the jobless of that year, whereas from 1929 onward they prevailingly took the view that the lack of a job might mean anything but not a lack of enterprise on the part of the individual. (To an extent, the "hard-boiled" attitude of reporters in 1914 was a natural reaction against the insolence of the I. W. W. which in that year was pestiferously active.) The Colorado Springs *Gazette*, commenting on "certain temperamental peculiarities displayed by the uninvited guests," said:

These peculiarities are chiefly an extraordinary spirit of pride and independence which lead the unemployed to refuse work when it is offered them, to complain of the quality of food given them at the soup-houses — in short, to demand all the comforts of home at public expense even though they are being fed and cared for as objects of charity. In Portland 500 men who had been receiving shelter at the expense of the city were offered work. Only fifty applied, and of these but twelve appeared at the place where work was furnished. Seven of the twelve quit during the first hour. In other words, five of the unemployed, or 1 per cent, of the total number receiving shelter, remained at work long enough to earn $1.50. At San Francisco, the number of the unemployed is estimated at 15,000, but only 800 of them, or less than 6 per cent, appeared for work when they were given a chance to wield pick and shovel.

Among the few papers to take the stand that something was to be said for the jobless was the Springfield *Republican:* "It is easy to conclude that the unemployed are a worthless lot of loafers, but this is not so; they are of all sorts. . . . One might almost fancy that the aim of the authorities was to make work so repulsive as to drive away as many as possible of the men seeking it. . . . It seems to be assumed that unemployment automatically gives the strength, knack, and endurance needed for hard manual labor, or else that only common laborers can be out of work."

April 20. A strike, led by the United Mine Workers of America, begun in the Colorado coal fields in September, 1913, mainly because of the refusal of the operators to permit the unionization of the mines, flared into a pitched battle at Ludlow in the course of which 25 persons, including 11 children and 2 women, lost their lives, by shooting or burning. Three days later the strikers retaliated by bombing and setting fire to mine properties and on the 28th they killed seven mine guards. The viewpoint of the miners, as set forth by the Denver *Express*, was:

Mothers and babies were crucified at Ludlow on the cross of human liberty. They tried to help their men folk rise in Rockefeller-ruled southern Colorado. Their crucifixion was effected by the operators' paid gunmen who have worn militia uniforms less than a week. The dead will go down in history as the hero victims of the burnt offering laid on the altar of [the] great god greed. With the operators enlisting gun-fighters in Denver today the end is not in sight.

That of the owners, by the New York *Sun:*

Unfortunately, a generation of truckling to the violent striker had bred in labor ranks a belief that the harrying of rival workers and the spoiling of plants was the strikers' accorded right. The words meant as a warning were taken up by the labor leaders as a challenge. Rifles and ammunition were distributed among the strikers. Inevitable bloodshed followed. The events in Colorado should lead to a re-awakening of consciousness of justice and individual rights.

From the inception of the strike eight months before there had been frequent outbreaks of violence, resulting in deaths and injuries. Following the violences of late April, Federal troops were sent to the district, where they remained until through the intercession of President Wilson the strike was ended in September, 1914.

April 21. Water was let into the Cape Cod Canal for the first time.

"Mother's Day"

May 7. A resolution introduced in the House of Representatives by Congressman (later Senator) Thomas Heflin of Alabama, providing that the second Sunday in May be designated "Mother's Day," was passed. On May 8, the Senate approved it and President Wilson issued a proclamation calling on the public to display the American flag "as a public expression of our love and reverence for the mothers of our country."

The idea took hold, and every year since has seen a widening observance of "Mother's Day." A development which the public has had to accept, as a small evil, has been the commercialization of the day by vendors of various sorts. Through advertisements in newspapers, talks over the radio, and even through the sending of personal letters, practically everybody is advised, a day or two ahead of time, that "Mother's Day" is coming and that the purchase of gifts is in order. The telegraph and cable companies, to facilitate the flow of sentiment, with profit to themselves, prepare ready-made messages, some of them in verse, so that all a patron has to do is pick out the one he likes best.

One worthwhile result of Heflin's resolution has been the directing of serious thought to the high mortality rate of mothers at child-birth, which in America is more than double that of other civilized countries, and the taking of steps to ameliorate that condition.

A Great German Ship — and Its Fate

May 14. The Hamburg-American liner *Vaterland*, largest ship ever built, left Cuxhaven on her maiden

voyage, reaching New York May 21. She was 950 feet
long, had 100 feet beam, a tonnage of 54,500, and a
total carrying capacity of more than 5,000. Her only
rival as mistress of the seas was the British Cunarder
Aquitania (49 feet shorter and in other dimensions cor-
respondingly smaller than the *Vaterland* but a colossus
among ships nevertheless), which sailed for New York on
her first transatlantic trip shortly after the *Vaterland*
left Germany. The *Vaterland* was destined to make but

The *Aquitania*.

two trips for her German owners. From August, 1914,
onward she was interned in New York Harbor, and
when the United States declared war on Germany in
April, 1917, she was taken over, renamed the *Leviathan*,
and used as a transport carrying the American Expeditionary Forces to Europe.

May 30.   A despatch from Berlin (in the New York
Times) pictured the Kaiser as delighted with a new invention: "It is a cinematographic contrivance, known as
'live targets,' which enables a person to shoot film repro-
ductions of human beings, animals, aeroplanes, or other
animate objects. He took 300 shots at Doeberitz this
week, and was so delighted with his experience that he has

ordered the apparatus installed in several cadet schools and naval training ships."

June 15. At Chicago the tango and hesitation and other extremes in dancing were put under a ban by the General Federation of Women's Clubs at the biennial convention. Suggestive stories in magazines also were disapproved in resolutions adopted.

June 15. Congress, at the request of President Wilson, repealed the clause in the Panama Canal Tolls Act of 1912 exempting American vessels from the payment of tolls.[4]

June 28. The Archduke Francis Ferdinand, heir to the Austrian throne, and his wife were assassinated at Sarajevo, Bosnia.[5]

July 31. Early morning cables announced the closing for an indefinite period, because of the beginning World War, of the London Stock Exchange, followed by similar action on every other important Stock Exchange in the world. Until nearly 10 A.M. the New York Stock Exchange refused to follow suit; but evidence submitted by international houses of an utterly overwhelming mass of foreign selling orders, cabled for execution "at the market" on the only open stock market of the world, settled the question. The New York Exchange suspended business "until further notice." It did not reopen until November 28, and then only for bonds; even when stock transactions were resumed, on December 12, all sales were required to be made for cash. Not until April 1, 1915, was unrestricted trading again permitted.

August 6. Mrs. Ellen Axson Wilson, first wife of President Wilson, died. (See p. 38.)

---

[4] See "Our Times," Vol. IV, for an account of the events leading up to this action.

[5] For an account of how news of this event came to America, see Vol. IV.

August 15.   The Panama Canal was formally opened to commerce.

September 26.   President Wilson signed the Act

One who does not view with alarm.

Webster in the New York *Globe,* August 6, 1914, thought that school children did not share in the general concern felt for Americans stranded in Europe by the war.

creating the "Federal Trade Commission," a body having for its function the policing of business.

The Books of 1914

"Our Mr. Wrenn," by Sinclair Lewis. . . . "Neighborhood Stories," by Zona Gale. . . . "The Titan," by Theodore Dreiser. . . . "Personality Plus," by Edna Ferber. . . . "The Woman in the Alcove," by Jennette Lee. . . . "The Hands of Esau," by Margaret Deland. . . . "Mothers and Children," by Dorothy Canfield Fisher. . . . "Penrod," Booth Tarkington's stories of boyhood; "the book went like wildfire." . . . "The Lay Anthony," by Joseph Hergesheimer. . . . "The Witch," by Mary Johnston. . . . "Marryers," by Irving Bacheller. . . . "Perch of the Devil," a romance of Montana, by Gertrude Atherton; in the same year appeared Mrs. Atherton's "California — An Intimate

Edna Ferber. Robert Herrick.

History." . . . "Love and the Soul Maker," by Mary Austin. . . . "Aliens," by William McFee. . . . "Kazan," by James Oliver Curwood. . . . "Saturday's Child," by Kathleen Norris. . . . "Charis Sees It Through," by Margaret Widdemer. . . . "Clark's Field," by Robert Herrick, an exposure of the "soullessness of the pampered, overprotected American women of the prosperous middle class." . . . "The Clarion," by Samuel Hopkins Adams. . . . "Cap'n Dan's Daughter," by Joseph C. Lincoln. . . . W. D. Howells was still dean of American letters, but all he produced in 1914 were a fantasy on Stratford-on-Avon and his reminiscences "Years of My Youth."

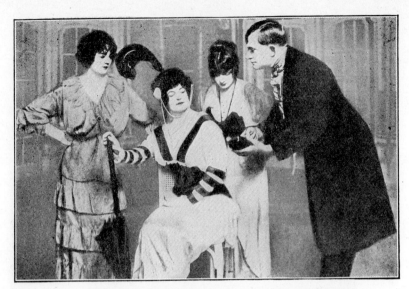

Raymond Hitchcock in a scene from the "Beauty Shop."

From a photograph by White.

Edith and Mabel Taliaferro in "Young Wisdom."

The Theatre in 1914

Maude Adams was appearing in J. M. Barrie's "The Legend of Leonora." . . . William Collier in "A Little Water on the Side." . . . Bertha Kalich in "Rachel." . . . Alice Brady in "The Things That Count." . . . Elsie Ferguson in "The Strange Woman," a satire on village life. . . . Frank Craven in his own play, "Too Many Cooks." . . . Laurette Taylor in three one-act plays by J. Hartley Manners, "Just as Well," "Happiness," and "The Day of Dupes." . . A farce-comedy, "The Rule of Three," was criticized by *The Theatre Magazine:* "Divorce as a subject for farcical treatment would hardly in any circumstances commend itself to audiences of the kind managers would seek to bring to their theatres. Much is made in this play of a child who speaks of and addresses its real father, the first husband of the mother, as father, the second as daddy, and the third as papa." . . . Billie Burke in "Jerry." . . . Raymond Hitchcock in a musical comedy, "The Beauty Shop." . . . Lew Fields in "The High Cost of Loving." . . . Julia Sanderson and Donald Brian in a musical play, "The Girl from Utah." . . . George M. Cohan's play, "The Miracle Man," with Gail Kane and William H. Thompson. . . . Fritzi Scheff and Charlotte Greenwood in "Pretty Mrs. Smith." . . . "Pygmalion," a play by George Bernard Shaw, "in one of his most extravagant moods," with Mrs. Patrick Campbell as star. . . . A revival of "Diplomacy," with a cast "scintillating with the names of stars," among them William Gillette, Blanche Bates, and Marie Doro.

1915

An Evangelist, Appropriately Named Sunday, Whose Unconventional Hortatory Style Attracted Both Penitents and Public Attention. The Telephone Expands Its Range. A Note about the Early Charlie Chaplin. Jess Willard Defeats Jack Johnson. Emergence of Two Political Figures Destined for a Long Stay in the Spotlight, One the Scion of a Family of Wealth, the Other the Son of a New York Truckman. Theodore Roosevelt Sued for Libel. Books and Plays of 1915.

January. 1915 was the Rev. "Billy" Sunday's big year. At Philadelphia, where he preached nightly for several weeks to crowds that overflowed his gigantic "tabernacle," he became more a topic for discussion than the World War. Philadelphians were of two minds about him, strongly pro and strongly contra. In *The North American*, a biographical sketch recited:

Twenty-nine years ago, on a midsummer Sunday afternoon, at South Clark and Van Buren Streets, Chicago, Ill., "Billy" Sunday, the ballplayer, sat with a crowd of his fellows at the edge of the sidewalk listening to the coaxing, pleading, persuasive melodies of a "melodeon" in a gospel wagon close by; in the wagon was Harry Monroe.

And the same night, in the old Pacific Garden Mission, "Billy" Sunday heard another simple exhortation, for Harry Monroe was a street worker for the mission, and Monroe's pleading in the afternoon had led "Billy" to seek solace for his troubled thoughts with the same kind of gospel cheer.

As he lingered, hesitating whether he should go in where he might hear the preaching, a veteran woman mission worker, Mrs. Sarah D. Clark, put her arm affectionately around Sunday's neck and whispered in his ear: "The Master loves you."

"Billy" Sunday had then, and he has now, the heart of a woman. He went forward like a shot from home plate to first base, and dropt at the altar, professing salvation.

Mrs. Clark had been waiting for a night like that for a long, long time. Hers was a simple exhortation, the simplest kind of pleading, in the simplest kind of language, but it went straight home to "Billy" Sunday; for "Billy" had been knocked about since he was a lad of seven years, doing a man's work in the field, sweeping out sixteen rooms in the public school in Nevada, Iowa; a little later, milking several cows, taking care of several Shetland ponies, and — when he had time — driving the hearse for the only furniture-dealer in the town.

When a feller needs a friend.

As Briggs, in the Cleveland *Plain Dealer,* viewed the advent of the New Year.

"Good-by, boys," "Billy" Sunday said to his baseball team-mates later, "I'm going to Jesus Christ."

And "Billy" has been on the job ever since.

Those who attended Sunday's revivals in Philadelphia listened to exhortations of a unique sort; unique in language; unique in the whirling-dervish and baseball-pitcher manner of their delivery. His statements, as taken down by a newspaper reporter, included:

Do you know what a decollete gown is? It's a dress with a collar around your waist. . . .

I'll give you hell enough before you get through. I'll give you all the hell in the Bible. The Lord put it there; and if you don't like it, fix it up with the Lord, not with me. . . .

I don't give a rap whether you like my preaching or not. You'll like it if you're decent, and if you desire to make other people decent, as I am trying to do. . . .

When I am at Heaven's gates I'll be free from old Philly's blood. I can see now the day of judgment, when the question of Philadelphia and of me is taken up by God:

© *Underwood & Underwood.*

Billy Sunday with Ma Sunday and their three sons.

"You were down in Philly, weren't you, Billy?" the Lord will ask me.

And I'll say to him, "Yes, sir, Lord, I was there."

"Did you give them my message of salvation, Billy?"

"I gave them your message, Lord. I gave it to them, the best way I could and as I understood it. You go get the files of the Philadelphia papers."

And the Lord will say, "Come on in, Bill; you're free from Philadelphia's blood." . . .

You can't pray "Thy Kingdom come," and then sit down at

some bridge-whist party, or look at God through the bottom of a beer-mug.

Every night during the revival Sunday would say, "Why, if I thought I could get any nearer God by kneeling or taking off my coat, I'd do it." And suiting his action to his word he would tear the coat from his back and fling it about to give emphasis to his utterances.

"Billy Sunday's way is coarse, rude, vulgar — but it works," remarked *The Independent*, whereupon *Life* commented cynically:

> What makes you believe that it works, and what is the exact condition of those upon whom it has worked? How does a "convert" differ from any ordinary person? Is he better? Is he worse? When you say it "works," maybe you mean that Billy Sunday draws a crowd.

January 2. The United States Senate, by a vote of 50 to 1, passed a bill providing a literacy test for immigrants. President Wilson vetoed it. Similar bills approved by Congress in the past had been vetoed by Presidents Cleveland and Taft.

"Hello" Across the Continent

January 25. Transcontinental telephone service was inaugurated. The event duplicated the one of March 10, 1876, at Boston, when the telephone was used for the first time. In 1915, the conversation, like that of 1876, was between Alexander Graham Bell, inventor of the telephone, and his assistant, Dr. Thomas A. Watson. Bell at New York, speaking into an exact copy of the 1876 instrument, said to Watson at San Francisco: "Mr. Watson, come here, I want you." In 1876, Watson had been in the next room, and came at once; in 1915, he was obliged to reply that it would take four days of rapid railroad travel for him to reach Bell's side. The difference was a measure of the progress that had been made in the forty years of the telephone's existence.

Many engineers co-operated for the successful accomplishment of trans-continental telephony, but it is not too much to say that success would have been impossible had it not been for the "loading-coils" invented by Dr. Michael I. Pupin of Columbia University, which were placed at intervals along the line. The function the Pupin coils fulfilled was to give "body" to a circuit and thereby make it possible for an electric impulse to be transmitted along it without diminishing in force. The effect may be likened to the play of children in whipping a wave along a rope. If the rope is too light the wave travels only a short distance and dies. If a heavier one is used (but not too heavy) the undulation can be made to travel a considerable distance. Hardly less important than the coils themselves was to know where to insert them along a circuit — if not placed exactly where they should be placed they were useless. It took Pupin years to solve this problem but finally he did it, with a formula taking into account all the complicated factors involved.

The make-up of the New York-San Francisco circuit included 3,400 miles of copper wire weighing 5,920,-000 pounds, supported on 130,000 poles (only ten miles of the circuit were underground), the whole representing an investment of over two million dollars. Three conversations could be carried on at once, without interfering one with another, and a number of telegraph circuits could be formed.

Talking to Honolulu

More spectacular even than this epochal advance in wire telephony were several achievements in the field of wire-*less* communication. On April 30, Naval wireless experimenters at Washington talked with the Panama Canal Zone. On July 27, radio-telegraphic service with Japan was inaugurated. On September 29, occurred the most phenomenal exploit since Marconi's transmittal of the letter "S" across the Atlantic thirteen years before.

On that day President Theodore Vail of the American Telephone and Telegraph Company in the offices of the company in New York City spoke into a telephone transmitter. From New York his voice was carried over wires to the radio-telegraphic station of the Navy at Arlington near Washington, D. C., where it was "put on the air." By pre-arrangement, at the moment President Vail began to speak, the chief engineer of the company, J. J. McCarty, at the Mare Island Navy Yard at San Francisco, adjusted a set of head-phones and "listened in." Faintly, and with its clearness marred somewhat by static, McCarty heard Vail's voice, was able to distinguish his words. Newspapermen present at the trial, both in New York and San Francisco, rushed off stories to their papers telling that wireless telephony had spanned the continent. It was not until four or five hours later, when some of the newspapers containing accounts of the event were on the street, that it became known that Vail's voice had been heard not only at San Francisco, but also at a point two thousand miles farther to the westward, in the Hawaiian Islands. While preparations were being made for the New York-Mare Island test, it had been decided to send one of McCarty's assistants, Lloyd Espenchied, to Honolulu, more in the hope than the expectation of results. Espenchied, who took with him only a receiving outfit, set up his instruments in a tiny hut at the foot of a towering antennæ mast on the shore at Pearl Harbor. Sitting there before his complicated apparatus of bulbs and coils and dials, he, too, heard Vail's voice coming to him through the air from New York almost 5,000 miles away. Lacking a way of communicating at once with McCarty or Vail, it was not until several hours had passed that he was able to send a cable to his associates from Honolulu advising them of the double success of the experiment.

February 2. Werner Van Horn, a German-American, made an unsuccessful attempt to dynamite the bridge across the St. Croix River.[1]

February. "Going to see Charlie Chaplin has become a habit all over the country. With his doleful countenance, his heavy feet, his characteristic French kick, his diminutive moustache, and his ridiculous actions, he has earned a place all his own in the realm of motion pictures. And it is only a few months ago that he walked unannounced into the office of Mack Sennet, director of the Keystone Company, and asked for a tryout as a comedian." — *Photoplay Magazine.*

March 14. Lincoln Beachy, aviator, was killed during a spectacular flight at the San Francisco Exposition.

Another "Battle of the Century"

April 5. Jess Willard of Kansas won the heavyweight pugilistic championship of the world from Jack Johnson, at Havana, Cuba. In the opinion of many fight followers Johnson was the greatest heavyweight of his time. Several inches over six feet in height, and weighing when in fighting trim something over two hundred pounds, he was a magnificent exemplar of physical power and prowess — an antagonist not for a man but a gorilla. A panther, in fact, Johnson was in the ring. His movements were like a panther's — graceful and incredibly swift and sure. His very nature was feline.

[1] For an account of the attempts by German agents and sympathizers to prevent by methods of violence the production and despatch of munitions and other war supplies for the Allies, see Chapter 8.

Every newspaper account of his fights spoke of his "golden smile" — there must have been several ounces of gold in his jaws — as well as the badinage he carried on with onlookers while in the ring. When fighting Jeffries in 1910[1a] he leaned his weight for a moment on the shoulders of the outclassed and tiring "white hope" and jeered at another old-time fighter, Jim Corbett, occupying a ring-side seat. "Jim," he said, "this big bum can't fight any better than you could." But Johnson smiled his golden smile and toyed with his opponents only when he knew they were not a match for him. Whenever a blow reached him that really hurt the apparent good nature vanished. Then he became a primal force, as dangerous and almost as deadly as a jungle cat braced for the kill.

After winning from Jeffries Johnson was for several years an expatriate, living in London and Paris. The dislike of Johnson in some quarters because of his supremacy over white fighters was intensified, and the groups where it was felt broadened, by Johnson's penchant for white wives, of whom he had had several, one of whom committed suicide. Johnson, before quitting his native land for those parts of Europe where his color was not a handicap but, if anything, an asset, had been locked up several times on charges ranging from disturbing the peace to bigamy.

Abroad, Johnson gloried in the adulation almost everywhere showered upon him; but in time even the glamour of the Paris boulevards palled before his longing to be back among his kind on the South Side of Chicago.

Best known, because of his picturesqueness, among the American heavyweight boxers of the day was a gigantic, gangling ex-cow-puncher, Jess Willard.

[1a] See "Our Times," Vol. III.

Willard was enormously strong — he could perform prodigies of strength such as bending a silver dollar with his fingers — but as a fighter he was only mediocre, not to be classed with Johnson even in the let-down condition of the negro after long dedication to the night life of Europe. Willard was not a "natural"; it wasn't instinct with him to fight, and what he knew about fighting had been painstakingly learned. He was too amiable, too innately good-natured, too reluctant to cause pain ever to be a "killer." Everybody liked Willard, though not many considered him of championship calibre.

To Johnson at Paris, lonesome for the Chicago black belt which was his home, came newspapermen and promoters with the suggestion that he should fight Willard. Johnson assented; quickly the details were arranged. The fight was to take place at Havana, just eighty miles away from the homeland for which Johnson longed.

On reaching Havana, Johnson dismayed his friends and backers by doing practically no training. Instead of going through the usual gymnasium and road work and boxing with sparring partners, Johnson spent most of his days in an automobile, driving about the city with his white wife and a shifting group of chance friends picked up in the lower strata of Cuba's sporting circles.

Complications arose. Cosmopolitan Havana, most tolerant of cities, from regarding Johnson when he first arrived as a curious and interesting phenomenon adding a piquant touch to the capital's Bohemian life, came in a short time to feel irritated with him. His ways, unlike those of the rather punctilious and Chesterfieldian Cuban negro, were annoyingly free-and-easy. By getting into disputes he attracted the wrong sort of attention to himself. His life at Paris had endowed him with a liking for the best restaurants, and it was to the best of Havana's hotels and cafés that he went for breakfast, lunch, dinner, and a ten-o'clock *cena*. That was all right, for the first few days after his arrival. But in time the novelty wore off and Johnson became increasingly *non grata*.

© *International News.*

Johnson vs. Willard fight, 1915.

Head waiters, on seeing him and his vari-colored retinue appear, became panic-stricken. They were timid about refusing him service lest in his anger he should do to them what he did to opponents in the ring. On the other hand, if they did admit him many of their white diners would walk out. In time the patience of the Cubans began to run short. Johnson, they concluded, was a for-

ward-pushing negro of a type they knew and disliked —
"*un negro pernicioso.*" So much racial feeling was
aroused that the Government felt compelled to post
soldiers at the race-track where the fight was held, and
to announce that any demonstration by whites or blacks
would be summarily dealt with.

The fight itself amounted to little. For twenty-two
rounds Willard and Johnson milled about under the
scorching Cuban sun, without either delivering a blow
with real force behind it. Then in the twenty-third
round something happened, opinions differ as to what —
whether a blow by Willard, or a sun-stroke, or whatever.
At all events Johnson was seen to sink slowly to the
canvas floor of the ring, stretch himself out at full
length — and raise his arms as if to shade his eyes from
the sun! Over him the referee counted ten, and then
held up Willard's right arm in token that the championship had changed hands. Once more it was in the keeping of a white man.

A short time after losing to Willard, Johnson returned
unobtrusively to the United States and made his way to
his beloved Chicago. He never fought again, though he
attended fights and saw his successors as heavyweight
champion — all white men — fight for purses running
into the millions of dollars. In 1933 he was conductor
of his own jazz orchestra and the father of the theory
that the bass viol is the noblest of all musical instruments.

Chicago Elects a Mayor

April 6. Emergence of a national figure destined to
a long and colorful and controversial place in the sun of
American politics, in the course of which he was to be
given the sobriquet "Big Bill the Builder," to fight a
bloodless war against King George of England, to intro-

duce a menagerie into political campaigning, to forestall the German Nazis in burning books he did not like — William Hale Thompson, of Chicago. "It is a woman's victory," exclaimed the happy wife of Chicago's new Mayor. "It is a Republican victory," said the equally jubilant Chicago Republicans, which "means a united party and a landslide for a Republican President in 1916." "It means," announced the Mayor-elect himself, grimly, that "the crooks had better move out of town before I am inaugurated." It is history that the crooks did not move out.

Alfred E. Smith Emerges

April 6. A State Constitutional Convention assembled at Albany, N. Y.; Elihu Root was elected President. The convention was called to frame a new draft of the State's fundamental law, which had become so bulky, involved, and antiquated that the lawyers expert in its mysteries were uniformly growing wealthy.[2] In the end the convention accomplished little except to suggest ideas that a delegate to the convention, later Governor, Alfred E. Smith, was to develop and bring to fulfillment a decade late. "Of all the men in the convention, Alfred E. Smith was the best informed on the business of the State of New York," said Elihu Root, after the convention had adjourned. "He was the most useful man in the convention," admitted George W. Wickersham, who had been Republican floor leader and was a former United States Attorney General.

April 19. A suit against ex-President Roosevelt for libel, brought by William Barnes, Jr., began at Syracuse, N. Y. The suit grew out of a statement issued by Roosevelt on July 22, 1914, which Barnes considered a reflection on his character. Barnes, who was Republican boss

2 "Alfred E. Smith," Henry F. Pringle.

of New York State, and Murphy, the Democratic boss, had purposes and interests, said the statement, that were "fundamentally identical" —

When the issue between popular rights and corrupt and machine-ruled government is clearly drawn, the two bosses will always be found on the same side openly or covertly, giving one another such support as can with safety be rendered. . . . It is idle for a man to pretend that he is against machine politics unless he will . . . openly and by name attack Mr. Barnes and Mr. Murphy.

Next day Barnes entered suit, asking $50,000 damages.

Roosevelt's hosts of enemies were gleeful with anticipation. Barnes's counsel, William M. Ivins, boasted to Elihu Root: "I am going to nail Roosevelt's hide to the fence." Root replied: "Ivins, let me give you a piece of advice. I know Roosevelt and you want to be very sure that it is Roosevelt's hide you get on the fence." As it turned out, Root was right. Barnes's lawyers, on the hunt for scandal, raked through Roosevelt's past, but without turning up anything of consequence. When questioned about the corporation contributions to his campaign in 1904, which the Democrats had relentlessly and without success been agitating off and on ever since that year, Roosevelt gave so convincing an exhibition of innocence that he actually emerged from the ordeal with heightened prestige. His defense was to the effect that no wrongdoing had occurred, but if there had he himself had not known about it. In a word, Roosevelt ran away with the trial, got vast fun out of it, tied the plaintiff's lawyers into knots and then gently untied them, sermonized on his philosophy of politics. The trial ended, May 22, with a verdict declaring Roosevelt's criticism of Barnes truthful, which constituted not only vindication for Roosevelt but congé for Barnes from dominance in New York Republican politics.

Some months later a friend in the course of a casual talk with Roosevelt asked him what sum the jury had awarded him. "Would you mind saying that again?" Roosevelt demanded, a look of glee spreading over his face. The friend complied. "My dear fellow" — Roosevelt's voice rose to its highest squeak — "*I* was the de-fen-dant."[3]

June 8. Secretary of State William Jennings Bryan resigned. (See Ch. 6.) June 23. Robert Lansing was appointed to succeed him.

July 8. To guarantee neutrality, United States naval authorities took control of the German wireless station at Sayville, L. I. (See Ch. 2.)

July 16. For the first time the Panama Canal was used by United States battleships, the *Missouri*, *Ohio*, and *Wisconsin* passing through.

July 24. 852 people were drowned when the excursion steamer *Eastland* turned over at her pier in Chicago.

Intervention in Haiti

July 27. Trouble broke out afresh in Haiti. A revolutionary mob led by Dr. Rosalvo Bobo stormed the Presidential residence at Port au Prince, driving President Vilbrun Guillaume Sam to seek refuge at the French legation. In retaliation, Guillaume's aides, still in control of the government, killed 160 political prisoners. Next day the revolutionists routed President Guillaume from his hiding place, tortured him to death, and dragged his mutilated corpse through the streets.

These disorders climaxed several years of struggle between Haitian factions, during which many lives had been lost, business brought to a standstill. Haiti with its 90-per cent negro population was fast sinking into sav-

[3] "Theodore Roosevelt," Henry F. Pringle.

agery; effective government had practically ceased. Protests over injury to their nationals by France, England, and other countries of Europe, and over Haiti's indifference to her financial commitments, went unheeded. There was talk of armed intervention in the Republic's affairs by France.

In this situation, and following the killing of President Guillaume and the rioting that ensued, Admiral Caperton, aboard the U. S. Cruiser *Washington* at anchor in the harbor of Port au Prince, sent a force ashore to establish order. Continuing anarchy throughout Haiti's half of the Island caused Caperton next to proclaim martial law in the territory occupied by his forces. A month later, September 16, he signed a treaty with the new President, Sudre Artiguenave, providing for American supervision over Haitian finances and in general for a virtual American protectorate over the country. The Customs had been taken over by the Americans and Caperton forced the Haitian Senate to approve the treaty by withholding funds required for necessary public services.

Immediately the Americans embarked on a program for improving the country. A native gendarmerie officered by Americans was organized and quickly became an efficient police force. Banditry was stamped out. Modern roads were constructed, and cities and towns were given the first thorough cleaning they had had since Columbus first visited the island. For one or another reason, however, the natives did not take kindly to the new order and never ceased to complain against it. Possibly their greatest cause for resentment was the unwillingness of the members of the American Intervention to accept them on a plane of social equality.

The occupation, intended at first to continue only until the Haitian Government was strong enough to stand by itself, was prorogued, after the first treaty expired in 1925, and was still in effect in August, 1933. In that month an "executive agreement" was reached between the Presidents of the United States and Haiti calling for the retirement of the Intervention on October 1, 1934.

July 30. Charles Becker, formerly police-lieutenant of New York City, convicted of complicity in the murder of Herman Rosenthal, was electrocuted at Sing Sing.[4]

August 10. The Plattsburg (N. Y.) camp for training American citizens for national defence was inaugurated. (See Ch. 9.)

August 17. Leo M. Frank was lynched. He had been convicted and sentenced to death for the murder of Mary Phagan, a girl employed in his Atlanta factory. Because Frank was a Jew, because of the morbid circumstances surrounding the death of the victim, and because of the skill and financial resources of the counsel defending him, the trial, and its subsequent reviewings in the higher courts on up to the Supreme Court of the United States itself, held the attention of the entire country. To the 1910's the Frank case and the Becker one were what the murders of Stanford White and Governor Steunenberg were to the 1900's, and the Bobby Franks and the Hall-Mills murders were to the 1920's.

Everywhere in the country, except the South and particularly the region about where the crime had been committed and the trial held, the belief was strong, in spite of the court's decision, that Frank was innocent.

While Frank was in prison awaiting execution of his sentence, Governor Slaton of Georgia, shortly before his term of office expired, commuted Frank's sentence of death to life imprisonment. Intense indignation swept over the State. A fellow-prisoner attacked Franks and

[4] For an account of the famous Becker trial, see "Our Times," Vol. IV.

seriously injured him. While he was recuperating he was forcibly removed from the prison by a group of twenty-five men, who took him to Marietta, the home of Mary Phagan, where they hanged him.

The lynching fanned into new flame for a moment the old animosities between North and South of fifty years before. "Georgia has vindicated her Kultur, too," observed the New York *World* with cutting sarcasm. Much of the comment of Northern papers was in like vein. In the South, while few reputable editors condoned the lynching, the feeling was general that the act was justifiable on the grounds as stated by the Marietta *Journal:* "The people demanded that the verdict of the court be carried out, and saw to it that it was. We insist they were, and are, law-abiding citizens of Georgia."

No new evidence bearing on the guilt or innocence of Frank has ever been revealed.

October 6. The engagement of President Wilson and Mrs. Edith Bolling Galt of Washington, D. C., was announced.

October 9. Gil Anderson, driving a Stutz car 350 miles at the rate of 102.6 miles an hour, won the Astor Cup and made a new automobile record at Sheepshead Bay, N. Y.

October 14. Forty-one persons were killed and 101 wounded in a raid by Zeppelins on London.

October 15. A $500,000,000 loan agreement between the British and French Governments and American bankers was signed in the office of J. P. Morgan & Co., New York. The amount asked for originally was $1,000,000,000, to be guaranteed jointly by the French and British governments, and was to be used in paying for munitions and other supplies bought by the Allies in the United States. American bankers demurred at making so large a loan; it was the largest ever floated in any country up to that time.   Protests against the loan came from pro-Germans and others.

October 19.   The United States recognized Gen. Venustiano Carranza as President of Mexico; eight Central and South American republics took similar action. The following day an embargo was declared on the ex-

Photographs by Underwood & Underwood.

British policeman (*inset*) spreading the alarm of a Zeppelin raid, *and* The damage done by a German Zeppelin in London.

portation of arms to Mexico, except to territory controlled by Carranza.

November 1.   The Arizona Anti-Alien law, providing that 80 per cent of the employees of any concern must be Americans, was declared unconstitutional by the U. S. Supreme Court.

November 7.   40,000 men paraded in a demonstration against the closing of saloons on Sundays in Chicago.

November 14.   Booker T. Washington, negro educator, died.   Of him, *Life* said:

He is the most lasting American who has died in a long time. He never held a political office, never influenced an election that is known of, never yielded to the delusion that salvation comes by votes; but where shall one match in a contemporary career the sum of his accomplishment in thirty-five years for this country? Mourn for Booker Washington! It is to lament that his years were not more, but they sufficed for a prodigious work.

December 10.   Henry Ford made his millionth automobile.

The Books of 1915

"The Harbor," by Ernest Poole, for which he was awarded the Pulitzer prize. . . . "Spoon River Anthology," by Edgar Lee Masters. . . . "The Genius," by Theodore Dreiser. . . . "Roast Beef Medium," by Edna Ferber, and in the same year her "Emma McChesney & Co.," which was called a "perfect picture of the tired business woman." . . . "The Song of the Lark," by Willa Cather — "a thing finished, sound and noble." "Every Soul Hath Its Song," by Fannie Hurst. . . . "Aunt Jane," by Jennette Lee. . . . "Around Old Chester," by Margaret Deland. . . . "Hillsboro People," and "The Bent Twig," by Dorothy Canfield Fisher, described by *The New Republic* as "gaily resolute, hopeful and unafraid — and wise as well." . . . "K," by Mary Roberts Rinehart. . . . "The Turmoil," by Booth Tarkington. . . . "Mountain Blood," by Joseph Hergesheimer. . . . "The Moral Obligation to Be Intelligent," by John Erskine. . . . "A Far Country," by Winston Churchill; *The Atlantic Monthly* called it "a thoughtful, broad-minded work." . . . "The Pentecost of Calamity," by Owen Wister. . . . "The Rivet in Grandfather's Neck," by James

Branch Cabell, a "story of the old South and its stiff-necked loyalty to its traditions." . . . "Speaking of Operations," by Irvin Cobb. . . . "Hempfield," by David Grayson (Ray Stannard Baker). . . ."Ar-

Theatre Collection, New York Public Library.

In the movies.

Left: Lillian Gish in "The Birth of a Nation." Right: Charlie Chaplin, who had become a habit with the country.

cadian Adventures with the Idle Rich," by Stephen Leacock. . . . "The Three Sisters," by May Sinclair. . . . Patrick Magill's "Children of the Dead End," which J. B. Kerfoot in *Life* called "one of the peculiar products of our time — a literature of essentially autobiographic fiction dealing interpretatively with the life of the lowly." . . . Julian Street's "big, fat American wander-book," "Abroad at Home."

The Theatre in 1915

"Hello, Broadway!" a musical show and burlesque of the season's plays, by George M. Cohan, with the author and Mr. William Collier in the cast. . . . "The Phantom Rival," a drama based on dream, adapted from the Hungarian, with a company headed by Laura Hope Crews and Leo Ditrichstein. . . . Ina Claire, back from London with what Metcalfe of *Life* described as "a slight taint of the London affected speech," played in "Lady Luxury." . . . Margaret Illington in "The Lie," by Henry Arthur Jones. . . . Hazel Dawn as the prima donna in a musical show "The Debutante.". . . John Barrymore in "Kick In," a melodramatic play about life in the underworld. . . . Marie Dressler in "A Mix Up." . . . "Dancing Around," with Al Jolson as star. . . . "Children of Earth," by Alice Brown, a play about New England life which won a $10,000 prize. . . . John Drew in a revival of "Rosemary." . . . "The Birth of a Nation," big moving-picture undertaking based on Tom Dixon's "The Clansman," covered the Civil War and the Reconstruction.

1916

The Appointment of Louis D. Brandeis to the Supreme Court Starts Angry Controversy. Another Isthmian Canal Is Contemplated. A Raid by Followers of Pancho Villa on an American Border Town Leads to the Sending of a Punitive Expedition into Mexico, which Fails to Catch Villa but Fights a Skirmish with Regular Mexican Troops. The Beginning of Federal Grants to States for Road Building. Purchase of the Danish West Indies. Independence for the Filipinos. Passage of the Adamson Act. The United States Intervenes in Santo Domingo. Books and Plays of 1916.

January 24. The constitutionality of the income tax law was upheld by the United States Supreme Court.

January 28. Louis D. Brandeis was nominated by President Wilson for Associate Justice of the United States Supreme Court to fill the vacancy left by the death of Mr. Justice Lamar. Mr. Brandeis, born in Louisville, Ky., in 1856, had been educated in the Louisville schools, and in Germany and at Harvard. He began the practice of law in Boston in 1879. During the fifteen years prior to his appointment to the Supreme Court his name had been unceasingly in the newspapers in connection with social legislation, law suits affected with public interest, disputes between labor and capital. A nation-wide discussion had been inspired by his statement before the Interstate Commerce Commission in 1911 that with competent management the railroads of the country could save one million dollars a day.

To Wall Street, according to the New York *Sun*, the announcement of Brandeis' nomination came as "a surprise and a shock." Liberals and radicals were elated. Reasons voiced by objectors to Brandeis, as summarized

by the Washington correspondent of the New York
World, Louis Seibold, were:

That Mr. Brandeis is a radical, a theorist, impractical, with
socialistic tendencies.
That he is given to extravagance of utterance, inspired by
prejudice.
That he is a "self-advertiser," seeking personal exploitation.
That he does not possess the "judicial temperament."

Among other protests — space is lacking to print half
of them — was that the appointee was a Jew. Argument
was made that it is doubtful if an Oriental mind can
successfully interpret a system of law which is the
product of Occidental minds.

Defenders of Mr. Brandeis were as numerous and as
zealous as his detractors, and as highly placed. Nine of
eleven members of the faculty of the Harvard Law
School expressed their unqualified approval of the selection.

The Springfield (Mass.) *Republican* saw "supreme
merit" in the nomination:

Unless Mr. Brandeis can be professionally or personally discredited by the enemies he has made, he deserves the favor of
the Senate for the reason that a man of his type on the bench
of the highest court would tend to make every trade-unionist,
every socialist, every anarchist even, more loyal to our government and to American institutions; and that not because
Mr. Brandeis is a trade-unionist, or a socialist, or an anarchist,
but because there are many thousands of citizens who believe
that the court should contain members who can see life from
their point of view and in whose fidelity to democracy they
entertain no shadow of doubt.

After hearings, he was confirmed.

February 10. Secretary of War Lindley M. Garri-
son resigned. To succeed him President Wilson on
March 7 nominated, and the Senate approved, Newton
D. Baker, former Mayor of Cleveland.

From a photograph © Harris & Ewing taken in the fall of 1916.

U. S. Supreme Court.

Top row: left to right: Louis D. Brandeis; Mahlon Pitney; James C. Mc-Reynolds; John H. Clarke. *Lower row: left to right:* William R. Day; Joseph McKenna; Chief Justice E. D. White; Oliver Wendell Holmes; Willis Van Devanter.

February 18. The United States Senate ratified a treaty with Nicaragua under which the United States secured two naval bases and the right to build a canal across Nicaragua, in return for $3,000,000. We already had one canal across the Isthmus of Panama, upon which we had expended more than $400,000,000. Why we should enter into a treaty giving us the right to construct another one at a cost more than double that of the first, gave rise to speculation. The Springfield *Republican* explained:

The acquisition in perpetuity of the Nicaragua Canal route is eminently desirable in safeguarding American interests in transisthmian transportation. The Nicaragua Canal route may never be utilized for a waterway, but . . . if a second canal should be needed the United States should construct it rather than some European Power. The Nicaraguan route becomes a valuable asset, too, in the light of the possibility, more or less remote, that the United States in some future war might lose the Panama Canal to an enemy.

Negotiation of the treaty aroused the hostility of other Central American countries, and two of them, Costa Rica and Salvador, brought suit against Nicaragua in the Central American Court of Justice. Though the suits were successful they were disregarded by Nicaragua and the United States.

March 9. A band of 1500 Mexican soldiers belonging to the forces of the revolutionary General, Pancho Villa, crossed the American border and attacked the town of Columbus, New Mexico, and the adjacent camp of the Thirteenth U. S. Cavalry, killing nine civilians and eight troopers. They were pursued by the American troopers who killed fifty of them on American soil and seventy more on the Mexican side of the border. The pursuit penetrated fifteen miles into Mexico.

The raid on Columbus came as a climax to years of disorders in Mexico during which American citizens and other foreigners had been robbed, kidnaped, murdered, and their property destroyed.[1] The United States had helped the sitting President of Mexico, Venustiano Carranza, into power in the hope that he as the strongest of several revolutionary leaders contending for control might be able to pacify the country. These hopes had been proven vain, and in Carranza the United States found it had raised up against itself a jingo who let no opportunity pass to badger the United States Government and to foster animosity towards it as a means of rallying nationalistic sentiment in Mexico to his support. Immediately, now, Carranza, through his Foreign Secretary,

---

[1] January 10, 1916, nineteen American employees of a mining company were taken from a train near Chihuahua, Mexico, and shot. February 17, the United States Senate received from President Wilson a report showing that 76 Americans had been killed in Mexico in three years (63 in 1915), in addition to 36 killed on American soil by Mexicans.

offered regrets for the murders at Columbus and promised that he would "use the most vigorous means to run
this man [Villa] to earth and avenge his horrible acts."
But Carranza had made similar offers before without
ever anything coming of them, so, in view of the coun-
try-wide indignation which insisted that Villa be pun-

Villa and his chief of staff.

ished, Washington decided to let Carranza capture Villa
if he could but also to take positive action itself. Accordingly, a military expedition of 6000 men, under command of Brigadier-General John J. Pershing, was
ordered into Mexico to pursue and capture Villa and
bring him back to the United States for trial. The expedition from its inception was doomed to failure. Had
Pershing been adequately equipped with airplanes he
might have been able quickly to search for Villa in
mountainous northern Mexico whither the bandit re-
treated after recrossing into Mexico. Lacking airplanes,
Pershing's progress was too slow to catch up with the
raiders before they had separated into small bodies and

hidden in the wooded ravines of the uplands. Meanwhile Carranza, true to form, had been making shrill demands that the American troops be retired from Mexican soil, and in other ways causing difficulties which made progress by the punitive expedition difficult. On June 16, General Jacinto Trevino, Carranza commander in the north, informed General Pershing that any devia-

Photograph by U. S. Army Signal Corps.

An official Mexican Army photograph of the American troops captured by the Mexicans during the Pershing expedition in pursuit of the bandit General Pancho Villa. When these soldiers were finally released they were received with blankets on the American side of the International Bridge, as their captors had appropriated their clothing.

tion of his column to south, east, or west would be considered a hostile act and a signal to commence warfare. On June 21, a clash occurred near Carrizal between Carranzista troops and part of Pershing's forces, resulting in the capture of twenty-three Americans. The situation continued tense until early in July when the Carrizal prisoners were released and Carranza in a conciliatory note to Washington promised once more to do all in his power to prevent the recurrence in the future of events such as the raid on Columbus. On January 28, 1917, the War Department announced that Pershing had been ordered to withdraw from Mexico; on February 5 the withdrawal was effected.

April 18. The State Department at Washington notified the German government that diplomatic relations would be severed unless Germany abandoned its methods of submarine warfare. (See Ch. 4.)

April 22. Despatches from London announced that Sir Roger Casement, an Irish Nationalist, with others, had been taken prisoner while landing arms from a German auxiliary cruiser in Ireland. The news of Casement's capture interested many Americans, especially those of Irish blood, who had been long observing the troubled state of Irish-British relations, which even before the outbreak of the Great War had reached a state of extreme tension due to the aspiration of South Ireland for independence. The day following the arrest of Casement an uprising occurred in Dublin, where a large force of armed men identified with the Sinn Fein party forcibly occupied Stephens Green, the Post Office, and houses on Sackville Street and along the quays. Troops were summoned and for days carried on a guerrilla warfare with the revolutionists, in the course of which a score of persons were killed and much damage done to property. The disorders continued until late in the month, when they came to an end following the surrender of Provisional President Pearse of the "Irish Republic," and a dozen other leaders. Pearse and seven of his companions were executed in Dublin May 3. Casement was hanged in Pentonville Prison, London, August 3, 1916.

June 5. Lord Kitchener, British Minister of War, and almost his entire staff were lost when the British cruiser *Hampshire*, on which they were travelling to Russia, struck a mine and sank off the Orkney Islands.

June 10. Charles Evans Hughes and Charles Warren Fairbanks were nominated for President and Vice-

President respectively by the Republican National Convention. Mr. Hughes resigned as Associate Justice of the United States Supreme Court and accepted the nomination. (For an account of the elections of 1916, see Ch. 11.)

July 11. The Shackleford Good Roads Bill was signed by the President. It provided for a Federal contribution to the States for the building of roads of $5,000,000 in 1917, $10,000,000 in 1918, and so on until the fifth year when the amount would be $25,000,-000. Subsequently large increases were made in the Federal conributions for the years from 1918 onward. A stipulation of the law was that Federal moneys turned over to the States for road construction must be matched dollar for dollar with State money. General supervision and a measure of control over the laying out of roads and the design and construction of them were retained by the National Government.

July 18. *The Official Gazette,* London, published the names of American individuals and firms placed on the blacklist under the British trading-with-the-enemy act. (See p. 96.)

July 30. Two explosions of munitions on Black Tom Island, Jersey City, N. J., caused the loss of a number of lives and several million dollars damage to property.

August 4. Secretary of State Lansing and Danish Minister Constantin Brun at Washington signed a treaty for the purchase of the Danish West Indies by the United States for $25,000,000. Ten days later the Danish Folkething approved the treaty and on September 7 it was ratified by the United States Senate. The United States took possession of the Islands March 31, 1917. A prosperous business in the export of rum, which the Virgin Islands enjoyed prior to their acquisition by the United States, was destroyed when the Prohibition law went into effect. Since then the economic condition of the Islands has been such as to cause President Hoover to remark, when he visited them in the winter of 1928, that they constituted an "effective poorhouse."

August 29. President Wilson signed an Act passed by Congress reorganizing the government of the Philippine Islands. Under the new law the Philippine Commission, of which the majority were Americans, went out of existence and the Islands became practically autonomous. It also extended the suffrage to 600,000 more Filipinos and required that Americans, to exercise the suffrage, become Philippine citizens. An amendment to the bill, passed by the United States Senate but rejected by the House of Representatives, provided for complete independence of the Islands at a time not later than 1920. In the bill as passed no fixed date for granting independence was set, but eventual separation was promised in the preamble which stated "that it has always been the purpose of the people of the United States to withdraw their sovereignty over the Philippine Islands and to recognize their independence as soon as a suitable government can be established therein." Independence, though agitated in season and out by politicians both in the Philippines and in the United States, did not make headway until 1933 when Congress passed and President Roosevelt signed a bill providing for a gradual assumption of full governing powers by the Filipinos, to be followed by American withdrawal at the end of about ten years.

September 3. The Adamson bill making eight hours the norm for certain classes of railroad workers was signed by President Wilson. The prosperity enjoyed by the railroads due to the heavy exports being made to Europe and, indeed, to all the world since shortly after the War began, had made the workers restive. Earlier in the summer they had demanded pay increases and shorter hours but had met refusal. A calamitous nation-wide strike seemingly being imminent, President Wilson sought by means of conferences with union officials and managers of the railroads to bring about a settlement. These failing, and a strike being called for September 4, the President on August 29 asked Congress to pass re-medial legislation. The result was the Adamson Act, hurried through all the legislative stages in less than 100 hours. In addition to regulating working hours the bill contained provisions for settling the controversies over wage rates. Much criticism was directed at the bill on the ground mainly that it established a precedent of gov-ernmental interference with business which would cause trouble in the future.

September 7. President Wilson signed the Shipping Bill, providing for a Government controlled $50,000,-000 corporation to build, buy, or lease merchant ships.

September 7. A bill giving to widows of men who served in the Civil or Mexican Wars or the War of 1812, and who had reached the age of seventy, pensions of $20 a month, instead of the former $12 a month, was passed by the United States Senate. It had already passed the House. The President signed it.

September 11. The second attempt to bridge the St. Lawrence River at Quebec resulted in a failure, with the loss of eleven lives, when the massive centre span, weighing 5100 tons, collapsed and fell into the river.

October 7. Flying the German man-of-war ensign, and carrying two deck guns conspicuously placed, the German submarine *U-53* arrived in Newport harbor and requested that a berth be assigned her. *Kapitän-Leutnant* Hans Rose, commanding her, called on the commandant of the Naval Station, stating that his object in entering the port was to "pay his respects," and that he intended to sail within a few hours. He invited American officers to visit his ship. While in port, the *U-53* was careful not to violate neutrality regulations, but after sailing from Newport she began sinking vessels, some of them within sight of our shores but outside the three-mile limit.

November 29. Captain H. S. Knapp in command of United States forces in the Republic of Santo Domingo,[2] acting on instructions, at 4 o'clock P.M. proclaimed American military intervention in the Island's government. All citizens having arms were warned to turn them in to the American military.

American interference in Santo Domingo dated back to 1905 when President Roosevelt undertook to adjust controversies arising from the country's foreign debts. The financial administration which he installed deprived European holders of defaulted Santo Dominican bonds of any excuse for action by their governments that might infringe upon the Monroe Doctrine. One act of the financial intervention was the writing off of $20,000,-000 of the European claims, which the American experts declared to be unjustifiable. With Americans in charge, the Customs Service for the first time yielded sums sufficient for the service of the foreign debt and for the greater part of the Government's domestic expenditures.

It had been hoped that the stabilizing of Dominican finances would put an end to political unrest, but the disturbances continued unabated. Nor did the betterments brought by the American fiscal administrators win plaudits from the Santo Dominicans, whose natural repugnance to foreign meddling in their affairs was augmented by unending fault-finding by newspapers and

---

[2] U. S. Marines had been landed earlier in the year, on one occasion to subdue disorders and another time to ensure the free election of a Provisional President to succeed General Juan I. Jiminez, resigned.

politicians. A display of anti-Americanism, whether by revolutionist avid for loot or by politician bent on advancing himself, was the one sure road to power, the unanswerable proof of patriotism.

Following the complete intervention inaugurated by Captain Knapp, the country was pacified, and the same program of internal improvements was embarked upon as had characterized American interventions in Cuba, the Philippines, and Haiti. Materially, the progress has not been inconsiderable, but on the whole the adventure has turned out to be a costly one for the United States. Trouble with Europe over the Monroe Doctrine has been obviated, but the intervention contributed to the tremendous swell of ill will against us in some of the Latin American Republics growing out of their suspicion of the largely phantasmagorial "imperialism" of the United States.

December 21. The New York Stock Exchange did the largest volume of business in fifteen years — 3,086,-000 shares — due to the frantic sale of "war stocks" following a statement of Secretary Lansing that the United States was being drawn into the war.

The Books of 1916

"Mrs. Balfane," by Gertrude Atherton. . . . "Casuals of the Sea," by William McFee, which was "seven years in the writing." . . . Irvin Cobb's "Local Color" and "Old Judge Priest." . . . "Mary-'Gusta," by Joseph C. Lincoln. . . . "The Prisoner," by Alice Brown. "A Hoosier Holiday," by Theodore Dreiser. . . . "God's Puppets," by William Allen White. . . . "Unfinished Portraits," by Jennette Lee. . . . "When a Man's a Man," by Harold Bell Wright. . . . "Windy McPherson's Son," by Sherwood Anderson. . . . "Life

and Gabriella," by Ellen Glasgow. . . . "The Rising
Tide," by Margaret Deland. . . . "Tish," by Mary
Roberts Rinehart. . . . "Penrod and Sam," by Booth
Tarkington; "The best stories of juvenile prankishness
[said *The Review of Reviews*] that have ever been writ-
ten." . . . Another Tarkington book, "Seventeen," was

*Reproduced by special permission from The Saturday Evening Post, copyright 1916 by The
Curtis Publishing Company.*

One of May Wilson Preston's drawings of Tish, Mary Roberts Rinehart's
famous character, with her two companions, Lizzie and Aggie.

published this year. . . . In biography, the most talked
of book of 1916 was Lord Charnwood's "Abraham Lincoln."

The Theatre in 1916

E. H. Sothern as Lord Dundreary in a revival of
"Our American Cousin," a play made famous by Mr.
Sothern's father more than fifty years before. . . .
"Stop! Look! Listen!" a girl and music show, of whose
central figure, the French actress Gaby Deslys, dramatic

Ethel Barrymore in a scene from "Our Mrs. McChesney."

Musical comedy stars featuring the last word in 1916 headgear
off and on the stage.

Left: The Dolly Sisters, dancers with the Winter Garden and Ziegfield "Fol-
lies." *Right:* Gaby Deslys in the musical revue "Stop! Look! Listen!"

critic Metcalfe said in *Life:* "War may have devastated Europe, its landmarks and cathedrals, but it hasn't touched Gaby Deslys. She escapes to us in all her infantile beauty with the baby stare of her baby blue eyes quite as innocent and intact as ever they were." . . . Grace George in "Major Barbara," by George Bernard Shaw, an argument against preparedness written ten years earlier. . . . Edna Ferber's "Our Mrs. McChesney," with Ethel Barrymore as the lady drummer in the petticoat line. . . . "The Merry Wives of Windsor," with Thomas A. Wise as "Falstaff." . . . "Henry the Eighth" done in spectacular form by Beerbohm Tree — the critics feared a deluge of Shakespearean plays to mark the tercentenary of the Bard. . . . Henry E. Dixey in "Mr. Lazarus." . . . Otis Skinner in "Mister Antonio." . . . David Warfield in a revival of "The Music Master." . . . John Drew in the title rôle of Thackeray's "Major Pendennis." . . . William Faversham in George Bernard Shaw's "Getting Married." . . . Mme. Sarah Bernhardt appeared in repertoire. The old magnetism and fire were still there enabling Bernhardt to demonstrate that in spite of her physical handicaps she was still great as an artist.

1917

The War Resolution. Prices Sky-rocket. Congress Votes a Vast Appropriation for Aviation. American Troops Marching in London Are Given an Ovation. Suffragettes Picketing the White House Are Arrested. The Government, as a War Measure, Fixes the Prices of Some Commodities. Books and Plays of 1917.

March 31. The United States took formal possession of the Danish West Indies, renaming them the Virgin Islands.[1]

April 2. Congress met in extraordinary session at noon "to receive [from President Wilson] a communication concerning grave matters of national policy which should be taken immediately under consideration." At half-past eight in the evening the President, appearing personally before the two Houses assembled, asked Congress to declare that a state of war existed between the United States and Germany. A few minutes after three o'clock on the morning of April 5, Congress passed a joint resolution providing "that the President is hereby authorized and directed . . . to carry on war against the Imperial German Government and to bring the conflict to a successful termination." Thus empowered, the President, April 6th, issued a proclamation that "a state of war exists between the United States and the Imperial German government."[2]

[1] See Chapter 29.

[2] There was point in saying "Imperial German Government," rather than "Germany" or "German Government." The distinction Wilson made and maintained between the German government and the German people is discussed on pp. 441–443.

April 4. The price of wheat on the Chicago Board of Trade passed $2 a bushel for the first time in a normal market. April 19, the price reached $2.40. On May 11, with May wheat selling at $3.25, the Chicago Board of Trade ordered discontinuance of trading.

April 19. The price of cotton on the New York Exchange reached 21 ¼ cents a pound, the highest price since the Civil War. It continued rising and on June 19 reached 27 cents.

July 4. Practical instruction of America's big army of aviators began, with the opening of the first Government training field at Rantoul, Ill. Camps at Dayton and Mount Clemens were to open July 15.

July 14. The House of Representatives voted $640,000,000 for an air fleet, without a dissenting vote. Members, to keep details of the great aviation program secret, did not debate.

July 27. Secretary of the Treasury McAdoo told the Senate Finance Committee that the first year's cost of the war to the United States would amount to $11,651,-194,000.

July 31. American trade figures for the fiscal year ended June 29, 1917, showed imports $2,659,000,000 and exports $6,294,000,000, an increase over 1916 in combined foreign trade of 35 per cent.

August 6. The Texas House of Representatives began an investigation of Governor James Ferguson. The State Senate, sitting as a court of impeachment, removed Ferguson from office. Subsequently Ferguson's wife, "Ma" Ferguson, was elected Governor, the first woman to hold that office in the history of the country.

August 15. Millions of people in London became ecstatic welcoming a large contingent of American troops who paraded through the city, escorted by all the famous bands of the guards. The Americans were reviewed by

Ambassador Page and Admiral Sims and later by King George at Buckingham Palace.

August 28. Ten suffragette pickets were arrested in front of the White House, Washington, D. C. On October 16, four of them were sentenced to six months in the penitentiary. On November 10 the picketing was

Photograph by U. S. Army Signal Corps.

First American troops to reach England marching across Westminster Bridge on September 5, 1917.

resumed and again it was broken up by the police, who arrested forty-one women, among them Mrs. Harvey W. Wiley, wife of the pure food advocate, and Mrs. William Kent, wife of a former Congressman from California. To some of the leaders sentences to imprisonment of from 6 days to 6 months were meted out.

September 5. Government agents raided I. W. W. (International Workers of the World) simultaneously in twenty-four cities, seizing important documents and books, and making ten arrests.

September 20.   President Wilson approved of the agreement made with copper producers fixing a price of 23½ cents a pound to the Government, the Allies, and the public. The figures were 3 cents below current quotations and 12 cents below the high price of the year.

September 23.   Secretary of the Treasury McAdoo

A group of suffragists who were imprisoned for picketing.

announced the distribution of two billion dollars' worth of war savings certificates throughout the country to make it easy for every one to help win the war through thrift.

October 4.   The War Department announced that contracts had been let for construction of 20,000 airplanes for use in the War. Five thousand of them were to be built abroad and 15,000 in the United States. Baron Richthofen, Germany's leading aviator, on being told of America's aviation project, scoffed. America could not put 20,000 trained pilots into active service, he said.

October 11.　President Wilson approved a schedule of prices agreed upon by steel manufacturers, fixing prices until January 1, 1918.

October 23.　Two Army deserters from Camp Mills were sentenced to ten years apiece at hard labor in the Federal Penitentiary at Atlanta.

October 25.　New York City Federal Food Administrator Arthur Williams urged on housewives two meatless and wheatless days a week.

October 25.　In an address to 100 members of the New York State Woman Suffrage Party in the White House President Wilson indorsed adoption of equal suffrage by States: "I am very glad to add my voice to those which are urging the people of the great State of New York to set a great example by voting for Woman Suffrage."

October 26.　Troops from Alabama and troops from the 15th Infantry, New York (negroes), clashed at Camp Mills, L. I. No casualties were reported, but the camp was kept under arms all night.

November 7.　The Treasury Department announced that subscriptions to the second Liberty Loan totalled $4,617,532,200 and that 9,500,000 persons subscribed.

November 10.　Seventeen members of the I. W. W. were tarred and feathered near Tulsa, Okla., by a posse calling themselves "Knights of Liberty."

December 3.　The expulsion from the United States Senate of Robert M. LaFollette of Wisconsin was urged by the American Defense Society in a brief submitted to the Senate committee investigating a speech by LaFollette at St. Paul in September, 1917.

December 5.　The Ford Motor Company was ordered to declare a dividend of $19,275,385 by Judge George S. Homer in a suit arising from a dispute between Ford and some of his partners.

December 6. In Halifax harbor a munitions ship bound for Europe collided with a Belgian relief vessel and blew up. Two square miles of the city were wrecked, with the dead totalling more than 2000, many of them buried in the ruins. The explosion was heard 61 miles away.

December 10. As a picturesque incident of the War

Though the war in Europe held the attention of the American people in 1917 to the exclusion of almost everything else, nevertheless there were many fields in which activity was carried on "as usual," which were touched by the war only slightly if at all. The Southdown Wether in the picture, bred by the U. S. Department of Agriculture at Beltsville, Md., and shown by J. C. Andrew of West Point, Ind., received the award of "Grand Champion" at the Chicago International Livestock Exposition.

exciting universal attention, newspapers published despatches from abroad stating that Jerusalem, for 673 years in undisputed possession of the Turks, had, after being surrounded on all sides, surrendered to the British forces under General Allenby.

December 14. The Federal Fuel Administrator ordered electric advertising signs darkened Sunday and Thursday of each week.

December 21. Professor Peabody of Harvard returned to Kaiser Wilhelm his decoration of the Order of the Prussian Crown.

December 28.   President Wilson placed the railroads under government control and management and named Secretary of the Treasury Wiliam G. McAdoo Director-General.

December 31.   New York State Fuel Administrator, to conserve coal, ordered six lightless nights per week; lighting permitted on Saturday nights only.

Prohibition

December.   So numerous were the advances made by Prohibition during 1917 that even the perennially optimistic "Mr. Dooley," America's best-known saloon-keeper, in a conversation with his friend, Mr. Hennessey, was moved to gloomy reflections:

King Alcohol no longer rules th' sea or th' land. Th' ladies have got that binivolent ol' dishpot on his knees beggin' f'r mercy an' they're sayin' to him, "Did ye have mercy on us?" an' ar-re gettin' ready to chop off his wicked ol' head. Take a dhrink, me boy, whether ye need it or not. Take it now. It may be ye'er last.

I used to laugh at th' pro-hybitionists; I used to laugh them to scorn. But I laugh no more; they've got us on th' run. I wudden't be surprised at anny minyit if I had to turn this emporyum into an exchange f'r women's wurruk. Whether ye like it or not, in a few years there won't be anny saloons to lure the marri'd man fr'm his home, furnish guests f'r our gr-reat asylums an' jails, an' brighten up th' dark sthreets with their cheerful glow. I don't care. I wudden't mind if all th' liquor in th' wurruld was poored into th' lake. It wud make people pay their wather tax with a lighter heart.

"I don't believe in this here prohybition," said Mr. Hennessy. "Th' man who dhrinks modhrately ought to be allowed to have what he wants."

"What is his name?" asked Mr. Dooley. "What novel is he in?"

Most important among Prohibition's triumphs were: *January* 8.   The United States Supreme Court upheld the constitutionality of the Webb-Kenyon law prohibiting the shipment of liquor from "wet" to "dry" States.

January 9.   The Senate passed the Sheppard bill prohibiting the manufacture, importation or sale of liquor in the District of Columbia. The law passed the House

The wets viewed the drys' activities as an affront to personal liberty.
— *Life, April 18, 1918.*

February 28, was signed by the President March 3, and went into effect November 1, 1917.

January 11.   The Senate passed a bill prohibiting the sending of liquor advertisements by mail into "dry" territory.

February 2.   Prohibition bills were signed by the governors of Oregon and Tennessee.

February 9.   The governor of Indiana signed a Prohibition Bill, to take effect April 2, 1918.

February 21.   The House adopted a measure originating in the Senate forbidding shipments of intoxicating liquors into States which prohibited their manufacture and sale. At midnight June 30, when the law went into effect, twenty-two States automatically became "bone dry."

April 17.   The Governor of New Hampshire signed a bill establishing prohibition, effective May 1, 1918.

July 16.   Porto Rico at a special election adopted Prohibition, to go into effect March 2, 1918.

August 1.   The Senate, by a vote of 65 to 20, adopted the Prohibiton Amendment to the Constitution. In the House some minor changes were made in it and it was passed, 282 to 128, on December 17, 1917. December 18 the Senate agreed to the House changes and adopted the resolution. It consisted of three articles, of which the third provided a limit of seven years for ratification by the States. The two pertinent articles read:

1. After one year from the ratification of this article the manufacture, sale, or transportation of intoxicating liquors within, the importation thereof into, or the exportation thereof from the United States and all territory subject to the jurisdiction thereof, for beverage purposes, is hereby prohibited.

2. The Congress and the several States shall have concurrent power to enforce this article by appropriate legislation.

The Amendment, to become part of the Constitution, had to be ratified by thirty-six, or three-quarters of the States. The thirty-sixth ratification was secured January 16, 1919, and on January 29 it was proclaimed ratified by the Secretary of State.

September 8.   By Government decree the manufacture of whiskey in the United States was prohibited from September 8, 1917. This was a war-time measure having nothing to do with the Prohibition Amendment itself.

December 10.   With a decision upholding the Idaho Prohibition Law, the United States Supreme Court gave an opinion that a citizen has no constitutional right to possess liquors for his personal use if a State wished to forbid it. Justice McReynolds, who gave the Court's opinion, held that a State "has power absolutely to prohibit the manufacture, gift, purchase, sale or transpor-

Spirits of 1917.
— *Nelson Harding in the Brooklyn Eagle, July 18, 1917.*

tation of intoxicating liquors within its borders without violating the Constitution; we further think it clearly follows from our numerous decisions upholding Prohibition legislation that the right to hold intoxicating liquors for personal use is not one of those fundamental privileges of a citizen of the United States which no State may abridge."

December 11. President Wilson, as a war measure, issued a proclamation reducing the alcoholic content of beer brewed after January 1, 1918, to 2¾ per cent by weight. He also prohibited the use in the manufacture of malt liquors of more than 70 per cent of the average amount of foods, fruits, food materials, and feeds used

Kathleen Norris.

Sinclair Lewis and James Branch Cabell.

in such manufacture during the one-year period ending on that date.

Books of 1917

"A Son of the Middle Border," by Hamlin Garland. . . . "The Dwelling Place of Light," by Winston Churchill. . . . "The Light in the Clearing," by Irving Bacheller. . . . "The Living Present," by Gertrude Atherton. . . . "The Ford," by Mary Austin. . . . "Salt," by Charles G. Norris. . . . "Martie the Unconquered," by Kathleen Norris. . . . "Parnassus on Wheels," and "Songs For a Little House," by Christopher Morley. . . . "Great Possessions," by David Grayson (Ray Stannard Baker), called by the Springfield *Republican* "a delightful book; rich in its wisdom, redolent of nature, and bespeaking a love for humble things and men of gentle will." . . . "Extricating Obadiah," by Joseph C. Lincoln. . . . "His Family," by Ernest Poole. . . . "Fanny Herself," by Edna Ferber. . . . "The Green Jacket," by Jennette Lee. . . . "The Three Black Pennys," by Joseph Hergesheimer, a study of three generations of Pennsylvania ironmasters. "Understood Betsy," by Dorothy Canfield Fisher. . . . "Bab: A Sub-Deb," by Mary Roberts Rinehart. . . . . . . "Marching Men," by Sherwood Anderson. . . . Two books by Sinclair Lewis, "The Job," and "The Innocents." . . . "A Daughter of Tomorrow," by Zona Gale.

The Theatre in 1917

Jane Cowl was playing the heroine in "Lilac Time," a war play but with "none of the horrors of war." . . . Another war play, "Out There," written by Hartley Manners, the heroine played by Miss Laurette Taylor, was considered by critic Metcalfe of *Life* "a stimulant to patriotism for Americans, coming just at the moment when America needs an incentive to the putting aside of individual gain and individual comfort for the country's good." . . . Miss Fay Bainter, as the heroine of "The Willow Tree," displayed "a grace of movement and a command of facile and vocal expression not often encountered in the new generation of the stage." . . . Nora Bayes, "almost an entire show in herself," was informing her audiences that if they checked their brains at the door with their wraps, "I'll educate you — down to me." . . . Marjorie Rambeau was starring in "The Eyes of Youth." . . . Guy Bates Post in "The Masquerader," was entertaining principally for the rapid changes he made from one character to another. . . .

Orme Caldara, Henry Stephenson, Lawrence Grant, W. Mayne Lynton and
Jane Cowl in "Lilac Time."

Left: Sarah Bernhardt as Portia, during her 1917 tour in this country. *Right:*
Ina Claire, who scored a hit in "Polly With a Past."

Julia Sanderson and Joseph Cawthorn in "Rambler Rose." . . . Ina Claire played a glove-fitting part in "Polly With a Past." . . . Mr. Raymond Hitchcock in "Hitchy-Koo." . . . George Arliss was attempting to impersonate our first Secretary of the Treasury in "Hamilton," but was handicapped, according to a critic, by "his stature, his comedy manner and his modern-English accent." . . . Pinero's "The Gay Lord Quex," with Mr. John Drew and Margaret Illington.

1918

Congress Passes a Constitutional Amendment Giving the Vote to Women. Charges of Incompetency Against the War Department Are Answered by Secretary Baker. A German Accuses Germany. War News from the Front. Scandal in the Aircraft Administration. A Proposal, by a United States Senator, for the Cancellation of the French War Debt. The Supreme Court Declares the Federal Child Labor Law Unconstitutional. Progress of the Air Mail. American Troops Fight the Bolsheviks. Spanish Influenza Sweeps Over the Country. Congress Goes Republican. Germany Collapses. The Armistice Is Signed. McAdoo Resigns. The President Sails for Europe. Books and Plays of 1918.

January 10.   By a vote of 274 to 136, the exact two-thirds required, the House of Representatives adopted the Susan B. Anthony resolution to submit the woman suffrage constitutional amendment to the State legislatures for ratification. In the Senate, despite a plea for its passage by President Wilson, it was defeated by a margin of two votes. In 1919, it passed the Senate and by August of 1920 enough State legislatures had approved it to make it part of the Constitution. Women everywhere voted in the Presidential elections of November, 1920, in which Warren G. Harding, Republican, defeated James M. Cox, Democrat.

January 10.   Secretary of War Newton D. Baker, appearing before the Military Affairs Committee of the United States Senate to answer charges by Senator Chamberlain and others that "the military establishment of America [had] fallen down because of inefficiency in every bureau and department of the United States Government," made a spirited defense of his management of the War Department. On this and succeeding days Baker answered hundreds of questions asked by the Committee, explained in detail what had been done to make America's power effective in the War. He admitted that delays had occurred in outfitting troops with clothing and in manufacturing ordnance and shipping it abroad, but insisted that all such conditions had been remedied. Never in history, he stated, had an army of the size of the American one been raised and equipped so quickly. "We will have," he said,[1] "500,000 men in France very soon and a million more ready to go, a total of 1,500,000 American soldiers in France before the end of 1918."

January 28. Maximilian Harden, Berlin editor, caused a sensation in Germany by putting the blame for the World War on Germany, admitting the justice of the Allies' viewpoint regarding Alsace-Lorraine, and printing the text of speeches of President Wilson and Lloyd George as bases for peace.

January 31. *Life* published an ode by Christopher Morley to the first soldiers of the American Army to die in action in France:

> Gresham and Enright and Hay!
> There are no words to say
> Our love, our noble pride
> For these, our first who died.

February 8. The first issue of *The Stars and Stripes*, official weekly publication of the A. E. F., appeared.

February 12. All theatres on Broadway, New York City, were closed, to save coal.

February 14. President Wilson directed Attorney-General Gregory to investigate alleged waste and extravagance in the construction of the Government's fabricating shipyard at Hog Island, Philadelphia, "with a

[1] January 28.

view to instituting criminal process in case the facts justify it."

March 29. Emotions of horror and intense indignation were aroused in America by despatches from Paris stating that seventy-five persons had been killed and ninety wounded, most of them women and children, when a shell fired by a German long-range gun fell on a church in Paris during Good Friday services.

April 6. President Wilson, in a speech at Baltimore, condemned German peace treaties forced on Russia and Roumania, and said America would meet German challenge with "force to the utmost."

April 12. Charles M. Schwab was made Director General of Emergency Fleet Corporation, to have entire charge of the government shipbuilding program.

April 23. In one of the outstanding feats of the War, British naval forces, with the co-operation of French destroyers, carried out a raid against Zeebrugge and Ostend with the object of bottling up those two bases of German submarines on the Belgian coast. They succeeded in blocking the canal at Zeebrugge by sinking two old cruisers filled with concrete in the channel. Marines and blue-jackets landed and stormed the mole to distract attention of the enemy. The British lost five small warcraft.

April 24. The first real engagement of American troops, at Seicheprey, took place.

May 3. Gigantic operations were going on back of the American lines, said a bulletin of the Committee on Public Information. In April, three hundred and fifty thousand tons of materials had been handled. Huge storage sheds and big docks and railroads were being rushed to completion.

May 7. A resolution introduced in the Senate by William S. Kenyon of Iowa, harbinger of a discussion which was to become practically a world controversy for long after the War ended, and which was still raging the year this volume was published (1933), provided that "all obligations of the Republic of France to the United States for moneys borrowed or funds advanced since the

Photograph U. S. Army Signal Corps.

American soldier making friends with French children.

commencement of the present War, including interest thereon, be and are hereby cancelled."

May 8. Increasing participation of American forces in the fighting in Europe was reported in bulletins issued by the Committee on Public Information:

American flyers are making a splendid record on the Western Front. They have wrested air supremacy from the Germans on the sector our troops are holding and are helping the Allies at other points. More planes are needed.

German forces attempted a vigorous raid on one of the American combat groups within a strong point in the Luneville sector this morning, but were badly beaten. Carried on with hand grenades, rifles, and revolvers, it was virtually a hand-to-hand encounter. The Germans beat a hasty retreat, carrying their dead and wounded. Our troops suffered no losses.

May 15. Widely published charges of graft and inefficiency against the military aircraft administration by Gutzon Borglum, the sculptor, caused President Wilson to appoint an investigating committee, with Charles Evans Hughes and Attorney-General Gregory as members.

May 15. Mrs. Cornelius Vanderbilt donated the use of her Fifth Avenue, New York, home for musical entertainments in aid of the Red Cross. This started a vogue, which was followed by, among others, Clarence H. Mackay, who on May 29 turned over his mansion at Roslyn, L. I., to the Red Cross.

May 21. Director-General of Railroads McAdoo issued a sweeping order suspending railroad presidents from active participation in the conduct of their various systems.

May 26. Theodore Roosevelt and William Howard Taft shook hands at an accidental meeting in a Chicago hotel. (For an account of the ending of the historic Roosevelt-Taft estrangement, see "Our Times," Vol IV, Ch. 23 *et seq.*)

May 28. General Wood, denied service overseas, laid his case before President Wilson. Friends of the General throughout the country were indignant. (See Ch. 23.)

June 3. The United States Supreme Court declared the Federal Child Labor Law of 1916, product of years of reform agitation, unconstitutional. This law made illegal the shipment in interstate commerce, within thirty days after manufacture, of all goods produced by children below the ages stipulated in the law for specified industries, and also of goods produced by children above the minimum ages working longer hours than those stipulated for specified industries. Immediately after the Keating-Owen Act's passage its constitutionality was challenged in North Carolina, with the result that it was

Photograph U. S. Army Signal Corps.

A pathetic episode of the Great War — French peasants four years behind the German lines, greet American "Doughboys" after the ebbing of the German flood.

declared invalid by the lower courts. This decision the United States Supreme Court ratified, on the ground that the law interfered with the powers reserved to States under the 10th Amendment and transcended the power of Congress over interstate commerce.

June 19. The Post Office Department announced that aerial mail service between New York, Philadelphia, and Washington, for the first month, carried 5⅜ tons of letter mail; the planes covered 11,109 miles, totalled in the air 157 hours 59 minutes; average speed was more than 70 miles an hour.

July 2.   War bulletin of the Committee on Public Information:

In the most important military operation they have so far executed, American troops last night captured the village of Vaux and the Bois de la Roche west of Chateau-Thierry, advancing their lines on a front of four kilometers and occupying strong strategic positions. A swift night thrust secured the key to Chateau-Thierry. American gunnery was superb and reduced the town to ruins and prevented an early counterattack. Practically a whole German regiment was wiped out in a fierce attempt to retake the captured positions.

July 4.   A great Fourth of July splash of American

Then and now — The rising cost of living.
—*From the New Yorker Staats Zeitung, February, 1918.*

shipping took place as nearly 100 ships were launched from ways throughout the country. (See Ch. 19.)

August 27.   Walter Hines Page, Ambassador to Great Britain, resigned on account of ill health.

August 27.   John D. Ryan, of New York, was named head of the Bureau of Aircraft Production, and Benedict Crowell, of Cleveland, Director of Munitions.

August 29.   Labor Department statistics showed an increased cost of living in New York between July, 1917, and July, 1918, of 17%.

August 31. President Wilson signed the new man-power bill and issued a proclamation setting September 12 as the day of registration for military service of all men between the ages of 18 and 45. (See Ch. 19.)

September 10. Mail was carried by airplane from Chicago to New York in 12 hours 55 minutes. The actual flying time was 10 hours 5 minutes. This was the first Chicago-New York air-mail trip to be completed in one day.

September 11. American troops were safely landed at Archangel, the headquarters and supply base of the Allied Expeditionary Force operating in the northern part of European Russia. September 24, American forces won their first fight against the Bolsheviki, repelling them south of Archangel.

July 16. Activities of American troops at the front in France were described in a war bulletin:

Fighting on the Western battle-front continues unabated from Chateau-Thierry to the Argonne, with the Allied lines holding firmly nearly everywhere. More complete details of yesterday's bitter fighting disclose that the American soldiers, who had never before played a part in this great struggle, withstood the savage rushes of the Germans like veterans and held them at a most vital point in the allied line. Chateau-Thierry was the pivot about which the Germans hoped to swing their lines, but the courage and tenacity of the Americans fooled them.

Men who have seen fighting throughout the war say that there has never been anything like the artillery preparation for this, the greatest drive yet made. The Germans laid a creeping barrage over the American sector which extended back for five miles. Back and forth, from front to rear, for ten long hours, successive curtains of steel swept the American sector at short intervals.

October 19. The last day of the Fourth Liberty Loan Drive. Subscriptions to the loan poured into the banks in such numbers that clerks worked all night tabulating them. The Treasury estimated that more than

20,000,000 persons, more than half the adult population of the United States, had bought bonds.

Spanish Influenza

October. PANDEMIC. In the early Fall of 1918, before the topic became sombre, almost one of terror, there was mild joking about it — one of the jests became almost a folk-quip:

> I had a little bird named "Enza."
> I opened the window and in-flu-enza.

A two-part cartoon showed a cloaked figure labelled "Spanish Influenza," muttering "Carramba!" and astounding John Public; then in the next picture his disguise had been snatched off — "Heck! I'm diskivered!" cried Old Man Grippe. But as September advanced this facetiousness waned. In the age of microbiology, of serums, of enlightened and triumphant medicine, here were death lists three or four times as long as those of the Black Death in London, the terrible Plague of 1665.

Some time in September the influenza struck the Atlantic seaboard. Apparently it had come from Europe — in the hysteria of the time there were charges that the germs had been disseminated deliberately, by German agencies, including submarines. A more thoughtful surmise said the germs might have been brought to Europe by the 200,000 North Chinese coolies imported to France for war work, who carried a form of pneumonic plague which had raged in China since 1910.[2] All that was known was that it had swept through Germany, flourished in Spain (whence the sobriquet). "Influenza" is merely Italian for "influence" — mysterious and ma-

[2] *The Medical Record,* New York, October 22, 1918.

lignant, its source wholly unknown,[3] its manner of progress guessed at only vaguely, its epidemic form unsolved
by science, its direct cure utterly beyond the power of

© *Western Newspaper Union.*

A street cleaner, protected by a gauze mask, during the "flu" epidemic.

medicine, this "influence" appeared first in Boston, New
York, Philadelphia.

The suddenness of the attack can be shown very
simply. In Boston in the year 1914 there were 12 deaths
from influenza; in the year 1915, 37; in the year 1916,
80; in the year 1917, 51. And in 1918 on September 4
alone there were 21 deaths. The rate rose steeply, until
the apex was reached on October 1 with 202 deaths,
followed by a period of 175 deaths a day, relaxing on

[3] The cause of the epidemic of 1890 in this country had been "Pfeiffer's bacillus,"
but in 1918 no one could say what bacillus lay at the root of the trouble.

October 18 to 60 deaths.[4] Most virulent in New England, Pennsylvania, and Indiana, the influenza spread like prairie-fire; by early October 23 States were affected, by mid-October 36, by the end of the year 46. Nearly one-quarter of the people in the country fell sick; out of every 1000 sick, 19 died.[5] The total deaths were between 400,000 and 500,000.

The newspapers printed rules of hygiene side by side with the death toll; the Red Cross appropriated $575,-000, Congress $1,000,000; the Provost Marshal in the week of October 7 cancelled 142,000 draft calls. Mines shut down, shipyards and munition factories were curtailed, telephone service was cut in half. In New York, health orders staggered the opening and closing of business firms, factories, and theatres to avoid public congestion. In Philadelphia, the normal death-rate went up 700%, and there was a shortage of coffins until J. G. Brill Company, the street-car makers, turned them out in their wood-working shop; in house after house in the poorer sections lay unburied bodies, often as long as a week. In Baltimore, where was the highest death-rate of all, cold weather prevented the burial of bodies and the plague loomed a real menace. Everywhere, doctors, nurses, and undertakers labored night and day, exposed themselves to the functioning of their own professions. The "flu" ravaged over 20 Army camps, killed half as many soldiers as fell in battle overseas. Somehow it left children and old people comparatively untouched; those between the ages of 20 and 40 it slaughtered by the legion. Not a street in the country but had its hasty funerals. In early 1919 the pandemic vanished, yet for years thereafter it left a train of Bright's disease, cardiac affections, and pulmonary tuberculosis — all from a little germ which no scientist could see, no doctor combat.

[4] *The Survey,* October 26, 1918.   [5] *The Survey,* February 22, 1919.

November 3. Collapse of the Austro-Hungarian armies was complete, whole regiments surrendering to the Italian General Diaz. He reported 100,000 prisoners.

November 5. Election day. Republicans won majorities in both the House of Representatives and the Senate. In New York Alfred E. Smith, Democrat, was elected over Charles S. Whitman, Republican. Henry Ford was beaten for the Senate in Michigan.

November 9. Charlie Chaplin announced that on October 23 he married Mildred Harris, moving-picture actress, at Los Angeles, Cal.

November 10. Germany collapses. Despatches from abroad stated that the greater part of Berlin was in control of the revolutionists, the former Kaiser had fled to Holland, and Friedrich Ebert, new Socialist Chancellor, had taken command of the situation. The revolt was spreading throughout Germany with great rapidity. The red flag had been hoisted over the royal palace and the Brandenburg gate, and the former Crown Prince's palace was also held by the revolutionists. The King of Wurttemberg had abdicated, and the Socialists were demanding that every sovereign in the Empire be dethroned and all princes exiled.

November 11. The Armistice was signed. Hostilities ceased:

At the armistice hour there was no demonstration by shouting, slapping each other on the back, dancing, and tossing of hats. When the noise of battle ceased there was a restful peace that passeth man's understanding or his ability to describe; there was no hilarity or jubilation. Among the Germans opposite there was considerable shouting, singing, beating of drums, and blowing of bugles, all up and down the line — a remarkable contrast to the actions of American troops.[6]

November 14. Giving as his reasons: "As a result

[6] Quoted from Kenneth Mayo, an American officer at the front.

of long overwork I need a reasonable period of genuine rest to replenish my energy," and "I must, for the sake of my family, get back to private life, to retrieve my

Photograph U. S. Army Signal Corps.

Home again!

Soldiers returning on the *Agamemnon* arrive at Hoboken, N. J.

personal fortune" — William Gibbs McAdoo, Secretary of the Treasury and Director-General of Railroads, wrote a letter of resignation to President Wilson. Among the many editorial comments evoked by McAdoo's retirement, most of them eulogistic with reservations, was one containing a comparison destined to become almost a classic, by the Brooklyn *Eagle:* "No Secretary of the Treasury since the days of Hamilton supported heavier responsibilities."

November 15.   The Board of Censorship established

Rolling out the NC-1 for a trial flight.

by Presidential proclamation October 14, 1917, was discontinued.

November 19.   The London *Daily Mail* cabled the Aero Club of America that its offer of a prize of $50,000 to the first aviator to fly the Atlantic was now open.

November 30.   It was announced that all records for the number of passengers carried in any type of airplanes were broken November 27 at the Naval Air Station, Rockaway, when the navy's newest type seaplane, the giant NC-1, largest in the world, made a flight with fifty men on board.

December 5.   Representative Carter Glass of Virginia was nominated by President Wilson as Secretary of the Treasury to succeed William G. McAdoo. The Senate approved.

December 8. The submerged steel net which had been stretched across the Narrows, New York Harbor, since this country entered the War, was taken up.

December 23. At New York, twenty-five miles of noise hailed the return of 3798 soldiers on the *George Washington* and *Cedric*.

December 26. King George and British officials met President Wilson at Charing Cross Station. The President slept in Buckingham Palace.

December 29. President Wilson, with Mrs. Wilson, visited his mother's girlhood home at Carlisle, England, and attended church.

December 31. New York had a "dry" New Year's Eve. (War-time Prohibition.)

Books of 1918

"Shavings," by Joseph C. Lincoln. . . . "Shandygaff," by Christopher Morley. . . . Two books by Mary Johnston, "Foes," and "Pioneers of the Old South." . . . "Keeping Up with William," by Irving Bacheller. . . . "In Secret," by Robert W. Chambers. . . . "The White Morning," by Gertrude Atherton. . . . "The Forty-niners," the first of the trilogy of historical novels about California by Stewart Edward White. . . . "His Second Wife," and "The Dark People," by Ernest Poole. . . . "The Earthquake," by Arthur Train. . . . "Belgium Under German Occupation," by Brand Whitlock. . . . "The Heart of a Fool," and "The Martial Adventures of Henry and Me," by William Allen White. . . . "Cheerful — By Request," by Edna Ferber. . . . "Humoresque," by Fannie Hurst. . . . "The Marne," by Edith Wharton. . . . "Home Fires in France," by

Dorothy Canfield Fisher. . . . "The Amazing Interlude," by Mary Roberts Rinehart. . . . "The Magnificent Ambersons," by Booth Tarkington. . . . "Gold and Iron," by Joseph Hergesheimer. . . . "The Hand of the Potter," by Theodore Dreiser. . . . "Mid-

Willa Cather.   Christopher Morley.

American Chants," by Sherwood Anderson. . . . "Birth," by Zona Gale. . . . "My Antonia," by Willa Cather, a portrayal of the hardships and tragic adventures of Nebraska homesteaders, perhaps the best of Miss Cather's novels.

The Theatre in 1918

Ethel Barrymore was playing in "The Lady of the Camellias." . . . John Barrymore in Tolstoi's "Redemption." . . . Wm. Faversham and Maxine Elliott portrayed the characters of "Lord and Lady Algy." . . . Marjorie Rambeau in a war drama, "Where Poppies Bloom." . . . Margaret Anglin in "Billeted," a war play, in which Miss Anglin, as the critics put it, "makes

Theatre Magazine.

Photograph by White.

Above: A scene from "Billeted" in which the heroine, Margaret Anglin, rec-
ognizes the officer quartered in her home as her long lost husband.
Below: Justine Johnson in the revue "Over the Top."

us forget the meatless, wheatless, coalless, boozeless days and the dread possibilities of the new tax laws." . . . Fred Stone in "Jack O'Lantern." . . . Mme. Nazimova in Ibsen's "The Wild Duck," "Hedda Gabler," and "A Doll's House." . . . Chauncey Olcott in "Once Upon a Time." . . . Mr. and Mrs. Sidney Drew in a comedy of business life, "Keeping Her Smiling." . . . "Under Orders," by Berte Thomas, a war drama with a cast of only two artists, Effie Shannon and Shelley Hull. . . . "Lightnin'," destined for one of the longest runs of the American stage. . . . Otis Skinner in "Humpty Dumpty." . . . Alice Brady in "Forever After." . . . "The Better 'Ole," Bairnsfather's comic war pictures made into a play.

INDEX

INDEX